The Unraveling of Representative Democracy in Venezuela

The Unraveling of Representative Democracy in Venezuela

Edited by
Jennifer L. McCoy and David J. Myers

The Johns Hopkins University Press
Baltimore and London

Printed in the United States of America on acid-free paper

Johns Hopkins Paperbacks edition, 2006
9 8 7 6 5 4 3 2 1

The Johns Hopkins University Press
2715 North Charles Street
Baltimore, Maryland 21218-4363
www.press.jhu.edu

The Library of Congress has cataloged the hardcover edition of this book as follows:

The unraveling of representative democracy in Venezuela /
edited by Jennifer L. McCoy and David J. Myers.
p. cm.
Includes bibliographical references and index.
ISBN 0-8018-7960-4 (hardcover : alk. paper)
1. Venezuela—Politics and government—1999– 2. Representative government and representation—Venezuela—History. 3. Political participation—Venezuela—History. 4. Venezuela—Economic policy.
I. McCoy, Jennifer. II. Myers, David J.
F2329.U67 2004
320.987—dc22
2004005542

ISBN 0-8018-8428-4 (paperback : alk. paper)

A catalog record for this book is available from the British Library.

To the memory of
Janet Kelly,
a courageous and brilliant analyst of Venezuelan
politics and economics and a dear friend

Contents

Foreword

A Saudi-like oligarchy that created a corrupt, exclusionary, and deeply flawed democracy in which poverty reigned despite the nation's immense oil riches. A charismatic army officer who gave voice to the anger and the hopes of the poor, who was able to gain power through fair and free elections, and who, once in government, launched an ambitious plan to correct decades of inequities and injustice. A bickering, incompetent opposition run and funded by the displaced elite, which was bent on recovering its historical privileges and willing to resort to any means, including a coup d'état, to oust a democratically elected president. These, in bold strokes, are the main elements of the common wisdom about Venezuela which informed international public opinion, expert commentary, and the responses of other governments to that country's recurring crises since the late 1990s. Common wisdom, as we know, is made of unassailable truths mixed with gross simplifications and, sometimes, obsolete facts.

This book will help dispel some of the myths that have clouded our collective understanding about Venezuela's surprising developments over the past decade. Venezuela's dizzying recent evolution and its tragic current predicament cannot be comprehended without understanding what happened during the forty years between the demise of the Marcos Pérez Jiménez dictatorship in 1958 and the collapse of the party system that formed the backbone of Venezuela's democracy until the mid-1990s. This period is the first focus of the chapters in *The Unraveling of Representative Democracy in Venezuela.*

The four and a half decades analyzed in this book are as interesting for what failed to happen in Venezuela as for what did happen. Venezuela, for example, did not suffer from major armed conflicts or the miserable economic performance so common among developing countries. While its neighbors were ravaged by wars, economic instability, and political turmoil, Venezuela was a functioning democracy in which fair and competitive elections took place every five years and in which opposition candidates won five of the eight elections held in that period. Venezuela was also a country that between 1920 and 1980 posted the world's highest yearly rate of economic growth and the planet's lowest inflation. Ironically, since the early 1990s, as other Latin American countries seemed to gain a more solid political and economic footing, Venezuela spiraled out of control in a self-destructive cycle that shows no signs of abating.

Thus, Venezuela entered the twenty-first century under dramatically different conditions, but conditions still as exceptional as they were during the second half of the twentieth century; now, however, instead of being exceptionally good, these conditions were—and still are— exceptionally bad. But is Venezuela's situation a relic of the past or a harbinger of things to come in Latin America and perhaps even elsewhere in the developing world? This volume addresses this question, as well, as it analyzes the rise of the Bolivarian Revolution and the nature of the political regime that replaced the Punto Fijo regime.

As for its role as a model for the region, there is no doubt that the politics of rage, race, and revenge so deftly utilized by Lieutenant Colonel Hugo Chávez to mobilize a wide base of supporters are echoed by new political movements sprouting throughout the region. Argentina's *piqueteros,* Brazil's *sin terras,* Bolivia's *cocaleros,* and Mexico's *zapatistas* are just some of the most notorious examples of new political actors that share agendas, modes of operation, and international supporters with Chávez's Bolivarian Revolution. Some of these groups are marginal and will either disappear or be co-opted by mainstream political actors. Others are bound to increase their power and influence. In all cases, however, their grievances have become part of the national political discourse.

Their grievances all stem from their countries' poor economic performance, the chronic inability of the governments to deploy more effective social policies, and an intense democratization process that has enabled the emergence of new political actors capable of challenging the traditional political parties. Even during the spells of economic bonanza which all Latin American countries seem to enjoy at one time or another when the winds of the international economy blow in their favor, governments fail to use their windfalls to make a substantial dent on poverty. When such failures are combined with the popular perception that these countries are "rich" in minerals, agricultural land, or other valuable resources, then it follows that the main, if not the only, explanation for the rampant poverty is the thievery of the rich and powerful—a pervasive theme throughout the region. Venezuela's oil riches coupled with its continuous economic decline and booming poverty in the past two decades make the country a paradigmatic example of what happens when the "corruption explanation" becomes the central organizing theme of political discourse and action.

Yet, although widespread corruption is inexcusable and an unquestionable Latin American reality, it is also unquestionable that bad public policies and a public sector that simply does not work are far more important than corruption in fueling poverty and human suffering. It is, of course, true that corruption is also a driver of bad polices and inept institutions. But the assumption that corruption is the single most important cause of poverty and inequality—and thus that its eradication is the single most important solution to these problems—has become itself an impediment to political, economic, and social progress throughout the region. The Venezuelan experience serves as an example of the collateral damages caused by an ineffective, misguided, and ultimately bankrupt war on corruption. Venezuela's decades-long anticorruption obsession actually fueled corruption, increased political instability and economic inequality, and prevented a more productive discussion of the problems facing the nation.

These nefarious effects stem from the widespread and paralyzing idea that if public sector thievery is the root of poverty then stopping it would immediately, and almost effortlessly, improve the lot of the poor. This message, endlessly repeated by politicians, intellectuals, international experts, schoolteachers, and, very important, the scriptwriters of *telenovelas,* has become the silver bullet that blocks the public discussion of most other policies. Why dwell on cumbersome educational reforms or debate methods to ensure that hospitals are adequately staffed and stocked if corruption will cripple any initiative? The widespread conviction is that only by getting rid of corruption will there be any hope of improving health, education, or, for that matter, any public service that matters to the poor. Thus a reduction in corruption is bound to translate not only into added prosperity but also into better social policies.

The dominant thought—especially in an oil-producing country—is that *the money is there; it's just a matter of distributing it better.* A survey conducted in 2000 found that 82 percent of Venezuelans thought that theirs was the richest country in the world (Naím, 2001). As several chapters of this book show, the reality is that *the money stopped being there a while ago.* In 1974 oil revenues contributed $1,540 per head to the government coffers. In the mid-nineties the number was closer to $200. GDP per capita in 2000 was the same as it had been in 1950. Corruption alone cannot explain this macroeconomic implosion. Bad policies, not bad morals, are the principal explanation of this catastrophic decline.

Nonetheless, Venezuela still is a country rich in oil, and a better use of its substantial oil income can improve social conditions. But a Venezuelan reality as important as its oil wealth—and one that is usually buried under the corruption explanation—is the country's dire poverty in terms of the other resources and conditions needed to create sustainable and equitable prosperity: reliable and effective institutions. Venezuela's schools, hospitals, ministries, universities, armed forces, judiciary, private sector, political parties, and regulatory agencies have a hard time fulfilling the goals for which they exist. Most don't. This volume highlights those institutional deficits and their roots in political culture and structural constraints. It usefully emphasizes, for example, the variables embedded in Venezuela's political culture (orientations toward democracy and consensus building, strong preference for tutelary leadership, and political learning) and their interplay with the nation's political economy (volatile oil revenues, demographic change, growing poverty, weak international linkages). Some of the chapters show how these factors have constrained and influenced the institutional development and choices of political leaders throughout Venezuela's democratic history.

Still, the corruption explanation and its collateral damage to the way in which the electorate, political and media leaders, or intellectuals interpreted Venezuela's woes and their solution are the subtext to several of the chapters in this book. In Venezuela, the corruption explanation was not unjustified; nor was it the only idea that influenced expectations, frustrations, policies, and politics during the period reviewed in these pages. But the failure of the Venezuelan elites both to address corruption and to prevent it from becoming the main explanation for everything that went wrong with the country is an important part of the story of Venezuela's surprising and painful implosion.

The central role played by corruption, its discussion, and the failures to limit it together with Venezuela's declining economic fortunes paved the way for the ascendancy of Lieutenant Colonel Hugo Chávez and his Bolivarian Revolution. Jennifer McCoy, David Myers, and their colleagues writing in these pages have given future historians a sound foundation on which to base their analysis of Chávez's revolution. Ironically, under Chávez corruption is still an important protagonist of Venezuelan history. Even though Chávez owes much of his political good fortune to his fiery anticorruption rhetoric and he enjoys almost completely unchecked leeway over almost all the levers of power, during his time in government corruption is still blatant and pervasive, and it still dominates everyone's mind. It will thus be interesting to see if future historians of the Chávez period will confirm the conclusion that Professor Charles Simic reached after studying other revolutions: "Despite what historians may pretend, in revolutionary times stealing is more important than ideas. While leaders of the revolution promise the moon, murder and looting are the only reality that the powerless know" (Simic, 2003).

It is hoped that, as a result of the chapters in this book and of other similar studies, future Venezuelan leaders will be able to identify ideas that will enable them to steer the country toward a situation in which revolutionary promises are replaced by real achievements and in which corruption, rage, and revenge are not the main sentiments that define the nation's political soul.

Moisés Naím
Editor in Chief
Foreign Policy magazine
Washington, D.C.

Preface and Acknowledgments

We initiated this project at the March 2000 LASA Congress after discussing the need to better understand the demise of Venezuela's Punto Fijo democracy in order to understand its replacement. We both had long and deep involvement in Venezuela, Myers going back to the late 1960s with his doctoral research and McCoy to the early 1980s with her doctoral research. Since then, we both continued to visit, study, and write on Venezuela and to collaborate with our academic colleagues in Venezuela and the United States.

Beginning in 1998, McCoy became involved in Venezuelan political developments in a more direct way through her leadership in the Carter Center's efforts, monitoring elections and referenda from 1998 to 2000 and then creating the Tripartite Working Group (OAS, UNDP, and Carter Center) that facilitated national dialogue and negotiations in 2002 and 2003. Myers served as an election observer for the Carter Center in several of those elections as well. Earlier, in 1987 and 1988, he polled and consulted for the 1988 presidential election campaign of Carlos Andrés Pérez.

We would like to acknowledge the support of both of our universities toward this project. Georgia State University provided funds for the translation of several of the chapters and for the indexing, as well as research and editorial assistance. Pennsylvania State University provided funds and technical assistance to produce the graphics. We are also indebted to James A. Buchanan of the U.S. State Department for hosting a conference in September 2000 during which many of the authors presented first drafts of their chapters.

Marcela Szymanski and Robert Barros translated several of the chapters from Spanish to English. Ines Rojas and Shawn Bingham of Georgia State University helped edit the chapters and the reference list. María Inclan of Pennsylvania State University revised the graphs and charts to ensure that they conformed to the specifications of the Johns Hopkins University Press. Grace Buonocore Carino provided patient and careful editorial assistance, Carol

Zimmerman managed the production editing of the book, and Henry Tom, executive editor at the Press, was patient and encouraging throughout the process.

We thank all our contributors for their willingness to go through several drafts to ensure coherence and readability for the volume. Finally, we want to recognize one of our contributors, Janet Kelly, now deceased, as one of the most cogent and courageous analysts of Venezuelan politics and economics in her adopted country.

Abbreviations

AA	Acción Agropecuaria (Agropecuarian Action)
AD	Acción Democrática (Democratic Action). Dominant political party of the Punto Fijo era; nationalist and social democratic.
ANC	Asamblea Nacional Constituyente (National Constituent Assembly)
CADIVI	Comisión de Administración de Divisas (The Exchange Control Agency)
CCN	Cruzada Cívica Nacionalista (Nationalist Civic Crusade). Political party founded in the late 1960s to support the return to power of General Marcos Pérez Jiménez.
CENDES	El Centro de Estudios del Desarrollo, Universidad Central de Venezuela (The Center for Development Studies, Central University of Venezuela)
CESAP	Centro al Servicio de la Acción Popular (Center for the Service of Popular Action)
CNE	Consejo Nacional Electoral (National Electoral Council)
CONATEL	Comisión Nacional de Telecomunicaciones (Telecommunications Commission)
CONIVE	Consejo Nacional Indio de Venezuela (National Indian Council of Venezuela)
COPEI	Comité de Organización Política Electoral Independiente: Partido Social Cristiano (Committee of Independent Electoral Political Organization: Social Christian Party). Second political party of the Punto Fijo era.
COPRE	Comisión Presidencial para la Reforma del Estado (Presidential Commission for State Reform). Created in 1985 and formed by representatives of different political parties, unions, professional associations, business associa-

	tions, and citizen groups to review relations between the state and Venezuelan society.
CORDIPLAN	Oficina Central de Coordinación y Planificación (Central Office of Coordination and Planning)
CTV	Confederación de Trabajadores de Venezuela (Confederation of Venezuelan Workers)
CVF	Corporación Venezolana de Fomento (Venezuelan Development Corporation)
FAPUV	Federación de Profesores Universitarios (Federation of University Professors)
FCU	Federación de Centros Universitarios (Federation of University Centers)
FDP	Fuerza Democrática Popular (Popular Democratic Force). Political party founded in 1962 to support the presidential candidacy of Admiral Wolfgang Larrazábal.
FEDECAMARAS	Federación de Cámaras y Asociaciones de Comercio y Producción de Venezuela (Federation of Chambers of Commerce and Production of Venezuela)
FEDEPETROL	Federación de Trabajadores Petroleros (Federation of Oil Workers). Venezuela's richest and most important labor union.
FEM	Fondo de Estabilización Macroeconómica (Macroeconomic Stabilization Fund. It later became Fondo de Inversión para la Estabilización Macroeconómica (FIEM; Investment Fund for Macroeconomic Stabilization).
FIDES	Fondo Intergubernamental para la Descentralización (Intergovernmental Fund for Decentralization)
FIN	Fuerza Independiente Nacional (Independent National Force)
FND	Frente Nacional Democrático (National Democratic Front). Center-right political party founded by Arturo Uslar Pietri. It participated in President Raúl Leoni's "Government of the Broad Front" (1963–65).
GE	Gente Emergente (Emergent People)
ICC	Independientes con el Cambio (Independents with the Change)
ID	Izquierda Democrática (Democratic Left)

IESA	Instituto de Estudios Superiores de Administración (Institute for Graduate Studies in Administration). Training in public and business administration.
IPCN	Independientes por la Comunidad Nacional (Independents for the National Community)
LCR	La Causa Radical (The Radical Cause). Political party founded by Alfredo Maneiro, a Communist guerrilla fighter of the 1960s, with roots in labor.
LUZ	Universidad del Zulia (University of Zulia)
MAS	Movimiento al Socialismo (Movement toward Socialism). Breakaway faction of the Venezuelan Communist Party that adopted a social-democratic ideology.
MBR-200	Movimiento Bolivariano Revolucionario 200 (Bolivarian Revolutionary Movement 200). Clandestine organization of young military officers organized by Hugo Chávez Frías in the 1980s. It staged the unsuccessful coup attempt of February 4, 1992.
MDD	Movimiento por la Democracia Directa (Movement for Direct Democracy)
MEP	Movimiento Electoral del Pueblo (Electoral Movement of the People). Faction of Acción Democrática that supported the presidential candidacy of Luis B. Prieto in 1968.
MIN	Movimiento de Integridad Nacional (National Integrity Movement)
MIR	Movimiento de Izquierda Revolucionario (Movement of the Revolutionary Left). Guerrilla organization, and later political party, of the 1960s with roots in Acción Democrática.
MVR	Movimiento Quinta República (Fifth Republic Movement). Political party established in 1997 to support the presidential candidacy of Hugo Chávez Frías
NGD	Nueva Generación Democrática (New Democratic Generation)
NRD	Nuevo Régimen Democrática (New Democratic Regime)
OAS	Organization of American States
OCEPRE	Oficina Central de Presupuesto (Budget Central Office)

ONDA	Organización Nacionalista Democrática Activa (Nationalist Active Democratic Organization
OPEC	Organization of Petroleum Exporting Countries
ORA	Organización Renovadora Auténtica (Authentic Renovating Organization)
PCV	Partido Comunista de Venezuela (Venezuelan Communist Party)
PDVSA	Petróleos de Venezuela Sociedad Anónima (Venezuelan Oil Company, Incorporated). State corporation composed of the private petroleum companies nationalized in 1976.
PPT	Patria para Todos (Homeland for All). Political party composed of breakaway factions from La Causa Radical.
PQAC	Por Querer a la Ciudad (For Love to the City)
RENACE	Rescate Nacional Electoral (National Electoral Rescue)
SI	Movimiento Solidaridad Independiente (Movement Independent Solidarity)
UCAB	Universidad Católica Andrés Bello (Andrés Bello Catholic University)
UCV	Universidad Central de Venezuela (Central University of Venezuela). The oldest and most prestigious university in the country.
UDO	Universidad de Oriente (University of the East)
ULA	Universidad de Los Andes (University of the Andes). The second oldest university in the country; for many years a stronghold of Christian democratic ideology.
URD	Unión Republicana Democrática (Democratic Republican Union)
VenAmCham	Venezuelan-American Chamber of Commerce and Industry
VU	Venezuela Unida (Venezuela United)

The Unraveling of Representative Democracy in Venezuela

Introduction

Jennifer L. McCoy and David J. Myers

The unraveling of an apparently consolidated representative democratic regime poses new theoretical challenges for comparative politics. Early literature on democratic transition and consolidation focused on identifying the conditions and paths by which those transitions would "consolidate" into institutionalized liberal democracies. More recently, scholars have questioned the notion of consolidation and emphasized instead the need to measure the quality of democracy, and they have further attempted to delineate important subtypes of democratic and quasi-democratic regimes (Collier and Levitsky, 1997).

These efforts have led scholars to take a second look at political regimes that are not fully democratic and liberal but which have ceased to be authoritarian and which exhibit some democratic characteristics. Such regimes have been characterized as "hybrid" (Hartlyn, 2002) and placed in a "gray zone" between liberal democracy and outright dictatorship (Carothers, 2002; Myers and McCoy, 2003). Political regimes in this gray zone may, of course, evolve into liberal democracies. On the other hand, they may become institutionalized in the gray zone. Carothers (2002) recognizes two kinds of gray zone regimes which appear with some frequency in the developing world. One, the "feckless democracy," is dominated by unresponsive hierarchical political parties. It allows for fair elections and limited civil liberties, but its policy outputs are unresponsive to mass demands. A second common variety, the "dominant power system," usually has some kind of electoral base, but elections are not fair, and there are severe restrictions on political liberties. Carothers views Venezuela's Punto Fijo democracy, especially as it functioned in the 1990s, as a "feckless democracy."

Other social scientists have identified alternative types of hybrid regimes which may be stable for significant periods of time and which do not represent a movement along the continuum of democratization. These include electoral authoritarianism (Schedler, 2002); competitive authoritarianism (Levitsky and Way, 2002); hybrid regimes (Diamond, 2002); delegative democracies (O'Donnell, 1994); limited pluralism (Gil Yepes, 1978); illiberal democracies (Zakaria, 1997); twilight zone democracies (Diamond, 1999); and exclusionary democracies (Remmer, 1985–86). However, there has been little progress in understanding how these regimes become institutionalized or how stable they are. In other words, we still lack a theory of change from one of these hybrid, or gray zone, political regime subtypes to another.

The demise of Venezuela's Punto Fijo democracy did not signal the end of democracy per se but of one variant of limited democracy which lasted over a forty-year period. The demise of that regime differs from the regime ruptures represented by the twentieth-century military coups and violent revolutions and from the political instability leading to frequent government and constitutional changes. The evidence suggests that the unraveling of representative (though limited) democracy in Venezuela and the transition to a more hybrid regime (one that combines elements of pluralism and authoritarianism, of representative and direct democracy, and of capitalism and statism) are charting a previously unobserved path of political change.

The rise of Venezuela's Fifth (Bolivarian) Republic under Hugo Chávez Frías raises theoretical challenges for comparative politics. Does it offer a new and more responsive variant of democracy—one that, as its proponents claim, favors politics that are direct, participatory, and less prone to corruption? Or is it a new incarnation of civic-military populism which updates the tenets of Juan Perón's Justicialismo and Marcos Pérez Jiménez's New National Ideal? Finally, regardless how scholars describe what has occurred in Venezuela, does the new political regime herald a future direction for Latin America?

This volume views Venezuela since the "Black Friday" currency devaluation of 1983 as an example of political regime change within the gray zone. It examines the unraveling of a long-lived limited democracy—the Punto Fijo regime of 1958–98[1]—and the rise of another regime type. The emerging regime type, as yet incompletely defined, shares many characteristics with Punto Fijo. In both, political elites operate in small circles, but they reach out on a limited basis to supportive economic and cultural elites. Decision making is centralized in each. Nevertheless, Fifth Republic Venezuela, when all is said and done, is less open and less pluralistic than its predecessor. Decision making within it relies heavily on one person—President Hugo Chávez. The authors of this book argue that both regimes lie within the gray zone.

Democracies, whether limited or fully pluralistic, are a type of political regime characterized by a particular set of rules and institutions governing access to power. The essential rules of the democratic political game constitute Dahl's notion of polyarchy (1971).[2]

Venezuela's second-wave democracy (the Punto Fijo regime) took root unexpectedly, as did its successor.[3] The former regime, as suggested earlier, functioned within the spectrum of Dahl's rules of polyarchy while remaining in the gray zone. We view the Punto Fijo regime as a *limited pluralist polyarchy*.[4] It had deeply entrenched political parties that shared power and operated multiclass patronage networks. These parties had difficulty renewing themselves, and over time they became isolated. Likewise, Hugo Chávez's Bolivarian Revolution, or Fifth Republic, is a kind of gray zone polyarchy, though it exhibits more hybrid characteristics than its predecessor. It blurs the relationship between the state and governing party, creates mechanisms of direct democracy while weakening mechanisms of representative democracy, and involves the military extensively in public policy formulation and implementation.[5]

Normalization of the Punto Fijo regime merits attention. The development was unexpected and long-lasting. After an initial period of uncertainty, marked by challenges from insurgencies on the right and on the left, post-1958 democracy normalized into a two-party-dominant competitive electoral democracy that lasted until 1998. North American scholars have focused on two factors, oil income and statecraft, to explain why post-1958 democracy took root in Venezuela while the rest of the continent experienced popular unrest and military domination. Michael Burton (Burton and Higley, 1987), John Higley (Burton, Gunther, and Higley, 1992), Daniel Levine (1973), John Martz (1966), and John Peeler (1992), some of the best-known scholars of the statecraft school, analyzed leadership agreements and institutional arrangements to explain how Venezuelan political elites managed conflicts that were rending the political fabric of other second-wave democracies. Scholars like Gene Bigler (1981), Fernando Coronil (1997), and Terry Karl (1987) attributed Venezuelan political stability after 1958 to characteristics embedded in the rentier state. The rentier state of that time displayed great capability to distribute resources based on its ability to extract revenue from the international environment. Distributive capability based on oil revenue thus shaped particular institutions and underlay the political pacts making it possible to have a democracy with very few losers.

These two contending perspectives, then, emphasized either the variables of policy making and choice or the structural characteristics of the political economy. At the same time, Venezuelan scholars noted that the alleged advantages for democratic consolidation bestowed in each of these perspectives also had their down side. Juan Pablo Pérez Alfonso (1976) pointed out the negative consequences of being flooded with oil, or the "excrement of the devil," and Miriam Kornblith and Thais Maingon (1984) analyzed how these negative consequences undercut the capabilities of the state to extract and distribute resources. José Antonio Gil Yepes (1978) discussed how Punto Fijo democracy limited responsiveness, and Juan Carlos Rey (1989) demonstrated how a political regime based on elite pacts tended to grow ever more closed as time passed.

The two contending schools that attempted to explain the unexpected normalization of Punto Fijo democracy also compete to illuminate why it unraveled. Some who examine political decay in Venezuela from the statecraft perspective argue that party pacts, because of their elitist nature, are always centralist and exclusionary. They argue that, to a large extent, the operational rules of post-1958 democracy reflected the disposition of newly triumphant party leaders to "circle the wagons" once they assembled a coalition of interests capable of dominating politics. With the passage of time social mobility decreased, and excluded groups turned on the ruling elite. The resulting legitimacy crisis could be overcome only if established national leaders were willing to provide new channels for interest articulation by the emerging civil society and elected officials in the regions and municipalities. This kind of power sharing was not part of the elite agreements that led to Punto Fijo in the first place, and the regime's elites resisted creating the new channels for interest articulation throughout the 1990s (Crisp, Levine, and Rey, 1995: 160).

Others in the statecraft tradition echo arguments made by Diamond, Hartlyn, and Linz for the region as a whole (1999: 1–70). In the case of Venezuela, their concern is with the conditions that prevailed when party system institutionalization was occurring and with the tutelary nature of post-1958 democracy (Coppedge, 1994; Oropeza, 1983). Coppedge and Oropeza claim that the structures crafted by elites to shape the institutions of Punto Fijo were designed to permit rapid and decisive actions by national leaders when threats appeared. On the other hand, the mentality present at the creation of Punto Fijo tended to restrict the options considered by the Caracas elite. Those at the center of power avoided strategies that expanded the number of effective political actors (Crisp, 1997: 161–63). This mind-set undermined the political regime when modernization produced a civil society that became more assertive and diverse.

Finally, another facet of the statecraft perspective focuses on the consequences of drawing lessons about how best to govern from earlier events and adhering to those lessons when conditions change (Jácome, 2000; McCoy, 1999, 2000). Scholars who focus on political learning in the Venezuelan context point out that the lessons learned from the military's overthrow of President Rómulo Gallegos in 1948 led to cooperative behavior that helped to stabilize Punto Fijo democracy during the 1960s. However, conditions were different after the Black Friday currency devaluation of 1983, and behavior that contributed to regime consolidation in an earlier era had the opposite effect. For example, power sharing among supporters of Punto Fijo democracy in the 1990s came to be viewed as exclusionary. It led most Venezuelans to search for a different kind of democracy.

The political economy perspective, with its emphasis on petroleum revenue and political power, includes work by Karl (1987, 1997), López (2001), Naím (1993), and Schael (1993). Three of these observers (Karl, Schael, and López) have similar concerns. They draw out implications of the fact that rentier states are unsuited to weather the boom-bust patterns of single-commodity economies and are vulnerable to decay. Naím, on the other hand, examines the politics of adjusting to sharp reductions in the distributive capabilities of the Venezuelan state. He explains how the neoliberal policies most likely to produce rapid economic growth may also destabilize the political regime. Turmoil leads to capital flight, loss of confidence, and economic implosion.

Finally, we note the recent collection edited by Steve Ellner and Daniel Hellinger (2003) which relies on class conflict to analyze why Punto Fijo democracy unraveled. The thrust of this collection is that after 1989 social polarization increased the distances and the tensions between unorganized sectors of the population and the privileged. Acción Democrática (AD; Democratic Action) and Comité de Organización Política Electoral Independiente: Partido Social Cristiano (COPEI; Committee of Independent Electoral Political Organization: Social Christian Party) had long served as vehicles to smother class conflict, but their failure to develop the country and their corrupt practices discredited both. The old order's loss of legitimacy made the urban poor receptive to Hugo Chávez's message of radical change. That message accentuated class conflict, linked Punto Fijo democracy to discredited party elites, and convinced Venezuelans to adopt a new constitution that promised a "different" democracy.

Argument of the Book

We contend that no single approach satisfactorily explains the Punto Fijo experience. The explanation posited by the analyses in this volume draws on three theoretical approaches: structural approaches emphasizing the political economy; institutional approaches emphasizing political choices; and cultural explanations emphasizing mediating political orientations and political learning.

We share Dan Levine's doubts about "Venezuelan Exceptionalism," with its assumption that commodity oil produces unique dynamics and determines the range of choices for institution building and statecraft. The political economy of petroleum, however, was important in the rise and fall of Punto Fijo democracy. Even more significant, in the views of the contributors to this volume, were the choices made about how to utilize oil wealth and manage conflict. These choices responded to cultural predispositions and political learning from recent Venezuelan history, especially the course of events after the passing of General Juan Vicente Gómez in 1935. Attitudes shaped by these two perspectives led to the creation of political institutions that channeled policy making along lines that allowed for the normalization of representative democracy between 1958 and 1975.

The internalization of political mechanisms and procedures to stabilize a regime can embed vulnerabilities that, when conditions change, may lead to its demise. This volume argues that the institutional and policy choices made by Venezuelan elites after the fall of General Pérez Jiménez (in 1958) and during the years when Punto Fijo became the accepted political regime (1958–73) embedded four vulnerabilities that led it to unravel in the 1990s. The first derives from reluctance by those who designed the regime to lessen the dependence of its institutions on income from petroleum. Second, the political regime's founders decided to neglect the state's deteriorated regulative capability, a vulnerability that impeded government's ability to allocate basic services when state income declined and hard choices had to be made. Failure to strengthen regulative capability also complicated attempts to control corruption. In other words, limited regulative capability intensified reliance on distributive politics.

Third, Punto Fijo's supposedly temporary power-sharing arrangements became institutionalized in ways that ensconced the Caracas-based leaders of AD and COPEI in positions that were all but impregnable. Party oligarchs were able to block the ascension of young leaders to power and conspired successfully to keep party organizations in the interior dependent on them (Molina, 1998).

The final embedded weakness of Punto Fijo derived from the very pacts that enabled party leaders, businessmen, and unionized labor to control the political regime while normalization was occurring. Subsequently, after the polity stabilized and the economy modernized, other groups wanted to make their voices heard. This increase in the volume of political demands severely stressed the political regime's capabilities because its political institutions remained exclusionary. The most important marginalized groups were the urban poor, intellectuals, and middle-class civil society.

Our analysis of the unraveling of Punto Fijo democracy highlights interaction between the distributive and representative crises that gained momentum after 1983.[6] This volume begins with an examination of the process by which that regime became normalized in a country where authoritarian rule and military dictators had been the norm. Part II, composed of seven chapters, focuses on Venezuela's most important political groups. We examine their political behavior over almost two decades of political decay (1983–98) and during the transition to the Fifth Republic (1998–2000). Each chapter also discusses and analyzes how these interests are faring as Hugo Chávez seeks to build a new and different democracy. The actors receiving the most attention here are the urban poor, the military, entrepreneurs, groups in civil society, intellectuals, and the U.S. government. This part closes with a discussion of the political party system that organized and brokered political demands throughout the Punto Fijo period, but the emphasis is on events after 1983.

Next, our volume focuses on public policy. Part III opens with an analysis of the struggle to decentralize. Advocates of decentralization in the Punto Fijo years attempted to bring about an institutional reorganization in the 1990s which would make the system more accountable and representative. However, decentralization ran counter to the directly consultative mechanisms favored by President Chávez, and he undid most of the decentralizing reforms. We turn next to the ebb and flow of economic decisions that accompanied the demise of representative democracy and the transition to the Fifth Republic. We also assess capital flight and the Fifth Republic's prospects for economic growth and development, a concern that also surfaces in Chapter 4, on Venezuela's beleaguered entrepreneurial elite. The last chapter in Part III studies public opinion and how it reflected the declining legitimacy of representative political institutions. It also identifies and analyzes the attitudes that opened the way for Hugo Chávez's election to the presidency in 1998 and 2000 and which fed subsequent dissatisfaction with his government.

Our conclusion draws from the individual chapters to develop themes and propositions that provide insights into how and why Venezuela's representative democracy unraveled. It also examines events in the transition to the Fifth Republic and speculates on the nature of the political regime that President Chávez seeks to impose. The conclusion closes with an assessment of whether Venezuela's gray zone political regime represents a new model of participatory democracy or a neopopulist model, one that may gain currency throughout the region in situations in which representative democracy has been slow to satisfy basic human needs and lost its legitimacy.

Part I / Antecedents

The Foundations of the Punto Fijo Regime of Representative Democracy

CHAPTER ONE

The Normalization of Punto Fijo Democracy

David J. Myers

The unbroken thread of Venezuelan democracy dates from January 1, 1959, when Rómulo Betancourt took the oath as president, less than a month after his victory in the national elections of December 5. This fledgling political regime, known as Punto Fijo democracy, withstood challenges over four decades from neighboring dictators, leftist guerrillas, disgruntled military officers, and urban rioters. At the height of the cold war, President John F. Kennedy praised Venezuelan democracy as the true alternative to communism and authoritarianism in the Western Hemisphere.[1] Yet the survival of the democratic experiment remained in doubt when Betancourt took the presidential oath on January 1, 1959. Venezuela had experienced less than one year of elected democratic governments in almost 130 years of independence, and powerful enemies—foreign as well as domestic—plotted to ensure that power would not be passed to a successor administration by means of free and popular elections.

Representative democracy did survive, and democratic norms and procedures became the accepted way of conducting political business. Venezuela's post-1958 regime gained widespread legitimacy and entrenched itself in the face of political turbulence that brought down democracies in many other Latin American countries during the 1960s. So successful did this democracy appear that observers of Latin American politics regularly spoke of Venezuelan exceptionalism.[2] This characterization proved premature. Punto Fijo democracy unraveled in response to a series of punctuated political and economic crises that began in 1983 and culminated in the election of Lieutenant Colonel Hugo Chávez Frías as president in December 1998. Seven years earlier Chávez had masterminded an unsuccessful coup that came within a whisker of toppling the government of President Carlos Andrés Pérez.

President Chávez administered the coup de grâce to Punto Fijo democracy in short order. His final moves against the dying political regime played on perceptions that the established political parties were arrogant and on their failure to create economic prosperity with petroleum revenue. Within a year of his inauguration the new president convinced the electorate to authorize a constituent assembly and to approve a new constitution.[3] The 1999 constitution substituted a highly centralized direct democracy for political rules that had been fundamentally representative, a centralized state for one that had grown more decentralized, and a strong presidency for a national executive that had been recently forced to share power with a newly assertive congress and judiciary.

Seven months after the 1999 constitution went into effect, President Chávez ran successfully for reelection to a new six-year term. His personal movement, the Movimiento Quinta República (MVR; Fifth Republic Movement), gained control of the National Assembly, the most important governorships, and a majority of the mayoralties. Four months later, in December 2000, MVR repeated its successes in elections for the municipal and neighborhood councils. This restructuring of the political system set the stage for efforts to bring about far-reaching social and economic changes.

The Bolivarians, as Hugo Chávez's inner circle was known, blamed Venezuela's post-1983 difficulties on Punto Fijo's ruling elite and on its close association with the United States. The president promised a "different democracy," one that would diminish the influence of those he blamed for the plight of Venezuelans who had been left behind. The villainous elites included wealthy businessmen, corrupt political party leaders, coddled professionals, and kept unions. Bolivarian leaders encouraged those whom the previous political regime had "exploited" to press for what rightfully was theirs. In other words, the Chávez government replaced rhetoric designed to suppress class conflict (the terms of political discourse favored by Punto Fijo democrats) with calls for the underprivileged to unite against those who had prospered between 1958 and 1998.

The five years that followed Hugo Chávez's ascension to the presidency were tumultuous times. The government maneuvered incessantly to weaken institutions that retained an autonomous power base in society, especially after the elections of July 30 and December 5, 2000. In response, President Chávez's opponents became ever more strident. Merchants, professionals, the middle sectors, and allied union workers staged marches and strikes with increasing frequency. Support from executives of the state petroleum corporation, Petróleos de Venezuela Sociedad Anónima (PDVSA; Venezuelan Oil Company, Incorporated), enabled opponents to disrupt oil production. In addition, opponents plotted with dissident generals and admirals to oust President Chávez, and on April 11, 2002, they succeeded. Their short-lived victory proved Pyrrhic. Confusion reigned within the provisional government, and support from the urban poor for Chávez led the armed forces to reverse themselves. After less than forty-eight hours they restored President Chávez to power. The provisional government's sorry performance reinforced suspicions that the opposition had no coherent plan for governing.

President Chávez passed the midpoint of his presidential term on August 20, 2003. Although his appeal among the poor remained strong, public opinion polls indicated that upwards of 65 percent of voters viewed him negatively. This encouraged opposition forces to focus on the provision of the 1999 constitution which outlined procedures for recall of the president. During the last quarter of 2003, therefore, efforts to recall President Chávez dominated Venezuelan politics. The government maneuvered to prevent or delay the recall election, and tensions between President Chávez and his opponents threatened to ignite violence at a moment's notice. Thus, the unraveling of representative democracy that began with the February 18, 1983, currency devaluation (Black Friday) continued with uncertainty and instability into the twenty-first century.

My task in this chapter is to set the stage to examine this volume's central themes: the unraveling of Venezuela's post-1958 representative democracy and the rise of a potential new model for Latin America—the Fifth, or "Bolivarian," Republic. In setting the stage I examine three developments that shaped the fledgling Punto Fijo democracy. First, attention centers on the precedent-setting elite settlement of 1957–59. I identify those who crafted it and examine how and why groups with a long history of hatred and distrust put aside their suspicions and cooperated in a risky political venture. The second development follows from the reluctance of some important actors initially to embrace the settlement. However, the first three Punto Fijo presidents (Rómulo Betancourt [1959–64], Raúl Leoni [1964–69], and Rafael Caldera [1969–74]) governed effectively and pragmatically. I examine the policies during these administrations which won support for Punto Fijo democracy from all but a few die-hard holdouts. In February 1974, on the eve of the inauguration of the fourth Punto Fijo president (Carlos Andrés Pérez), most Venezuelans supported the Punto Fijo regime. That support persisted well into the 1990s.

Finally, this introduction examines the embedding of four vulnerabilities into the political regime during the period in which regime-supportive leaders expanded support for the 1957–59 settlement. For almost two decades these vulnerabilities seemed unimportant. However, in the changed conditions that followed the 1983 currency devaluation and the 1989 urban riots, these vulnerabilities crippled efforts by Punto Fijo leaders to adapt to the political and economic storm that eventually destroyed their democratic regime.

The Elite Settlement of 1957–59 and Elite Convergence

The Settlement: Actors, Process, and Motives

On January 23, 1958, an alliance of civilians and disgruntled factions of the armed forces ousted General Marcos Pérez Jiménez, and the new civic-military ruling junta scheduled elections for late in the year. Power flowed to political party leaders, many of whom had struggled for almost a decade against the military dictatorship. Acción Democrática (AD; Democratic Action) and the Comité de Organización Política Electoral Independiente: Partido Social Cristiano (COPEI; Committee of Independent Electoral Political Organization: Social Christian Party) controlled most important societal groupings. These included organizations of peasants, workers, educators, and professionals. Both political parties played an important role in drafting the elite settlement. AD boasted the larger institutional infrastructure, and it included guerrilla cadres that had fought in the underground against General Pérez Jiménez. COPEI, on the other hand, enjoyed backing from the church. The Unión Republicana Democrática (URD; Democratic Republican Union), the third settlement-drafting political party, depended heavily on the charismatic appeal of its founder, Jóvito Villalba. After two decades of destructive and often brutal conflict, these three parties desired a new and less destructive mode of competition.

AD and COPEI (and to a lesser degree URD) were hostile toward the fourth important political party, the Partido Comunista de Venezuela (PCV; Venezuelan Communist Party). They froze PCV out of the 1957–59 settlement even though PCV cadres had shed their blood in the clandestine struggle against Pérez Jiménez's dictatorship. Senior AD, COPEI, and URD leaders viewed PCV as more loyal to international communism than to Venezuela, and they doubted that national Communist leaders would commit to the kind of procedural democracy they intended to establish (Alexander, 1982: 426–28). In addition, AD, COPEI, and URD concluded that they needed the U.S. government's blessing if their pact was to evolve into a stable democracy, and they calculated that close association with PCV would jeopardize that blessing.

The most important nonparty elites entering into the 1957–59 settlement were entrepreneurs and the ecclesiastical hierarchy. Entrepreneurs turned against military populism, and prominent industrialists consulted with the leaders of AD, COPEI, and URD in New York during December 1957, just before the three parties issued their joint declaration in support of overthrowing the dictatorship. Business and ecclesiastical elites remained generally supportive of the new democracy even after Rómulo Betancourt, the AD leader they most distrusted, won the December 1958 presidential election.

Two other traditional elites, large landowners and the military, had even more misgivings about the 1957–59 settlement than either business or the church did. Landowners loathed AD from the moment of its birth, for the party's program called for the breakup of Venezuela's landed estates. During the initial period when AD governed, the so-called Trienio (1945–48), landowners fought against the agrarian reform initiated by AD governments. A decade later, after the overthrow of General Pérez Jiménez, rural landowners remained suspicious of AD, even when the second Betancourt government backed away from large-scale land redistribution. However, AD's moderation suggested that the second Betancourt government might be less militantly egalitarian than the provisional one over which Betancourt presided between October 1945 and February 1948.

Venezuela's officer corps included some AD loyalists during the Trienio. Between 1948 and 1950 opponents of democracy purged those most closely linked with AD; however, many in the military were uncomfortable with the undercurrent of brutality that marked Pérez Jiménez's exercise of power. Thus, it fell to the general's infamous police force, the Seguridad Nacional, to terrorize and liquidate his enemies. Nevertheless, most Venezuelans identified Pérez Jiménez's regime with the armed forces, and the institution's prestige plummeted when his dictatorship fell. The officer corps was powerless to prevent the return of the democratic political leaders whom they had exiled. Fifteen months into Rómulo Betancourt's presidency, in April 1960, opponents of the regime led by retired air force chief of staff General José María Castro León attempted to reestablish military rule. A nationwide outpouring of support for the elected government doomed this adventure, but military officers displayed the ambivalence toward Punto Fijo democracy which would be typical of their attitude toward that political regime for as long as it lasted (Agüero, 1995: ch. 10; Alexander, 1964: 110–11).

No faction of the elite despised the 1957–59 settlement more than Pérez Jiménez loyalists did. In addition to having lost its dominating position in the military, this inner circle had played a leading role during the 1950s in commerce, industry, and the professional associations. When General Pérez Jiménez fled, these loyalists lost their privileged position, and the defeat of Castro León dashed their hopes of quickly returning to power. In addition, after Castro León's rebellion, democratic leaders used the state to undermine the influence of those Pérez Jiménez loyalists who refused to mute their opposition to the elite settlement of 1957–59. But whether openly hostile or discreetly quiet, Pérez Jiménez loyalists remained a force with which democratic political parties had to reckon well into the 1970s.

The new democracy also faced challenges from radical leftists throughout the 1960s. Radicals commanded PCV, held important positions in AD and URD, and dominated student organizations at the most prestigious universities. Hostility from militant leftists, which continued over the forty-year life span of the Punto Fijo system, delayed the normalization of representative democracy for more than a decade. With the exception of PCV's founding generation, radical leftists in the 1960s came to prominence as combatants during the 1950s, in the clandestine struggle against General Pérez Jiménez. Venezuelan radical leftists romanticized the Cuban revolution, hoped to implement socialism, and loathed the United States. They also distrusted the senior leaders of AD, COPEI, and URD, viewing them as little more than spectators in the decade long antidictatorial struggle. Once militant leftists understood that the settlement between Venezuela's social, economic, and political party elites would delay, perhaps indefinitely, implementation of their radical agenda, they turned on the fledgling democracy. Many took up arms against the popularly elected (but "deceitful") governments of Rómulo Betancourt and Raúl Leoni. Fidel Castro, who quickly grasped the depth of this political cleavage, trained leftist insurgents and funded their struggle. Support also came from the international Communist movement.

Points of Agreement

The representative democracy spawned by Venezuela's partial elite settlement got under way before many of its rules could be codified. These rules appear in five documents. The first is the previously mentioned communiqué issued by the senior leaders of AD, COPEI, and URD from their exile in New York City. It called upon Venezuelans to replace Pérez Jiménez's dictatorship with a multiparty coalition government. The second is the Avenimiento Obrero-Patronal (Worker-Owner Accord) signed in April 1958 by the labor wings of the four political parties, including PCV, and the business federation; it committed business to respect the democratic order and workers' rights and committed labor to wage restraint and consultative contract negotiation mechanisms (McCoy, 1989).

Party, business, and church elites agreed to the third and fourth documents just prior to the December 1958 national elections. The former, the Pact of Punto Fijo, laid out power-sharing arrangements between the three participating political parties. The latter, Declaration of Principles and Minimal Program for Government, set boundaries in the political economy between the public and private sectors. Accompanying it were informal assurances to church leaders that Catholic education would prosper in the new democracy. Finally, during 1959 and 1960 the Bicameral Commission for Constitutional Reform drafted the 1961 constitution, which was the written source of other important provisions of the partial elite settlement (Alexander, 1982: 420–28; Herrera Campíns, 1977: 111–16; Karl, 1987: 81–89; Levine, 1973: 92–111).[4]

Six points of agreement marked the partial elite settlement: power sharing, reconciliation of old antagonisms, respect for individual liberties, reliance on the state as an engine of economic development, postponement of proposals that would redistribute wealth until procedural democracy was secure, and support for the United States in the cold war. The first commitment, power sharing, began with the agreement to institute a democratic form of government. Equally important, the dominant AD promised not to monopolize government, to consider the interests of other political parties when crafting political decisions, and to mute partisanship in its exercise of control over such linked social groups as organized labor and peasants. During AD's initial period in power (1945–48), opponents found the party wanting on all these accounts. They portrayed the November 1948 military coup that removed President Rómulo Gallegos as an understandable reaction to AD's refusal to allow other elites a meaningful voice in running the country. AD leaders, by entering into the elite settlement, signaled that they had learned from their "mistakes" (Karl, 1987: 78–79; Planchart, 1988: 361–62; Stambouli, 1979: 34).

The promise to share power, although necessary to gain the elite settlement, was not sufficient to normalize democratic rules of the political game. Leaders who had distrusted, despised, and brutalized one another over decades had to agree that they would treat one another with respect, even while acknowledging that they would be at odds over many issues of policy. The New York City declaration by AD, COPEI, and URD leaders demonstrated a new interelite civility, and the Pact of Punto Fijo established mechanisms for power sharing between government, the political parties, and important societal interests. However, all involved acknowledged that the new political regime would gain widespread legitimacy only if its supporters succeeded in crafting institutions that appeared nonthreatening, procedurally fair, and capable of providing rewards to a broad spectrum of groups (Betancourt, 1956: 313; Brewer-Carías, 1988: 380; Planchart, 1988: 370).

The third point of agreement, respect for individual rights and liberties, grew out of bitter experience with state terrorism that became commonplace during the General Pérez Jiménez dictatorship. The 1961 constitution sought to end capricious police behavior with guarantees of human rights and personal liberty. These included freedom of speech, assembly, and religion and a form of habeas corpus. The 1961 constitution also transformed the general public prosecutor of the republic into a kind of ombudsman charged with ensuring respect for constitutional rights and guarantees. Nevertheless, settlement supporters had no intention of allowing constitutional rights and guarantees to shield hostile groups seeking to overthrow the government by force. They created a strong presidency with the power to suspend constitutional rights and guarantees by decree (Crisp, 2000b; Planchart, 1988: 364, 373–76).

One of the most important disagreements between Venezuelan elites after 1945 involved the economic role of the state. Entrepreneurs initially preferred a limited role for government, whereas party leaders viewed the state as an engine of economic development. The 1957–59 settlement favored the latter's position. However, most businessmen had already concluded that they could coexist with an interventionist state and even benefit from selected intervention. Cooperation with the Pérez Jiménez government had shown the business community that state regulation of the economy could be useful for limiting foreign competition. The 1961 constitution, with its emphasis on the social function of property,[5] economic rights of the nation, and the state's role in supervising national economic progress, provided many such opportunities. Still, the business community accepted the 1961 constitution with some reservations. Its empowering of the state to reserve selected industries and operations for the public sector, and its highlighting of the right to restrict industrial and commercial freedoms, fed long-standing suspicions that Venezuela's political parties would not allow a vigorous private sector to develop (Karl, 1987: 84–85; Kornblith, 1995: 78–79; Planchart, 1988: 375–76).

An informal agreement between elites not to pursue issues of wealth and power redistribution, at least until support for procedural democracy had solidified, reassured the private sector. As a gesture of good faith AD senator Raúl Leoni (chairman of the Bicameral Commission for Constitutional Reform) chose the 1953 Pérez Jiménez constitution, rather than the egalitarian constitution of 1947, as the starting point for crafting the Punto Fijo constitution. Leoni feared that if the commission built on the 1947 constitution it would conjure up the hatreds and tensions associated with the redistributive conflicts of 1945–48. PCV efforts to use the 1947 constitution for this purpose were deflected by the settlement-supporting political parties: AD, COPEI, and URD (Brewer-Carías, 1988: 382–83).

Finally, the 1957–59 settlement fixed democratic Venezuela's position in the cold war. AD's Rómulo Betancourt, a longtime critic of U.S. policy toward Latin America, was at first glance an unlikely ally. However, Fidel Castro's attempts to extend his revolution throughout the Caribbean Basin led Betancourt and other settlement-supportive elites to view Cuban communism as an immediate threat. In addition, Presidents Dwight D. Eisenhower and John F. Kennedy signaled a new policy: that the United States now viewed democracy as the only viable alternative to communism in Latin America. This shift away from support for anti-Communist dictators dissipated resentment toward the United States (Rómulo Betancourt, interview with author, Barquisimeto, Lara, June 28, 1978). It became possible for democratic leftists such as Betancourt to side with Washington against Havana and Moscow. On the other hand, Washington's conciliatory attitude toward AD undercut traditionalists who had equated opposition to the AD with anticommunism. This rapprochement between the U.S. government and the center-left infuriated PCV, the leftist factions in AD and URD, and university students (Alexander, 1964: 145–47; Amerson, 1995: 119–203).

Convergence: The Second Phase

The convergence years, 1958–75, were ones when most Venezuelan elites united behind the 1957–59 settlement. Elections during December 1958 brought settlement supporters to power, but, as suggested earlier, important factions remained skeptical or hostile.

The 1957–59 settlement demanded a leap of faith by historical antagonists. Between 1959 and 1975 settlement supporters scrutinized one another to see if each was honoring the terms to which they had agreed. Evidence of good faith mounted, and by the early 1970s establishment elites concluded that they were prospering in a representative democracy dominated by mass-based political parties. Presidents Betancourt and Leoni had expanded the state's economic role, effectively denying the private sector the opportunity to develop heavy industry, but neither sought to nationalize existing companies. Businesses profited from selling to state enterprises, and the private sector acquired a voice in national economic planning (Friedmann, 1965; Gil Yepes, 1978; Salgado, 1987). In addition, important cabinet portfolios, such as minister of the treasury and president of the Central Bank, usually went to individuals with close ties to the private sector. AD also delivered on its promises to the church by normalizing relations with the Vatican, increasing clerical subsidies, and assisting Catholic schools (Levine, 1973). Not surprisingly, as the 1960s progressed, support for the elite settlement grew among business and ecclesiastical leaders.

Members of AD, COPEI, and URD did indeed treat one another with a new civility. As partners in government all three political parties cooperated with President Betancourt, and they received important cabinet positions.[6] AD leaders also shared power with their partners in the interest groups they dominated: industrial unions, teacher organizations, and peasant leagues (Ellner, 1993; McCoy, 1989; Powell, 1971). In addition, COPEI and AD counted significant followings in the professional associations (Martz and Myers, 1994). Nonallied political movements were free to organize as long as they rejected violence. However, except for the Frente Nacional Democrático (FND; National

Democratic Front), the several political parties that emerged in the 1960s were never strong enough to acquire and dispense meaningful patronage. None demonstrated staying power, and after going off by itself, URD declined. COPEI, on the other hand, grew stronger. Its founder, Rafael Caldera, won the presidential election of 1968. AD returned to power in 1974, but COPEI's presidential candidate finished a strong second. Thus, what began as a multiparty democracy became a two-party system dominated by AD and COPEI. Each viewed the other as a "loyal" opponent, and their leaders cooperated to monopolize power (Navarro, 1995).

Two fence-sitting elites, the military and the owners of landed estates, became supporters of the regime. Several factors explain change in the former. First, from the beginning President Betancourt's budgets favored the armed forces, guaranteeing modern equipment and privileged status. In addition, party leaders redefined military responsibilities, adding defense of constitutional democracy to the traditional task of guarding the frontiers. The responsibility to protect the political regime from its enemies became especially important after 1962, when radical leftists mounted a nationwide insurgency with backing from Fidel Castro and international Communists. This defense of the 1961 constitution created a bond between the military and governing civilians (Ewell, 1996: 216–17). It also increased contact between Venezuela's armed forces and the U.S. military at a time when the U.S. government was touting procedural democracy as the only viable alternative to communism in Latin America. Venezuela's once hostile military officer corps became guardedly supportive of democracy.

Large landowners made a similar journey between 1958 and 1975. They breathed a collective sigh of relief when Presidents Betancourt and Leoni confined land reform to distributing estates either confiscated from Pérez Jiménez's inner circle or already owned by the state. In addition, the three convergence-era governments provided agricultural credits while arranging for the state to purchase primary products. Disagreements surfaced over what constituted a "good price" for those products, but neither large landowners nor Punto Fijo politicians permitted tensions to become regime threatening.

Hostility from Pérez Jiménez loyalists, PCV, and leftist factions within AD and URD presented elite settlement supporters with an ongoing challenge. As long as these groups remained hostile and powerful, the future of Venezuelan democracy was in doubt. The Punto Fijo state confiscated the wealth of General Pérez Jiménez's inner circle, but many businessmen and professionals who had prospered during his dictatorship remained affluent, influential, and opposed to party-dominated democracy. Still, advocates of returning the generals to power did not hold center stage during the convergence process. They did reenter the political arena in the 1968 national elections, winning almost 10 percent of the total legislative vote, and for one brief moment Pérez Jiménez's supporters believed that they might return him to the presidency through democratic means.

PCV hostility to the elite settlement of 1957–59 deepened during Rómulo Betancourt's presidency. To a large extent the leaders of AD welcomed this development. AD governments during the Trienio had marginalized PCV, but the party regained popularity as the result of its important role in the anti–Pérez Jiménez underground. Popular support for PCV congressional candidates in the national elections of 1958 exceeded 10 percent, and the party's prospects appeared bright. PCV congressmen and senators, despite expressing some reservations, occupied the congressional seats to which they had been elected. However, from the moment he took office, President Betancourt dispersed patronage in ways intended to weaken and marginalize PCV. In contrast, he assisted Rafael Caldera in developing the institutional infrastructure of COPEI. PCV leaders responded to the government's political and economic attacks on their party by joining with other opponents of the 1957–59 elite settlement in a violent insurgency. The immediate goal was to prevent "bourgeoisie democracy" from renewing its popular mandate.

Leftist factions within URD, like the entire PCV, opted to use armed force against the first two Punto Fijo governments. One young charismatic leader, Fabricio Ojeda, accepted a Cuban army commission in 1962 and organized a highly publicized but short-lived guerrilla unit (Alexander 1964, 101–102).[7] Other URD leaders and sympathizers, most notably Luis Miquelena and José Vicente Rangel, supported Ojeda's insurgency and other violent efforts to bring down the Punto Fijo political regime. They never accepted its legitimacy. Indeed, thirty years later Miquelena and Rangel played a pivotal role in the Bolivarian Revolution that abolished the 1961 constitution and eliminated AD and COPEI as dominating political forces.

Many AD youths shared the outrage of URD leftists and PCV when it became clear that senior AD leaders intended to compromise with the traditional elites. They joined the insurgency (Martz, 1966: 174–83) in the third year of Rómulo Betancourt's presidential term. Led by Américo Martin and Domingo Alberto Rangel, these dissidents formed the Movimiento de Izquierda

Revolucionario (MIR; Movement of the Revolutionary Left). MIR's ideological appeal to students decimated AD's youth organizations, and radicalized students became the core of MIR's guerrilla cadres. MIR and PCV insurgents cooperated in the unsuccessful attempt to derail the 1963 presidential elections. Guerrilla warfare continued until the early 1970s, but military countermeasures and the skillful dispensing of patronage by AD and COPEI governments marginalized the insurgents.

PCV leaders were the first hostile elite to abandon the struggle against Punto Fijo democracy (Alexander, 1969). In 1968 party leaders demobilized their guerrilla forces and agreed to participate in the national elections under the banner of the Unión para Advancar (Union for Advancement). Those who agreed to play by the political rules of the 1961 constitution received amnesty. President Rafael Caldera extended this amnesty to other insurgents during his first term (1969–74), granting terms that were similar to those offered by his predecessor to PCV in 1968. Most accepted. In the 1973 national elections MIR ran candidates for Congress; however, the one-time guerrilla movement captured less than 1 percent of the total vote, slightly less than the moribund PCV.

Disagreements over how to disengage from the guerrilla struggle and over how to react to the Soviet Union's invasion of Czechoslovakia in 1968 splintered PCV. Most traditional party leaders backed Moscow, but most youths identified with the reformers who crafted the "Prague Spring" (Ellner, 1988: 41–63). These tensions led PCV dissidents to form an independent socialist political party, the Movimiento al Socialismo (MAS; Movement toward Socialism). José Vicente Rangel, running as the MAS presidential candidate, finished fourth in the 1973 presidential balloting, and MAS elected more congressmen than any other leftist force. Only 1 percent voted for PCV. Over the next decade MAS evolved into a reluctant supporter of the 1957–59 elite settlement. PCV became a historical curiosity, although some of its intellectuals surfaced in the 1990s as advisers to Lieutenant Colonel Hugo Chávez Frías.

To summarize, as of 1975 most Venezuelans accepted the Punto Fijo political regime as normal and legitimate. Jennifer McCoy (1988) and Kevin Neuhouser (1992) argue that this consolidation was the fruit of class compromise, but the more widely accepted view attributes it to the 1957–59 settlement between national elites (Burton, Gunther, and Higley, 1992; Burton and Higley, 1987; Higley and Burton, 1989; Higley, Burton, and Field, 1990; Karl, 1987). John Peeler (1992, 1998) was the first to argue that this settlement was partial because for more than a decade many important groups were either hostile or indifferent to its central tenets. Peeler sees full normalization and legitimization as occurring only after an extended period of convergence. However, neither Peeler nor other scholars who examine the early years of Punto Fijo democracy analyze convergence as a regime-legitimating process.

Rectification of this omission is important because the weaknesses embedded in post-1958 democracy during convergence policy making affected how and why the regime unraveled. On the other hand, policy making between 1959 and 1975 strengthened backing for the political regime in the short run. The process allowed supportive elites to reassure one another that they would honor the elite settlement, fence-sitters to become settlement supporters, and the opponents of Punto Fijo democracy to be either co-opted or marginalized.

Embedded Vulnerabilities

After 1975 most Venezuelans supported Punto Fijo democracy. An undercurrent of opposition persisted, but those who carried that torch were marginalized, and they would remain in the political wilderness for another twenty-five years. Still, the ability of groups and leaders who had been on the fringe for more than three decades to coalesce behind Lieutenant Colonel Hugo Chávez in the 1990s and take control of national politics suggests important weaknesses in the very fabric of the Punto Fijo regime. These deficiencies first revealed themselves in the late 1980s, and they were to prove so damming that they discredited those who crafted the 1957–59 settlement, undermined the hard-won consensus on behalf of its tenets, and shattered one of Latin America's oldest and most respected representative democracies.

Four critical weaknesses proved devastating. First, the ruling elites, those who controlled AD, COPEI, the national labor confederation (Confederación de Trabajadores de Venezuela CTV; Confederation of Venezuela Workers]), the private sector, and the Roman Catholic Church, relied inordinately on distributive policies to govern. This choice derived from what appears as an almost intuitive understanding that the techniques of control favored by distributive policy making placed minimal stress on the tenuous interelite unity that coalesced around the 1957–59 settlement. Establishment elites calculated that income to the state from the international sales of petroleum would provide new resources to satisfy their institutional needs (and to buy off others who might acquire power and influence). Second, this reliance on distributive output came at the expense of regulatory solutions; thus Punto Fijo elites failed to rebuild the deteriorated regulative capability of the state that they inherited. Third, post-1958 democracy remained highly centralized while its operational rules were being institutionalized. Its leaders never reached a consensus in regard to how much decentralization there should be and the forms it should take. Finally, the power-sharing arrangements that developed during elite unification overlooked two groups whose importance was increasing, the urban poor and the middle classes. Implementation of the 1957–59 elite settlement also relegated the military to a twilight zone in which the officer corps accepted political demobilization in return for modern equipment, professional schooling, and economic security.

Heavy reliance on distributive policies, the first embedded weakness, was not unique to Punto Fijo governments. During the revolutionary Trienio (1945–48), governments mixed redistributive and distributive legislation, and in the 1950s General Marcos Pérez Jiménez relied heavily on regulations intended to stifle dissent and control population movement. Those who crafted the 1957–59 settlement viewed the redistributive policies of the Trienio as an important cause of the 1948 coup against President Rómulo Gallegos. They also believed that General Pérez Jiménez's implementation of regulations against his opponents intensified tensions that contributed to his ouster. Specifically, in 1956 and 1957 Caracas slum dwellers refused to obey regulations that required them to take up residence in recently constructed high-rise apartments. At the same time, the military responded to increasingly draconian regulations against the dictator's opponents with plots to overthrow his government. When Marcos Pérez Jiménez fled the country, on January 23, 1958, the regulative capability of the Venezuelan state was in shambles (Doyle 1967).[8] Memories of these disasters cast a powerful shadow over Punto Fijo democracy between 1958 and 1975.

Distributive politics, as we have seen, activated mechanisms of control which Venezuelan elites viewed as less stressful than their regulative or redistributive counterparts. After 1962 democratic governments received important new resources as the country pulled out of an economic recession. Steady growth continued into the 1970s. This trend depended on incremental increases in income from petroleum sales and on continuing political stability. Given these conditions, distributive policy making as a strategy to accommodate political demands was the rational choice. Political parties, labor unions, entrepreneurs, and the church received new resources, as did the military. Nevertheless, until the 1973 national elections, which produced a bipolar political party system and finally marginalized the regime's most intransigent opponents, elites who supported Punto Fijo democracy viewed their hold on power as precarious. They behaved in ways calculated to minimize strains within their coalition and reduce incentives for mass protest. This explains why they favored policies that could be implemented by distributing new resources over ones whose implementation required redistributing wealth or crafting additional regulations.

Distributive policy making between 1959 and 1975, although not free of corruption, was more honest than during the regime of General Marcos Pérez Jiménez. Indeed, the first three governments of the post-1958 democratic era enjoyed some success in professionalizing the bureaucracy and imposing accountability. These accomplishments proved short-lived. AD and COPEI needed to provide employment for party activists, and by the time most elites had unified behind the Punto Fijo system, the two dominant political parties controlled hiring and promotion in the bureaucracy. Patronage concerns increasingly trumped professionalism. After 1975, when the "petrobonanza" brought unimagined income to the state, AD and COPEI became more dependent than ever on public sector goods to satisfy their clients.

Subsequent chapters discuss how the weaknesses embedded in Punto Fijo democracy manifested themselves during the regime's decline and fall. Distributive policy proved an inadequate tenet for governing as revenues rose and fell, and unraveling progressed. The available resources were insufficient to satisfy the expectations of establishment interests, let alone new ones that emerged in the 1980s and 1990s. In addition, decades of allocating new resources while mechanisms of accountability decayed had fostered carelessness and a disregard of standards. These characteristics intensified the negative consequences in hard times of having the political regime's legitimacy so tied to distributive capability.

The neglect of capabilities to make and implement regulative policies accompanied heavy reliance on resource distribution. This neglect is rooted in events that surrounded the overthrow of General Pérez Jiménez and the transition to Punto Fijo democracy. That change in regime was violent, and political order hung by a slender thread for more than a decade after Punto Fijo democracy triumphed. Those who negotiated the 1957–59 elite settlement feared that making and implementing regulative policy would stress the fragile political order. Their concern in this regard is supported by Theodore Lowi's work (1964, 1972) that views regulative policy making as activating mechanisms of control which increase the likelihood that government will have to employ coercion. In Lowi's terms, the application of coercion tests support for the rules of the political game, and regulative policy making and implementation require more coercion than distributive policy.

Punto Fijo elites sought to minimize the number of instances in which the application of coercion would be necessary. Again, the lesson learned from the fate of General Pérez Jiménez loomed large. In late 1957 the general lobbied political and economic elites to support new regulations that would prolong his rule, but his efforts laid bare underlying disgust and opposition. When he ignored these attitudes and imposed regulations that prolonged his rule, he evoked a firestorm that forced him to flee the country. Subsequently, peasants streamed into Caracas and other large cities. The regulations that had controlled internal migration became unenforceable. Admiral Wolfgang Larrazábal's provisional government maintained order only by implementing a massive program that transferred income from petroleum to the urban poor for "make-work." These events illustrate why Venezuela's democratic elites favored distributive policy making. An unintended consequence of this preference was their failure to rebuild the state's regulative capability.

The third core weakness embedded in Punto Fijo democracy derives from the centralized nature of regime policy making. This characteristic stood in contrast to the position taken by democratic leaders during the struggle to oust Pérez Jiménez. At that time they promised to strengthen popular participation and increase the influence of regional leaders. The first three Punto Fijo governments backed away from these promises, citing the need to maintain tight control from Caracas in order to defeat the insurgency that was seeking to topple the fledgling democratic regime. The resulting disconnect between practice and promise during the period of elite unification meant that Punto Fijo elites remained divided over how to decentralize. Throughout the 1960s interests from the interior anticipated that once national leaders had marginalized the disloyal opposition they would increase the powers of regional political institutions. However, consolidating the democratic regime took longer than expected, and by the time its enemies were defeated, the leaders of AD and COPEI had become addicted to controlling distribution from the national capital. The resources available to their distributive networks at that time all but silenced calls for regional empowerment. Even the long-standing demand for the popular election of regional governors got lost in the mad scramble to tap into national distributive networks and accumulate personal wealth.

The first important concession to the long-frustrated expectation that democratic consolidation would lead to decentralization occurred in 1978, with reforms that established separate municipal elections and created the office of city manager. National elites argued that the separation of municipal balloting from national and regional elections fulfilled their long-standing promise to strengthen local autonomy. The reforms of 1978 gave municipal councils power over the newly created post of city manager.

Autonomous municipal councils and nonpartisan city managers never became part of the local political landscape. Municipal councilmen continued to be elected on party slates by means of proportional representation. This allowed the national party organizations of AD and COPEI to impose candidates who would do their bidding, and centralized party control undercut the autonomy of city managers.

Finally, Punto Fijo elites weakened post-1958 democracy by blocking access to policy making for several important groups that once supported General Pérez Jiménez and only grudgingly accepted the new political order. The urban poor constituted the largest of these groups. Between 1959 and 1973, especially in Caracas, slum dwellers voted for movements that opposed how AD and COPEI were implementing the 1957–59 elite settlement. These movements, as we have seen, included URD, PCV, backers of Admiral Wolfgang Larrazábal, and loyalists who sought the return of General Marcos Pérez Jiménez. The urban underclass appeared dangerous and threatening to AD and COPEI. Their governments attempted to dampen hostility among slum dwellers by distributing goods that included subsidized food, public services, housing, and public sector jobs. However, neither of the establishment political parties succeeded in organizing the urban poor. Slum dwellers as a group subsequently split their vote between AD and COPEI but remained distrustful of both.

The middle sectors, initially suspicious of the 1957–59 settlement, became supportive as time passed (Myers and Martz, 1997). During the first two AD governments (Rómulo Betancourt, 1959–64; and Raúl Leoni, 1964–69) middle sector attitudes toward the political regime were mixed. Pockets of support existed in the cities of eastern Venezuela, Maracaibo. and Barquisimeto, but in general the middle class did not see the AD party as representing its interests, and it viewed the 1961 constitution as the partisan creation of AD. After COPEI captured the presidency in 1969, the middle class became supportive of the political regime. Over the next two decades Punto Fijo governments created jobs, mostly in the public sector, which employed the middle class. AD and

COPEI expanded their professional secretariats, and these organizations became gateways to middle-class employment and lucrative consulting contracts. Like the urban poor, however, the middle classes remained on the periphery of power. Marginality fueled resentment and sparked efforts to create organizations that could lobby the government directly, in effect bypassing the political parties. In other words, the normalization of Punto Fijo democracy gave rise to middle-class demands for a more responsive and autonomous style of interest aggregation. Delay in responding to these demands undercut support for the regime among the middle sectors.

Tensions marked relations between the armed forces, AD, and COPEI over most of the six decades during which these two political parties played a major role in public life. Neither AD nor COPEI ever fully trusted the military. After 1958, even though the armed forces worked closely with Presidents Betancourt, Leoni, and Caldera to quell the leftist insurgency, few in the military displayed much enthusiasm for the dominant political parties. Despite public shows of unity and support, most officers believed that AD and COPEI never fully trusted them.

The armed forces, of course, were not monolithic. Factions existed within each uniformed service which allied themselves with AD or COPEI. Still, many officers chafed over the secondary role that Punto Fijo leaders assigned to the armed forces, especially given the tradition of placing military leaders at the center of public policy making. And even regime-supportive military factions resented the intrusion of AD and COPEI into the internal affairs of the armed forces, especially in matters of promotion. The military, then, remained ambivalent toward AD and COPEI and pragmatic in its backing for the Punto Fijo regime.

Stability and Crisis

Support among Venezuelan elites for the 1957–59 settlement appeared broad and deep as of 1975. Prosperity and political stability legitimated limited pluralistic rules of the political game in a country that had almost no experience with democracy. Yet this moment of unbridled optimism was all too brief. Petroleum prices plummeted during 1982, and in February 1983 President Luis Herrera Campíns ordered a massive devaluation that exploded the myth that there was enough wealth for all Venezuelans to enjoy the good life. Hard times, as the following chapters discuss, marked the remainder of the decade.

Part II / The Actors

Making Political Demands

CHAPTER TWO

Urban Poor and Political Order

Damarys Canache

The convergence of economic and political crises throughout the 1980s and 1990s contributed to the unraveling of Venezuela's representative democracy. As a result of these crises, mass dissatisfaction with the institutions and policies implemented by the Punto Fijo regime paved the way for the emergence of a charismatic leader who appealed to sectors previously excluded. The arrival of Hugo Chávez Frías and his efforts to consolidate the Bolivarian political project cannot be fully understood without attention to the role of the urban poor.

The urban poor were vulnerable to the negative effects of both economic crisis and economic reform. This became starkly evident as Venezuela's economy faltered in the 1980s and as the government implemented severe austerity programs starting in 1989. Economic measures that drastically reduced purchasing power, coupled with a discernible lag in the formulation of new social policies (Kelly, 1995: 307), highlighted the precarious position of the urban poor. Reacting to this changing economic environment, the urban poor played a leading role in the bloody riots of February 1989 (Civit and España, 1989; Coronil and Skurski, 1991; Hellinger, 1991: 192). These riots arguably signaled the changing political role of the millions of residents of Venezuela's shantytowns. In the next years, the political role of the urban masses would be characterized by their rejection of traditional political parties and an increasing social and political mobilization.

This chapter analyzes the changing character of the urban poor. It advances a simple two-part thesis. First, the economic crisis that began in the early 1980s heightened the urban poor's concern with public policy. Second, the crumbling of Venezuela's two-party political system opened a window of opportunity for citizen participation. Diminished party control over politics and government paves the way, at least potentially, for new perspectives to be heard.

Using public opinion data from the second half of the 1990s, this analysis compares the political attitudes and preferences of the urban poor with those of other Venezuelans in an attempt to understand the role of the urban poor in the demise of the Punto Fijo regime and the emergence of the Bolivarian regime.

The Decline of Punto Fijo: The Role of the Urban Poor

The developing world is rife with crowded metropolitan areas overflowing with citizens living in impoverished conditions. Venezuela is no exception. As in other nations, the percentage of Venezuelans living in urban areas increased dramatically in the past fifty years, both because of population growth within those urban areas and because of migration from rural areas to the cities. For a large portion of urban dwellers, living conditions are extremely harsh. In Venezuela's shantytowns, or barrios, residents live in feeble shacks, and access to clean water and sanitary facilities is limited. Many of Venezuela's barrios perch on the sides of hills and mountains, placing the residents at grave risk from the mud slides that accompany torrential rains. This was demonstrated in December 1999, when a tragedy of virtually incomprehensible magnitude occurred—by some estimates, more than thirty thousand Venezuelans perished when incessant rain caused hillsides, and the barrios they housed, to disintegrate. In the early 1980s, immediately prior to Black Friday, just over 70 percent of Venezuelans lived in urban areas, more than double the proportion that had lived in urban areas only thirty years before (Fossi, 1984). In nations such as Venezuela, urban poverty is typical, not exceptional. In 1990, more than half of the residents in Caracas were classified as impoverished, with 7 percent labeled as extremely poor. Similar conditions existed in Venezuela's other urban centers. In these areas, more than 70 percent of residents were classified as poor in 1990 and 12 percent as extremely poor (Gruson, 1993).

The Urban Poor and Political Tranquility

One need not examine the history of Venezuela's urban poor too deeply before discovering a seeming paradox in the years prior to 1983. In the Punto Fijo era, many policy initiatives were designed to aid the urban poor. Likewise, the leading political parties competed for political support among this sector. Nevertheless, the urban poor arguably were the group that was represented least effectively by Acción Democrática (AD; Democratic Action) and Comité de Organización Política Electoral Independiente: Partido Social Cristiano (COPEI; Committee of Independent Electoral Political Organization: Social Christian Party), for three reasons. First, to a large extent, the experiences of the urban poor in Venezuela mirrored those of the urban poor elsewhere. All people are not equally likely to participate in politics. Rather, the tendency toward involvement in politics increases with factors such as education and income. Apart from sheer strength in numbers, residents of Venezuela's barrios lacked the resources needed to promote active involvement in politics. Ray (1969) noted that people in the barrios perceived themselves as lacking the competence necessary to be effective political participants. As a consequence, party membership among the urban poor was minimal. To the extent that the urban poor were less politicized than were other sectors of Venezuelan society, the electoral incentive for the nation's parties to attend to the urban poor was weakened.

Although the very fact that they are impoverished partly explains the politically disadvantageous position of the urban poor in most nations, there often is more to the story. A second factor in Venezuela was that, in the early years of the democratic era, the urban poor in essence bet on the wrong horse. The Punto Fijo era was dominated by AD and COPEI, but other parties also were active in this period, especially in the first two elections of the democratic era, the elections of 1958 and 1963. In retrospect, one likely problem for the urban poor was that they did not side with AD or COPEI from the beginning. The most popular party among the urban poor was Unión Republicana Democrática (URD; Democratic Republican Union) in 1958 and Fuerza Democrática Popular (FDP; Popular Democratic Force) in 1963. Partido Comunista Venezolano (PCV; Venezuelan Communist Party) also was influential among the urban poor in the late 1950s. When Venezuela evolved into a stable two-party political system, URD, FDP, and PCV were relegated to the periphery of national politics. The urban poor slowly gravitated toward AD and COPEI, but their status as newcomers to these parties possibly cast them in a disadvantaged position relative to the parties' core constituencies.

The third, and probably most important, political constraint on Venezuela's urban poor is that the loyalties of this sector were divided between AD and COPEI for most of the Punto Fijo period. Both organizations functioned as catch-all parties, and both attempted to appeal to all groups in society. The fact that both parties found support among this sector served to divide, and thus mute, the urban poor as a political force. As Ray explained (1969: 158), the Venezuelan political system neutralized "the collective strength of the barrio people by dividing their allegiances among several antagonistic parties, thereby leaving them unable or, perhaps more precisely, unwilling to unite and speak with a single voice on the big issues of their barrio existence."

Even though the urban poor did not constitute a united political group, their policy interests were not ignored under Punto Fijo. Resources from the oil industry meant that the government had the capacity to implement programs designed to benefit the poor. Moreover, leaders of all parties agreed that such action was appropriate. When a democratic system was installed in Venezuela in 1958, there was consensus that that system must represent all citizens, including the poor. The provisional government, under the leadership of Wolfgang Larrazábal, allowed numerous urban settlements through land invasions, provided these new communities with public services, and implemented a massive employment program (Plan de Emergencia). The political climate of the time helped to entrench among the poor a sense of clientelistic politics. That is, leaders of Venezuela's emerging democracy encouraged the poor to look to government to satisfy their social and economic needs. At the same time, the nation's fledgling political parties endeavored to develop an organizational presence in Venezuela's barrios. Further, to help build support among the urban poor, elected officials from AD and COPEI relied on political patronage, working closely with representatives of barrio organizations (juntas) on projects concerning barrio improvements. The government also implemented broad programs that brought general benefits to the urban poor, including programs headed by agencies such as the Ministry of Public Works, the National Institute of Sanitary Works, and the Division for Community Development within the Oficina Central de Coordinación y Planificación (CORDIPLAN; Central Office of Coordination and Planning) (see Fossi, 1984; Gilbert, 1981; Ray, 1969).

The Urban Poor and Political Turmoil

Two interrelated developments—the economic crisis beginning in 1983 and the corresponding decline of Venezuela's two-party political system—were of direct consequence for the urban poor. If the economic position of the urban poor was precarious before Black Friday (February 18, 1983), it was catastrophic after. The ranks of the poor swelled, and the conditions of the poor worsened. Declining wages threw countless members of the lower middle class into poverty, and the existing poor spiraled into extreme poverty (Cartaya and D'Elia, 1991; Levine, 1998a). On the political front, the link between the urban poor and Venezuelan politics had been the clientelistic policies of two catch-all parties. As those policies were weakened and dismantled, and as the strength of AD and COPEI deteriorated, the political role of the urban poor was forced to change. The plight of the urban poor was dire, and this sector's limited avenue of political representation had narrowed. Not surprisingly, these tandem forces compelled the urban poor to engage in new and very different forms of political expression.

What avenues of political participation were open to the poor as Punto Fijo democracy began to unravel? One route was for the urban poor to engage in unconventional participation—that is, to join in political protests and riots. An outbreak of severe social and political unrest erupted in February 1989 in response to the adjustment program announced by the Pérez government. Although these riots were among the most severe in Latin American history (Coronil, 1997: 376; Salamanca, 1989), they were not isolated events. Based on content analyses of media reports of political protests in the period 1989–94 (Canache, 2002: ch. 1), 851 incidents of political protest were recorded in this period, and 58 percent of these were violent. Although students, workers, and members of the middle class participated in many protests (e.g., Coronil and Skurski, 1991), the urban poor were especially drawn to this avenue of participation. Years of inadequate representation and escalating economic despair pushed the urban poor to the breaking point, and this frustration manifested itself in a prolonged wave of sociopolitical turmoil.

Beyond participation in protests and riots, Venezuela's emerging civil society offered a second and peaceful avenue of participation to the urban poor. In sharp contrast with the elite-led pattern of political participation instituted by the Punto Fijo model in 1958, the 1980s and 1990s witnessed the growth of new social and political actors who struggled fiercely to establish independence and autonomy from the traditional political structure. These new actors sought to represent and articulate the interests of specific sectors of Venezuelan society (e.g., neighborhood associations, workers, women's groups, environmentalists).[1]

Although civil society offered the urban poor a plausible avenue of participation, the promise of civil society has been somehow unmet for this critical sector. As with any form of political participation, effective involvement in social organizations requires resources lacked by the urban poor. Social organizations, and especially neighborhood associations, have become significant avenues of participation for Venezuela's middle class, but the consequences of the emerging civil society have been less noteworthy for the urban poor.[2]

During the stable years of the Punto Fijo era, the urban poor did not coalesce as a united force in Venezuelan politics. However, economic crisis during the 1980s and 1990s provided the urban poor with a heightened incentive to mobilize, and the declining power of AD and COPEI opened a window of opportunity for class-based political action. Protest allowed the urban poor to express their frustration, but protest alone would not yield political change. Whereas Venezuela's emerging civil society was especially important for the middle class, other new political actors endeavored to enlist the sympathy of the urban poor. One such actor was the political party La Causa Radical (LCR; The Radical Cause).[3] LCR emerged as a political organization that rejected the hierarchical and vertical forms of organization characteristic of Venezuela's traditional parties. Instead, LCR stressed a participatory and egalitarian ethos. After years of intensive political work in unions and poorer neighborhoods, the party's efforts were rewarded with a successful showing in the first separate regional and municipal election, which was held in 1989. The party's electoral success continued in subsequent elections, including victory in the 1992 contest for mayor of Caracas.

The success of LCR in mobilizing the support of Venezuela's urban poor was only one of two significant events in 1992. In February of that year, Lieutenant Colonel Hugo Chávez led an attempted military coup. Although the coup was quickly suppressed, it was Chávez and his fellow coup leaders, not the government, who enjoyed mass support. Chávez was especially popular with Venezuela's poor. In the weeks following his arrest, thousands of Venezuelans demonstrated in support of him (McCoy, 1999). When Chávez was released from prison, he mounted a campaign to wrest control of the Venezuelan government through peaceful rather than coercive action. At this same time, the urban poor were no longer content to sit on the sidelines of Venezuelan politics; nor had they remained loyal to AD or COPEI. Hugo Chávez became the figure around whom the urban poor finally could unite. His election as president of Venezuela in 1998 solidified the status of the urban poor as a significant force in Venezuelan politics. As the 1990s came to an end, two important transitions had taken place. Punto Fijo democracy had given way to the Fifth Republic, and the urban poor had transformed from a relatively weak and divided bloc to a stronger and more united political coalition.

Rise of the Fifth Republic: Politics among the Urban Poor

Using data from public opinion surveys conducted in 1995 and 1998, I have analyzed the attitudes and preferences of the urban poor and contrasted them with those of the nonpoor in three areas: attitudes regarding the economy, attitudes regarding public policy, and the extent to which the urban poor contributed to the electoral victory of Hugo Chávez.[4] The 1995 survey includes data from Caracas and Maracaibo. The 1998 survey includes a national sample, but analyses here are limited to respondents from urban areas.[5] In 1998, respondents originally were classified into one of five economic strata: very poor, poor, middle, upper middle, and upper. Widespread poverty in Venezuela means that a sizable majority of respondents are classified as poor or very poor. Poverty loses meaning as a descriptive category if virtually everyone is poor. Hence, I used the following categories in 1998: lower stratum (those originally classified as very poor; 39.8%); middle stratum (38.5%); and upper stratum (21.7%). Respondents on the 1995 survey were not categorized by economic strata, but numerous items provide data that are used to create an index of economic status. To facilitate comparison with 1998, I used the 1998 thresholds to stratify the sample. That is, in both years, the lower stratum is defined as the bottom 39.8 percent of respondents in terms of economic status, the middle stratum is the next 38.5 percent, and the upper stratum is the top 21.7 percent.

The Urban Poor and Perceptions Regarding the Economy

Two types of data are available to assess perceptions regarding the economy. First, in both 1995 and 1998, respondents were asked whether they expected the nation's economy to improve in the future and also whether they expected their own personal finances to improve. The 1995 item used a five-year time frame, whereas a one-year time frame was used in 1998. In research on economic voting, the national items are commonly referred to as measures of *prospective sociotropic* perceptions, and the items concerning personal finances are measures of *prospective pocketbook* perceptions.[6] At question is whether the urban poor are more pessimistic about the economy than are the nonpoor.

The second set of survey items of relevance to the economy asked respondents to identify the important problems facing Venezuela. In 1995, respondents were asked to name the one issue they viewed as being the most important problem Venezuela faced. In 1998, respondents were shown a list of issues and were asked to select up to three that they viewed as important problems that the next government must address. Using the 1995 data, we can calculate the percentage of respondents who named an economic matter as Venezuela's most important problem. In 1998, the top two economic concerns were unemployment and inflation. These data are summarized using separate indicators so that we can determine what percentage of respondents named unemployment as Venezuela's top problem and what percentage named inflation.

The data reported in table 2.1 reveal that attitudes regarding the economy did vary across economic strata in 1995, although little comparable variance existed in 1998. In 1995, 63 percent of the urban poor identified some facet of the economy as Venezuela's most important problem, versus only 53 percent for the middle stratum and 43 percent for the upper stratum. In short, the economy topped the issue agenda of the poor to a greater extent than it did for the nonpoor. Additionally, respondents from the lower stratum were more pessimistic about the economic future than were other respondents. This is true for both the prospective pocketbook and the prospective sociotropic indicators. Values above 50 percenton these items indicate that respondents, on average, foresee an improvement in the economy; values below 50 percent, in contrast, indicate that respondents expect economic conditions to worsen. Although respondents from all economic strata predicted that their personal finances would improve, projections were much more negative regarding the national economy, especially among the urban poor.

In 1998, differences in economic perceptions across economic strata were minimal. Upper-stratum respondents were less concerned with unemployment than were their lower-stratum and middle-stratum counterparts, but no other effects reached statistical significance. With respect to prospective judgments, it is illuminating to contrast the attitudes of the urban poor in 1995 and 1998. In 1995, the urban poor were more pessimistic about the future than were

Table 2.1. Perceptions Regarding the Economy, 1995 and 1998

	Economic Strata Lower	Middle	Upper
1995			
Proportion of respondents naming the economy as the nation's most important problem	63%	53%[a]	43%[a,b]
Prospective pocketbook perceptions	0.59	0.70[a]	0.71[a]
Prospective sociotropic perceptions	0.37	0.45[a]	0.51[a]
1998			
Proportion of respondents naming unemployment as one of the nation's three most important problems	55%	56%	46%[a,b]
Proportion of respondents naming inflation as one of the nation's three most important problems	30%	35%	36%
Prospective pocketbook perceptions	0.67	0.71	0.69
Prospective sociotropic perceptions	0.48	0.52	0.54

[a] Statistically significant difference vs. column one, $p < .05$.
[b] Statistically significant difference vs. column two, $p < .05$.

other respondents. Middle-stratum and upper-stratum respondents were no more optimistic in 1998 than in 1995, but lower-stratum respondents did become more optimistic. That is, in 1998, the absence of differences in prospective judgments across economic strata reflects a growing sense of optimism on the part of the urban poor. In 1998, at a time when the election of Hugo Chávez appeared certain, the urban poor perceived that the economic future would be brighter. For Hugo Chávez, this optimism on the part of the urban poor was a blessing, if only in the short term. Economic programs designed to aid the urban poor constituted a central portion of Chávez's campaign, and this strategy clearly hit the intended mark.

The Urban Poor and Public Policy

In 1995, the urban poor were moderately more concerned with the economy than were other residents of Caracas and Maracaibo. At least to some extent, it follows that the policy preferences of the urban poor were likely to differ from those of the nonpoor. Policy-making resources are inherently limited. Given the relative salience of the material needs among the urban poor, it appears probable that this sector would have awarded economic matters an especially high place on Venezuela's policy agenda. But what is not yet clear is whether the poor and the nonpoor held different preferences *within* the domain of economic policy. In assessing the attitudes of the urban poor, it is important to keep in mind that the urban poor experienced a roller coaster of economic policy in the decades prior to 1995. Relatively well funded protectionist policies that existed in the period of political tranquillity gave way to neoliberal reform in 1989, and this reform, in turn, was reversed following the election of Rafael Caldera in 1993. With these dramatic changes in mind, consider a simple thought experiment. If the urban poor were given sole control over economic policy making in Venezuela, would the resulting public policy have differed from what would exist in a scenario in which the nonpoor controlled this aspect of policy making? If the answer to this question is yes, then the renewed politicization of the urban poor potentially is of tangible significance.

Several comparisons are possible regarding the policy preferences of the poor and the nonpoor. In 1995, respondents were asked whether they felt that greater government intervention in the economy was needed and whether it was the government's responsibility to ensure that all Venezuelans had access to jobs and to health care. Respondents also were asked whether political change in Venezuela should be gradual or radical.[7] Two of these questions, whether greater government intervention in the economy was needed and whether change should be gradual or radical, were asked in 1998. In 1998, respondents also were asked whether the government should increase economic privatization. Outside the realm of economic policy, 1998 respondents were asked whether the Venezuelan Congress should be dismantled. Hugo Chávez had promised to do so during his initial presidential campaign, and he carried out this promise in 1999.

Data from these items are reported in table 2.2. In 1995, the policy preferences of the urban poor appear to be unique at every turn. Compared with other urban residents, the poor more strongly supported government intervention in the economy and radical rather than gradual political change. On the first of these items, the difference in support for government intervention is especially vast between lower-sector and upper-sector respondents. On the second item, most Venezuelans indicated a preference for gradual rather than radical change, but support for radical change ran more than twice as high among the poor as among the nonpoor. Turning to the last two items from 1995, we see that poor and middle-sector respondents supported government provision of employment and health care in greater numbers than did respondents from the highest economic sector.

Table 2.2. Public Policy Preferences, 1995 and 1998

	Economic Strata		
	Lower (%)	Middle (%)	Upper (%)
1995			
Proportion of respondents who support government intervention in the economy	68	58[a]	29[a,b]
Proportion of respondents who prefer radical rather than gradual political change	21	09[a]	08[a]
Proportion of respondents who feel that government should guarantee employment	96	92	73[a,b]
Proportion of respondents who feel that government should guarantee access to health care	95	92	80[a,b]
1998			
Proportion of respondents who support government intervention in the economy	86	84	80[a]
Proportion of respondents who support greater privatization	34	42[a]	41[a]
Proportion of respondents who prefer radical rather than gradual political change	24	13[a]	17[a]
Proportion of respondents who support dissolution of Congress	24	19	16[a]

[a] Statistically significant difference vs. column one, $p < .05$.
[b] Statistically significant difference vs. column two, $p < .05$.

By 1998, support for government intervention in the economy had increased among all sectors, although the wealthiest urban residents remained marginally less supportive of economic intervention than the poor. Conversely, the poor were more strongly opposed to privatization than were the nonpoor. Support for radical rather than gradual political change also increased among all sectors from 1995 to 1998, but it was again the urban poor who found radical change to be the most appealing. Finally, all sectors rejected the suggestion that the Venezuelan Congress should be suspended, but the urban poor were somewhat more receptive to this reform than were the wealthiest urban residents.

Collectively, the data on economic preferences can be interpreted in one of two ways. The urban poor clearly differ from other urban respondents in terms of policy preferences. Simply put, the poor expect more from government: more government intervention in the economy, more efforts to ensure that jobs and health care are available, and more dramatic rather than incremental change. However, with the exception of government intervention in the economy in 1995, majority consensus exists across economic strata on every item. Hence, these data arguably provide little evidence of a class-based rift. It would be unwise, though, to dismiss the class effects identified here. Results in the previous section demonstrated that the urban poor were especially concerned with the state of Venezuela's economy. We now see that these concerns prompted the urban poor to support government intervention in the economy and to oppose further privatization. Consequently, the heightened politicization of Venezuela's urban poor in the 1990s brought the articulation of unique policy preferences.

The Urban Poor and Political Behavior

The catch-all nature of the nation's two major political parties meant that the unique political interests of the poor were unlikely to be represented effectively. At the same time, Venezuela's continuing economic crisis caused the financial situation of the urban poor to become increasingly perilous. Faced with the convergence of these dual pressures, many among the urban poor reacted with behavior outside the channels of conventional political participation. In the late 1990s, however, new actors emerged which facilitated the reentry of the urban poor into the conventional political arena. At question is whether these changes have produced tangible effects on the political behavior of the urban poor and whether politicization of this sector has, in turn, influenced the current composition of Venezuelan government.

To explore these questions, data on two issues are examined: voter turnout and support for Hugo Chávez. If the urban poor felt politically alienated in the early 1990s, then we should see relatively low electoral participation among this sector at that time. Conversely, if efforts to mobilize the urban poor in the mid-1990s were successful, then turnout among the urban poor should have been higher in 1998 than earlier in the 1990s. Likewise, in the early and mid-1990s, it would have seemed more likely that Chávez would gain power by force than by peaceful election. The poor were especially supportive of Chávez's failed 1992 coup attempt (McCoy, 1999). Here, we can consider whether this support followed Chávez when he moved from coup leader to presidential candidate. That is, did the urban poor represent an especially strong component of the Chávez electoral coalition?

In 1995, data on voter turnout are from an item that asked respondents whether they had voted in the 1993 elections. In 1998, turnout data are from an item regarding whether the respondent planned to vote in the upcoming election. Voter turnout data typically suffer from overreporting by respondents, and there is no reason to expect otherwise here. A further complication in 1995 is that the survey was administered thirteen months after the 1993 election; this time gap may have heightened the level of misreporting. However, there is no reason to expect overreporting or misreporting to vary by economic status. As a result, general comparison of the 1995 and 1998 data is possible.

In 1998, support for Hugo Chávez was measured with data on whether the respondent planned to vote for Chávez. A somewhat more complicated Chávez measure was used in 1995. On the 1995 survey, respondents were asked to name the individual they viewed as being the most influential person in Venezuela. A follow-up item then asked whether the named individual also was influential for the respondent's own personal views. In most cases, the named individuals were both nationally and personally influential. Using these data, support for Hugo Chávez is operationally defined to exist if the respondent selected Chávez as the most influential person in Venezuela and the respondent also indicated that Chávez influenced the respondent's personal views. If some other individual was named as being both nationally and personally influential, in contrast, then the respondent is assumed to have lower support for Chávez. Data are omitted if no individual was named or if the identified figure was nationally but not personally influential. The resulting measure is a reasonable, albeit imperfect, indicator of support for Chávez. The validity of the measure hinges on the reasonable assumption that a person who believed that Hugo Chávez was the most influential person in Venezuela in early 1995, and who also claimed that Chávez had influenced his or her own personal views, had positive affect toward Chávez.

Hugo Chávez's victory in the 1998 presidential election was impressive on two counts. First, voter turnout was 64 percent in 1998, a slight increase versus the turnout rate of 60 percent in 1993. Second, Chávez received 56 percent of the vote, compared with 40 percent for Salas Römer, who finished second. Data in table 2.3 reveal that the urban poor contributed to both noteworthy aspects of the Chávez victory. The results for voter turnout corroborate the contention that political mobilization among the urban poor increased between 1993 and 1998. Only 58 percent of poor respondents claimed to have voted in 1993, whereas 86 percent reported that they intended to vote in 1998. Nonpoor respondents also reported high expected turnout in 1998, but it is the

Table 2.3. Electoral Behavior, 1995 and 1998

	Economic Strata Lower (%)	Middle (%)	Upper (%)
1995			
Proportion of respondents who indicated that they voted in the 1993 presidential election	58	61	73[a,b]
Proportion of respondents who perceived Hugo Chávez to be personally and nationally influential	24	20	07[a,b]
1998			
Proportion of respondents who planned to vote in the 1998 presidential election	86	88	92[a]
Proportion of respondents who expected to vote for Hugo Chávez	55	44[a]	47

[a] Statistically significant difference vs. column one, $p < .05$.
[b] Statistically significant difference vs. column two, $p < .05$.

swing in turnout among the poor which is most dramatic. For instance, poor respondents lagged behind upper-stratum respondents by 15 percentage points in 1993, but this gap was reduced to only 6 percentage points in 1998.

The urban poor also provided Hugo Chávez with his strongest base of electoral support. On the 1998 preelection survey, 55 percent of the urban poor indicated that they planned to vote for Chávez, whereas only about 45 percent of the nonpoor expected to back Chávez. It also appears that many among the urban poor had sided with Chávez for quite some time. In 1995, 24 percent of poor respondents held positive affect for Chávez, versus only 7 percent of the wealthiest respondents. Mobilization of the urban poor in 1998 brought a twofold benefit for Hugo Chávez. His election gained perceptual legitimacy because turnout increased versus 1993 and because his margin of victory was large—factors that were both affected by the actions of the urban poor. This dynamic of support also was at play in the 2000 election. Focus on the 2000 presidential election reveals a persistent support of the poor toward Chávez. In his study of Venezuelans' electoral behavior, Molina (2002) demonstrates that poor voters significantly favored Chávez in the 2000 elections.[8]

Conclusions: The Urban Poor in Bolivarian Venezuela

The unraveling of Punto Fijo democracy and the rise of Venezuela's Bolivarian Republic shed light on the dynamics of political change that may occur in polyarchies located in the gray zone between full liberal democracy and dictatorship. In revisiting the Venezuelan experience, this chapter has confirmed that a critical condition for the transition from limited pluralism to a more hybrid regime has been the political transformation of the urban poor. The interaction of multiple factors that corroded the capabilities and bases of legitimacy of the Punto Fijo democracy paved the way to entrance of previously excluded social sectors. Twenty years ago, prior to the onset of Venezuela's economic crisis, the rise to power of a charismatic, populist political leader unaffiliated with one of the nation's two leading parties would have been highly improbable. Since then, however, a series of developments combined to create ideal conditions for the emergence of such a figure. Because they bore the brunt of Venezuela's economic crisis and because they were quick to discard allegiance to Venezuela's traditional parties, the urban poor were central players in the developments that brought Hugo Chávez to power.

The transformation of the urban poor in Venezuela comports well with past historical examples. Because their economic situation is inherently unstable, the urban poor in any nation are highly susceptible to the ill effects of a stagnant economy. We have seen that in Venezuela the effects of economic crisis on the urban poor were compounded by the nature of representation in the Punto Fijo era. The urban poor often are ripe for mobilization by a flash party (Converse and Dupeux, 1962), or populist movement, and this was the case in Venezuela in the 1990s.[9] This sector provided Hugo Chávez with his earliest base of support, and the urban poor were Chávez's most loyal constituency in 1998 and 2000.

Although the involvement of the urban poor in the rise of Hugo Chávez represents a familiar pattern in mass politics, it does not follow that what lies ahead is also easily predicted. Chávez's relationship with the urban poor perhaps is best depicted as a race against the clock. The pragmatism of the urban poor is demonstrated by the data reported in this chapter. The urban poor are concerned with the economy, they seek heightened government involvement in economic matters, and—as the decline of AD and COPEI shows—they are willing to break political allegiances in times of crisis. Venezuela's middle class began to grow skeptical about Chávez's Bolivarian Revolution early on, but the urban poor continued their support of the president. Largely because of this support, the Chávez presidency enjoyed a prolonged honeymoon period, but the pragmatism of the urban poor suggests that this honeymoon will not last indefinitely.

Chávez's failure to transform symbolic action into substantive results has created mounting frustration among a wide spectrum of Venezuelan society, including a significant portion of the urban poor. The inspection of opinion data gathered throughout the Chávez presidency reveals the erosion of popular favor. In February 1999 Chávez began his government with an impressive 92 percent approval rating, and he was able to maintain the support of a majority of the population (on average 67%) the following year. By early 2001, however, the level of approval of the government declined sharply, and since then support has eroded further.[10]

Generalized frustration has given rise to a new wave of political turmoil. Two major events—the attempted toppling of the regime in April 2002 and the two-month-long strike in late 2002 and early 2003 which paralyzed much of Venezuela, including the critical oil industry—show two important lessons. They denote that for many Venezuelans Chávez already has failed in fulfilling the promise of economic and social advancement. But they also show that, at least as these events occurred, some sectors of the urban poor continued to provide Chávez with critical bases of support.

In April 2002, Chávez arguably regained power largely because of the efforts of the Círculos Bolivarianos—state-sponsored social organizations developed by Chávez—to mobilize the urban poor on his behalf. The formation and growth of the Círculos Bolivarianos constituted one of the most intriguing and controversial developments in the Chávez era. First created in 2000, the Círculos Bolivarianos initially were depicted as human networks for the defense of the revolution. Some observers viewed them as being comparable to the Revolution Committees in Cuba. Chávez subsequently redefined the Círculos Bolivarianos as neighborhood- or community-based organizations, a status that made them eligible for financial support from the government. Part of the controversy surrounding the Círculos Bolivarianos concerns claims that some of the organizations have had a hand in promoting social unrest, and even political violence, since late 2001. Although full understanding of the political significance of the Círculos Bolivarianos does not yet exist, it is clear that they provided Chávez with important mechanisms to maintain and mobilize support for the regime.

During the December 2002–February 2003 general strike, supporters of the president led by Círculos Bolivarianos staged various mobilizations to pressure managers and employees to end the strike in the oil industry. Thus, the unwavering support of the poor has been important for the survival of Chávez's regime. That Chávez sought since 2000 to promote the Círculos Bolivarianos in Venezuela's slums provides evidence that he recognizes the significance of the urban poor for the maintenance of his regime.

Whether and for how long Hugo Chávez will continue to reap benefits from his strong standing among the urban poor is a matter of vital importance for the Bolivarian political project. Recent public opinion data have begun to bring bad news for Chávez. Some indicators depict a dramatic decline in his support, even among the poor. For example, a national survey conducted in May 2003 indicates that 67.5 percent of Venezuelans hold negative views of Chávez's government. This rejection is now majoritarian even in the two lower strata of the population (strata D and E), where it reaches 67.4 percent and 59.9 percent, respectively.[11] The failure of the Bolivarian government to implement policies that produce tangible benefits for Chávez's most loyal supporters, the urban poor, has began to take its toll. Increasing activism of popular sectors in opposition demonstrations and protests, as well as in supporting a national referendum to revoke Chávez's mandate, signal that the Bolivarian regime no longer remains in widespread high esteem among this most critical of sectors, the urban poor.

CHAPTER THREE

The Military

From Marginalization to Center Stage

Harold A. Trinkunas

On the evening of April 11, 2002, the third day of a general strike against the government, the Venezuelan armed forces rebelled against their president, Hugo Chávez Frías. Reacting to the bloody outcome of clashes between pro- and antigovernment demonstrators near the presidential palace, the commander of the army, General Efraim Vásquez Velasco, announced in a nationally televised address that he would no longer obey presidential orders. High-ranking generals and admirals soon followed him on the airwaves, expressing their solidarity with the army commander and their opposition to the president. Within hours, the senior military officer in the Venezuelan armed forces, General Lucas Rincón Romero, announced President Chávez's resignation. Remarkably, the transitional government formed by a leading figure of the opposition, businessman Pedro Carmona, and backed by many senior military leaders lasted less than forty-eight hours. By April 14, 2002, President Hugo Chávez had returned to power, and his civilian and military opponents scrambled to pick up the pieces of their failed political adventure.

In the months following the April 11, 2002, coup, Venezuela's political leadership has tried to minimize the importance of divisions and conflict within the armed forces, but to no avail. Public hearings by the National Assembly have heard from most of the major participants in the April event, and it is clearly apparent that the Venezuelan armed forces are profoundly politicized and divided. Former senior commanders such as General Manuel Rosendo, once the number three figure in the armed forces, have been highly critical of the efforts of the Chávez administration to influence the political cast of the senior officer corps (Poleo, 2002; Weffer Cifuentes, 2002).

This degree of politicization and civil-military conflict is nearly unprecedented in Venezuela's recent democratic history. Although some presidents had experienced public difficulties with military officers during the Punto Fijo period (1958–98), these incidents were rapidly resolved in favor of civilian authorities (Maso, 2000). However, in the Fifth Republic, open military politicization has gone hand in hand with increasing levels of military participation in government decision making and policy implementation. This suggests that a fundamental transformation of civil-military relations has occurred in Venezuela and calls into question whether elected officials have authority over the armed forces in this country. It is clear that any future democratic government in Venezuela, whether led by President Chávez or his successor, will have to contend with the reemergence of the armed forces as a political actor.

Since the election of President Chávez in 1998 and the transition to the Fifth Republic, the role of the Venezuelan armed forces has expanded rapidly, deemphasizing external defense in favor of internal missions. This change has been not only in scope but also in the degree of participation by military personnel in state policy making. Simultaneously, through the process of writing and enacting a new constitution in 1999, President Chávez dismantled the mechanisms that previously allowed civilians to monitor—albeit inadequately—the armed forces and exclude them from political activity.

Changes in the roles and missions of the armed forces and the institutions of civil-military relations suggest that civilian control in Venezuela has been eliminated. The shortcomings of this approach to civil-military relations are made clear by the aftermath of the April 11, 2002, coup. In the event of further civil-military conflict during this or any future administration, elected officials will find themselves deprived of the institutional means by which to assert their authority over the armed forces or protect the security of the regime. In effect, Venezuelan civil-military institutions, as is the case with many other features of this country's political regime, have unraveled to such a degree that they can no longer be compared to similar institutions in consolidated democracies. In fact, Venezuelan civil-military relations also inhabit a "gray zone" somewhere between democracy and outright military praetorianism (Myers and McCoy, 2003).

Expanding the Role of the Armed Forces

Since the inauguration of President Hugo Chávez in 1999, the role of the armed forces in Venezuela has rapidly ballooned from a relatively narrow focus on external defense to a broad focus on internal security and development. Although the armed forces had always retained residual internal security missions during the Punto Fijo period, by the 1970s these were largely carried out by the Guardia Nacional, a national gendarmerie force under the authority of the Ministry of Defense. After the defeat of a Cuban-backed Marxist insurgency in the 1960s, the army, navy, and air force concentrated on traditional external defense missions. However, among the first acts of President Hugo Chávez upon taking office was to order the armed forces to carry out a broad civic action program called Plan Bolívar 2000, which has brought the military into a wide range of domestic security and development activities. This reorientation of the armed forces toward internal roles is of concern because it has increased civil-military friction while at the same time decreasing the professionalism of the Venezuelan armed forces.

Military Roles and Missions during Punto Fijo Democracy

The Venezuelan armed forces have always oscillated between an internal and external security orientation since their rebirth as a professional garrison force during the Gómez dictatorship (1908–35). General Juan Vicente Gómez used this professional force to manage his large personal estates and control the population through regional garrisons, allowing his political cronies and their armed supporters to carry out the few external defense duties that arose during his regime. This bias toward an internal orientation persisted during the regimes that followed, although the armed forces increasingly acquired the necessary armaments for an external defense role during the 1945–48 democratic Trienio and the dictatorship of General Marcos Pérez Jiménez that followed (Trinkunas, 1999: 44–52).

After the 1958 transition to democracy, the Betancourt administration initially focused on establishing civilian control by containment, limiting the areas of national policy in which the armed forces participated. However, the new regime's need to use the armed forces in a counterinsurgency role beginning in 1961 undermined this policy. Venezuela's Marxist insurgency had its origins in an internal division of the governing Acción Democrática (AD; Democratic Action) party which led its wing of mostly leftist youths and their allies in the Venezuelan Communist Party to take up arms against the new regime. Rómulo Betancourt, the first president of the Punto Fijo period, used Cuba's support of the guerilla movement to convince the armed forces that they faced an external threat to the country, one that could be defeated only through unconditional support for the new democratic regime and subordination to duly constituted civilian authorities. Successful civil-military cooperation against this insurgency reconciled the armed forces to the democratic regime. By the time Rafael Caldera took office in 1969, the insurgency was largely defeated, and the new president implemented an amnesty program for remaining guerrilla forces. The military's acceptance of Caldera's pacification program, despite some grumbling within the officer corps, indicates the extent to which civilian control of the armed forces had been consolidated at this time (Trinkunas 1999: 170–87).

With the end of counterinsurgency operations, few missions remained for the regular armed forces other than external defense, which suited elected officials who wanted to minimize military participation in national politics. Internal security duties were assumed by civilian police forces and the Guardia Nacional. Most of the officer corps quietly buried itself in the peacetime routine of training, procurement, and military exercises. However, this reorientation produced dissatisfaction within some elements of the armed forces who sought to justify a continuing internal role for the military.

One way in which the internal orientation of the officer corps was perpetuated was through the military educational system. Beginning in the 1970s, the Venezuelan armed forces experienced a generational break within the military hierarchy as educational reforms in the national military academies produced a new generation of elite, highly trained junior officers with a strong sense of leadership, élan, and nationalism.[1] Under the Andrés Bello educational plan developed by the armed forces, Venezuela's military academy was transformed into an accredited undergraduate institution, graduating its first classes at this level in 1974. Not coincidentally, President Chávez was a member of this first graduating class (Norden, 1996: 158–59).[2] This plan was designed to emphasize leadership training in the new classes of cadets. Not only were the professional aspects of military education reemphasized, but the program aimed to inculcate a mystique of honor, discipline, and self-sacrifice in this new generation of officers (Tarre Briceño, 1994: 143–46). The Plan Andrés Bello also reinforced a populist, egalitarian, and ultimately utilitarian perspective toward democracy, one that was in tune with the politics of Venezuela's heady oil boom of the 1970s. However, it is not surprising that, confronted with the uncertainties and disorder of the Venezuelan political process, which seemed to place party interests ahead of national interests, most young officers formed a greater attachment to Venezuela's glorious Bolivarian past instead of its inglorious present.

At the same time, the Venezuelan armed forces began a search for a new doctrine to replace the focus on counterinsurgency which had dominated the institution during the 1960s (Manrique, 1996: 64–75). National security doctrine (NSD) was adapted to a democratic regime through an emphasis on security through development. Military educational institutes that taught this new doctrine encouraged a populist, equity-oriented vision of development which was well matched to political discourse of the country during the oil boom of the 1970s.[3] Under the influence of this "soft" version of NSD, military leaders successfully lobbied Congress for legal provisions legitimizing their participation in national economic affairs, adding development to the traditional mission of defense of sovereignty (Manrique, 1996: 159). These desires were frustrated in practice by a political system that ensured that all military participation in development planning was confined to ritualistic and formal exercises.[4] Blocked in its efforts to redefine its mission, the Venezuelan officer corps increasingly concentrated on institutional power struggles for resources, promotions, and assignments.

External defense was not entirely neglected during this period as Venezuela used its windfall profits from the 1970s oil boom to rearm, converting its military from a light counterinsurgency army to a modern conventional force. Venezuela's traditional regional rivalry with Colombia revived, and illegal immigration, drug smuggling, and Colombia's left-wing insurgency remained perennial irritants to bilateral relations. Venezuela and Colombia had several substantial border disputes on which most Venezuelan officers took a hard-line attitude, opposing any concessions. Venezuela also claimed sovereignty over a large proportion of the territory of its neighbor, Guyana, creating another potential area for international conflict. Furthermore, given the large amount of revenues produced by petroleum exports, the armed forces increasingly raised concerns over protecting the shipping routes of Venezuelan oil.

An unintended consequence of rearmament, and of the oil boom in general, was the growth in corruption and malfeasance among senior military officers and civilian politicians. High-level government officials, military procurement officers, and well-placed civilian intermediaries enriched themselves with suspiciously large commissions on defense purchases. Acquisitions were made with little attention to the compatibility of new military equipment with the existing arsenal or its suitability for its use in a Venezuelan context.[5] Venezuela's activist foreign policy during this period, which included financial and military support for Eden Pastora's southern front during the revolution against Somoza in Nicaragua in 1979 and for the Christian Democratic government in El Salvador during the early 1980s, provided an additional source of illicit enrichment for civilians and some military officers.[6] The concern these practices generated among officers, particularly at the junior level, became a source of tension within the armed forces and deepened the divisions between senior officers and the new generations of idealistic officers coming out of the national military academies.

The military generational split intensified when the Venezuelan armed forces were rudely reintroduced to their internal security role by the 1989 urban riots. Almost immediately upon taking office, President Carlos Andrés Pérez introduced a package of neoliberal reform measures designed to deal with an impending economic crisis. In reaction to the sharp rise in gasoline prices which resulted from this package, a popular uprising occurred on February 27, 1989, in Caracas and other major cities. Since the police and the Guardia Nacional were overwhelmed by the extent of the riots and looting, President Pérez ordered that the uprising be repressed by the regular armed forces, which it did at the cost of several hundred civilian casualties. The large number of civilian casualties is one indicator of the extent to which the regular armed forces had deemphasized training and equipment for internal security duties, using conventional weapons and tactics where riot control methods would have been more appropriate.

Facing persistent popular protests, civilian politicians continued to rely on the armed forces to protect the regime. Public protests rose rapidly during late 1991 and early 1992, exceeding nine hundred major events in a seven-month period. Senior military commanders were amenable to this role, given their concern that the rising tide of lawlessness would destabilize the political system. However, the civilian authorities' need to use the military for ongoing internal security duties undermined junior officer confidence in the political regime (Burggraff and Millet, 1995: 60–61).

The experience of propping up Punto Fijo democracy produced a strong negative reaction in the junior officer corps. Many of the officers who eventually participated in the failed 1992 coup attempts report that their participation in the repression of the riots of the Caracazo crystallized their feelings of disgust toward the ruling civilian political elite. This reaction also helped the coup plotters of the Movimiento Bolivariano Revolucionario 200 (MBR-200; Bolivarian Revolutionary Movement 200), the military conspiracy founded by Hugo Chávez in 1982, to gain new adherents for their cause of overthrowing Venezuelan democracy (Gott, 2000: 45–49).

The 1992 failed coup attempts led to further expansion in the armed forces' internal roles, although at the behest of civilian politicians rather than as a result of military pressure. As Venezuelan political and bureaucratic institutions further deteriorated, the second Caldera administration (1994–99) used the military to resolve public policy crises, deploying soldiers to maintain emergency services in the face of strikes by public sector employees. For example, rather than allow Caracas public transportation to be shut down during a strike by Metro (subway) employees, Caldera ordered the army to keep the trains running (Villegas Poljak, 1996). This participation in public service was welcomed because it resonated with the national security doctrine of "democracy and development" current within officer corps. However, President Caldera's principal goal was to restore civilian authority over the armed forces by providing them with new tasks that would distract them from the political crisis Venezuela faced.

As part of his program of restoring civilian authority, President Caldera also reemphasized the external defense mission of the armed forces by ordering them to suppress the activities of Colombian insurgents in border areas. Increasing activities by Fuerzas Armadas Revolucionarias de Colombia (FARC; Revolutionary Armed Forces of Colombia) guerrillas in Venezuela's frontier regions resulted in numerous attacks on military outposts and significant Venezuelan casualties between 1994 and 1998. Caldera responded by creating two military theaters of operations to combat guerrillas along the Colombian frontier. These theaters of operations gave military commanders expanded authority over the civilian population, but within a limited area of the national territory. Thus, they were less threatening to civilian control than a full-fledged military participation in internal security missions (Trinkunas, 1999: 330–32). The main objective of this limited role expansion was to assign the armed forces new professional duties that would both sustain the democratic regime and distract the officer corps from the conspiratorial activities that followed the failure of the 1992 coup attempts.

Expanded Roles and Missions under the Fifth Republic

In the Fifth Republic, the armed forces have become one of the principal executors of government programs and policy. Since the beginning of his term, President Chávez has argued that the only way to meet the current national crisis in Venezuela is to take advantage of the human and technical resources provided by the armed forces (Leal, 1999). Furthermore, President Chávez has explicitly called on the armed forces to join and support his revolutionary project (Mayorca, 2000c). The proposed reform of organic law of the armed forces, prepared by the Ministry of Defense, identifies eighteen missions for the armed forces, compared with six in the existing law—Anteproyecto de Ley de las Fuerzas Armadas. The military has played a prominent role in public policy through the Plan Bolívar 2000 social program, in disaster relief and internal security following the floods in Vargas state in December 1999, and in staffing key positions in the government bureaucracy. The result produced substantial tensions within the armed forces which contributed to the withdrawal of military support for President Chávez during the first days of the April 11, 2002, coup attempt.

Among the first programs announced by President Chávez was Plan Bolívar 2000, aimed at the broad incorporation of the armed forces into domestic political and economic affairs. Plan Bolívar 2000 includes infrastructure refurbishment and construction, health care for the poor, combating illiteracy and unemployment, and food distribution. Initially established as a six-month emergency program that hired unemployed civilians and placed them under the direction of military officers, it now appears to have become a permanent part of the Chávez administration's policies.[7] Under Plan Bolívar 2000, the armed forces have gone so far as to use soldiers to sell basic goods at below market prices to hold down costs in lower- and working-class marketplaces. The air force now provides low-cost rural air transport through its Rutas Sociales. Approximately 29,000 soldiers (out of a total force of 85,000) participated in this program in its first year (Cardona Marrero, 2000).

Although these military-led efforts at poverty alleviation and economic development may provide public benefits, they have come at the expense of civilian leadership in these areas. The Chávez administration has starved opposition governors and mayors of resources with which to address these problems (Maracara, 1999). This has occurred even as Venezuela benefited from a sharp rise in world oil prices during 1999 and 2000, which peaked at more than thirty dollars per barrel, generating a large sum of windfall revenues with which the central government funded discretionary spending. Even though the government was legally required to channel a substantial amount of this funding to the state and local governments, it failed to do so (Monaldi Marturet, 1999). Specifically, President Chávez avoided disbursing windfall profits from the sale of oil set aside in a macroeconomic stabilization fund, part of which was originally destined for the use of regional governments. Instead, military garrisons, as principal executors of Plan Bolívar 2000 in each state, have benefited from these revenues and have been able to replace the state and municipal governments as the principal agents for regional development and poverty alleviation.[8]

Another significant expansion of the military mission occurred as a result of the December 1999 floods, which devastated the coastal state of Vargas and left tens of thousands homeless. In response to this crisis and the wave of looting which followed, President Chávez deployed regular army troops to provide security and disaster relief. They acted in cooperation with the police and the Guardia Nacional, the forces that traditionally have performed internal security missions (La Rotta Morán, 2000). This type of deployment is not an uncommon mission for any armed forces, even in well-established democracies. What has been unusual in the Venezuelan case is the extended length of the operation, which continued for more than two months after the disaster, and the accusations of human rights violations which quickly surfaced in the wake of the military's deployment (Lastra Veracierto, 2000). President Chávez and his administration initially discredited the reports of human rights violations by army troops, and some elements of the government harassed the journalist who had reported them (López, 2000b). Further investigation has resulted in the indictment in civilian courts of two low-ranking soldiers for crimes committed during the Vargas emergency, although the security forces have resisted cooperating with prosecutors (Reinoso, 2000).

President Chávez's administration has also been noted for its reliance on active-duty and retired military officers to staff political and bureaucratic positions. Retired and active-duty military officers have held up to one-third of the portfolios in the presidential cabinet, including the Ministry of Interior, Ministry of Infrastructure, and the governorship of the federal district during the transition to the Fifth Republic. As of October 2000, more than 150 active-duty military officers held senior ministerial or administrative positions within the government. Military officers have been appointed as president and vice president of the state oil company, Petróleos de Venezuela Sociedad Anónima (PDVSA; Venezuelan Oil Company, Incorporated), as well CEO as of its U.S. subsidiary, CITGO. Active-duty military officers have held positions as the president's chief of staff and personal secretary. An active-duty general heads the state agency charged with building public housing, including new homes for victims of the 1999 Vargas disaster, as well as the Office of the Budget. Chávez has also been careful to appoint officers who supported him in the 1992 coups to head the political and judicial police forces. A number of mid-ranking officers have also been transferred to administrative functions in traditionally civilian bureaucracies, particularly in tax collection and customs posts. More controversial, the president encouraged several active-duty military officers to run for office in the 2000 elections on his party's ticket. So far, all these officers have submitted resignations prior to taking up political activity (Colomine, 2000; Trinkunas, 2002: 66).

The expansion of military roles and missions has generated considerable debate within Venezuela. Retired military officers have critiqued the expansion of the military's role as a threat to the professionalism of the institution (Huizi Clavier, 2000). Former prosecutor general Eduardo Roche Lander reported several cases of corruption in relation to irregularities in the administration of Plan Bolívar monies (López, 2000a). Former presidential candidate Francisco Arias Cardenas has accused the government of decreasing military readiness as a result of excessive emphasis on Plan Bolívar 2000. Other critics have questioned the diversion of government resources into funding a civic action plan under the auspices of the military, which has used secrecy regulations to shield its activities under the plan from scrutiny (El Gobierno Debe Aclarar, 1999). Although all these critics have valid grounds for their specific concerns, the danger lies not only in the expansion of the military's role but in that it is occurring at the same time that institutional mechanisms of civilian control are being dismantled.

Civil-Military Institutions in the Fourth and Fifth Republics

After Venezuela's 1958 transition to democracy, civilians consolidated control of the armed forces based on institutions that fragmented the military and satisfied the personal and professional interests of the officer corps. Control by oversight was minimal, restricted to superficial congressional reviews of officer promotions and the defense budget—although these reviews did have the benefit of creating incentives for self-policing and preemptive compliance with civilian policies within the military. Control by containment succeeded in barring military participation in politics in Venezuela between 1962 and 1992, a notable achievement considering the wave of authoritarian reversals which swept over almost all Latin American democracies during the 1960s and 1970s. Furthermore, this pattern of civilian control was instrumental in preventing the success of the coup attempts in 1992. Once Hugo Chávez was elected president in 1998, he set about dismantling the mechanisms and procedures that had once prevented his accession to power. The result has been the deinstitutionalization of civilian control over the armed forces.

Civil-Military Institutions under Punto Fijo

In 1958, political leaders, and some military officers, guided by a strategy of "divide and conquer," reformed military institutions to ensure that any future participation by the armed forces in policy making would be contained to issues of national defense. During the transitional period, civilian leaders decreed the elimination of centralized military command structures, particularly the General Staff, and granted administrative and operational autonomy to each of the individual military services. The ensuing competition for power and resources between the army, navy, air force, and Guardia Nacional reduced possibilities for interservice cooperation. This fragmentation was compounded when each service created a system of independent training centers, garrisons, and commands. Punto Fijo governments also responded to the potential threat of military intervention through institutions of appeasement, granting rising budgets for the armed forces, a strong military social safety net, and deference to their interests in security affairs.

Under this system of control by containment, any incursion by the armed forces into rebellion, or even public policy, was swiftly punished during the first democratic administrations as presidents zealously preserved their prerogatives to appoint military leaders, approve senior promotions, and command the armed forces. The fragmentation of the officer corps and the satisfaction of many of its members with their professional and personal opportunities inhibited conspiracies and reconciled the armed forces to democratic rule. By 1973, the armed forces retained a high degree of autonomy within the relatively narrow area of state policy they controlled, national defense. Even though the armed forces preserved a nominal role in maintaining public order after the conclusion of counterinsurgency warfare in the early 1970s, this mission was carried out by the Guardia Nacional, a militarized national police that was viewed with suspicion by other services, particularly the army (Trinkunas, 1999: 286–97).

Once civilian control became consolidated, Venezuelan elected officials interacted with the military only in matters related to defeating the insurgency by disaffected leftists who received help from Fidel Castro and the Communist internationale. By institutionalizing strategies of "divide and conquer" and appeasement, civilian politicians felt confident that they had contained the threat of military intervention. Beginning with the election of Carlos Andrés Pérez in 1974, civilian presidents paid less attention to supervising military affairs. Nevertheless, they retained the capacity to decide defense policy on an ad hoc basis, examples of which include the decision to end counterinsurgency operations in 1969 and management of a serious border incident with Colombia in 1987.[9]

Military autonomy in defense issues remained high owing to legal provisions that protected military budgets and operations from civilian oversight. Congress approved overall defense expenditures by the four services but remained in the dark as to how money was spent; nor did it participate in the preparation of detailed military budgets. No member of either the Senate or Chamber of Deputies defense committees had any experience in military affairs (Norden, 1996: 151). Furthermore, rather than falling under the oversight of a civilian inspector general or Congress, the armed forces had their own auditor, who reported directly to the president. Sometimes, even the minister of defense did not know how his own service chiefs spent their budgets. Secrecy laws prevented the publication of detailed defense expenditures or a thorough discussion of defense policies in the media (Trinkunas, 1999). Congressional journalistic investigation of corruption scandals was discouraged, and the armed forces urged the prosecution of journalists who overstepped these boundaries (Agüero, 1995: 150–51).

AD and Comité de Organización Política Electoral Independiente: Partido Social Cristiano (COPEI; Committee of Independent Electoral Political Organization: Social Christian Party) used institutional means to circumvent the barriers posed by military autonomy. The 1961 constitution established the need for congressional and presidential approval for any promotion at the rank of colonel or general—or for their equivalents in the navy. This created opportunities for political manipulation, particularly by the civilian president. Although the overall number of promotions affected was small, many senior officers felt the need to align themselves preemptively with one of the two principal parties—AD and COPEI—to protect their careers.[10] This also created incentives for officers to police their own behavior to ensure it did not attract the unfavorable notice of politicians. Luis Herrera Campíns, president from 1979 to 1983, confirmed this when he once commented that generals should be appointed on the basis on trust rather than merit.[11] Moreover, a thirty-year limit on military careers, together with a policy of yearly rotations of officers among different positions and commands, created fierce competition over choice assignments that well-connected officers could resolve in their favor (Agüero, 1993: 199).[12] It also created a mechanism by which senior military officers practiced self-regulation to avoid offending civilian politicians, providing the government with a means of controlling the armed forces at a very low cost in resources and civilian expertise.

The politicization of promotions and assignments was particularly galling to junior officers, who were held to strict ethical and professional standards during their careers. Career assignments are made on a competitive basis at lower ranks, based principally on the educational achievements of individual officers.[13] The conduct of young officers and their ethical handling of professional and personal duties weigh heavily in the process as well. For officers recently graduated from the military academy and therefore most strongly indoctrinated with professional standards, promotion on the basis of political preference instead of merit led them lose respect for their military superiors and civilian politicians. Politicization in the military promotion process allowed civilians to overcome institutional autonomy on important issues but also increasingly split the civilian and military elite from the junior officer corps (Agüero, 1995: 149).

By the 1980s, civil-military relations had settled into a stable, if somewhat dysfunctional, pattern in Venezuela. So long as institutions designed to appease and fragment the officer corps were in place, open discontent in the military was avoided, and the armed forces' substantive authority over state policy was contained to a narrow range of issues related to defense and frontier policy. Nevertheless, civilian inattention to defense issues, growing civilian and military corruption, and politicization of the armed forces created the latent potential for a break between the armed forces and the civilian regime. The high degree of military autonomy from civilian oversight also meant that the growing alienation of many officers went undetected by the civilian government. Politicians had become complacent, confident that they could rely on their connections with the military high command to maintain supervision over the armed forces. The growing distance between the generals and admirals and their subordinates thus undermined the ability of politicians to detect military unrest.

Transforming Civil-Military Institutions in the Fifth Republic

There has been a clear trend toward eliminating any mechanisms for civilian control by oversight or by containment in Venezuela since Hugo Chávez assumed the presidency. This shift is especially apparent in the 1999 Bolivarian constitution, which eliminates the barriers to cohesive military action in the political arena enforced during the Punto Fijo period and makes institutionalized civilian control of the armed forces almost impossible. The absence of institutionalized control became apparent during the April 11 coup attempt. Paradoxically, President Chávez has reacted by attempting to deepen his personal control over the officer corps rather than reinstitutionalizing government control of the military.

Article 328 of the 1999 constitution redesignates the Venezuelan armed forces as the National Armed Force (note singular) and directs them to operate in an integrated manner. This change is more than semantic, since the intent of the constituent assembly was to increase centralization in the military command structure (Duarte, 1999). This created a centralized organization in charge of military administration, planning, and operations, replacing the weakly articulated Joint Staff of Punto Fijo democracy, which had responsibility only for planning (Mayorca, 2000b).

Article 331 eliminated the right of the legislature to approve military promotions and assigns this task to the armed forces themselves, establishing that promotions should be decided on the basis of merit, seniority, and vacancy. The new armed forces organic law specifies in its Article 157 that a single integrated list based on merit and seniority is to be prepared every six months. It also requires that this list be the only tool used to select officers for promotion and reassignment (A. Romero, 2000). In practice, President Chávez has arrogated this power to himself, and he reportedly alters promotion lists to reward officers for loyalty to the "revolution" and move key supporters into command positions (Designado Manuel Rosendo, 2003).

These reforms eliminate two of the mechanisms for containment and oversight of Punto Fijo democracy: decentralized military command structures and legislative approval of military promotions. During the Punto Fijo period, each military service had administrative independence. Although the defense minister was the titular head of the armed forces, each military service chief could plan, administer, and operate independently from the wishes of either the Ministry of Defense or the Joint Staff. This deterred military intervention in politics by increasing the risk that a coup d'état would fail owing to lack of coordination, and it encouraged each service to compete with the others for resources and attention from elected officials. The transition to a general staff within the armed forces is likely to concentrate power in the armed forces in the hands of a single officer, thus reducing the amount of control and information available to civilians which previously emerged from intramilitary competition.

The elimination of the constitutional requirement for legislative approval of military promotions for the ranks of colonel and general makes civilian control by oversight much more difficult because no other elected officials besides the president have effective means to remove potentially disloyal officers from the armed forces. During the Punto Fijo period, legislative approval of military promotions overtly affected less than 5 percent of officers in any given year, according to former minister of defense, García Villasmíl. This manipulation generally took place in the executive branch, prior to the submission of the promotion list to Congress. However, it had the important effect of self-censoring ambitious military officers into compliance with the policies of elected officials.

As commander in chief, President Chávez is the only civilian elected official in Venezuela who currently has authority over the armed forces. Below him, all members of the chain of command and defense bureaucracy are active-duty or retired military officers. Since there is no bureaucratic entity within which civilian defense expertise and practical knowledge can develop, all future defense bureaucrats are likely to remain either active-duty or retired military officers. The widespread participation of generals and admirals in the April 11, 2002, coup attempt—close to one hundred, according to some estimates—reveals the shortcomings of such an approach to maintaining control of the military (Chávez at Bay, 2002).

In addition, the change in the relationship of the legislature to the military under the 1999 constitution further reduces opportunities for civilian oversight. The new constitution does provide for the possibility of legislative oversight by the National Assembly through a defense committee that has the power to produce and approve defense legislation (Galicia, 2000a). However, the dominance of the governing Polo Patriótico (Patriotic Pole) during the early Chávez administration and the legislative deadlock that characterized the post-April 11 environment make it unlikely that oversight will be exercised in any instance in which it is contrary to the will of the president. An early indicator of the weakness of legislative oversight is that the draft of a new armed forces law was written by military officers in the Ministry of Defense rather than by legislators (Mayorca, 2000d). Thus, it seems unlikely that the National Assembly will set any precedents for regularized civilian oversight of military activities during its first five-year mandate. Although Chávez's military experience and knowledge of the Venezuelan officer corps made it possible for him to exercise personal authority over the armed forces (most of the time), the absence of any civilian institutions for oversight and control in the Fifth Republic will make the task of civilian control impossible for his successors.

Civil-Military Relations in the Wake of the April 11 Coup

The failed April 11, 2002, coup attempt demonstrates the shortcomings of President Chávez's effort to control the armed forces personally by manipulating assignments and promotions of officers. His strategy backfired by accentuating divisions between pro- and anti-Chávez forces in the military. Key pro-Chávez members of the military high command, including General Manuel Rosendo, head of the unified armed forces command, and General Lucas Rincón Romero, armed forces inspector general, played significant roles in supporting the initial phases of the coup.

The coup attempt, which collapsed after two days because of the errors committed by the transitional Carmona government and the counterefforts of pro-Chavista military officers, damaged the credibility of the civilian opposition to President Chávez. The hijacking of the transitional government by the most conservative elements in Venezuelan civil society, their mistakes in handling civil-military relations, and the subsequent failure of the coup could only create doubts within the officer corps about the wisdom of working with the opposition. More important, the unconstitutional decrees of the Carmona government confirmed for many officers the truth of President Chávez's claims about the opposition, namely, that it was led by a right-wing conspiracy between a corrupt oligarchy and the owners of the media. This charge could especially resonate among junior and mid-ranking officers most likely to favor President Chávez and, more significant, most likely to lead combat units. As a result, important elements of the armed forces would distance themselves from those civilians who opposed the president.

What all civilians in Venezuela faced, whether in the government or in the opposition, were armed forces too divided to act coherently yet more politically significant than ever. The anti-Chávez military faction, concentrated among senior officers, was hard hit by its defeat on April 14. The disjointed nature of its rebellion against the president revealed a lack of preparation, even though some had been plotting for nearly a year. It also highlighted the enduring rivalries between the services. The unseemly scramble for high position among rebellious officers during the Carmona interim government contributed to the failure of the coup and is likely to have discredited them among their subordinates. Notably, a significant number refused to obey their superiors' orders. In the army, these detentions were largely concentrated in the logistics and aviation branches, confirming reports that rebellious senior officers in fact controlled few combat troops.

Pro-Chávez military forces emerged from the rebellion with a mixed record. Key senior officers closely identified with the president's revolutionary program during the preceding three years sided with the rebels on April 11. As a result, almost the entire military high command was replaced. On the other hand, some officers demonstrated that they were committed supporters of President Chávez. The presidential guard never transferred its loyalty to the Carmona interim government, allowing Chávez supporters to regain control of the presidential palace soon after the coup. Reports emerged in the media of efforts by junior and mid-ranking officers to undermine the detention of President Chávez during April 12 and 13 by providing him with cell phones and bringing him messages. Similarly, in Maracay, where Venezuela's air, armor, and airborne units are based, military commanders never joined the coup attempt. After the rebellion ended, Brigadier General Raúl Baduel, who commanded the loyalist Forty-second Paratrooper Brigade based in Maracay during the coup, was promoted to command the most powerful unit in the Venezuelan army, the fourth division, and was consulted frequently by the president on the promotion of other loyalist officers to key command positions (D. Romero, 2002b).

Most important, the institutionalist majority in the Venezuelan armed forces emerged from the April 11, 2002, coup as the "swing voter" in both a military and political sense, although this was hardly what many of these professionals would wish. By deposing the government in reaction to the death of peaceful protesters on April 11, the institutionalists showed that they were willing to place limits on the actions of President Chávez. By contrast, the institutionalists' support for democracy led them to support the defeat of the Carmona interim administration after it issued unconstitutional decrees. This suggests that the Venezuelan armed forces are not willing to support an outright dictatorship, although their behavior during the December 2002 general strike would later demonstrate a high tolerance for government quasi-repressive activities. Although institutionalist officers may desire to avoid politics, the turmoil in the Venezuelan political system is likely to draw them back in. Civilians in government and the opposition were likely to continue to focus part of their efforts on the key actor in a divided military, the institutionalist majority.

The December 2002 General Strike and Beyond

Government restraint in the use of the armed forces in internal security roles greatly decreased during the sixty-three days of the general strike that began on December 2, 2002. Organized by the Democratic Coordinating Committee, the Confederación de Trabajadores de Venezuela (Confederation of Venezuelan Workers), and the Federación de Cámaras y Asociaciones de Comercio y Producción de Venezuela (FEDECAMARAS; Federation of Chambers of Commerce and Production of Venezuela), the general strike was intended to force President Chávez from power, by either his resignation or his acquiescence to a recall referendum (Oposición Convocó, 2002). President Chávez's popularity among the general public plummeted, with approval ratings dropping to 29 percent (Giusti, 2002). To survive the general strike, President Chávez turned to the armed forces to provide internal security, distribute goods and services, and assist in the restoration of oil production.

Political tension between the government and the opposition reached a peak when President Chávez ordered the armed forces to take over the Caracas metropolitan police force, which was under the control of the opposition mayor, Alfredo Peña. The government accused the police force of being partial to the opposition because it protected the latter's demonstrations from clashes with pro-Chávez activists, such as the Círculos Bolivarianos. The government went so far as to accuse the metropolitan police of deliberately targeting its supporters. The armed forces prevented the police from operating and put troops on the streets of Caracas to ensure their control of the city. This striking use by the government of the armed forces to intervene in domestic politics formed the backdrop to the decision to call a general strike (Cardona Marrero, 2002; Ruiz Pantin, 2002).

The armed forces enabled President Chávez to remain in power during the general strike; the Guardia Nacional and the army military police, in particular, acted to quell civilian opposition demonstrations on a number of occasions, and the military was used to intimidate civilian food producers participating in the general strike (Camel Anderson, 2002; González, 2003). The armed forces occupied the police stations of the Caracas metropolitan police force, preventing the civilian police from operating. The military occupied oil facilities and assisted in breaking the production strike by PDVSA workers. When the oil tankers of the Venezuelan merchant marine refused to load oil or operate, they were boarded by navy marine commandos, and their crews were reportedly intimidated (Camel Anderson and Castro, 2002). After President Chávez took the step of breaking up the existing organization of PDVSA and firing almost half of its employees, military officers were brought in to support the pro-government minority of oil workers and managers who returned to work (Camel Anderson, 2003). Finally, as supplies and services ran short in most metropolitan areas of Venezuela, the navy was used to ship supplies from neighboring countries, and the army was used to organize street fairs at which citizens could buy necessities and access health and government services (Buque Cargado de Alimentos, 2003). With the rest of the state largely inoperative, wavering (the Supreme Court), or actively opposing the president (the Consejo Nacional Electoral [CNE; National Electoral Council]), only the armed forces allowed the government to continue operating with some measure of physical security, access to resources, and the threat of violence to compel its adversaries to end the general strike. However, it is significant that the use of the armed forces in internal security missions was limited to specialized units, such as the Guardia Nacional, army military police, and the naval commandos, rather than to units of the regular military as a whole.

Conclusion

The broad expansion of the military's participation in government policy making and implementation, combined with the elimination of institutions of containment and oversight, indicates that Venezuela's institutions of civilian control have unraveled. As the events of April 11, 2002, demonstrate, elected officials no longer have the ability to defend the regime against military conspiracies or carry out their constitutional duty of ensuring that the activities of the defense bureaucracy match the policies of the civilian government. The return of Chávez to power after being deposed was a product of the political ineptness of the interim Cardona administration rather than any institutions. In the wake of this experience, Chávez did not choose to restore institutionalized control but has resorted to ever more politicized and personalized mechanisms for controlling the officer corps (D. Romero, 2002a).

How can we explain that a democratic regime deliberately dismantled its authority over its own military? Why not attempt to restore an institutionalized basis for government control in the wake of the April 11, 2002, coup? Aside from the ideological convictions that motivate President Chávez in this area, his substitution of personal control over the armed forces for institutionalized democratic control is, in part, a response to his experiences as a military officer and a coup leader. The dysfunctional aspects of civil-military institutions were well known and understood by military officers during the Punto Fijo period. Certain aspects, such as the political manipulation of promotions and the alliances based on corruption between senior military officers and politicians, were particularly galling to officers of Chávez's generation. Furthermore, the difficulties that Chávez faced in achieving success in the 1992 coup attempts were also a result of the institutionalized decentralization of military authority, which inhibited the ability of the MBR-200 conspiracy to recruit members from services other than the army. Eliminating these dysfunctional institutions was a means for Chávez to gain support within the armed forces and correct problems he experienced during his military service. However, the consequence—intended or otherwise—of these institutional reforms was to reduce government authority over the military.

President Chávez's decision to expand the roles and missions of the armed forces was also, in part, a reflection of his distrust for the civilian political parties and state bureaucracies that would otherwise participate in this process. Once in government, the parties making up his electoral alliance, the Polo Patriótico, were more noted for internecine squabbling and competition for power than an interest in government policy making (Galicia, 2000b). Hardly noted for its efficiency during the Punto Fijo period, the civilian state bureaucracy of the Fifth Republic achieved new depths of poor performance. In comparison, the armed forces were much more responsive to the president's orders and adopted their new social and economic missions with alacrity. In the first year of the program, the army estimated that 1.6 million people would receive assistance through its social programs (Plan Bolívar 2000, no. 2, 26). Ideological convictions aside, Chávez's decision to expand the role of the armed forces can be at least partly explained by the contrast between the performance of the armed forces and that of the civilian politicians and bureaucrats.

The reorientation of security forces toward internal roles and missions has traditionally been a leading indicator of civil-military conflict and authoritarian rule in many states (Trinkunas, 1999: 8–12). Military readiness has been eroded by its participation in domestic activities because the skills used for domestic security and development do not readily translate into combat. The use of the armed forces to support elections, carry out their assignments under the Plan Bolívar 2000, and support the government during the general strike is likely to have left many units less ready for combat, despite disclaimers by senior officers in this regard.[14] In addition, the expanded level of military participation in economic development and internal security is likely to expose the armed forces to substantial corruption. Accusations of such irregularities in the Plan Bolívar 2000 have already emerged (Cortés, 2000). In the wake of the April 11, 2002, coup and the December 2002 general strike, it is clear that the Venezuelan armed forces were no longer under civilian control yet they were also unwilling to support an outright dictatorship. For the foreseeable future, the Venezuelan armed forces will remain at the center of a tug-of-war between the opposition and the government and thus will continue to hatch pro- and anti-Chávez conspiracies. The result will be a less professional and less capable armed forces, one that is highly politicized as long as President Chávez remains in power and a substantial political headache for any future administration.

CHAPTER FOUR

Entrepreneurs

Profits without Power?

Nelson Ortiz

Venezuela's private sector, in contrast to most of its regional counterparts, was diverse and powerful in 1958 when the Pacto de Punto Fijo was signed.[1] At the beginning of the twentieth century, when agriculture and commerce predominated and petroleum played no significant role, names such as Vollmer, Boulton, Phelps, Delfino, Mendoza, Zuloaga, Machado, Branger, Velutini, Sosa, and Perez-Dupuy dominated the economy. These same family groups controlled Venezuela's private sector throughout most of the twentieth century, although beginning with the 1973 oil boom they were forced to share economic power with other private groups that benefited from the infusion of new resources. The complex alliances and rivalries of traditional and emerging elites determined private sector policy through the remainder of the Punto Fijo era and into the Fifth Republic.[2]

Venezuela's prosperous private sector derived from a strong and successful economy, one that was envied not only in Latin America but also throughout the world. The country's gross domestic product (GDP) grew rapidly after the mid-1930s, increasing by an annual average of more than 8 percent throughout the 1950s and 1960s. At the same time, the rate of inflation was among the lowest in the world, averaging less than 1.5 percent per year (Baptista, 1991). Not only was the economy growing at a fast rate, but per capita GDP was substantially higher than in the rest of Latin American and even surpassed that in countries such as France, Spain, Italy, and Japan.

Although oil accounted for much of this impressive development after 1935, this was not the full story. Such spectacular results were not matched by other oil-producing nations at the time, and Venezuela itself failed to replicate this success during subsequent oil booms. Thus, the key lay with those who managed these oil revenues, that is to say, policy makers and institutions. In addition, a significant portion of oil revenue was redistributed to a private sector that invested at very high rates, kept its savings in the country, had vast interests in most sectors of the economy, and participated in administering the state.

Forty years later the situation had changed dramatically. Per capita GDP had fallen to a fraction of that in those nations Venezuela had outperformed in earlier decades.[3] Paradoxically, this decline coincided with periods in which the state received unprecedented income from oil sales and at times when Latin America experienced sustained economic progress.

The private sector collapse was far greater than Venezuela's economic decline. Few of the dominant economic groups of the early 1990s were major players a decade later. The extent of this destruction can be gleaned by looking at the precipitous fall in market capitalization of the Caracas Stock Exchange, which includes most of the country's largest companies. Whereas it exceeded $13 billion in 1991, twelve years later it had dropped to a paltry $3 billion or less. This decline is only the tip of the iceberg. These figures do not reflect the control and management of a large number of the major agricultural, commercial, industrial, and financial companies that passed to foreign ownership. In fact, the value of companies actually controlled by Venezuelan investors at the end of June 2003 was less than $1 billion. These figures are starker still given that stock market capitalization rose significantly in the rest of the region, as shown in figure 4.1.

Of the five hundred largest Latin American companies, ranked by sales, at the end of 2002, only one was owned and controlled by Venezuelans: Empresas Polar, which ranked seventy-sixth (Ranking de las Mayores Empresas, 2003). Many heirs and descendants of Venezuela's ruling classes, as well as a substantial portion of the middle class, reacted to the shrinkage of the private sector by emigrating. Joining this exodus were descendants of immigrants who came to Venezuela after World War II, mainly from Italy, Spain, and Portugal. The

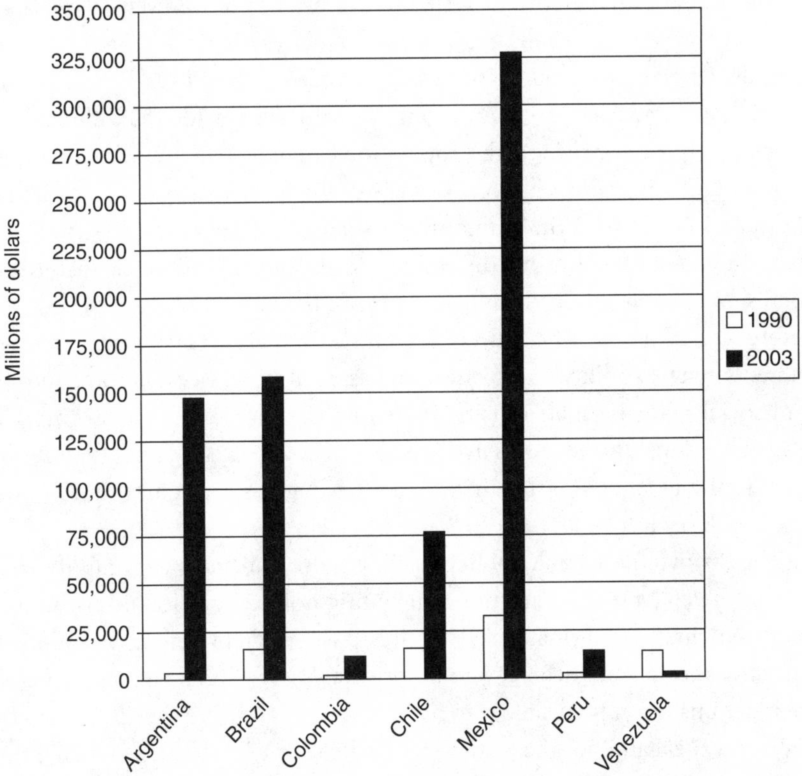

Fig. 4.1. Market capitalization in selected major economies in Latin America, 1990 and 2003. *Sources:* Ibero-American Federation of Exchanges and Caracas Stock Exchange.

1990s brain drain is equal to or more dramatic than the destruction of physical and financial capital which occurred at the same time. This situation worsened in the Fifth Republic, owing mainly to Chávez's radical speech and policies and an alarming increase in crime. In 2003, according to official figures, every sixty-nine minutes a person was murdered, every two days a person was kidnapped, every day 9.6 people were raped, every hour 10 people were robbed, and every day 141.7 vehicles were stolen (Tarre, 2003).

This grim scenario forms the backdrop to Punto Fijo democracy's demise. The socioeconomic disintegration experienced by Venezuela since Black Friday of February 1983 would be puzzling even if financial resources had been scarce.[4] In a time of plenty, it is almost beyond comprehension.[5] So what was the role of the private sector in this process of unraveling?

The single most important factor in the process of unraveling appears to have been institutional collapse. The dominance of oil in the economy created a model whereby the state distributed resources derived from the sale of that natural resource. Hence, gaining control of the state made the difference between being poor or rich. As the population expanded, oil prices dropped, and per capita income from petroleum sales declined, the struggle for control of the state intensified. Within the private sector, this led to the destruction of institutional constraints on competition for resources and of the institutions themselves. Public policy making became an increasingly chaotic struggle for resources with few mechanisms of accountability. This transformation undermined the state's ability to provide even basic public services such as education and social and personal security. It also had an impact in transforming oil from a blessing into a curse as in the typical case of rent seeking (attempting to capture the revenue the state has gained from selling natural resources) outlined by Terry Karl (1997).

The distorting of public policy making by the business community had a role in the collapse of institutions, including political parties, in institutional arrangements, and ultimately in the fall of post-1958 representative democracy. But how and to what degree? Should private sector elites be blamed based on their actions or on their failure to act? How influential are they in contemporary Venezuela and how have they changed? Are we likely to see a turnaround in the deteriorated condition of private sector institutions in the near or medium term? These are the principal questions addressed in this chapter in an attempt to understand the interaction between the business community and politicians during the unraveling of Punto Fijo democracy and in the Fifth Republic. Discussion of the private sector mainly takes into account large Venezuelan-owned companies rather than multinational corporations.

Business Elites under Punto Fijo

The private sector model of the Punto Fijo era originated with two important changes in the mid-1930s. The first, a democratic opening, included two dimensions: broader participation from groups in civil society—including private sector elites—and institutional development. Institutional development occurred when the state established a professional military and created a number of important public institutions. Meanwhile, workers, with help from the political parties, set up the Confederación de Trabajadores de Venezuela (CTV;

Confederation of Venezuelan Workers). A few years later private sector interests formed an umbrella business confederation, the Federación de Cámaras y Asociaciones de Comercio y Producción de Venezuela (FEDECAMARAS; Federation of Chambers of Commerce and Production of Venezuela). The second important change reflected the increasing importance of petroleum production. Until the early 1930s this mineral was second to agriculture in importance. Subsequently, petroleum shaped Venezuelan development. This trend would continue into the twenty-first century.

Agricultural production drowned in a sea of oil during the 1940s, a classic example of the so-called Dutch disease.[6] Decades later Domingo Alberto Rangel (1972) would describe Venezuela as a nation of merchants and bureaucrats, implying that only these activities could flourish in an oil-dominated economy. Still, Venezuela did industrialize between 1943 and the late 1970s, assisted by high protective tariffs. Protectionism facilitated one of the longest and most intense periods of capital formation growth experienced by any twentieth-century nation (Baptista, 1991).

Venezuela's traditional ruling classes turned industrialization to their own advantage. Many of the agricultural era's prominent families evolved into important manufacturing and trading groups during the 1940s and 1950s. Evidence of private sector power can be seen in the role businessmen played in overthrowing the dictator Marcos Pérez Jiménez. This involvement gave them great influence during the transitional government of 1958. Eugenio Mendoza served in the provisional Junta de Gobierno, and other businessmen, such as Oscar Machado Zuloaga and Arturo Sosa, were part of one of the most economically powerful cabinets ever assembled in Venezuela. Other private sector captains who served included Oscar García Velutini, René de Sola, Oscar Palacios Herrera, Carlos Eduardo Galavís, Juan Ernesto Branger, Héctor Santaella, and Héctor Hernández Carabaño. They supported the transition to democracy while setting in the stage for a permanent presence in public policy making. They also strongly supported the development of political parties.

The economic primacy of petroleum led to a redistributive state and an overvalued currency. Therefore, private enterprise needed assistance from government in order to compete with foreign goods. Public works contracts, Corporación Venezolana de Fomento (CVF; Venezuelan Development Corporation) loans, price controls, licenses, import tariffs and quotas, and export bonds, inter alia, became the instruments that linked government and business. Indeed, much private sector investment during the Punto Fijo period was financed with state resources or state guaranties, a practice that dated from the early days of the petroleum economy.

Major business groups could exist during the Punto Fijo era mainly by establishing at least one of the ties just described. For a merchant, the issue was tariffs and exemptions, whereas for industrialists it was the permits needed to build a plant, as well as price controls and tariffs to alienate foreign competition. Builders negotiated public works, and bankers managed deposits from government entities. Profits were dependent on appropriate decisions by bureaucrats or party leaders, and businessmen became commensurate lobbyists. The consequence was a deeply skewed system in which most players had *rabo de paja* (implicated in corruption) and *bozal de arepa* (tuned out to what was going on), leading to a society of kept accomplices (*sociedad de complices*).[7]

The Decline of Punto Fijo

How can we explain the fact that many operational characteristics of the Punto Fijo period remained unchanged throughout the full forty-year period? In both the early, successful period and the years when the political regime unraveled, income from the sale of petroleum flowed into the economy through government spending, much of it filtered through channels that linked the private and public sectors. In good years and bad Venezuelan business elites (bankers, contractors, industrialists, merchants, and linked professionals) participated actively and directly in public policy making, often holding high positions in the bureaucracies charged with overseeing their conduct.

The characteristics of Punto Fijo democracy which persisted over its entire lifetime do not provide the most important insights into why the political regime fell. Focusing on factors that were present or absent when that regime functioned well and when it unraveled provides a better route for understanding the private sector's decline. Particularly helpful is an examination of how the country's institutions unraveled and the rifts between business elites which surfaced after the oil windfall of 1973.

During the first fifteen years of Punto Fijo, Venezuelan institutions and institutional arrangements appeared successful. At the same time, the business elite had a relatively coherent approach to government. After 1974, institutions began to deteriorate and were increasingly unresponsive. It was then that rifts appeared within the business community. Also after 1974 Venezuela appeared to develop into the typical model of the petro-state described by Terry Karl (1997).

Institutional Collapse

The post-1974 institutional collapse can be explained by bad decision making, in particular by two costly mistakes that led Venezuela to abandon the three macroeconomic rules—fixed exchange rate, fixed interest rates, and fiscal expenditures equal to fiscal revenues-which, according to Ricardo Hausmann (1995), were the key behind the economic success of several decades: first, the misuse of revenue from the 1973 oil windfall; and second, mismanagement of the drop in oil prices after 1982. In fact, we could say that Venezuela was a textbook case of large windfall revenues leading to poor decision making by government (Stevens, 2003).

The fiscal windfall of 1973 had a major effect on the economy and policy making. President Carlos Andrés Pérez (1974–79; 1989–93) established the Venezuelan Investment Fund in his first term to avoid distortions of the increasing inflow of foreign exchange by investing most of the surplus abroad. These good intentions were soon abandoned. Huge conglomerates of resource-hungry state-owned enterprises sprang up. They initially included only basic industries but later encompassed practically every sector in the economy: iron and steel, petroleum, electric power, aluminum, petrochemicals, construction, tourism, aviation, shipping and shipbuilding, banking, broadcasting, and telecommunications. Their demands more than soaked up revenue from the petroleum bonanza.

The state, intent on participating in each of these sectors, secured additional financing by contracting foreign debt at an average rate of more than 7 percent of GDP per annum over eight years. Half of the debt was incurred directly by state-owned enterprises, which borrowed with little central government supervision. Loans were granted under very favorable terms given Venezuela's AAA credit risk qualification. The private sector also exploited international markets for financing, though with greater caution. At the end of 1982, the public external debt stood at close to $28 billion, while the private external debt was slightly over $5 billion, a sharp contrast to the rest of the region, where most debt was private.

This policy of state capitalism had important consequences for the private sector. First, it limited scope for entrepreneurial activity, excluding private investment in many of the more profitable economic activities, notably those associated with oil. Second, the fact that business was conducted directly with the state at every level increased private sector dependency on the official sector from procurement of the basic inputs to construction of sophisticated plants. Third, bureaucratic managers shifted their focus toward activities in the more autonomous state-owned corporations. Fourth, the exponential growth of public expenditure led to the collapse of public finances. In 1974, fiscal expenditures rose more than 300 percent, and just a single item, salaries and wages, came to $7 billion in 1980 whereas in 1973 the total government budget was $3.2 billion. Finally, the huge fiscal expansion added to the overvaluation of Venezuela's currency (the bolivar), which in turn further constrained the private sector action.

When oil prices fell and interest rates rose in international markets in 1982, the state capitalistic economic model collapsed. Venezuela's government tried in vain to maintain existing interest rates and to keep the exchange rate fixed, but capital flight accelerated. On February 18, 1983, President Luis Herrera Campíns abandoned the fixed foreign exchange policy, devalued the currency, and imposed exchange controls.

Devaluation was the easiest to manage from a political perspective. Private sector leaders, displaying remarkable shortsightedness, felt that they had a great deal to gain from this policy in light of their high levels of external savings. They had begun to export their savings and accumulate foreign assets in the late 1970s after they perceived a lack of investment opportunities and decided that the government's interest rate policy was irrational. At the time of the February 1983 devaluation, it was estimated that the overseas assets of Venezuela's private sector exceeded $30 billion, a figure equal to the country's entire foreign debt (Rodríguez, 1984).

What the private sector had failed to grasp was that devaluation was destroying the purchasing power of its local consumers by effectively transferring wealth to the public sector. After 1983, real wages declined year after year, bringing down the real sales of Venezuelan companies and their ability to invest. Local business leaders also displayed lack of foresight when they supported the adoption of differential exchange rates in 1983 which provided for a preferential exchange rate for private sector liabilities of up to $5 billion, or in other words, one-sixth of their foreign assets. There was a catch, however. The assets in question belonged to individual businessmen, but it was the corporations that incurred the indebtedness. This led then president Luis Herrera Campíns (1979–83) to remark that Venezuela was a country of bankrupt companies with wealthy entrepreneurs. Nevertheless, this regime of exchange controls and differential exchange rates lasted six years, increased corruption, and became yet another instrument for increasing the dependency of the private sector on the public sector.

These economic policy decisions had long-term implications for the country, particularly the private sector. Between 1983 and 2002, the accumulated current account surplus in the external sector exceeded $50 billion. This situation should have led to an important revaluation of the bolivar, rather than to devaluation to less than 1 percent of its early 1983 level. Venezuela's fiscal situation, however, had deteriorated markedly. Moreover, as owner of the oil and the country's foremost exporter, the government turned devaluation into its principal instrument for filling the fiscal gap.

Rifts between the Leading Classes

Until 1973, Venezuelan private sector elites were relatively united despite some political differences and rivalries associated with business competition. After 1974, government policies led to more intense divisions. President Carlos Andrés Pérez encouraged policies that favored the formation of new business groups. In theory, this seemed a good idea; it is, after all, a function of government to promote economic competition and avoid the rise of monopolies and oligopolies. In practice, however, Pérez appeared to be favoring his friends and financiers, policies that estranged him from Acción Democrática (AD; Democratic Action), the government party. It became conventional wisdom that the new economic elite was corrupt and destructive of sound fiscal management. Sociologist Pedro Duno, a writer who later influenced Hugo Chávez, attached a derogative label that stuck to this emergent entrepreneurial cabal, the "Twelve Apostles" (Duno, 1975). The cabal's favored treatment infuriated the groups that traditionally dominated private sector activities, such as the Mendoza and Delfino cement producers, whose oligopoly was undercut by the imposition of price controls and granting of building permits to firms controlled by the Twelve Apostles.

The appearance of new actors also affected FEDECAMARAS, one of the Punto Fijo system's most emblematic institutions. This umbrella organization, which brings together sectoral and regional business associations, had been from its inception in 1944 the institutional link between business and government. In 1979, amid bitter conflict, control of this institution passed from traditional economic groups to Ciro Añez Fonseca, a former general manager of FEDECAMARAS who represented an alliance of the emerging groups and long marginalized business elites from the interior. The traditional groups would never regain control.[8]

FEDECAMARAS played a part in negotiating the Pact of Punto Fijo, the interelite agreement that facilitated normalization of democracy (as discussed in Chapter 1). Post-1958 governments constantly summoned its leaders, along with those of the CTV, to consult on a broad range of policy issues. FEDECAMARAS also played a leading role in the elections that carried Hugo Chávez to power in 1998. However, it would be after the general strikes of December 2001 and December 2002 that FEDECAMARAS would play its highest-profile political role.

Beginning in 1989, new government policies again divided the private business community. In particular, incentives that opened up the economy brought about meaningful competition between business groups for the first time. In a 1984 article, "La Empresa Privada en Venezuela: ¿Qué Pasa Cuando se Crece en Medio de la Riqueza y la Confusión?" (Private enterprise in Venezuela: What happens when growth is accompanied by wealth and confusion?), Moisés Naím argued that market oligopoly leads some companies to adopt highly aggressive tactics intended to destroy the competition while others seek entry into cartel arrangements. Naím himself, as minister of development, was responsible for implementing the policy of economic openness which would cause even greater strife in Venezuelan business.

Post-1989 conflict between the business factions went beyond mere competition. Emerging groups that struggled to acquire petro-bonanza wealth in the 1970s sought in the 1990s to control two of the country's flagship corporations, Banco de Venezuela and Electricidad de Caracas. These struggles for control, both of which occurred during Pérez's second administration, saw the traditional oligarchy challenged by emerging groups including some once known as the Twelve Apostles. Banco de Venezuela changed hands; Electricidad de Caracas did not.

Control of the media was also an important focus of conflict. For many years a balance existed in which the two dominant television channels were owned by the rival Cisneros and Phelps groups. This equilibrium was shattered in the early 1990s when the Cisneros group and certain banks, mainly those involved in the hostile takeover of Banco de Venezuela, bought a third channel —Televen. The Televen license purchased by the Cisneros group was the only VHF signal available for private broadcasting in addition to the two already granted to Cisneros and the rival Phelps group. In 1988, President Lusinchi had given that license to businessman Omar Camero, a close confidant of the president. This conflict surrounding Televen, especially given the political influence that accompanied control of an important broadcast outlet, increased the level of tension, already high because of fallout from the Banco de Venezuela takeover. Several other financial groups, owned basically by emerging groups, also purchased newspapers, radio networks, regional TV stations, and even telecommunication companies. Ironically, few of these media-oriented groups survived the banking crisis in 1994.

The rifts and disputes between major business conglomerates would have important consequences for Punto Fijo democracy. The struggles were high-profile conflicts, and the ensuing "dirty wars" involved high-ranking government officials and political party leaders. This intensified the perception that the political regime was corrupt and paved the way for the 4 de Febrero and 27 de Noviembre coup attempts in 1992, as well as opening the way for Rafael Caldera's election to the presidency the following year as a critic of AD and Comité de Organización Política Electoral Independiente: Partido Social Cristiano (COPEI; Committee of Independent Electoral Political Organization: Social Christian Party).

The Opening of the Economy and Its Impact on the Private Sector

Neoliberal reforms in 1989 dramatically altered the economic environment for the private sector. As Antonio Francés and Moisés Naím (1995) pointed out, the most relevant changes occurred in its relationship with the state and the way businessmen approached markets and treated their clients. Venezuela's private sector, as discussed earlier, had developed in a strongly protected environment, and government-business collusion had led to unprecedented corruption during the three previous administrations (1974–89).

The private sector had an important role in changing the government's economic corporatism. After the Black Friday devaluation of 1983, a prominent group of businessmen, "el Grupo Roraima," prepared and publicly supported a series of concrete proposals that advocated market-oriented policies. The members of this group were mainly businessmen and top executives tied to traditional Caracas families, but the less traditional group Cisneros also worked very hard for a change toward more market friendly policies. The Grupo Roraima invited former policy makers, such as Pedro Pablo Kuczynski of Peru and Miguel Boyer of Spain, to visit Venezuela and meet with government and political leaders, give lectures at universities, and appear in the media.

These efforts led President Carlos Andrés Pérez to incorporate into his cabinet a large number of successful individuals linked to the private sector. However, by either coincidence or design Pérez brought in representatives of rival groups: Eduardo Quintero and Gustavo Roosen (Grupo Polar), Jonathan Coles (president of Mavesa—linked to Grupo Phelps), Pedro Tinoco (president of Banco Latino—tied to Grupo Cisneros), and Gabriela Febres-Cordero (Cementos Caribe). These captains of the private sector were complemented by a group of talented academics, most notably Moisés Naím (Ph.D. from the Massachusetts Institute of Technology's Management School) and Miguel Rodríguez (Ph.D. in economics from Yale University). Others with similar academic credentials were recruited for second- and third-level positions. The rest of Pérez's cabinet was populated by AD party members, who the president hoped would make up for the businessmen's and technocrats' lack of political skill.

The post-1989 economic openness and reforms presented opportunities to the private sector. After some ten years without making investments, the private sector began to act on the assumption that domestic investment in the country would return substantial profits. This time around, however, there were different rules. There was no longer a CVF, or subsidized loans, or preferential dollars, or import quotas. Tariffs were substantially reduced according to a preplanned schedule. These policies encouraged the private sector groups to risk money, leading to a rise of more than 700 percent in the Caracas Stock Exchange between 1990 and 1991, unprecedented in any country in modern history.

The Banking Crisis

Financial institutions participated enthusiastically in the Pérez neoliberal experiment. They purchased or created companies in the broadcasting, cellular phone, tourism, agricultural, and real estate industries, as well as state corporations that were privatized. Given the absence of public sector financing, banks were in a privileged position to take advantage of the best opportunities, along with other less favorable ones using other people's money. However, most of these ventures never had the time to prove their worth. The political crisis of 1992 brought the process of economic openness to an end.

Political instability coincided with a new downturn in the oil market. The flow of investment became a trickle, which diminished the value of Venezuelan assets and undermined the quality of bank portfolios.

The return to power of Rafael Caldera in February 1994, following an election campaign in which he attacked President Pérez's turn to a market economy, accelerated this trend. Within weeks the Banco Latino collapsed, an event that led to the failure of dozens of financial institutions over the ensuing eighteen months. The fate of the Banco Latino was highly symbolic. Not only was that institution one of the country's largest banks, but its principal shareholders controlled the new business groups that had emerged in the 1970s, the so-called Twelve Apostles of Carlos Andrés Pérez. The Banco Latino's guiding light throughout most of the Punto Fijo period was Pedro Tinoco, an individual whose talent for coordinating economic and political power was legendary. Friend and foe alike agreed in declaring him one of the most brilliant minds in the country. During the first Caldera administration (1969–74), Tinoco was minister of finance; he later founded a right-wing party and ran unsuccessfully for president in 1973. Subsequently, he became a financial backer of Carlos Andrés Pérez and served as president of the Central Bank in the second Pérez administration.

As president of Banco Latino, Pedro Tinoco had unprecedented economic and political power. Politicians espousing different views and beholden to competing business groups allied with him, including some who would finance Lieutenant Colonel Hugo Chávez's election campaign and join his future Fifth Republic. After Tinoco's death (in early 1993), his successor, Gustavo Gómez López, continued his mentor's tradition of supplementing economic power with political influence. The Banco Latino became a major financier of the electoral campaign of Oswaldo Alvarez Paz, the candidate of COPEI who lost to Rafael Caldera. Not only Banco Latino but nearly all banks had close ties with the political and bureaucratic world. Consequently, the political ingredient of the financial crisis was high. Coincidentally, whereas many of the affected bankers had been close to Carlos Andrés Pérez, private sector groups that had backed President Caldera came through the storm unscathed.

Venezuelan banks had evolved into business conglomerates by the early 1990s. Several controlled large corporations, including media outlets, and most maintained close corporate connections. Therefore, the financial crisis of 1994 led to the demise of a large group of Venezuelan entrepreneurs. This had a major long-term consequence for the economy and investment and also affected the balance between the private sector and the government, a factor that would prove critical for the failure of the general strike of December 2002.

The disappearance of such important banking and entrepreneurial groups in a single financial crisis was unthinkable; it was also unthinkable that such powerful and intimidating entrepreneurs were not able to coordinate a unified response to the Caldera government en masse. As in 1989, when it was unable to stop the government from liberalizing trade, the private sector was once again a paper tiger (Naím, 1993). Part of its problem was the general perception among the population that business sector wealth had been acquired through corruption and unfair practices. Relations between businessmen and politicians had become an explosive issue. Groups that obtained favors from the state were portrayed as corrupt by those who did not. Suspicions among politicians intensified when one faction or the other appeared more successful in its search for private sector financing. Almost every government was accused not only of having favorites but also of getting even with those who prospered during the preceding administration. The presence of any business leaders in high government positions increased tensions. Excluded entrepreneurial groups charged that businessmen in the bureaucracy favored their cronies, and politicians viewed the presence of private sector individuals as depriving talented party members of key posts. Indeed, this issue had been sensitive for quite some time. One of Carlos Andrés Perez's promises during his 1988 campaign—which he kept—was that his minister of finance would be chosen from the ranks of the AD party.

The resources commanded by business groups give them significant political influence in most democracies, especially during primary and general election campaigning. In Punto Fijo Venezuela, however, private sector influence bordered on the obscene. Whereas the average cost per vote in developed country elections ranged from two to three dollars in 1978, in Venezuela the cost approached fifty dollars (Myers, 1980). Such elevated costs solidified a two-way arrangement between political parties and business groups. Long-term arrangements became common in which private sector groups financed political parties, or factions within the parties, and were repaid with business for their "investment."

Finally, in assessing the private sector elite's responsibility for the unraveling of post-1958 democracy, it is necessary to address the charge that the private sector abandoned politics and government. Nothing could be further from the truth! The private sector participated in all Punto Fijo governments, without exception. And because of political party dependence on business groups for campaign financing, this relationship was ongoing and close. Competition between groups, however, ensured that entrepreneurs never controlled the political system. Nevertheless, penetration of the latter by the former was extensive. It was not uncommon for an entrepreneurial group to "place its bet" on a young politician in the hope that he would reach a position of influence from which he could repay his benefactor.

Mechanisms for dialogue over the future of Venezuela persisted throughout the Punto Fijo era, not only between business and government but also between the private sector leaders and other elites. The most prominent examples were the Santa Lucía and Jirahara groups. The first—a collection of economic, political, religious, labor, military, academic, media, and civil society leaders—was named after the island where its first meeting was held in 1977. The second, boasting a similar membership, brought together influentials from the regions. It was named for the hotel in Barquisimeto which hosted its annual meetings. Finally, FEDECAMARAS provided a forum that brought together all sectors of the economy and all regions of the country to debate national issues. FEDECAMARAS also maintained channels of communication with top party and government leaders. Venezuela's private sector, then, was politically engaged and well informed throughout the Punto Fijo era.

Rise of the Fifth Republic

Prominent members of the business and social elite supported Hugo Chávez's Bolivarian movement in the late 1990s even though Chávez himself attacked the private sector for its backing of Punto Fijo democracy. Among them were businessmen such as Reinaldo Cervini (agro-industry, iron, and steel); Luis Vallenilla, a banker and financier of Fundapatria, an organization that opposed Caldera's petroleum policy; and Henry Lord Boulton, principal shareholder and chairman of Avensa, Venezuela's largest airline.

For some time an antiparty sentiment, fueled in part by the ongoing media discourse, was growing among the population. Just as the middle and lower classes wanted to punish AD and COPEI, some business leaders viewed supporting Chávez as a protest vote, regardless of ideological considerations. Nevertheless, most business groups limited their support for Hugo Chávez to modest campaign contributions. The Chávez campaign did receive marginally greater support from business leaders outside Caracas (the capital) and Maracaibo (the second city in size and importance).

At the close of the polemical and bitter 1998 presidential election campaign, Chávez selected FEDECAMARAS as the location for his encounter with the private sector. His address sought to reassure the private sector. Especially noteworthy at this meeting was the presence of Venezuela's most traditional business groups. Some of these traditionalists had abandoned FEDECAMARAS for the Venezuelan-American Chamber of Commerce and Industry (VenAmCham), where they considered themselves to be better represented. This shift could be traced to the appearance of Ciro Añez Fonseca and to their loss of control of FEDECAMARAS.

Relations between the media and the Chávez campaign followed a distinct path. During the first part of the campaign, when polls found that the intention to vote for Chávez barely surpassed 10 percent (far behind Irene Sáez and Claudio Fermín), the only major media outlet that paid much attention to the defrocked lieutenant colonel was the newspaper *El Nacional.* This changed when the Sáez and Fermín candidacies imploded and the race became a contest between Chávez and the governor of the state of Carabobo, Henrique Salas Römer, who quickly gained the support of two of the most conservative major media outlets, the newspaper *El Universal* and Radio Caracas TV. The decision by these media outlets to support Salas Römer brought the expected response from their competitors, the newspaper *El Nacional* and rival media outlets (Venevisión and Televen), which consequently gave greater coverage to Chávez. Immediately following Chávez's victory, decisions by media entrepreneurs to support candidates paid dividends for those who backed the winner. The site chosen by the newly elected president for his first address to the country (on election night) was the Ateneo de Caracas, a cultural institution closely tied to *El Nacional.* On the following day, the new president and the first lady spent the entire morning at Venevisión as guests on several of its morning programs.

The messages transmitted to the country from the Ateneo and Venevisión were conciliatory, and they defused tensions. The Caracas Stock Exchange, which had been depressed as a result of the Asian crisis, the drop in oil prices, and the heated election campaign, rose more than 40 percent in the next two days. The question of the day in business circles was which of the other prominent leaders in the Spanish-speaking world Chávez would most resemble: Argentina's Carlos Menem, Peru's Alberto Fujimori, or Spain's Felipe

González. All three presidents had won with inflammatory populist electoral rhetoric. On assuming power they had implemented pragmatic, market-oriented policies. There was near unanimity among business leaders that, thanks to Chávez's strong political backing and popular support, Venezuela would be in a position to outperform other countries in the region economically.

When business leaders began to lobby for contracts and ties with the new government, the president-elect's more antiestablishment supporters recoiled, viewing these approaches as yet one more example of those who had benefited during the Punto Fijo regime attempting to retain their ill-gotten privileges. Chávez shared these reservations, and contrary to previous presidents-elect, he kept his distance. There were no celebrations at the homes of the private sector's heavy hitters; nor would the president make any visits after his inauguration. The onetime lieutenant colonel from Barinas was appalled by the appearance of several lists, apparently prepared by the Caracas business establishment, which proposed candidates for the new cabinet. Some time later, during one of his Sunday radio broadcasts, President Chávez confirmed rumors of private sector efforts to influence him to appoint businessmen to high-level positions in his government.

The first Chávez cabinet included only one businessman, Alejandro Rivera, the minister of agriculture. Rivera, an entrepreneur with interests in beef and sugar, was well known in the country's interior. He had supported the Bolivarian movement since 1994, when President Caldera released Chávez from the Yare prison. Rivera held the Ministry of Agriculture portfolio for less than two months, and no other entrepreneur had received a cabinet nomination until Francisco Natera, a former president of FEDECAMARAS, was appointed in 2002 as minister for the development of special zones. Natera did not have any influence within the government, and his ties to the private community were almost nonexistent.

Business leaders were not alarmed initially when President Chávez excluded them from his cabinet. They accepted the fact that he was keeping individuals identified with the private sector at arm's length in order to avoid possible conflicts of interest. Here it is necessary to remember that Chávez came to power on a radical, anticorruption platform, and he really did view the presence of businessmen in public-policy-making positions as inappropriate. His position seemed to be "No businessmen in government, no kitchen cabinets, and no private socializing with business leaders." On the other hand, the new chief executive attempted a rapprochement with the business community by participating in a permanent dialogue and meeting with businessmen upon request. On his first few overseas trips, President Chávez even offered invitations to any businessman who wished to accompany him. This policy was later abandoned because of the large retinue of travelers which signed on, few of whom had significant business clout.

The radical tone that marked the several electoral events leading up to approval of the 1999 constitution, and the populist reelection campaign in 2000, ended the honeymoon between President Chávez and the business community. Particularly inflammatory was Chávez's statement (on October 24, 1999, in his weekly television broadcast) that Venezuela and Cuba "sailed toward the same sea of happiness," coming as it did in a moment when businessmen had decided that the proposed new constitution was too far to the left. In response, FEDECAMARAS took a strong political stance for the first time in its history and publicly urged Venezuelans to vote "no" in the referendum on Chávez's constitution. Chávez immediately assumed the offensive by meeting with supportive businessmen. Although the group of pro-Chávez business leaders was small and unrepresentative, it served to convey that some important business figures (including some former presidents of FEDECAMARAS) supported the Bolivarian Revolution. Relations between FEDECAMARAS's current leadership and the government deteriorated notably after this event, as did relations within FEDECAMARAS between members who favored and those who opposed "the process."[9]

Following the election of Pedro Carmona, an economist with substantial diplomatic experience, as president of FEDECAMARAS in July 2001, there was a short second honeymoon. Chávez invited Carmona to join him in an official visit to Chile, and at a meeting with the Chilean private sector leaders, the Venezuelan president praised Carmona and proclaimed a new period of close dialogue between FEDECAMARAS and his government.

This new cordiality lasted two months; it ended when the government approved a package of forty-nine laws, most of them at the heart of the economy and individual rights that dramatically increased state intervention in the economy. Furthermore, those laws were approved under an enabling law that managed to exclude not only the private sector but the whole nation from the discussion that dramatically increased state intervention in the economy. FEDECAMARAS and the middle class viewed the package as a threat to private property, and Carmona reacted by calling a national strike on December 10.

The strike attracted popular support and hardened opposition to the government's leftward drift. President Chávez responded by taking ever more radical steps. One proved especially costly—his attempt to seize Petroleos de Venezuela, the state oil company. Opposition to this power grab triggered a general strike that led to the April 11, 2002, coup, which temporarily removed the president from power.

Relations between the government and the media provide another case that contributes to our understanding of President Chávez's relationship with the business community. The divide that opened between these two in 2002 was largely of the president's making. Tensions became public when the president charged media outlets with providing inaccurate and insufficient coverage of his government, and it deepened to the extent that President Chávez accused the media of lies and distortions. On these grounds, he justified ongoing demands for radio and television airtime.

Although the media had no choice but to acquiesce, their owners and their allies continued to criticize President Chávez. They pointed out that his domination of the other branches of government meant that there was no public institution that could hold the executive accountable for bypassing the public administration and using the military to allocate resources, for corruption, or for weakening regional and local governments through constitutionally questionable maneuvers. The media also raised questions about the administration's inability to use some $50 billion in state revenues from petroleum (2000–2001) to reduce poverty and crime. *El Nacional,* a leading Caracas daily, opined in its editorial of June 4, 2002, "The President is right in not being happy with the media because without media he would be a happy revolutionary." Even more so than in the case of FEDECAMARAS, the fight that Chávez picked with media owners served to unify opposition to him among interests that long had been divided by personal feuds and competition for market share.

The Fifth Republic and Venezuela's Transformed Private Sector

Most of the profits since President Chávez's inauguration have been made through government contracts, even more so than previously. The national executive shapes Venezuela's financial and real estate sectors, and it is in these areas that profits have been the greatest. In the case of the former, government placed deposits at low rates in selected banks while at the same time borrowing at rates that were up to 40 percent higher. In the case of real estate, Chávez's administration implemented a massive program to construct low-income housing. Management of these programs and transactions between some financial groups and the government gave rise to some of the Fifth Republic's most notorious corruption scandals. Given the lack of accountability, the fragility of surveillance, and the lack of veto points within the government, corruption levels seem to have far surpassed those of the Punto Fijo era. Chávez himself has not been involved in any scandal, but one wonders why he has been so permissive with some of his closest collaborators.

The private sector of the Fifth Republic, smaller but more unified than its Punto Fijo predecessor, continues to press its case. The current imbalance of power between the state and business interests stems largely from the 1994 financial crisis, which wiped out more than two-thirds of the private sector. As of late 2003, only two major private sector groups were considered major global players: Cisneros and Polar. Each followed a distinctive business strategy. Cisneros's growth was basically outside Venezuela in media and telecommunications. Within the country Cisneros sold most of its interests in soft drinks, retail stores, supermarkets, and banking to foreign investors; maintaining a presence only in television, telecommunications, and beer. In contrast, Polar focused on the domestic arena. Its strength lay in beer, soft drinks, and agribusiness, although Polar capital was present in other sectors (oil, petrochemicals, banking, supermarkets, and real estate).

The individuals who hold sway in the Polar and Cisneros groups include many with names that came to prominence only in the 1990s. As mentioned earlier, most of Venezuela's early-twentieth-century business elite survived the changes that accompanied the country's transformation from an agrarian to an oil-based economy and from primitive dictatorship to representative democracy. However, many of them lost their businesses in the 1994 crisis. The family names that currently dominate the private sector, including a few traditionalists, are Camero, Carrero, Cohen, Curvello, Escotet, Gama, Gill, Macedo, Maza-Tirado, Mezerhane, Souto, Sultan, and Vargas. Most, however, are immigrants or first-generation descendants of immigrants. They are among the few locals making significant investments in Venezuela today.

Foreign capital now plays the largest role in most sectors of Venezuela. In contrast to the Punto Fijo times, when overseas investors entered into agreements with local partners, they now tend to act alone. Few capitalists, either local or foreign, invest in industry or minerals for export. Rather, they focus on food production and distribution and the tertiary sector: banking, insurance, real estate, telecommunications, health care, and retailing.

The lack of understanding of these structural changes within the Venezuelan private sector, as well as the lack of understanding that the Venezuelan democracy evolved from a limited pluralist democracy to a dominant power or hybrid regime (Myers and McCoy, 2003), was crucial in the failure of the strike of December 2002. The formal private economy employs only about 13 percent of the population. In addition, the most sensitive sectors are either fully or partially controlled by foreign companies, which is the case with electricity, telecommunications, food, and banking. The government, besides being the largest formal employer, with about 15 percent of the population, also has vast financial resources to draw on, and, as in a typical dominant-power regime, it sees no lines between the state and the ruling political forces when it comes to using money. Owing to the financial independence of the government, it does not need to negotiate with the private sector in the opposition. The tragedy of the strike episode was that many small and medium-size firms never reopened and several others were still struggling to survive in the hope of a turnaround that may never occur in the Bolivarian Republic.

This failure had an important impact within FEDECAMARAS. Carlos Fernández, acting president, left the country after the strike. When he tried to run for election as FEDECAMARAS's president in July 2003, he lost to vice president Albis Muñoz, despite the support of most former presidents. But more important, the image of FEDECAMARAS and its ability to mobilize the population may be damaged for some time to come. A silver lining to the decline of FEDECAMARAS, however, was the reopening of space for the political parties.

Conclusions

The unraveling of Punto Fijo democracy was intertwined with the implosion of economic institutions, including the private sector. The private sector imploded before the political system collapsed, but after the capability of public institutions had declined precipitously in the crisis of distribution. Support for Punto Fijo public policy making rested on the government's capability to distribute resources, and this capability depended on high levels of income from the sale of petroleum on the international market.

Conventional wisdom has ascribed responsibility for the shrinkage of Venezuela's private sector and its inability to compete internationally to the loss of the risk-taking ethos by second- and third-generation entrepreneurial families. However, many victims of the 1994 economic crisis carry family names that came to prominence during the petroleum boom, and these companies were still run by the first generation. This suggests that defects in the institutional framework that integrated entrepreneurs into the political economy are a more plausible explanation for private sector weakness. On the other hand, businessmen can be blamed for failing to use their integration into public policy making to change that structure. The substantial expenses associated with presidential election campaigns, held at five-year intervals, gave private sector leaders an opportunity to influence each new government of the Punto Fijo era. However, instead of lobbying for measures that would have made enterprises competitive and less dependent on government subsidies, business groups expended their political capital on maximizing rent creation and capture. The other aspect for which Venezuelan entrepreneurs could be blamed was the lack of understanding of what it means to do business in a petro-state, that is, in an environment of high macroeconomic volatility and of high incentives to compete for government business.

The basic conditions that limited private sector power during the Punto Fijo era persisted in the Fifth Republic: a weak institutional framework, a long-term decline in terms of trade, Dutch disease, crowding out, the increasing role of the state, bad decision making, and rent seeking (Stevens, 2003). In addition, the complaint that most discredited Punto Fijo democracy—that people were getting poorer not because of bad economic and social policies but because someone was stealing their share of the country's wealth—was heard again. What was different in the Fifth Republic was that the private sector had shrunk while increased petroleum revenue strengthened the national executive. The imbalance was made even more pronounced by public policies that encouraged multinational capital to displace domestic entrepreneurs. President Chávez had no intention of empowering a new economic elite capable of challenging his government, although at the institutional level he has encouraged and given financing for the creation of institutions parallel to FEDECAMARAS without success.

During the successful years of Punto Fijo, corruption and rent-seeking behavior existed, particularly prior to the adoption of reforms to reduce state intervention in the early 1990s. At the same time, however, in the early 1960s institutions worked, policy making produced a stable macroeconomic environment with ever higher standards of living, and the private sector invested in Venezuela and had a more coherent approach to government. These conditions changed after the mid-1970s, and they continue to change today. Consequently, the outlook for recovery of the private sector in the short and medium term is bleak.

CHAPTER FIVE

Civil Society

Late Bloomers

Luis Salamanca

The crisis and decline of the political system governed by the parties, which were once the fundamental channels for citizen representation and participation, as well as channels for articulating popular demands, left a vacuum that spurred the politicization of social and cultural actors, such as civil society organizations and the media. These actors have attempted to fill this vacuum not through the implementation of a deliberate strategy but as a side effect of the unfolding political dynamic. As the traditional political actors imploded in 1998, civil society organizations and the media became sui generis political actors seeking to influence and direct the public administration, even while not directly competing for power. This chapter examines this turn in the activity of organizations that had previously been occupied by social issues.

The Concept of Civil Society

The search for a definition of civil society still has not produced a consensus among theorists on how far the concept extends, how it differs from the concept of the state, who is part of civil society, how it functions, and whether it should be regulated by the legal system.[1] There is not even agreement on its name. In order to provide a more efficient conceptual delimitation, a number of authors have suggested new categorizations for specific components of civil society, such as nonprofit sector (Salamon and Anheier, 1999), third sector (Jeréz, 1997), and promotion and social development organizations.

Civil society constitutes itself with respect to concrete configurations of dominant political power at each moment (the church, the monarch, the state, or the party) and/or with regard to the modalities whereby these forms of power operate (exclusionary or inclusionary, arbitrary or legal, military or peaceful).[2] Civil society is not a condition intrinsic to the political system but a historical product. It begins to form when sectors excluded from the political realm begin to mobilize in order to influence political decision making, though not to hold power. This mobilization is the least common denominator among definitions of civil society; it makes civil society a dynamic and changing arena whose dynamism shifts according to the open or closed character of the configurations of power at each historical moment.[3] The concept of civil society changes according to the type of relationship which is established between society and political power. Therein lies a good part of its origins in Venezuela, where civil society appears in opposition more to the dominance of the political parties than to the dominance of the state in society.

In Venezuela, the concept of civil society has grown since the 1970s, probably as a result of the diffusion of Antonio Gramsci's writings in political and intellectual circles. Before the seventies, the notion of civil society was not an important element of political discourse in Venezuela.

Civil Society during Punto Fijo Democracy

Venezuelan civil society during the Punto Fijo period can be characterized as a space of nonparty, nonstate, voluntarily formed, nonprofit, citizen organization which arose outside the interest group and labor union world and whose purpose was to attain better living conditions both for its own members and for other sectors of the population. Civil society as a space of heterogeneous actors arose on the margins of a system of state-society relations established by the Pact of Punto Fijo, which made the political parties the fundamental actors in the democracy just initiated. Social organizations, in particular the workers' organizations, were assigned secondary roles. This initial experience marked the model of state-society relations which would develop in the Punto Fijo democratic period with two important characteristics. On the one hand, these relations were channeled and virtually monopolized by the political parties, especially the two largest parties (Acción Democrática [AD; Democratic Action] and Comité de Organización Política Electoral Independiente: Partido Social Cristiano [COPEI; Committee of Independent Electoral Political Organization: Social Christian Party]), though the minor parties—Movimiento al Socialismo (MAS; Movement toward Socialism) and the Movimiento Electoral del Pueblo (MEP; Electoral Movement of the People), among the most important—were not excluded from the process. The smaller parties followed the same working logic as the larger ones. Although criticizing and challenging AD and COPEI, the small parties used the same methods and sought to displace and control the positions held by the large parties.

On the other hand, the parties were linked with society by way of a few large organizations representing social interests, among these a large central labor union (Confederación de Trabajadores de Venezuela [CTV; Confederation of Venezuelan Workers]), a business organization (Federación de Cámaras y Asociaciones de Comercio y Producción de Venezuela [FEDECAMARAS; Federation of Chambers of Commerce and Production of Venezuela]), and an important peasant federation Federación Campesino de Venezuela (FCV; Venezuelan Peasant Federation). This matrix did not exclude the legal or political existence of alternative peak organizations, but these were hardly, if at all, taken into account in decision making. The main peak organizations played the role of social interlocutors with the state and the parties. At the same time, they monopolized the channels of participation of social interests before the state, mediating and containing the same social bases through a tight network that, in addition to political links, included personal and clientelistic ties.

This model would, in different proportions, combine diverse mechanisms of control administered in appropriate doses of (a) party penetration and control of social organizations; (b) nonrecognition and dissuasion of politically and ideologically distant social organizations; (c) direct repression of such contrary organizations; (d) co-optation of union, interest group, and community leadership by way of social policies to benefit the working class, peasantry, professional sectors, and urban poor; and (e) granting of representational monopolies to kindred social organizations, such as the CTV, to the detriment of other currents in the labor movement, including the Communist-leaning Confederación Unitaria de Trabajadores de Venezuela (CUTV; Unitary Confederation of Worker of Venezuela). This representational monopoly turned the CTV into the official interlocutor with the state in the area of labor politics, thereby marginalizing the CUTV. Finally, this model included the incorporation of the numerically most important and politically closest organizations in decision making on socioeconomic public policies (McCoy, 1985; Salamanca, 1998).

The model did not retard but, as we have stated, stimulated the existence of other labor confederations and business associations of lesser rank which were not considered to be interlocutors of the state but which still received some state subsidies. Similarly, the model allowed other forms of participation, though these had neither the centrality nor the importance of involvement in the large organizations. In fact, the state increasingly recognized as legal subjects other forms of social organization such as neighborhood associations and women's organizations. Nevertheless, only the large organizations had access to public decision making. The model functioned as limited associational pluralism.

At the margins of this model other types of social organization emerged. These new associations were organized around issues arising out of urban life (neighborhood associations), class (popular action groups), the popular economy (cooperative and microfirms), the environment, gender, and human rights, among others. All these associations sought a direct relationship with the state without the involvement of the parties. Many of these associational forms were not new in Venezuela, but their mode of action introduced a new tone to relations with the state and the parties. On the one hand, they sought autonomy from the parties; on the other, they not only demanded public services but also transformed themselves into modest providers of social services, as well as mobilizers of resources that were drawn from the state and international agencies and directed toward local levels and the poorest sectors of the country. This new type of relationship with the state and the parties was imposed with varying degrees of success—in some cases, quite high levels. During the 1970s and the 1980s, the new organizations participated in some important efforts, such as the neighborhood protests against uncontrolled urban growth, women's involvement in civil code reform, and ecological protests.

The formative stage of the new civil society in Venezuela occurred during the 1960s and 1970s. Its principal characteristic was the appearance of autonomous urban organizations oriented toward improving the living conditions of neighborhood and women's groups, promoting and providing educational work in communities, and aiding environmental and cooperative struggles. These groups were composed of middle-class and, to a lesser extent, popular sector activists. It was a stage characterized by the search for alternative channels to the political parties as well as by mutual suspicion between the state and the organizations. From the perspective of some leftist organizations, the state was perceived as a capitalist instrument standing against the popular sectors. To these organizations, the state was an enemy, whereas the state viewed civil organizations as vehicles of the far left. The political parties sought to capture the territorial expressions of other organizations—such as the neighborhood and environmental groups—and to a large degree were successful in this effort (García-Guadilla, 1991: 46). Nevertheless, the growth of organizations continued, and new types emerged (CISFEM-UNICEF, 1992: 213–32; EcoNatura, 1993). Groups formed which over time would become nationally significant, including the Centro al Servicio de la Acción Popular (CESAP; Center for the Service of Popular Action), today the largest in the country and one of the largest in Latin America.

Public opinion began to identify, without great conceptual precision, the notion of civil society as organizations that had their own characteristics and were distinct from peasant and union organizations. The associational forms that took shape in Venezuela during the 1970s and especially the 1980s are generally associated with the term *civil society*. This term was not applied to the earlier associational forms that erupted upon the death of Juan Vicente Gómez in 1935 and accompanied the process of establishing representative democracy in the 1930s and 1940s. These early forms were basically centered on the political parties, in contrast with the new forms emerging in the 1970s.[4]

Over time, the discourse of the new civil society centered on replacing the democracy of the parties with a democracy of citizens. This development, however, did not take the form of a struggle against the parties but rather a silent and titanic work of building a new political culture. This culture was oriented toward the participation of the population in the solution of its own problems. It sought to overcome the paternalism of the state and the indifference of the citizenry by promoting a new type of citizenship based on experiences in public policy management, usually in alliance with the state but occasionally with multilateral agencies. Resistance to party domination, more than state domination, thus became the characteristic that defined the backbone of civil society during Punto Fijo. In contrast to the union, professional, and peasant organizations of the first cycle, who accepted the political project of the newly formed parties and collaborated in their organization prior to the Punto Fijo period, the civil society organizations that emerged during the

1970s rejected the parties and refused to be controlled and mobilized by them, although not all of them were successful at this.

The parties of the Punto Fijo period lacked a program with which to mobilize social energy and could only offer to contain the social bases clientelistically—a strategy that became ever more precarious as the resources for distribution in Venezuela's modernization process were exhausted (Salamanca, 1997). The parties organized themselves as quasi-corporatist structures that encapsulated social activism by sector: union, youth, woman, peasant, and professional. AD was the prototype of this party modality. Professional associations and unions became interlocutors between the parties and the social bases. In practice, the professional associations ended up functioning as unions, and many of them became affiliated with the CTV.

When this first mode of relationship between party and organized society went into crisis, the appeal to the notion of civil society began. This appeal arose as a critique and rejection of the parties' penetration and control of the action programs of workers, peasants, and professionals, as well as any other citizen space that might be of electoral importance. The fact that the parties served as interlocutors between the mass organizations and the state institutions led to the inefficiency and corruption of the parties. For this reason, civil society targeted its criticisms principally at the parties and only secondarily at the state. Rather than being antistatist, Venezuelan civil society has above all been antiparty. This orientation can be seen in the extent of agreements and negotiations between the social organizations and the state, at both the national and local levels, despite their mutual mistrust and the complete absence of any mutual understanding reached with the parties. In fact, numerous analysts have noted that a high proportion of these associations were created and subsist thanks to state financial support (Janssens, 1997; Mascareño, 2000).

The Decline of Punto Fijo Democracy: The Role of Civil Society

The second stage of new civil organization began in 1989, a key year in the crisis of the Venezuelan political system and the search for solutions. Here it is not possible to provide a detailed review of this evolution, but a brief sketch of a growing presence of civil society organizations in public life can begin in the 1980s, the decade during which the living standards attained in preceding decades began to erode as petroleum-based modernization stagnated. Various critical conjunctures stimulated the growth of associations, and gradually, not without favoritism, these associations convinced the state of their capacity to manage areas of social policy critical to the population.

The underlying reason for the dynamic growth of civic associations was so-called Black Friday (February 18, 1983), the day that state support for the currency ended. Following the collapse of public finances, a number of events occurred which led to greater growth of social organizations: the government's pursuit of a sharp economic adjustment package and its development of a social program to alleviate the effects of the adjustment on the poorest sectors of the population; the social explosion of February 27 and 28, 1989, known as the Caracazo; and finally, the implementation of a policy of decentralization in the form of the direct election of governors and mayors. The joint effects of all these factors contributed to the unprecedented growth of civil organizations.

The Caracazo resulted in the creation of an important human rights organization, the Comisión de los Familiares de las Víctimas del 27 de Febrero (COFAVIC; Commission of Relatives of the Victims of February 27). In addition, attempts were made to build links between organizations, at times between organizations dedicated to the same activity, such as the Coordinadora de ONG de Atención al Niño (CONGANI; Coordinator of NGOs Serving Children), or between nongovernmental organizations (NGOs), such as the Zuliana Network. It is estimated that there are now twenty networks (SINERGIA, 1998).

Although there are no reliable and up-to-date inventories and statistics on the number of civic associations in Venezuela, different estimates suggest that since 1989 civil society has assumed an ever growing quantitative and qualitative presence in public life. The available statistics are largely influenced by the definition of civil society used; accordingly, the numbers vary significantly. In an earlier work, on the basis of unofficial information, I reported that there were some 10,000 associations in the country (Salamanca, 1995a). At the 1993 National Encounter of Civil Society in Caracas, 1,500 associations were expected (Conferencia Episcopal Venezolana, 1994). Recent studies (Janssens, 1997) report that there are 1,200 Organizations of Promotion and Development, a category that excludes a large number of associations. The most ambitious attempt to quantify the number of social organizations, a study carried out by the Centro de Investigaciones en Ciencias Sociales (CISOR; Center for Research in the Social Sciences) and the Instituto de Estudios Superiores de la Administración (IESA; Institute for Graduate Studies in Administration) as part of an international study on the nonprofit sector (Salamon and Anheier, 1999), counts 24,628 organizations (González, 2000). The CISOR itself estimates 54,266 organizations in all of Venezuela (González, 1998: 74).

Decentralization is the most important factor behind associational growth in the country. More organizations began to contract with the state for a variety of social programs, especially at the regional level. Mascareño (2000: 151) gathered information on 3,526 associations in the states of Carabobo, Lara, Sucre, and Zulia which were involved in the management of decentralized public policies. The type of association which appeared to be growing the fastest was the neighborhood association, the pioneer in the formation of a new civil society.

There were also self-sustained experiences that rejected financial support from the state, such as the Ferias de Consumo (Consumer Fairs) in the state of Lara (Vethencourt, 1999), a clear example of the cooperative popular economy. The programs of the multilateral agencies and international organizations also stimulated the growth of associations, particularly as they manage resources that are often greater than those of the public sector. The media increasingly covered private associations as they assumed new policy roles. This, then, was the state of civil society at the moment the new government assumed power in 1998.

The Rise of the Fifth Republic: The Politicization of Civil Society

As civil society and the electorate in general broke away from the two traditional parties, the parties became progressively weaker, and presidential elections were carried by personalistic candidates such as Rafael Caldera (1994–99) and the current president, Hugo Chávez, elected in 1998. After his inauguration, Chávez set in motion a process of institutional changes which began with the convocation of the Asamblea Nacional Constituyente (ANC; National Constituent Assembly). From this point on, political dynamics were fundamentally characterized by conflicts between government actors and the many strategic elites in the nation, including prominent civil society organizations.

The issues triggering confrontation were centered in two large areas: constitutional and institutional change. First, an intense political-juridical struggle arose over how far the new government's desire to effect constitutional changes should extend. In dispute was whether the government's power to change the constitution was original, that is, free from any restraint by the standing juridical-constitutional order in force, or whether, on the contrary, the government's power was derivative or ordinary, that is, subject to the established juridical order, with faculties limited by the 1961 constitution, then in force. After the first semester of 1999, the now extinct Corte Suprema de Justicia (CSJ; Supreme Court of Justice) managed to make juridically viable the convocation and election of the ANC, which was seated on August 3, 1999, and acted under the more far-reaching original powers.

Second, the government set off a sharp showdown against the social and political powers established after 1958—except for the military—through the range of institutional changes that the government sought to carry out. The government shook the foundations of these powers but, at the same time, created strong resistance among the groups targeted by the government. The traditional and nontraditional political parties, the church, most of the business sector, labor unions, professional associations, the peasant federation, the mass media, the judiciary, and the legislative power were simultaneously subjected to an offensive to weaken them and, in some cases, to conquer them. Civil society did not escape from the clash triggered by the government.

Civil Society As Defined by the 1999 Constitution

The convocation of the ANC opened a new chapter in the history of Venezuelan civil society. A significant number of civil society organizations participated in the assembly's discussions, and many of their proposals were incorporated into the new charter. Civil society organizations were thus crucial to the constitutional design of the new political system. Again, civil society is an abstract and confusing concept, which is used to identify a referential space more than a homogeneous subject of social participation and change. In it, dissimilar organizations act, organizations that are *of* civil society but do not themselves constitute civil society. Nevertheless, the same term ended up being incorporated into the constitution as a subject of participation, with rights and duties in diverse areas of public power. Along with the state, the new constitution made civil society responsible for the security of the nation in the economic, social, political, geographic, environmental, and military realms as established by Article 326 of the 1999 constitution.

Alongside this enormous responsibility, the constitution also confers the following attributes to civil society: Article 206 says that civil society should be consulted by the state-level Legislative Councils on matters of interest to the states (these replace the former state Legislative Assemblies), and Article 296 indicates that civil society nominates three members to the Consejo Nacional Electoral (CNE; National Electoral Council). As a result of these new provisions, *civil society* became a term plagued not only by conceptual problems but also by problems of juridical interpretation. These juridical dimensions were aggravated by the proliferation of terms used to identify the subjects of collective rights (society, organized community, people, neighbors, etc.). For example, what is the meaning of the notion that civil society is in part responsible for national security, even in the military realm? Who nominates the three persons who are to be members of the CNE for civil society? These are only two of the questions that arise regarding the role of civil society as provided for under the 1999 constitution.

Civil society's constitutional role is framed among the diverse forms of direct citizen participation in public affairs, which, theoretically at least, assume primacy over mechanisms of representation, or indirect participation. On paper, representative democracy gives way to participatory democracy, as Article 62 of the constitution establishes the right of all citizens to intervene in all public affairs at all levels, and Article 70 establishes mechanisms of participation which define not only participatory democracy but also direct democracy (Salamanca, 2000).

This broad range of forms of participation generated strong expectations in civil society, which saw in these channels recognition of long-unmet demands. Nevertheless, the activation of participatory democracy spawned quite a bit of disillusionment and sharp political confrontations, as well as problems of juridical interpretation regarding who should be the bearer of rights to intervene in public affairs (the people, society in general, neighbors). In practice "participatory democracy" ended up causing organized civil society's right of participation to vanish while promoting the participation of individual citizens in new forms of direct democracy.

Far from benefiting organized civil society, these dynamics harmed civil organization because of the process of regulation which took place to determine who should be considered part of civil society. The Supreme Court handed down various rulings aimed at settling the issue of just who "represents" civil society. These rulings have constructed a jurisprudential definition of civil society which does not encompass the richness of the Venezuelan experience. In one opinion, drafted by Judge Jesús Eduardo Cabrera, civil society is delimited as being different from the state and from the bodies that constitute it (states, municipalities, etc.), leading to the conclusion: "Foundations, associations, corporations or groups, totally financed by the state, even when they are private in character cannot represent [civil society], unless they demonstrate that in their directorship and activities the state has no influence" (Tribunal Supreme de Justicia [TSJ; Supreme Tribunal of Justice], Sentencia de la Sala Constitucional, November 21, 2000, cited in Pierre Tapia, 2000: 205).

In the same decision, the TSJ argued that since civil society is embodied by means of representation in political society, participation by civil society is superfluous: "The chamber notes that the representation whereby political society acts (especially the National Assembly) produces a real delegation of the majoritarian will of society in general which, in most cases, renders superfluous or redundant, the political participation of the majority, at least in the form in which it is practiced in civil society."

In response to a writ of habeas corpus, presented by a group of people involved with the Red de Veedores (Network of Monitors) of the Andrés Bello Catholic University, the TSJ addressed the problem of representation, noting that as long as a law does not create "the mechanisms to determine who can represent civil society in general or sectors of it, in particular, and under what conditions that representation will be exercised, groups of people who on their own initiative claim this representation cannot be admitted as legitimate representatives of civil society, of the citizenry, etc., without knowing what their support in society is nor what their interests are; and without being able to control to which interests they respond: economic, political, supranational, national or international" (TSJ, Sentencia de Sala Constitucional, August 23, 2000: 8). In the previously cited November 2000 decision, the TSJ established that civil society ought to be Venezuelan, that "civil society, taken into account by the Constituent [Assembly], is Venezuelan civil society"; therefore, "those who represent it cannot be foreigners, nor organisms led, affiliated, subsidized, financed, or directly or indirectly sustained by states, groups or movements influenced by those states, nor by transnational or world associations that pursue economic or political ends for their own benefit" (TSJ, November 21, 2000: 208).

In some aspects, the TSJ's jurisprudential construction of civil society meshes with established international doctrines, but in other aspects, it runs totally against these doctrines. Since civil society is the expression of diffuse, collective interests, national boundaries can hardly be established for collective problems that involve organizations and governments of different countries. Similarly, the exclusion of groups financed by the state contradicts the nature of civil associations: as these move within a public space, they interact with the state and develop different forms of cooperative relations with it, with the goal of helping the state better fulfill its ends. This implies state financing in different forms, given that many associations lack their own resources. Thus, the TSJ's jurisprudence is exclusionary insofar as thousands of associations in Venezuela function under contracts financed with public funds as well as support and donations from the Venezuelan state and international organizations. Furthermore, for reasons of national identity it is in the state's interest to promote and strengthen many organizations of civil society, given their contribution to social development and national culture. The ruling of November 21, 2000, establishes a rigidly regulated space that isolates civil society from the international world and virtually liquidates civil society by questioning and then rejecting the multiple forms of international cooperation which allow for the survival of most of the civil organizations. If these considerations are not modified in the future, the probable effect is that many of these organizations will disappear.

It is surprising that in a democracy that defines itself as participatory the Supreme Court concerns itself with representation and not participation. To legally establish who represents civil society is one way to distort and curtail a space that arose out of voluntary efforts and is formed by a diversity of organizations, some twenty-five thousand.[5] These origins and diversity make it impossible for one or some of these organizations to "represent" the rest, and for this reason there is no such thing as a confederation of civil society organizations: the interests that civil society embodies cannot be homogenized as can professional and union interests. In civil society, one organization cannot represent another, let alone thousands of others; at best, an organization represents itself. The fact that some leaders of some organizations are frequently consulted by the media and/or generate a greater number of public initiatives does not mean that they represent civil society.

What really defines civil society is participation, the individual's personal deliberation over issues that interest him or her, in contrast to representation or the delegation of her voice. Representation is the intermediation of an interest by means of a delegation of authority; participation is a personal commitment to an interest which accepts neither delegation nor representation. Through its ruling, the Supreme Court introduced a political-cultural paradigm (that of representation) that distorts the participatory and direct nature of the world of civil society.

The inclusion in the constitutional text of an ambiguous notion—civil society—inevitably set off a political struggle over the "representation" of civil society. It led the supporters of President Hugo Chávez to try to create their own "Boliviarian" civil society, organizing various interests such as Círculos Bolivarianos and a Bolivarian workers' federation.

Furthermore, the elucidation of just who represents civil society has a major impact on the distribution of public resources. In this context, the polemic over civil society and who represents it must be related to the reform of the Ley de Creación del Fondo Intergubernamental para la Descentralización (Law Creating the Intergovernmental Fund for Decentralization), initiated by the president of the republic, whereby 20 percent of state resources are assigned directly to communities. Article 24 of the law states, "At least twenty percent of the resources annually budgeted to the Governments and Mayor's Offices will be used to finance projects that the organized communities, neighborhood associations, and non-governmental organizations present to these entities" (Gaceta Oficial No. 37.022, August 25, 2000). This clause raised the stakes in the struggle to define who belongs to civil society and followed the creation of a network of social organizations supporting the president's political project.

The Course of Democracy in the Fifth Republic: Challenges from Civil Society

The most important event following the approval of the constitution was the calling of national elections for May 28, 2000, convoked and organized by the new CNE, which had been designated by the ANC toward the end of December 1999. The electoral preparations were arduous and full of irregularities, which led a number of lawyers to introduce writs of habeas corpus against the electoral process. These writs were declared inadmissible by the TSJ. Many civil associations filed and failed with similar writs. Nevertheless, day by day it became evident that the electoral process was suffering from important delays and disorganization, despite the assurances that the directives of the CNE sought to convey.

In this context, Elías Santana, the coordinator of the civil association Queremos Elegir (We Want to Choose), a neighborhood association promoting conscientious voting, and Liliana Ortega, a member of the human rights organization COFAVIC, introduced a new writ requesting the suspension of the elections, a writ that no one thought would be successful. Surprisingly, the events ended up favoring their position, and the Constitutional Chamber of the TSJ announced to the country, on May 24, 2000, the suspension of the elections until a later date.[6] Days later, under strong pressure from the public, the full directorate of the CNE resigned. The Comisión Legislativa Nacional (National Legislative Commission), led by Luis Miquilena, the former president of the ANC, assembled to designate a new CNE directorate.[7] In this process, civil society played an important role by proposing a "Table of Dialogue" composed of civil organizations and members of the Legislative Committee, which finally chose the members of the CNE directorate. This event, the most important in the history of the civil associations, raised the prestige and public presence of civil society organizations, converting them into a political actor. The organizations participating for civil society were COFAVIC, Queremos Elegir, Veedores de la Universidad Católica (Monitors of the Catholic University), the Red Cross, and the Evangelical Council, as well as the Universidad Central de Venezuela (Central University of Venezuela), FEDECAMARAS, the Contraloría General de la República (Controller General of the Republic), and Defensoría del Pueblo (Public Defender).

The experience of the Table of Dialogue between civil society and the National Legislative Commission was not long lasting. The conciliation forced by the events of May 24 gave way to a conflict over the new date and the organization of the elections, which were unilaterally decided by the Legislative Committee. *Civil society* began to be used as an umbrella term encompassing many sectors, not only the social organizations. During the second semester of 2000, an intense debate took place, perhaps the broadest in Venezuelan history, over the concept of civil society. At the same time that many of civil society's activities were increasingly being presented and extolled in the press, criticisms and self-criticisms were being expressed regarding the deficiencies and limitations of civil society.

The government soon noticed the extent of organized civil society's impact and began to attack it with two arguments: one regarding the actors who represent it and the other on who forms part of it. Luis Miquilena set off the controversy when he asked the now famous question of the year 2000—"How do you eat that?"—in response to a journalist's query regarding civil society. Contemptuously, he was asking, "What is it?" "What does civil society mean?"

At the same time, organizations identified with the government began to appear. The Red Social No Hay Marcha Atrás (There Is No Retreat Social Network) was founded by 16 organizations with the participation of 450 other organizations in June 2000. According to some of its members, the objective was to "coordinate efforts among different popular and communitarian organizations that are committed to and back the transformations underway in the country led by President Chávez." They further maintain that those groups "self-nominated as representatives of civil society are anti-popular." They consider organizations such as Queremos Elegir and COFAVIC to be expressions of "the oligarchical interests in the country, who seek to legitimate themselves through financial support from the United States and the National Endowment for Democracy" (Reyes, 2000).

According to government authorities, the goal of this new organizational process was to promote a new civil society: "The process of change requires the emergence of a new civil society that incorporates the middle sectors and the organized expressions of the popular movement" (statement of Francisco Cedeño Lugo, president of *Fundacomún,* in *El Universal,* September 4, 2000, 11). In June 2001, President Chávez announced his decision to create the Círculos Bolivarianos from the offices of the Ministerio de la Secretaría de la Presidencia (President's Chief of Staff) and the Comando de la Revolución (Revolutionary Command)—a new political instrument to defend the Bolivarian Revolution. According to the official information, the Círculos Bolivarianos are the basic organizational forms to mobilize and direct the participation of individuals and communities in the revolutionary process, with the goal of building the free society and nation of which Simón Bolívar dreamed. The Círculos Bolivarianos can be organized in each street, neighborhood, town, and city of Venezuela, just as in any ministry, institution, university, school, and public and private enterprise. The Círculos Bolivarianos can be founded by seven to eleven members, and they must be presented to President Chávez at Miraflores Palace following political orientations provided by the president and the Comando Supremo Revolucionario Bolivariano (Supreme Bolivarian Revolutionary Command). Among the goals of the Círculos Bolivarianos are to form revolutionary cadres, loyal to and coherent with the revolutionary ideal, and to defend the Bolivarian Revolution.

One immediate practical consequence of civil society's activism and the rulings of the TSJ was that the National Assembly, in accordance with the TSJ's decisions, decided not to allow social organizations to participate in the Comités de Evaluación de Postulaciones del Poder Ciudadano (Committees for the Evaluation of Candidates to Citizens' Power), contradicting Article 279 of the constitution of 1999, whereby social organizations were to be convoked by the Consejo Moral Republicano (Republican Moral Council).[8]

The pro-government parties and the government adopted the thesis on representation formulated by the TSJ. The president of the republic took it upon himself to be the representative of civil society because a large majority of the people had voted for him. The ANC's denial of participation to civil society led to a direct confrontation between the president of the republic and the spokesperson for Queremos Elegir, who threatened to call for a campaign of civil disobedience—a form of action recognized by the constitution—if the legislature selected officers for the new powers without citizen participation.[9]

Trade Unionism at the Crossroads of the Fifth Republic

Analysts of labor movements have made a number of observations regarding the model of trade unionism which arose out of the Pact of Punto Fijo. Subject to control by the parties, the unions became a route to state and party leaderships, and over time the union movement itself, led by the CTV, became the object of criticisms and pressures for reform from the public. The labor movement was criticized for several reasons: it was organized fundamentally in the public sector and was subsidized by the state; its leadership was accused of corruption and patronage-influenced elections; it was given privileged status by the state as the exclusive interlocutor on labor questions; and it was hardly autonomous from the parties. As long as the economy continued to grow and inflation was low, workers gained an important share of national income, and collective bargaining gained ground. Salary increases and union victories were often attained without working-class mobilization. In this context, the model of labor relations strengthened. But once the social and economic crisis broke out in the 1980s, pushing more than 50 percent of the labor market into the informal sector, this situation changed dramatically, and criticisms of the labor movement reached new heights, especially after the January 1989 Caracazo and the February 4, 1992, coup attempt. The union leadership initiated a broad reform agenda but made little progress on it. The victory of Chávez in 1998 and the convocation of a new constituent assembly took place with the Venezuelan trade union movement in a weakened state.

Once the ANC had decreed a national emergency, reorganized the judiciary, and restricted the functions of the legislative power, all measures that sparked sharp protests and confrontations in 1999, it tried to intervene in the labor movement. It backed off when confronted with the danger of sharp conflicts and strong union resistance and shifted to a strategy of opening a dialogue with all union confederations. Alongside the existing labor confederations—the AD- and COPEI-controlled CTV, the Social Christian Confederación General de Trabajadores (CGT; General Confederation of Workers), the Communist CUTV, the Social Christian Confederación de Sindicatos Autónomos (CODESA; Confederation of Autonomous Unions), and El Nuevo Sindicalismo (The New Syndicalism), the workers' organization of La Causa Radical (LCR; The Radical Cause)—appeared the recently founded Frente Constituyente de Trabajadores (FCT; Constituent Front of Workers), formed by pro-Chávez workers and representatives to the constituent assembly.

There were two fundamental points on the labor reform agenda: the unification of the labor movement and the realization of a consultative referendum as a means to arrive at unification. In its penultimate session, the ANC made a number of decisions to promote a new framework of labor relations in the public sector. These decisions included the suspension of collective bargaining in the oil industry for 180 days and the creation of the National Union Electoral Commission, composed of three representatives from each of the national union confederations (the CTV, CGT, and CUTV), four representatives of nonconfederated labor organizations, four representatives from El Nuevo Sindicalismo, and four representatives from the FCT. This decree was intended to guarantee union liberty by assuring the realization of direct, democratic elections in labor organizations. Similarly, the ANC instructed the organs of the Citizens' Power (composed of the attorney general, ombudsman, and comptroller general; for more detailed discussion, see Chapter 12) to investigate crimes and ethics violations committed by labor union leaders during the discharge of their union activities, as well as any unjustified wealth, and when appropriate to take precautionary legal measures against them. These charges were also to be carried out by the National Legislative Commission, which would replace the ANC.

However, on July 6, 2000, the CNE announced that all union elections would be suspended except for those elections deemed by the National Legislative Commission to be too important to suspend. This decision was made amid labor conflicts, aggravated by unilateral government decisions on salaries (which disregarded the legally sanctioned tripartite mechanism of labor, business, and state agreement on increases). Further aggravating the labor conflicts were the increased unemployment and informalization of the economy, debates over social security which initially excluded the CTV and business representatives from the presidential commission charged with the reform, talks over the oil workers' contract, and the division of the FCT, which broke away from *chavismo.*

In response, on September 1, 2000, the Movimiento Quinta República (MVR; Fifth Republic Movement) created its union branch, the Fuerza Bolivariana de Trabajadores (Bolivarian Force of Workers). The inaugural meeting was attended by the vice president, the president of the ANC, the minister of labor, and prominent MVR figures, many of them former members of the constituent assembly. Chávez closed the ceremony, declaring, "Bolivarian Force will raze the leadership of the CTV" (*El Universal,* September 4, 2000, 2:3). He also proposed a national, nonunion referendum to decide whether to unify the labor movement into a single labor confederation and to require direct, secret vote of its leaders within six months. The referendum was approved by the ANC and scheduled to be held on December 3, 2000, jointly with municipal elections. The opposition political and labor forces viewed the president's proposal as a declaration of war, whereas other actors gave it lukewarm backing. The confrontation took on an international dimension, as the International Labor Organization (ILO) intervened and sustained the position that the referendum implied government intervention into union activity, an arena regulated by private law and to be voted on only by union members, not the public at large. Nationally, the conflict led to street demonstrations, with violent clashes between supporters and opponents of the referendum. Once again, faced with the possibility of a new official labor organization, society was divided. The CTV held its own internal elections at the federation and confederation levels, on the basis of the organization's own statutes.

The days of consensus were long past when the union referendum convoked by the ANC proceeded. The outcome was favorable to unification, but the level of abstention was high enough to affect the legitimacy of the vote. According to official data, 2,632,523 people voted in the referendum, that is, only 23.3 percent of registered voters, an abstention rate of 76.8 percent. Some 1,632,750 voted "Yes"; 719,771 voted "No"; and 280,002 votes were invalid.

As a consequence of the referendum, the leadership of both the Federación de Trabajadores Petroleros (FEDEPETROL; Federation of Oil Workers), the most important federation in the country, and the CTV, the principal union confederation, resigned. Thus, the central bulwarks of the traditional labor movement were subject to the government's project. By mandate of the referendum, the transition toward a new model of union organization, which included holding elections, had to take place within 180 days. The resignation of the union leaders did not mean the capitulation of the traditional unions. The CTV created the Junta de Conducción Sindical (Council of Union Management) to prepare for the elections, composed of working-class notables and leaders who were not members of the former leadership and who brought together the principal currents within the union movement. For its part, the Fuerzo Bolivariano de Trabajo (FBT; Bolivarian Workers Force) proposed a series of measures to continue the onslaught against CTV unionism: the convocation of a national constituent assembly of workers, a category without legal standing; the formation of regional councils of workers to fill the vacuum left throughout the country by the resignation of union leaders; the enactment of a law of union protection and guarantees; and, finally, the formation of a roundtable for a national dialogue.

The dynamics of 2000 revealed the weakness of the Bolivarian labor force. On the one hand, it did not achieve its goal of rapidly displacing, according to its own criteria, the traditional unions. Its proposal to create a new union confederation apart from the CTV within the framework of a constituent assembly of workers failed. On the other hand, the labor force ended up participating in union elections that relegitimated the standing confederation on October 25, 2001. The FBT and its candidate to the presidency of the CTV, Aristóbulo Isturiz, were defeated by Carlos Ortega of the traditional CTV leadership, amid several irregularities and the accusation of electoral fraud and disorganization by the command of the FBT and other union groups. Ortega won with 57.5 percent of votes against Isturiz's15.8 percent. Nevertheless, the government refused to recognize the election results or Ortega as president of the labor movement. Since then, the CTV has been involved in the most important activities opposing President Chávez, such as the national work stoppage (*paro nacional*) of December 10, 2001, particularly the events of the indefinite work stoppage (*paro nacional indefinido*) convoked on April 11, 2002, and ending in the removal, provisionally, of Chávez from the presidency, as well as the two-month strike in December 2002–February 2003.

The new and the old civil society had allied against Chávez, clashing in April 2000. High-level members of the armed forces disobeyed the president and demanded his resignation, announced by General Lucas Rincón Romero. The president of FEDECAMARAS took power, dissolving by decree all the public powers, which generated a crisis that took him from power and brought Chávez back to Miraflores within two days.

The protest and open conflict persisted. The Democratic Coordinator, led by the political parties but including civil society organizations, was born, reenergizing the parties and diminishing the space of the new civil society. The street demonstrations became a routine but were ineffective in ousting Chávez. This led the Democratic Coordinator to take more radical action, calling a general national strike on December 2, 2002—with unclear objectives and with differences among the NGOs, political parties, labor, and business regarding the strategies to follow. The government survived the strike, and the strike ultimately failed. The confrontation then moved to the institutional context, looking to revoke Chávez's presidential term through the new constitutional provisions for a recall referendum.

Conclusions

This chapter has placed the origin of organized civil society in the struggle between the military and civilians which has dominated Venezuelan political history. The formation and development of civil society can be viewed in terms of two different modalities: first, a traditional variant formed by unions and professional associations that were co-opted by the political parties prior to 1958 and in the early years of Punto Fijo, and, second, a new civil society that arose at the margin of the system of representation established within the framework of the Pact of Punto Fijo. The political system was concentrated in the party representation and in the distributive role of the state controlled by the political parties. The political parties invaded and controlled almost all the citizen spheres, which led to crises of representation and distribution. As a response to these crises, the new civil society emerged, and the 1958 party system deconstructed. This new civil society is not only nonstate in character but also a nonunion, nonprofessional, and, most important, nonpartisan association. The new civil organizations have attempted, with mixed success, to preserve their autonomy from the parties and the state. Venezuelan civil society experienced tremendous growth during the latter years of Punto Fijo democracy, peaking at some twenty-five thousand associations.

With the rise to power of Hugo Chávez and MVR and the vacuum created by the collapse of the Punto Fijo party system, civil society became an even more important political actor and reincorporated labor unions and business organizations opposed to the governing party. Chávez's polarizing policies led to an increase in civic mobilization. For the first time, civil society directly confronted the powers of the state and the government on issues of national import, demonstrated by the suspension of the May 28, 2000, national elections and the largest demonstration in Venezuelan history carried out on April 11, 2002, protesting against Chávez's policies and demanding his resignation.

The growing role of civil society in Venezuelan political life was further spurred by its increased access to the media after 1998, the decentralization policies begun in 1989, and the recognition of civil society in the 1999 constitution as an important actor. At the same time, civil society's heightened stature set off a struggle over the "representation" of civil society and efforts by pro-government forces to create a "new" civil society identified with President Chávez.

Faced with attempts by the Chávez administration to dominate all arenas of public life, civil society has engaged in important political struggles, of which only some have been addressed in this work. Owing to the weakness of the opposition parties, civil society groups, now including the national umbrella organizations of labor and business, mounted the only significant opposition to the government's policies. They led a drive in 2002–3 to oust President Chávez through various means—demands for resignation, constitutional amendment to shorten the term, recall referendum, and even a coup supported by some sectors.

Nonpartisan, diffuse opposition groups, whose leaders were largely unknown, used legal means and mobilized sectors of the population against attempts to concentrate power and politicize education. Their opposition, with the help of many of the new organizations, also demanded that the participatory democracy laid out in the 1999 constitution be put into practice. These developments indicate that amid the sociopolitical crisis in Venezuela a new social power has taken shape and has become a counterbalance to the Fifth Republic's undemocratic tendencies.

The media's recent attention to and treatment of the civil society theme have strengthened civil society's political ascendancy, but they have also unfortunately reinforced the conventional wisdom that civil society is a unitary actor and not a heterogeneous and conflictive space. This understanding has led many to view the topic as a notion free of problems, at times without any history, and as a homogeneous space that can be "represented" by specific political and social organizations or individuals. Such a view runs against the very nature of civil society, which is defined not by representation but by participation. For this reason, any pretension to represent civil society collapses in the face of a sphere formed by independent organizations that exist to have a direct voice in public affairs. The very trajectory of these organizations makes this participatory aspect clear, particularly the problems the organizations have in articulating themselves as part of a common social project.

The ascendancy of civil society has unleashed a political process of struggles to conquer and defend the spaces that for years have been taking shape in the area of social services. One consequence of this public confrontation has been the popularization of the concept of civil society and the extension of its coverage to other forms of association during the Fifth Republic. President Hugo Chávez has stated that we are all civil society, some politicians have maintained that the political parties are also part of civil society, and some analysts have gone so far as to claim that the military are members of civil society.

The confrontation that began in 2000 has moved along two fronts. On the ideological and theoretical front, sharp clashes have occurred over the very definition of civil society. On the political front, we observe the formulation of a politics of creating civil society from above by the state, with the mediation or intervention (or both) of the governing political party. This is not the first time that civil society faces a political challenge: in the past there have been attempts at political control by the state and governing parties, but they have not been as direct and crude as now. They were attempts at party control and union co-optation which took place without much fanfare, in contrast to today, when the challenges are directly launched by the president and the top leadership of *chavismo.* Thus, a battle is being waged over the control of civil society, which is also expressed as a conceptual struggle over the meaning of the term.

The Fifth Republic's attempt at statist incorporation has led civil society to an open and direct political confrontation with the state and the government parties, resulting in the further politicization of civil society. A democratic model composed only of civil society, without political parties, is not feasible for Venezuela. Rather, the Venezuelan democratic model will include, from now on, a politically mobilized civil society that can influence and hold more accountable political parties and the government.

CHAPTER SIX

Intellectuals

An Elite Divided

Richard S. Hillman

Comprehensive examination of a political regime in the "gray zone" (Carothers, 2002; Myers and McCoy, 2003) requires analyzing diverse inputs from its environment (Easton, 1966). This chapter addresses the role of writers, journalists, and scholars, whose engagement in opinion formation by articulating positions on political issues defines them as intellectuals or members of the intelligentsia—an elite group that influences mass political perspectives.

Theories of political legitimacy and elite settlements provide a framework for examining the role of intellectuals in political change. These theories view the informal political processes of demand making by weakly organized groups, such as intellectuals, as important complements to interest articulations by formal institutions in the policy-making process (Diamond, Hartlyn, and Linz, 1999; Klarén and Bossert, 1986; Wiarda and Kline, 1996). Weakly organized groups have been shown on occasion to play an important role in encouraging cooperative behavior among elites (Higley and Burton, 1989; Lijphart, 1984; Peeler, 1989). Intellectuals can provide ideological justifications for courses of action which hitherto have been perceived as unacceptable or impossible (Dahl, 1971; Huntington, 1991). Conversely, intellectual opposition that contributes to negative perceptions of the existing rules of the political game has a delegitimizing effect that can lead to institutional decay.

The Venezuelan case raises important questions about the relationship between intellectuals and political change: Did the Venezuelan intelligentsia as a group craft negative portrayals of post-1958 democracy which contributed to its unraveling? Did this group make it impossible to transform that regime into a more representative polyarchy? Have Venezuelan intellectuals provided a coherent ideological underpinning for *chavismo*? These are important question to which we hope to provide some preliminary answers.

Intellectuals in Historical Perspective

Social commentary by intellectuals has contributed a variety of perspectives to the Venezuelan political landscape. Venezuelan intellectuals have been policy makers, critical outsiders, voices for the powerless, and spokespeople for repressive power structures. Their roles and views are diverse. They do not fit into neat categories.

Historically the intelligentsia has been an important element in Venezuelan political dynamics. *Pensadores* Simón Bolívar and Andrés Bello provide characteristic testimony to the nineteenth-century preoccupation with the clash between liberty and authority (Martz and Myers, 1983: 226-27). Struggling with contradictions between democratic theory and traditional Hispanic political culture, these thinkers belonged to an intellectual milieu that included a variety of often conflicting ideologies. In the twentieth century some intellectuals advocated authoritarianism, and others spoke on behalf of democracy. Laureano Vallenilla Lanz's (1983) *Cesarismo Democrático* explained away Juan Vicente Gómez's brutal dictatorship as necessary to end decades of internecine strife. Novelist Rómulo Gallegos's *Doña Bárbara* (1948) agreed to a point, but he also attacked that dictatorship as "barbaric." Similarly, in *Venezuela: Política y Petróleo* Rómulo Betancourt (1956), the Punto Fijo president who evolved from a Communist revolutionary to a reformist democrat, penned an influential criticism of Marcos Pérez Jiménez's dictatorship.[1]

Universities also influenced Venezuelan political debate. The Universidad Central de Venezuela (UCV; Central University of Venezuela) provided a venue for organizing protests as interest articulators for the masses (Hillman, 1994: 85–86). University students fought in the independence wars and subsequently opposed an array of civilian and military tyrants. In 1928, antigovernment speeches at the UCV culminated in a strike that provoked popular demonstrations against General Gómez. Whether incarcerated or in exile, leaders of this student "Generation of 28" exerted a crucial influence on politics for more than five decades. The best known (Rómulo Betancourt, Raúl Leoni, and Jóvito Villalba) organized movements that became important political parties. Another group, the "Generation of 1936" (led by Rafael Caldera), followed the Christian Democratic tradition. Student leaders in the late 1950s also helped to overthrow the Pérez Jiménez dictatorship (1958) and make the transition to Punto Fijo democracy.

During the closing decade of the twentieth century newspaper and magazine editorials, radio and television talk shows, academic books, articles, lectures, and pamphlets excoriated the political parties and pacts that shaped democratic consolidation in the 1960s. Indeed, public opinion makers escalated their criticism of Acción Democrática (AD; Democratic Action) and Comité de Organización Política Electoral Independiente: Partido Social Cristiano (COPEI; Committee of Independent Electoral Political Organization: Social Christian Party) in the wake of the 1983 Black Friday crisis, blaming their governments for rising costs, deteriorating living standards, and governmental corruption. This criticism fueled the civil unrest that led to urban riots known as the Caracazo (1989),[2] two attempted *golpes* (coups; 1992), and the end of major party control of the presidency (1993). Hence, the role played by Venezuelan intellectuals is one of the keys to explaining the demise of Punto Fijo democracy.

Intellectuals during the Punto Fijo Regime

Venezuelan intellectuals participated actively in political debate between 1983 and 1998. These intellectuals included Roman Catholic thinkers and writers, Marxists, and nationalists. There was considerable overlap among the three categories. Catholic liberation theologians influenced by Marxist analysis of class conflict advocated far-reaching social transformation, and the Jesuit think tank Centro Gumilla regularly took post-1958 democracy to task (Myers, 1996: 250). Gumilla's influential magazines, *Revista SIC* and *Revista Comunicación*, published articles that criticized the failure of Punto Fijo governments to reduce poverty or address the issues of socioeconomic inequality, injustice, and human rights violations. After 1989 the Jesuits mounted a ferocious attack on the neoliberal programs of Presidents Carlos Andrés Pérez and Rafael

Caldera. The rise of neoliberalism even led military intellectuals whose praetorian vision involved saving the nation from politicians' incompetence to issue class-based analyses that excoriated the political regime.

Favored access to information and social status allowed intellectuals from the UCV to exercise influential roles in the political debates that raged in the 1990s. Organizations representing students in the Federación de Centros Universitarios (FCU; Federation of University Centers) had been highly politicized in the 1960s. At that time, the major forces had been the "youth wings" of AD, COPEI, Partido Comunista de Venezuela (PCV; Venezuelan Communist Party), Unión Republicana Democrática (URD; Democratic Republican Union), Movimiento de Izquierda Revolucionario (MIR; Movement of the Revolutionary Left), Movimiento Electoral de Pueblo (MEP; Electoral Movement of the People), and Bandera Roja (Red Flag). Concomitantly, the Federación de Profesores Universitarios (FAPUV; Federation of University Professors) represented twenty-five thousand university professors in fifteen universities. Few of these professors supported AD and COPEI, although by the end of the 1970s they appeared to have reconciled themselves to domination by the two political parties.

After the Caracazo, university politics were marked by frequent shutdowns (Hillman, 1994: 95–111). Students projected civic cynicism, glorifying electoral abstention and active resistance to political authority. Among the most prominent UCV intellectuals, Domingo Alberto Rangel denounced the second Pérez government for its "complicity with United States imperialism."[3] Other intellectual critics of the regime's pro-U.S. policy included Teodoro Petkoff (1960s *guerrillero* leader, former Movimiento al Socialismo [MAS; Movement toward Socialism] presidential candidate, and currently editor of the Caracas newspaper *Tal Qual)* and Américo Martin (also a former insurgent turned intellectual activist). Antonio Montilla (director of the School of International Studies at the UCV) was one of the few prominent intellectuals with a positive view of Punto Fijo democracy. This imbalance led governments during the 1990s to claim that subversives had taken over the universities. Sociologist Orlando Albornoz disagreed, arguing that protests at the UCV, as well as at important universities in the interior, "were driven by fundamental social discontent about explosive social problems that required political reform, without which radical movements would gain strength."[4]

The Universidad de Los Andes (ULA; University of the Andes) in Mérida, perhaps the most important university outside Caracas, was strongly influenced by Christian Democratic ideology and the COPEI party. However, criticism from the ULA declined after 1997, when Rafael Caldera adopted his neoliberal Agenda Venezuela program. Universidad del Zulia (LUZ; University of Zulia) in Maracaibo and the Universidad de Oriente (UDO; University of the East), with campuses in Puerto La Cruz, Cumaná, and Ciudad Bolívar, began as bastions of AD support. By the late 1970s they were dominated by MAS activists and radical Marxists. In the 1990s they were centers of criticism of Punto Fijo democracy. In the capital city of Caracas, Catholic intellectuals like Luis Ugalde and Jesuit Arturo Sosa clustered around the Universidad Católica Andrés Bello (UCAB; Andrés Bello Catholic University). They attacked neoliberal policies using the perspective of Christian communitarianism. Pro-capitalist intellectuals like José Antonio Gil Yepes, Pedro Palma, and Moisés Naím met at the Instituto de Estudios Superiores de Administración (IESA; Institute for Graduate Studies in Administration) and the Metropolitan University.

Most mainline academic journals, such as *Politeia* and *Cuadernos CENDES,* contained articles by intellectuals from the UCV, LUZ, and UDO which criticized Punto Fijo democracy frm a Marxist perspective. As an antidote to this antiestablishment activism, long a tradition in Venezuelan academic life, AD and COPEI had founded the Simón Bolívar University. They intended that this institution of higher learning be developed on the North American model with its emphasis on research and balanced teaching. The Simón Bolívar University political science masters program, in an ironic twist, counted among its alumni Irene Sáez, Francisco Arias Cárdenas, and Hugo Chávez, individuals who would play a major role in destroying the representative democracy dominated by AD and COPEI!

Intellectuals from traditional families, the most prominent of whom was Arturo Uslar Pietri, contributed to the political discourse throughout the Punto Fijo period. Uslar's critiques of Venezuelan oil policy, population problems, education, and political crises became classics (Uslar Pietri, 1989). In the 1990s he became a vociferous critic of the failure of neoliberal governments to provide a safety net for the poor. Members of a powerful media-owning family, Ruth and Carlos Capriles, published a compendium of cases denouncing the governments of Jaime Lusinchi (1984–89) and Carlos Andrés Pérez (1989–93) for "misuse of public funds, abuse of power, fraud, illicit enrichment," and other "crimes against the country" (Capriles, 1992: iv). Conservative pundit Carlos A. Ball M. wrote scathing critiques of Venezuela's "sad state of affairs" from a neoliberal perspective (Ball, 1992). Finally, prior to the 1998 presidential election, the establishment opinion magazine *Primicia* devoted an entire issue to the "democratic crisis after forty years" (September).

Even before the currency devaluation of Black Friday on February 18, 1983, intellectuals based at IESA were questioning the consequences for economic development and political accountability of systemic domination by the two hierarchical political parties. The best-known works of this type were the volume edited at IESA by Moisés Naím and Ramón Piñango (1985) and the first major book by José Antonio Gil Yepes (1981), who subsequently developed Datanalisis, Venezuela's leading public opinion polling company. Closely related to these intellectuals was the Grupo Roraima, a forerunner of the 1990s civil associations. Led by television talk show host Marcel Granier, Grupo Roraima included Arístides Torres, José Antonio Gil Yepes, Herbert Koenecke, German Campos Aymara, A. De García, Rafael Castillo, Imelda de Hardy, Kisaira Márquez, and María Isabel Gómez. They agitated for increased popular participation and a reduction in the state's role in the economy (Granier and Gil Yepes, 1987). The Grupo Roraima also maintained links with the Comisión Presidencial para la Reforma del Estado (COPRE; Presidential Commission for State Reform), Carlos Blanco, and others who wanted to increase popular participation but were less interested in privatization.

Military intellectuals gathered at the Instituto de Altos Estudios de la Defensa (Institute for Advanced Defense Studies) in Los Chorros (now on Avenida Los Ilustres), where the reformed guerrilla tactician Teodoro Petkoff gave classes. In the mid-1980s many of the institute's students and younger instructors gravitated to Hugo Chávez and Francisco Arias Cárdenas. They became the nucleus of the Movimiento Bolivariano Revolucionario 200 (MBR-200; Bolivarian Revolutionary Movement 200). At that time the Bolivarians counted in their ranks fifteen officers and approximately two thousand soldiers. Other Bolivarian military leaders who wrote on behalf of the MBR-200 included Yoel Acosta Chirinos, Francisco Urdaneta Hernández, and Jesús Ortiz Contreras (Garrido, 2000).

The cumulative effect of the dominant hostile intellectual currents was to discredit the legitimacy of AD/COPEI domination and the entire post-1958 democratic enterprise. The political parties attempted to counter this negative portrayal by founding their own think tanks: AD sponsored the Fundación Raúl Leoni, directed by political sociologist Andrés Stambouli, and COPEI's Eduardo Fernández developed the Fundación de Pensamiento y Acción. These think tanks held conferences and conducted high-profile seminars, but they produced no meaningful defense of the political parties. Unanswered criticism of the central institutions of Punto Fijo democracy took its toll. Neither the parties nor the political regime ever recovered from being portrayed as closed, pathologically corrupt, and beyond redemption (Capriles Ayala and del Naranco, 1992; Ochoa Antich, 1992; Zago, 1998).

Intellectual opposition failed to produce consensus on a viable alternative to the existing political regime. Public opinion surveys in the 1990s confirmed that support for Punto Fijo democracy was in a free fall, and anger grew as the economy contracted. AD and COPEI appeared detached and isolated to most citizens (Consultores 21 S.A., 1996). This left the door open for a radical solution. The few middle-class intellectuals who argued in favor of reforming the political regime were less persuasive than those who advocated dismantling it and moving on to something different.

Intellectuals and the Rise of *Chavismo*

In the 1990s newspaper editorials, television talk shows, academic writing, and even televised soap operas became vehicles for expressing citizen frustration at being excluded from meaningful political participation by AD and COPEI. The failure of national politicians to respond to these expressions of discontent increased alienation from AD and COPEI. After the attempted *golpes* of 1992, polls showed broad opposition to Carlos Andrés Pérez and extreme dissatisfaction with established party leaders. Nevertheless, most intellectuals still favored democracy over all other forms as a system of government, although after the failed coup of February 4, 1992, many greeted one another with the ubiquitous *Por ahora* ("For now").[5] This greeting confirmed the widespread impact of (although not necessarily support for) the Bolivarians' attempt to overthrow the government of President Carlos Andrés Pérez. Arturo Uslar Pietri argued that "the *golpe* [of February 4] was not an isolated incident, but a sign of Venezuelans' desire for a democracy that functions with decency."[6]

A loose association, known as the Group of Notables, came together following the failed February coup. The group strongly criticized Pérez and the secretary general of COPEI, Eduardo Fernández. Following the coup, Fernández had committed COPEI to propping up Carlos Andrés Pérez by joining in a government of national unity with AD. By taking this position Fernández diminished COPEI's image of being something distinct from AD. The Group of Notables included Rafael Caldera, General Alberto Rojas Müller, Arturo Uslar Pietri, and Luís Raúl Matos. These individuals can be considered politician-intellectuals, for each had held a major government position at one time in his career. On the academic side, Aníbal Romero (1994) published a highly regarded work that pointed out grave consequences for democratic accountability in the Punto Fijo system which derived from centralized domination by AD and COPEI. Equally telling criticism came from el Centro de Estudios del Desarrollo (CENDES; the Center for Development Studies, UCV), especially in a volume by CENDES director Heinz R. Sonntag and Thaís Maigón (1992). Intellectuals at the ULA and LUZ and the Jesuits from the Centro Gumilla also stepped up their criticism as the government of national unity implemented only minor changes.

The second failed coup attempt (November 27, 1992) led to increased activity by the intellectuals. Roman Catholic intellectuals at the UCAB and the Episcopal Conference organized a high-profile conference around the theme "An Encounter with Civil Society." At that gathering more than one thousand social and intellectual groups developed proposals for the transformation of Venezuela.[7] Finally, two volumes resulted from the cooperative efforts of Caracas-based intellectuals and scholars in the United States (Goodman, Forman, and Tulchin, 1995; McCoy et al., 1995). These academic analyses had considerable influence on the intellectual communities in the United States and Venezuela, but they contained little of practical value to policy makers. Neither volume anticipated the rise of the MBR-200 to electoral dominance.

Writers seeking to dismantle the Punto Fijo system focused on the personality of Hugo Chávez after the coup attempt of February 4. In this context it is important to acknowledge the "resurrected" influence of militantly Marxist social scientists who visited Chávez in prison and the reappearance of José Vicente Rangel, Luis Miquilena, and other members of the moribund URD. Ironically, the sons of some supporters of the Medina government (1940–45) who resented the revolution of October 1945 wrote about how removing Carlos Andrés Pérez from power would redress the wrongs committed during that 1945 revolution, a tear in the political fabric that brought AD and Betancourt to power for the first time. Another militant leftist, muckraking journalist Alfredo Peña, cast his lot with Chávez during the 1998 presidential campaign. Peña had chronicled Punto Fijo corruption and nurtured grudges against AD which went back to the 1945 revolution. During the initial months of Chávez's government Peña served as the president's chief of staff, and with the backing of the Movimiento Quinta República (MVR; Fifth Republic Movement) he was elected to the post of *alcalde mayor* (metropolitan mayor) of Caracas in the mega-elections of 2000. Most journalists in the Colegio de Periodismo (Journalist Guild), however, unlike Peña, had histories of supporting AD, COPEI, and MAS. But in the late 1990s their tepid defense of these political parties fell on ears that were more attuned to President Chávez's promises of a "social revolution" (Roberts, 2003: 55–72).[8]

Fifth Republic *Chavista* Intellectuals and Their Ideology

Hugo Chávez and his supporters crafted a theory to explain moral decomposition in Venezuela which predated their contacts with leftist intellectuals after the failed coups of 1992. Their initial concept of "social revolution" derived from Chávez's desire to reinvigorate democracy by returning the government to the people. Bolivarian thought, as discussed earlier, advanced the model of "participatory democracy" as an alternative to post-1958 democracy's representative paradigm. In his inaugural address President Chávez proclaimed that the Bolivarian Revolution was the result of a "storm that broke out over the last decade of the 20th century in Venezuela," which "generated a wave" that Chávez "navigates as helmsman."[9] During his first year in office, President Chávez tasked the armed forces to oversee the grassroots participation that he intended to mobilize through Círculos Bolivarianos—civic groups. In addition, he began to use national resources to further Venezuelan international objectives through leadership in the Organization of Petroleum Exporting Countries (OPEC). The new president also portrayed his followers as the heirs of Simón Bolívar's army of liberation. Therefore, they cannot "remain indifferent to the immense level of corruption that plagues all areas of our nation and bestows great privileges on the few. It is unacceptable not to punish those whom we all know have taken public funds improperly, implemented economic policies that have operated in opposition to the lower classes, and sold our basic businesses to foreign consortiums. These policies have led to the deterioration of our health care system and other public services, thus making it impossible for "the great majority to satisfy their basic needs."[10]

The intellectual basis of the Chávez regime appears to be grounded in a nationalism that its creators ascribe to Simón Bolívar.[11] Elementary Bolivarian thought claims to be a syncretic ideology based on the "tree of three roots"

(Simón Bolívar, Simón Rodríguez, and Ezequiel Zamora). A more convoluted version encompasses elements from chaos theory, national security doctrine, the right to rebellion, repudiation of "savage" neoliberalism, antiglobalization, and promotion of a multipolar international balance of power. Some military intellectuals supportive of the Bolivarian Revolution have also appealed to Rousseau's social contract. These Rousseaueans view the military institution as incarnating the general will of the people. In an ironic twist for a military that had been anti-Castro, the Bolivarian officers advocated leftist principles that closely resembled those pursued by the government of Fidel Castro. As of this writing (February 2004) Chávez's confused ideological mix has led neither to nationalization nor to statism—embracing completely neither the Left nor the Right.

Chávez's demonization of opponents and apparent desire to punish everyone who prospered during Punto Fijo democracy have led to intense debate about the meaning of this worldview, its ability to provide a legitimating ideology, and whether it is compatible with democracy in any meaningful sense. Nevertheless, *chavismo* filled the political void left by a regime that lost its legitimacy, even if the Fifth Republic's "rhetorical radicalism . . . greatly exceeds its practical implementation" (Lombardi, 2003: 5). Chávez's populist discourse resonated in what he called the *soberano*—the numerous informal and marginal sectors of Venezuelan society. Yet concern over whether the Fifth Republic can actually improve the lot of the poor continues to divide Venezuelan intellectuals.

Intellectuals and the New Regime

The intellectuals who backed Chávez in the late 1990s had no doubt that the Bolivarian Revolution would right the wrongs of Punto Fijo democracy. Some of those intellectuals, as indicated earlier, had been marginalized between 1958 and 1998 and harbored great resentment against AD and COPEI. The Fifth Republic's most important apologists included Luis Miquilena and José Vicente Rangel. In the 1930s the former had been a Communist Party labor leader, and in the 1940s he joined URD. Miquilena defended *chavismo* as the truly progressive alternative that opponents of Pérez Jiménez's dictatorship had intended to establish in 1958, when AD captured the anti-imperialist Venezuelan revolution and sold out to international capitalism. Miquilena helped to finance Chávez's faction within the army officer corps and headed a group of intellectuals who favored scrapping the representative democratic constitution of 1961. He broke with Chávez over the Bolivarian Revolution's increasingly authoritarian policies in January 2002. José Vicente Rangel, a veteran leftist politician and journalist who became vice president, also held a long-standing grudge against the Punto Fijo establishment, in this case dating from the 1945 revolution. AD founder Rómulo Betancourt had expelled his father from the AD and made his life as a businessman quite difficult.

Professionals associated with the traditional leftist parties (MEP, MAS, and PCV) prepared antiestablishment position papers for the new regime. Luminaries in this group included Jorge Pérez Mancebo, director of the UCV Escuela de Economía and member of PCV; Felipe Pérez Martí, a prominent UCV professor; Francisco Mieres, former president of Corpoindustria and ambassador to Russia; and Francisco Rodríquez, previously at Harvard and then of UCAB. Finally, Planning Minister Jorge Giordani (Ph.D. from Sussex) had served with the Economic Commission on Latin America (ECLA), and he infused Bolivarian economic policy with the ECLA's preference for Import Substitution Industrialization (ISI), suspicion of international capitalism, and a concern for social justice.

The Bolivarians also attracted a new group of intellectuals who viewed direct democracy as a desirable alternative to party control over government. Most prominent in this group was Carlos Lanz Rodríguez, a radical sociologist who advised the minister of education and crafted the government's education plan. Lanz's plan included state-appointed roving supervisors to oversee the secondary schools and to ensure the teaching of revolutionary values that rejected individualism, competitiveness, and the concentration of property among privileged classes. Equally prominent was Alí Rodríguez, the 1960s insurgent who became a leading expert on oil. Chávez named Alí Rodríguez to such pivotal posts as minister of energy and mines, president of Petróleos de Venezuela Sociedad Anónima (PDVSA; Venezuelan Oil Company, Incorporated), and secretary general of OPEC. Other pro-Chávez intellectuals included Alberto Jordán Hernández, attorney, journalist, and member of the Asamblea Nacional Constituyente (ANC; National Constituent Assembly). Augusto Hernández, humorist/journalist from Nueva Esparta (an island state of eastern Venezuela); Alfredo Toro Hardy, ambassador to the United States; Juan Barreto, communication adviser and journalist; and Virginia Contreras, attorney and Venezuelan representative to the Organization of American States (OAS). Finally the controversial Argentine sociologist Norberto Ceresole was for a time the government's most influential international adviser on national security (LaFranchi, 1999: 1). Ceresole's view on "social revolution" held that national security requires economic development and that, therefore, the military must become involved in its promotion. His affinity for Arab causes also inclined Chávez to support the Palestinian cause in the Middle East.

Venezuelan intellectuals, as indicated above, were not monolithic. There were no autonomous associations or writers' guilds similar to the organizations in civil society which emerged in Eastern Europe and cooperated to bring about the collapse of Soviet domination. Most professional associations were tied to the two major political parties. Beginning in the late 1980s, however, Venezuelan civil society did give birth to a number of institutions that produced and circulated propaganda critical of AD and COPEI. The most important of these were Pro-Venezuela, Venezuela Positiva, Sinergia, and Queremos Eligir. However, there was little cooperation among the intellectuals linked to these institutions. There were also private academic symposia (like "La Peña de Manuel Ugueto") and occasional academic colloquiums that attracted attention for brief periods. These rather elitist forms failed to establish a common perspective among opponents of the Punto Fijo regime. They neither strengthened the Bolivarian movement nor created support for groups seeking to reform and deepen post-1958 democracy. They had little impact beyond academia.

Once Chávez became president, the leftward authoritarian drift of his government led some prominent public policy intellectuals, writers, and military leaders who supported his presidential bid in 1998 to turn against the Bolivarian Revolution. Ricardo Combellas, former president of COPRE who had written for many years of the need to change the centralistic orientation of the 1961 constitution, concluded that the Fifth Republic was moving in the opposite direction. Two prominent lawyers who had written extensively on the lack of due process during the Punto Fijo years, Hermann Escarrá and Javier Elechiguerra, viewed with dismay what they viewed as even less regard for law in the Chávez government. Finally, José Antonio Olavarría, a retired general considered one of the army's leading professionals in matters of modernization, decried politicization of the officer corps. Perhaps most surprising, Francisco Arias Cárdenas, long the second most important leader of the MBR-200, clashed publicly with President Chávez over the government's plan to control parochial education which surfaced during the drafting of the constitution of 1999. Arias Cárdenas, a devout Roman Catholic, was serving as governor of Zulia at that time. When differences with Chávez became irreconcilable, Arias made common cause with a group of Catholic intellectuals at the LUZ. These intellectuals provided the governor with ideological arguments and policy positions as part of Arias's presidential bid in the mega-elections of 2000. However, Arias's dour public persona proved no match for Hugo Chávez's charismatic exuberance. After his loss to Chávez, Arias marshaled Catholic social thought to continue his challenge to the Bolivarian Revolution and its drift into Marxism.

Conclusion

The behavior of Venezuelan intellectuals between 1983 and 2004 supports this volume's unraveling thesis. Venezuelan intellectuals undermined post-1958 democracy by crafting images of Punto Fijo institutions and leaders after the Black Friday crisis of February 1983 which were overwhelmingly negative. Their writings both reflected and shaped public perceptions. Some intellectuals advocated reform, arguing that modifications to the institutions of the 1961 constitution would be sufficient to facilitate a more responsive and transparent democracy. Others argued that representative democracy as it had evolved in post-1958 Venezuela favored the privileged, marginalized everyone else, and was irretrievably flawed. Whether writing from the perspective of the reformers or the revolutionaries, Venezuelan intellectuals as a group attacked and discredited AD and COPEI, viewing them as sectarian, corrupt, and beyond redemption.

The debate among intellectuals over the shortcomings of Punto Fijo democracy and over how the political regime should be changed had far greater influence among the middle sectors than with the working classes and marginal groups. Most in the middle class favored reform rather than revolution. They wanted representative democratic institutions that would strengthen regional and local political institutions, give regional leaders more bargaining power with the central government, and increase their influence with Caracas-based elites. Nevertheless, some held that representative political institutions shielded political leaders from the popular will. They favored mechanisms that allowed the people to focus their demands directly on politicians. Therefore, at a basic level the contest between Venezuelan intellectuals to chart the future of Venezuelan political evolution was a contest between Lockean and Rousseauan visions of democracy. Even the Lockeans, however, were disillusioned with how post-1958 representative democracy had evolved in Venezuela. Their criticism of the Punto Fijo regime after 1983 did almost as much to undermine its legitimacy as did the attacks of their Rousseauan rivals.

Hugo Chávez tilted toward the Rousseauan vision, if for no other reason than his belief that representative political institutions had allowed Punto Fijo democracy to shield unresponsive political parties from popular demands. However, Rousseauan intellectuals, like the Lockeans, were divided into numerous subgroups. Chávez was exposed to these subgroups following his release from prison in 1994, while he was completing course work for his M.A. in political science at Simón Bolívar University in Caracas. The political science graduate school at Simón Bolívar University offered the premier program of its kind in Venezuela, and its professors prided themselves on their incorporation of the latest analytical techniques from universities in the United States and Western Europe. The political science graduate program at Simón Bolívar University was also the location where leading intellectuals from other Venezuelan universities and policy think tanks came to exchange ideas and debate how best to change and repair their country's flawed democracy.

No consensus about which changes would improve the quality of economic and political life emerged from the 1990s debate among Venezuelan intellectuals. Those who joined in these debates during the period when Chávez was a graduate student at Simón Bolívar University remember him as ill at ease when arguing political issues with scholars and policy analysts. These exchanges appear to have made him disdainful of intellectuals. In contrast, he thrived in the company of groups united in their faith that Marxist solutions would resolve Venezuela's problems. Many of the leftists with whom Chávez preferred to associate were older, in their middle sixties. They had been marginalized three decades earlier by the leaders of AD and COPEI when these institutions gained dominance and consolidated the Punto Fijo regime. Whereas the leaders of AD and COPEI had presented their institutions as open to all classes, the radical leftists around Chávez had taken up the cause of the poor and dispossessed against the middle class and the elite. This populist and conflictual approach hit a responsive cord with Chávez, himself a son of the Venezuelan *llanos* (plains), a region that historically resented the privileged position occupied by elites from Caracas. Chávez incarnated the plains people's suspicions of those elites and their foreign friends who exerted far too much influence on the cultural, economic, and political life of the country.

In the end, Chávez sided with the leftist, antisystem intellectuals. He shared their view of the Punto Fijo regime as a system imposed on Venezuela by international capitalists based in the United States and Europe. He viewed representative institutions as designed to thwart the popular will and protect privilege. Venezuelans were susceptible to Chávez's vision in the 1990s in no small measure because intellectuals (Lockeans as well as Rousseauans) had fixed blame on representative institutions for the country's pervasive corruption and declining economy. Chávez and his intellectual allies preached a different democracy, one in which government would respond directly and rapidly to the will of the majority.

CHAPTER SEVEN

The United States and Venezuela

From a Special Relationship to Wary Neighbors

Carlos A. Romero

Venezuela at the beginning of the twenty-first century is much changed from the country that U.S. policy makers dealt with during the first three decades of the Punto Fijo era. Three changes have great import for Venezuela-U.S. relations: (1) the country is in the midst of a prolonged political and economic crisis; (2) the once admired model of representative democracy is now criticized in Venezuela as well as in the United States; and (3) the cooperative attitude in matters of bilateral and multilateral foreign policy which once could be taken for granted has become confrontational, especially on issues that require not only agreement but negotiation. Tensions are especially pronounced in matters relating to the promotion of democracy, the fight against drugs, intellectual property protection, human rights, the environment, and security issues related to civilian air traffic.

Lack of enthusiasm for Venezuela's representative democracy increased among many U.S. citizens with experience in Venezuela, and their concerns filtered back to Venezuela at an increasing rate during the 1980s and especially during the early 1990s. Many of the same groups (both in government and in the academic community) that had praised Punto Fijo democracy during the cold war now emphasized the system's corruption, lack of responsiveness, and minimal accountability. Such pivotal institutions as organized labor, business associations, and the two dominant political parties (Acción Democrática [AD; Democratic Action] and Comité de Organización Política Electoral Independiente: Partido Social Cristiano [COPEI; Committee of Independent Electoral Political Organization: Social Christian Party]) received especially harsh criticism. It is worth remembering in this context that when it comes to promoting democratic principles, the Lockean model (predominant in the United States and England) prioritizes the rights of the individual in relation to a (potentially) abusive government. In contrast, the prevailing Latin American interpretation of democracy (influenced by the Roman tradition, Rousseau's views, and "Bolivarian" ideals) emphasizes each citizen's proper role within society and the polity. The differences between the Rousseauian and Lockean models of democracy was an important factor giving rise to the criticism of Punto Fijo democracy which came from the United States. Advocates of Lockean values and preferences had little patience with a "democratic" political system that accepted clientelism, paternalism, and sometimes a less than vigorous defense of human rights (Kelly and Romero, 2002; C. Romero, 1986).

After the victory of Hugo Chávez Frías in the presidential race of 1998 and the new constitution of 1999, which attempted to establish what the Bolivarians called participatory democracy, criticism from the United States intensified. These criticisms questioned the "depth" of Venezuelan democracy as reflected in Lockean prejudice for limits to presidential power, electoral transparency, and the insulation of the military from politics (Gómez Calcaño and Patruyo, 2000). Chávez, however, has remained an unrepentant Bolivarian. He continues to promote throughout all of Latin America the proposition that participatory democracy is superior to its representative counterpart. It is in fact a political alternative with Marxist roots, which oscillates between representative democracy and delegative democracy.

U.S.-Venezuelan Relations in the Twentieth Century

Relations between the governments of the United States and Venezuela ranged from cool and ambivalent to highly supportive over the first six decades of the twentieth century. U.S. policy makers viewed Venezuela as a country that naturally fell within Washington's sphere of influence, and they opposed any threat to this positioning. Thus, President Theodore Roosevelt's disdain for Cipriano Castro (1899–1908) and his horror at the chaos that accompanied Castro's rise to power did not prevent the Roosevelt administration from coming to Venezuela's assistance when European powers blockaded the Venezuelan coast. During the long rule of Juan Vicente Gómez (1908–35), Venezuela appeared on the radar of U.S. policy makers only when their concerns focused on petroleum, a commodity that Venezuela possessed in abundance and which proved crucial in World Wars I and II. Venezuela also supplied petroleum during the Korean conflict and remained the largest source of U.S. petroleum imports. During the mid- and late 1950s, Washington supported the dictatorship of General Marcos Pérez Jiménez on the assumption that his government provided the easiest means for securing an uninterrupted flow of Venezuelan petroleum to the United States and its NATO allies.

The overthrow of General Pérez Jiménez and the triumph of representative democracy forced the U.S. government to rethink its relations with Venezuela. A new model of interaction between the two countries emerged, and its basic parameters persisted over more than forty years (1958–99). First, building on an axiom that dated from the Gómez era, policy makers in both countries continued to treat Venezuela as unique in Latin America because of its massive petroleum reserves. These reserves and the Venezuelan government's willingness to supply energy to the United States at an acceptable price, coupled with Washington's interests (strategic and economic) in having a secure source of petroleum close to home, led to good and solid relations between the two countries throughout the Punto Fijo period.

Normalization of a stable system of representative democracy between 1959 and 1973 gave rise to a second dimension of Venezuelan uniqueness. In a region characterized by military coups, insurgencies, and revolutions, Venezuela appeared as an island of stability, despite guerrilla movements, leftist and rightist coup d'état attempts, mass mobilization, and political violence during the early sixties. The armed forces remained apart from policy making except for issues dealing with border security and the purchase of military armament. For more than thirty years (1959–89), Venezuela avoided the cycle of "democracy–military coup–dictatorship–democracy" which undermined Latin American democracies.

One important consequence of this second dimension of uniqueness was that the U.S. government supported the democratic leadership of Venezuela's dominant centrist political parties, AD and COPEI. The representative democratic system of Venezuela, its success in integrating former guerrillas into electoral politics, and its military's acceptance of civilian rule made the country a model for advocates of democracy throughout South America (Ellner, 1997; C. Romero, 1986). In addition, between 1958 and 1999 Venezuelan politics and political development did not readily fit within any of the scholarly classifications used by mainstream social scientists in the United States and Western Europe. Academics, like their counterparts in government, saw Venezuela's successful experiment with representative democracy as "exceptional."

The Venezuelan political system came to be seen as a limited democracy or, as McCoy and Myers say in the introduction of this book, "a limited pluralist polyarchy" far short of an idealized liberal Western democracy. The unraveling of this limited democracy led to another type of limited democracy defined by McCoy and Myers as a "hybrid regime." In terms of U.S.-Venezuelan relations, American governments worked for many years with a "middle of the road" democracy, and when U.S decision makers, politicians, and academics criticized the Venezuelan case, they hoped to see a liberal democracy emerge. Instead, the political system unraveled, and the United States now must deal with a new regime that is not yet consolidated but is moving toward a hybrid regime.

During the Punto Fijo years, few Venezuelan policy makers questioned Washington's supremacy in the Western Hemisphere, and a consensus developed over the desirability of strengthening representative democratic institutions and favoring the development of a mixed economy along the lines advocated by European social democrats. This pleased most Washington policy makers and petroleum executives. Venezuela's petroleum industry continued as one of the most efficient in the world, and the United States remained Venezuela's most important trading partner. The business culture of New York and Houston had had considerable influence in shaping the local private sector, which cooperated in a plethora of joint ventures in Venezuela with U.S. corporations (Rangel, 1972).

In the arena of multilateral diplomacy, successive Punto Fijo governments attempted to set Venezuela's positions apart from those of the United States by adopting activist roles within the United Nations, Organization of Petroleum Exporting Countries (OPEC), and Organization of American States (OAS). However, there was no expression of anti-Americanism, except for a few open disagreements such as the status of Puerto Rico, the U.S. invasion of the Dominican Republic in 1965, and Washington's support for the United Kingdom against Argentina during the Falkland/Malvinas War in 1982.

As a matter of fact, only a few governmental institutions controlled relations between Venezuela and the United States until the final decade of the Punto Fijo period. On the one hand, these included the Venezuelan presidency, the Ministry of Foreign Affairs, and the Ministry of Energy and Mines; on the other, the U.S. Departments of State, Trade, Defense, and Energy. Nongovernmental contacts occurred only with the U.S. petroleum company representatives residing in Venezuela (although these diminished after the nationalization of the oil industry in 1976) and occasionally with lobbyists and academics in Washington and New York City. Few disagreements marred relations between the governments of Venezuela and the United States between 1958 and 1999. The most important involved the role of Venezuela in OPEC and Washington's unwillingness to support the Betancourt Doctrine (a policy of the Venezuelan government launched in the 1960s which called for condemnation of any coup d'état against an elected democratic government and expulsion from the OAS).

A greater distancing between the two countries developed during the first government of Rafael Caldera (1969–74), when Caldera publicly attacked the existing trade agreement between the United States and Venezuela. Caldera's government also established diplomatic relations with Communist countries, including the Soviet Union (relations between Moscow and Caracas had been suspended since 1952), and other socialist countries. During the first government of President Carlos Andrés Pérez (1974–79), Venezuela built on the Caldera policy of developing closer links with states in the Caribbean Basin and restored relations with Cuba. (Havana and Caracas broke relations in 1961, when Fidel Castro was attempting to subvert existing governments throughout the Caribbean Basin—including Venezuela's own elected government). Pérez became the first Venezuelan president to pursue relations with several third-world countries in Asia and Africa.

Venezuela and the United States drew closer in matters related to promoting democracy and human rights. Cooperation with its powerful northern neighbor appeared more feasible to Venezuela after the U.S. government accepted Venezuela's nationalization of its petroleum, gas, iron, and aluminum industries in 1975 and 1976. During this phase, Venezuelan presidents portrayed their country to policy makers in the United States as a democratic nation promoting democracy in the hemisphere and as a steady and reliable supplier of petroleum to the United States and Western Europe. This was the essential message of governments headed by Carlos Andrés Pérez, Luis Herrera Campíns (1979–84), and Jaime Lusinchi (1984–89).

The Decline of Punto Fijo: The Importance of the U.S.-Venezuelan Relationship

With the second administration of Carlos Andrés Pérez (1989–93), Venezuela's vaunted political stability began to deteriorate soon after Pérez's inauguration, when economic belt-tightening led to riots in ten cities. New political and economic realities in Venezuela influenced relations between Caracas and Washington. Pérez applied the economic policy of the moment, a package of neoliberal programs for economic development suggested by the International Monetary Fund and the World Bank, also known as the "Washington Consensus." These policies required measures to implement them which went against the operational characteristics of Venezuela's post-1958 representative democracy: clientelism, subsidization of consumption, and protectionism. This departure provoked a deeply negative reaction among the masses, the salaried middle class, managers of public corporations, and the owners of subsidized enterprises.

President Pérez decided to revive an activist multilateral foreign policy, similar to the one he pursued during his earlier term. To some extent this came at the expense of seeking closer links with the United States. Pérez practiced what came to be called the "two-hand policy." On the one hand, he positioned Venezuela to play a key role in the third-world community, pleading for closer north-south cooperation and trade. On the other hand, his foreign ministry promoted regionalism, expanded free trade, and supported democratization. The "two-hand" policy did not affect relations between Caracas and Washington. However, President Pérez's extended travels abroad in support of this policy led to growing irritation with him within Venezuela, as did the commitments into which he entered without consulting either his own political party or the national Congress. This domestic discontent was an important source of two unsuccessful coup attempts against the Pérez government during 1992 (C. Romero, 1998b).

Carlos Andrés Pérez departed the presidency before finishing his term, in May 1993, and an interim president, Ramón J. Velásquez, governed until February 1994. During these months, the United States openly showed its disapproval of military coups when antidemocratic forces broached the idea of a military government with policy makers in Washington. President William J. Clinton fully supported Velásquez's government until the interim president handed over power to his elected successor, in February 1994.

The second presidency of Rafael Caldera (1994–99) was marked by continuing gradually deteriorating relations between Caracas and Washington. Although no important strategic disagreements that would lead to a climate of confrontation or submission surfaced between the two countries, tactical differences crystallized. They appeared mostly in the trade arena, where Caldera, still considering Venezuela to be a privileged trade partner of the United States, maneuvered to maintain autonomy in the face of pressure from President Clinton to join the Free Trade Area of the Americas (FTAA). Caldera had strong reservations about the FTAA. He viewed it as a series of commercial integration policies based on the liberal economic principles of the Washington Consensus, and during the first half of his term in office, he attempted to restore the legitimacy of Punto Fijo democracy by reviving state control over the economy.

Additional tensions between the Caldera and Clinton administrations derived from Washington's backing of the candidacy of former Colombian president César Gaviria for the post of secretary general of the OAS. Caldera strongly supported the candidacy of his minister of foreign affairs, Miguel Angel Burelli Rivas. Caldera also moved closer to Brazil and went so far as to adopt Brazilian president Henrique Cardoso's position that South America would be better served by forging stronger regional trade links first (for instance, between the subregional trade blocs of Mercosur and the Andean Pact) and only then move toward economic integration with the United States, Mexico, and Canada. President Clinton viewed this position as one more signal of Venezuela's determination to drag its feet and resist meaningful economic integration into the FTAA. Rafael Caldera's alignment with Brazil was also intended to send the message that Caracas would not be an active participant in Washington's efforts to promote neoliberal reforms, the war against drug trafficking, and human rights as priorities in Latin America. In turn, President Clinton strongly criticized the human rights situation in Venezuela, and his administration restricted the import of certain Venezuelan products such as tuna fish, lead-free gasoline, and Orimulsión, a nonoil asphaltlike product. Venezuela countered by refusing the use of its airspace and territorial waters to American aircraft and ships.

Interaction between Venezuela and the United States continues to be influenced by both global and hemispheric changes. Nevertheless, for the United States, one element that remains constant in its relationship with Venezuela is that country's role as a vital source of petroleum, the most important source outside the volatile Middle East. The primacy of national security interests that underpin the importance for Washington of retaining Venezuela as a dependable source of petroleum, however, has been undercut since the 1990s by tensions related to other important issues. These include the environment; drug trafficking, terrorism, money laundering, intellectual property, and human rights.

From the perspective of a shared political vision, relations between Caracas and Washington appeared extremely cordial at the beginning of the 1990s. The reservations about U.S. intentions which prevailed among the political elites that crafted post-1958 democracy had given way to a more pragmatic view of the relationship with the United States. This accommodation did not entail uncritical acceptance of American culture or capitalism, and political leaders shared an attitude of guarded resistance to U.S. influence in the business and academic sectors. Nevertheless, Venezuelan policy makers found a way to combine the populism of AD and COPEI with a mixed capitalist-socialist system that accepted private property, gave an important role to business in national economic development, protected political freedom, and moved toward the rule of law.

Economic relations expanded during the Punto Fijo era, and by the end of the twentieth century, the United States consumed 50 percent of all Venezuelan exports. U.S. goods made up 45 percent of Venezuela's total imports. This placed Venezuela as Washington's third most important trading partner in Latin America (preceded by Mexico and Brazil). In 1999, exports to the United States amounted to $11.3 billion (85% were oil and oil products). Imports were valued at $5.4 billion (Toro Hardy, 2000). Venezuela's publicly owned oil company, Petróleos de Venezuela Sociedad Anónima (PDVSA; Venezuelan Oil Company, Incorporated) enjoyed solid business relations with U.S. companies, with investments in the United States worth more than $7 billion and one strong fuel distributor on the East Coast, CITGO. U.S. banks also held deposits from Venezuelans estimated to exceed US$125 billion.

The U.S. government also exerts influence in Venezuela through its large Military Assistance Group, a diverse team of army, air force, and navy personnel which regularly trains its Venezuelan counterparts. Other actors (the political parties, civic groups, professionals, and the population in general) seek contacts with Americans and favor good relations with the United States. The most notable exception to this pattern is in cultural circles where diverse points of view exist, including rabid anti-Americanism. In other words, at the end of the twentieth century, populist and corporatist criticism of neoliberal capitalism had given way to ideals associated with democracy as practiced in the United States. These included the need for transparency in government, free market economics, individualist democracy, and civil society (Bigler, 1981; Kelly and Romero, 2002; Myers, 1993).

The traditional bilateral exchanges conducted exclusively by governments declined in importance during the 1990s. Groups in Venezuelan civil society had become more important, and they were developing ties with their counterparts in the United States and Western Europe. In addition, the Venezuelan private sector went beyond oil-related commerce and established trade relations with American partners. The presence of Venezuelan businesspeople in the United States created a counter to the long-held image of the "typical" Venezuelan immigrant (married to American citizens or an occasional highly skilled citizen looking for better opportunities). In other words, since the mid-1980s there have been growing numbers of a new kind of Venezuelan immigrant to the United States: blue- and white-collar workers, students, artists, academics, and nongovernmental organization employees.

Within Venezuela, U.S. economic influence has remained strong despite current political events. The presence of U.S. executives continues to shape the tenor of business transactions, especially in areas relating to the petroleum industry but also in commercial ventures intended to develop the different regions of the country (Ministry of Foreign Affairs, Libro Amarillo, 1959–99). In addition, the U.S. Embassy in Caracas still promotes technical assistance to Venezuela's public sector and exchanges in the arts, humanities, social sciences, and technology. Educational institutes based in the United States have opened centers in many of Venezuela's large cities, and these institutions promote the study of the English language and modern marketing techniques. American-style consumer behavior has become common among the middle class. This socialization has added layers of complexity to Venezuela-U.S. relations. Gone is the old dichotomy between those who view the United States as a model and ally and those who consider it dangerous and corrupting.

The Fifth Republic and the United States

Following Hugo Chávez's assumption of the presidency in February 1999, Venezuelan foreign and domestic policy set out in directions that the U.S. government viewed with skepticism. The first concern centered on open participation in policy making by an important faction of the armed forces.

Washington was uneasy with the leftist orientation of this faction and feared that its leaders lacked a firm commitment to democracy and free enterprise. This introduced an element of instability which policy makers in the Clinton and Bush administrations viewed as unfriendly to investment by national and foreign capitalists. New departures taken by President Hugo Chávez also threatened to interrupt the steady supply of Venezuelan oil to the North Atlantic, to intensify anti–United States cooperation with pariah states like Iraq and Iran, and to strengthen the Fuerzas Armadas Revolucionarias de Colombia (FARC; Revolutionary Army of Colombia) insurgents in Colombia.

The growing complexity of relations between the United States and Venezuela did not eliminate the apprehension that many Venezuelans felt toward U.S. culture and power. It is no secret that President Hugo Chávez attempted to reduce U.S. influence in his country. He envisioned a revitalized Venezuelan culture that would return to its Bolivarian roots and serve as a nationalistic beacon for all of Latin America. However, Chávez insisted that his government did not want confrontation with the United States but rather sought cordial relations within a climate of selective cooperation and mutual respect. In the first eighteen months of the Chávez government, U.S. ambassador John Maisto seldom responded to the president's periodic outbursts of anti-Americanism, implementing the Clinton administration's policy of "wait and see." In other words, the United States hoped to retain the cordiality that characterized relations between the two countries as long as the Chávez government respected the rule of law and the personal integrity and property of American citizens in Venezuela, abstained from nationalizing American businesses, and remained a secure source of petroleum for the United States (Kelly and Romero, 2002).

President Chávez pursued policies that sometimes flew in the face of the conditions for cordial relations laid out by the Clinton and Bush administrations. Examples abound. Venezuela opposed the American position (reiterated in 1999, 2000, and 2001) that condemned Cuba's violation of its citizens' human rights. President Chávez also refused to join the United States in condemning similar violations by the governments of China and Iraq, and he condemned the "occupation" of Kosovo by the United Nations in 1999 and the U.S. war in Iraq in 2003. Within the OAS, Venezuela promoted the concept of "participatory democracy" and opposed efforts by the U.S. government to use the OAS to make representative democracy the hemispheric standard. To summarize, Chávez articulated foreign policies that differed from those pursued by his predecessors; these included initiatives that were more egalitarian, anti–status quo, and laced with rhetoric that supported third-world claims against the industrial countries.

Foreign policy differences between the United States and Venezuela became more acute during 2001. At the center of this widening breach was President Chávez's commitment to strengthening multipolar tendencies within the international community. This commitment found expression in Venezuela's rapprochement with Cuba and China and in its promotion of a hemispheric security system without the United States, as described later in this chapter. Other Chávez initiatives designed to dilute U.S. influence included moving Venezuela into a leadership position in OPEC, publicly expressing support for some goals of the Colombian insurgents, and slowing efforts to implement free trade within the Western Hemisphere. For its part the United States began to voice "doubts" over the state of democracy in Venezuela's Fifth Republic and concerns about its leftward drift.

The Chávez economic policy retained the mixed state-market policies of Punto Fijo governments while giving them stronger populist overtones. These overtones took the form of programs in which the national government directly distributed resources, especially in poor neighborhoods. Distributions were portrayed as the honest and just use of Venezuela's petroleum wealth, a marked contrast to the corruption and cronyism that permeated policy implementation by previous governments. Not surprisingly, President Chávez brought in a new group of leaders to allocate resources.

Hugo Chávez appeared to relish the role of *enfant terrible* in Latin American international politics as he finished the third year of his presidency. His witty remarks, populist promises, and love of the "photo opportunity" created a hyperactive style of diplomacy, but it yielded few tangible results. He continued to stir the foreign policy pot in ways that exacerbated tensions, especially between the United States and its southern neighbors, but his ultimate intentions remained unclear. Chávez's most vehement opponents raised the specter of subversive Bolivarian revolutions that would sweep away existing governments from Bolivia to Colombia, an alarmist scenario intended to cause consternation in Washington. Specifically, the Chávez government drew Washington's ire when it sheltered the fugitive intelligence chief (Vladimiro Montesinos) of Peru's ousted president, Alberto Fujimori (Ewell, 1996; Kelly and Romero, 2002; A. Romero, 1988; C. Romero, 1986).

The issues that separate Bolivarian Venezuela and George Bush's America are complex. One part of the equation is Venezuela's independent, ambivalent, and sometimes hostile position toward post-1988 U.S. initiatives that promote Latin American economic integration. Another involves ongoing issues with histories that extend back in time over decades: trade restrictions, Venezuelan dependency on commerce with the United States, terms for the payment of Venezuela's external debt, and the magnitude of Venezuelan capital flight to New York and other U.S. financial centers (Cardozo de Da Silva, 1992; Guerón, 1983; Martz and Myers, 1977; Petrásh, 2000). The public's sensitivity toward these matters is a relatively recent development. Until the early 1990s oil and democracy monopolized Venezuelan foreign policy concerns. Foreign policy making was the exclusive prerogative of the president and his ministers of foreign affairs and energy. Only in the rare instances when defense of the national boundaries became a major issue was a broader spectrum of interests mobilized into the foreign policy arena (Guerón, 1992). Even the national Congress generally remained on the periphery. This changed during the second Pérez government, spurred by the president's efforts to transform the national economy and to integrate Venezuela into the global capitalist system. By the turn of the century, there was greater participation in foreign policy making by the legislative branch of government and a higher public awareness of the foreign policy choices open to the Venezuelan government (A. Romero, 1997).

President Chávez's public attitude toward the United States has been contradictory. On the one hand, he has shown respect and even admiration for the United States and its political system. Chávez sent a gracious congratulatory message to president-elect George W. Bush after one of the most divisive elections in American political history. In this communication, the Venezuelan president congratulated the American people for the good functioning of their democratic institutions and stressed Venezuela's determination "to forge close links and work together, within the framework of international law, to achieve peace, human rights and prosperity in this region of the world" (Caracas Practicará Política, 2000, 1:4). During his visit to Puerto Rico to attend the inauguration of Governor Sila María Calderón, President Chávez avoided any direct reference to the issue of Puerto Rico's independence and downplayed the clash between San Juan and Washington over the future of the U.S. military base in Vieques. Although he did state that Puerto Rico should "make its own decisions," he also characterized Vieques as an issue internal to the evolving relationship between Puerto Rico and the United States. President Chávez also used the occasion of his visit to Puerto Rico to express his hope that the U.S. government would disregard the derogatory gossip about him and actually see him "as what [he is], a democratically elected president" (Presidente Chávez Ofrece su Apoyo, 2001, A:2).

On other occasions, Chávez has been more confrontational and has seemed to delight in challenging U.S. preeminence in the hemisphere. For example, soon after his reelection in mid-2000 he attempted to circumvent U.S. government policy in Colombia with an autonomous effort to mediate in the conflict between the government and the FARC guerrillas. Coolness in Washington toward this initiative led President Chávez to state openly that Venezuela would not support the U.S. military cooperation with Andrés Pastrana's government (Plan Colombia). His criticism centered on the plan's potential to change the military and strategic equilibrium in northern South America. Nevertheless, Venezuela's president stressed that his opposition to Plan Colombia did not imply lack of support for the Colombian governments' efforts to pacify the countryside (Márquez, 2000, A:2).

The Venezuelan government's curtailing of U.S. Navy overflights, rejection of help from the U.S. Navy during the December 1999 floods, and the disputes over fighting terrorism and the Colombia guerrillas all put stress on the bilateral military relationship. The Venezuelan government has been collaborative with the United States in drug-related matters but less friendly in issues such as the U.S. support to the Colombian government to fight guerrilla operations on the Colombian-Venezuelan border. In interpreting these stands, it is important to take into account Venezuela's long-standing resistance to outside intervention (Kelly and Romero, 2002).

Hugo Chávez's friendship with Fidel Castro made headlines in Venezuela, in the United States, and throughout the Western Hemisphere. During Castro's first official visit to Venezuela, October 26–30, 2000 (he had visited six times previously), the Cuban president praised the Venezuelan political process and the Bolivarian Revolution. He stated in public that if Cuba's revolution had thrived in a country located only ninety miles from the "Colossus of the North," Venezuela, land of heroes and Bolívar, would do even better with Chávez at the helm (Villegas Poljak, 2000, 1:2).

This lovefest with Castro evoked an editorial published in the *Washington Post* (The Next Fidel Castro, 2000) which called upon the next president of the United States to limit the chances for Chávez "to export his ideology." Negative reaction to this editorial prompted Secretary of State Madeleine Albright to deny that the Clinton administration equated Hugo Chávez with Fidel Castro; however, she expressed concern about some of the domestic procedures favored by Bolivarian revolutionaries (EE.UU. No Compara, 2000, A:2). Another editorial, published in the *New York Times* (The Ambitions of Hugo Chávez, 2000), attracted the attention of Venezuela's president. This article called upon the U.S. government to proceed cautiously with Chávez, who had chosen to become a powerful symbol of resistance against U.S. influence, but it also argued that Washington "should refrain from unnecessary confrontation." Taking this commentary to be less hostile, Hugo Chávez stated that Venezuela has "the obligation to maintain [its] relationship with the United States, [U.S.-Venezuela] relations are condemned to be good" (Casas, 2000, D:1). Good relations have been the pattern observed in recent times.

Hugo Chávez and his Bolivarians professed to see no incompatibility between maintaining good relations with Washington and seeking to reduce U.S. influence throughout Latin America. In November 2000, the Venezuelan government released a position paper dealing with hemispheric security ("El Comportamiento Militar Latinoamericano y la Seguridad Hemisférica, Ministerio de la Defensa de la República Bolivariana de Venezuela, 2000"). The Ministry of Defense distributed this document during the summit of Latin American defense ministers (Manaus, Brazil, October 2000). The Defense Ministry's position paper explained that beginning in 1823 (the year that the United States proclaimed the Monroe Doctrine), it was possible to identify the rise of militarism in the foreign policy of the United States. U.S. militarism paved the way for "territorial expansion, military conquest and the construction of an American community according to their views." The position paper also called for implementing a new concept of hemispheric security, one that would set all nation-states on equal political footing. It would also create mechanisms for cooperative action designed not only for times of crisis but also to deal with ongoing problems. Finally, the Defense Ministry position paper called for the elimination of the Inter-American Treaty of Reciprocal Assistance, which it labeled "outdated" (Soto, 2000b, A:2), and for the creation of a confederation of Latin American armed forces, without the participation of the United States.

Shortly after the summit in Manaus the international media published a comment attributed to Peter Romero, the outgoing U.S. assistant secretary of state for Latin America. In that statement, Romero supposedly linked the Chávez government, Colombia's FARC guerrillas, and several other insurgencies that were simmering throughout Andean America. President Chávez responded with indignation over what he characterized as interference by the U.S. government in Venezuela's internal affairs. The Clinton State Department dismissed Romero's allegations of ties between the Chávez government and South American insurgents as the unauthorized ruminations of a single individual and instructed its new ambassador to Caracas, Donna Hrinak, to state publicly that Washington desired closer relations with the Chávez government in order to advance an agenda of cooperation and increased exchanges (Soto, 2000a, E:3).

In the multilateral arena, Bolivarian Venezuela has assumed a militant role within OPEC which included the adoption of pricing strategies with a high probability of increasing friction with the U.S. government (Kelly and Romero, 2002).

The cumulative effect of all these events was to create a frosty environment for U.S.-Venezuela relations. This extended to Chávez government policies in both the domestic and foreign policy arenas, especially in the areas of civil-military relations and in the exercise of U.S. influence throughout Latin America. President Chávez's redefinition of internal security in ways that facilitated political and civic participation by the military flew in the face of official Washington's preference for civilian control over the military. In addition, Venezuelan opponents of this policy found support for their position among nongovernmental groups in the United States. In the foreign policy arena, the Chávez government's antagonism toward Plan Colombia encouraged Colombia's FARC insurgents, angered the Colombian government, and challenged a cornerstone of Washington's Caribbean Basin policy. In this context, calls for eliminating the Inter-American Treaty of Reciprocal Assistance only confirmed the U.S. government's view of Chávez as obstructionist and annoying.

President George W. Bush's prioritization of the FTAA in early 2001 elevated the importance of a policy arena marked by long-simmering disagreement between the U.S. government and Venezuela. During the Summit of the Americas (Quebec, April 2001), Venezuela again became the dissenting voice, the only state to sign the final declaration with "reservations." The Venezuelan government's main objections were to provisions that committed signatories to promote representative democracy and which set January 2005 as the date for concluding free trade negotiations. President Chávez went out of his way trumpet his preference for direct democracy over representative democracy. (He also pointed out that Venezuela's 1999 constitution adopted a different emphasis in regard to human rights and civil-military relations.) In addition, the Venezuelan president refused to abandon his often stated preference for public sector intervention and state control over economic activity. Still, President Chávez muted his opposition to the emerging Quebec consensus. He viewed the FTAA as peripheral to Venezuela's core interests, which he considered to be more closely intertwined with actions that could be taken in cooperation with fellow members of OPEC. Venezuela eventually agreed to the Quebec Declaration, but the grudging manner in which President Chávez signed it intensified doubts as to his real commitment toward the FTAA (C. Romero, 2001).

U.S. reservation toward Hugo Chávez clearly surfaced in the Bush administration's ambivalent attitude toward the coup that on April 11, 2002, led to his replacement by an interim government headed by Caracas businessman Pedro Carmona Estanga. For a brief moment, Washington appeared supportive of the Carmona government and failed to condemn the ouster, but when, after less than thirty-six hours, loyal officers restored Chávez to the presidency, the United States reversed itself quickly. In the aftermath of these events elements in the international media and others suspicious of the Bush administration attempted to find connections between the coup's perpetrators and the U.S. government. Conspiracy theorists pointed out that in addition to earlier cited differences, President Bush himself had been appalled by Chávez's weak responses to the September terrorist attacks on New York and Washington and by his criticism of the military campaign that displaced the Taliban government in Afghanistan. It was also common knowledge that numerous opponents of the Venezuelan president, including some who had been at the center of the Carmona government, had made the rounds of official Washington in the months immediately preceding the coup. Nevertheless, the preponderance of evidence suggests that the Bush administration refused to be involved in any coup against Venezuela's popularly elected president.

Most U.S. Embassy and State Department personnel appear to have been supportive, at least in their hearts and minds, of constitutional processes that would have replaced President Chávez. The model held up in private conversations with them is the one that produced a satisfactory outcome in Peru, following the fraudulent elections of 2000 (resignation of the president, appointment of a new chief executive by the national legislature, respect for the judiciary, and preservation of regional and local governments). Still, the U.S. government did approve the OAS resolution condemning the April 11 coup attempt and issued no other official opinion on the matter. This measured reaction to those calamitous events suggests that Washington viewed relations with Caracas as too important to allow provocateurs of any persuasion to force precipitous intervention into Venezuela's internal political quarrels. It was observed during the December 2002–January 2003 strike and the PDVSA workers' strike that the U.S. government stayed "on the corner" watching the events and repeating its commitment to look for a political and democratic solution to the Venezuelan crisis. It was also seen in the same attitude toward the Tripartite Working Group sponsoring of the Mesa negotiations and agreements between the Chávez government and the opposition.[1] The U.S. government remarked that a political solution could be found only through the electoral route, specifically the constitutional provision for a presidential recall referendum. The same behavior was seen in the U.S. participation in the Group of Friends of Venezuela.[2] Nevertheless, the Bush administration remained dissatisfied with Hugo Chávez's government and would shed few tears were the president to be removed from power by democratic means.

Conclusions

Venezuela's relations with the United States have led some analysts to emphasize a bilateral perspective and others to focus on operational characteristics of the geopolitical region (Western Hemisphere) which both share. Bilateralists stress Venezuela's attributes as a middle-size power able to cooperate with the United States in certain joint endeavors. Regionalists portray Venezuela as a country pursuing a constrained agenda in close proximity to the planet's only superpower. Both ascribe the autonomy that Caracas enjoys to its oil wealth and recent democratic history. Further, both agree that Venezuela's status as an autonomous regional power depends in large measure on acquiescence by the United States (Ewell, 1996; Lanza, 1980). Most Venezuelan foreign policy makers have longed to convert their country's dependence to a special relationship with the United States.

This research finds that Venezuela, despite its best efforts, has never been accepted as a special partner by the United States. Neither in the past nor in the present, even when Washington has recognized the strategic value of access to Venezuela's natural resources, have United States policy makers accorded Venezuela the special status that it desires. The U.S. government has long crafted its Latin American policy based on calculations derived from the global balance of power. From this perspective European considerations received highest priority, followed by developments in Asia. Latin America has occupied (perhaps) third place, and even within this context Venezuela's importance usually has been secondary. This calculation has led to relative neglect, which in turn has been an important factor in the ability of Caracas to adopt policies, from time to time, that run counter to U.S. interests.

Recent polls of mass opinion reveal that the attitude shared by most Venezuelans toward the United States is situational—neither aggressively hostile nor uncritically positive. When the perception of participation in a mutually beneficial venture predominates, attitudes toward the United States and Americans are positive. But when the U.S. government is seen as unilaterally imposing its policies on Venezuelans, attitudes turn negative. This pattern was also observed during the 2003 Iraq war. The Venezuelan government's reaction to the war and the Venezuelan opposition efforts to link Iraq and Venezuela in the eyes of the White House did not provoke an important political dispute among Venezuelans. As a matter of fact, traditional anti-Americanism prevailed among the masses, and a pro-American attitude prevailed only in the higher circles and in a part of the middle classes (Kelly and Romero, 2002; Myers, 1993). Finally, for most Venezuelans, it is "a matter of honor" not to "latinize" their country's status vis-à-vis the United States. In other words, Venezuelans never want their powerful northern neighbor to take them for granted (Toro Hardy, 2000).

Since the 1930s, relations between Venezuela and the United States have "floated" on oil, specifically the capability of the former to supply crude to the American market. It is the only issue area in which Venezuela enjoys a special status in Washington. A consensus exists among economic and political elites in the United States to reduce dependence on oil supplied from beyond the hemisphere. This leads to Venezuela's occupying a relatively favored place when the U.S. government provides incentives for overseas investment, trade, and cooperation. Thus, during President Clinton's 1997 visit to Caracas he signed a treaty committing Venezuela and the United States to increase cooperation in developing renewable energy sources, efficiently using nonrenewable energy, and exploring for natural gas (C. Romero, 1998a).

Important departures have reshaped Venezuelan foreign policy since the inauguration of President Hugo Chávez. These begin with the pursuit of closer links to states that have resisted U.S. influence (China, Cuba, Libya, Iraq, and Iran) and assumption of a leadership role within OPEC. Chávez has continued to support production cuts to raise prices, whereas the United States has tried to convince OPEC that it should increase production quotas to lower prices. Venezuela promoted the idea within OPEC that the group should hold firm because neither the United States nor Europe should complain so much about higher prices, given that a large part of what consumers pay for gasoline, especially in Europe, takes the form of their own governments' taxes on petroleum imports. Chávez's government reverted to the traditional stance of OPEC loyalty and high prices at the expense of production, creating the first current quarrel between the two countries.

A second current quarrel is based on Chávez's reaction to the Iraq war of 2003. The Venezuelan government did not deliver any statement on the war and refused to support Hussein. Nevertheless, some pro-government political leaders, congresspeople, and decision makers did not hide their sympathies for the Iraqi government. Strategic concerns of the United States became evident with its lack of reaction to the PDVSA strike and the dismissal of more than eighteen thousand workers in early 2003, during the buildup to the Iraq war. The U.S. government did not issue a specific statement on the worker dismissals, although some American human rights advocates and journalists did. In this case, the White House appeared to be acting globally, prioritizing its access to Venezuelan oil supplies over human rights concerns.

Closer to home, under Chávez Venezuela has lobbied for hemispheric security institutions that exclude the United States, opened contacts with the insurgencies in progress throughout the Andean region as well as leftist movements, and remained aloof from President Bush's War on Terrorism. This suggests that Chávez's government is more broadly active than its predecessors. Caracas no longer assumes multiple identities depending on the arena but consistently presents itself as an oil-rich, third-world militant. Helping to promote this image, the United Nations provides Venezuela with a prestigious, high-profile forum in which it can project this "progressive" image and promote third-world causes (Fishbach, 2000). At the OAS, Venezuela has rejected United States–sponsored initiatives to transform that regional organization into the hemisphere's guarantor of democracy and human rights, the supervisor of internal electoral mechanisms and electoral observation missions, and the institution that defines and supervises the role of nongovernmental organizations (Perina, 2000). The Chávez government also has restricted participation by Venezuela's armed forces in the Inter-American military cooperation system. These policies have added to the freeze that was engulfing relations between Venezuela and the United States in 2003.

The points of contention, then, in relations between the United States and Venezuela appear at three levels: global, hemispheric, and bilateral. In terms of the global arena, Caracas and Washington hold distinct visions of how international politics should be conducted and structured. These differences often lead policy makers in the two countries to pursue goals that are incompatible and conflictual. Venezuela under Chávez promotes a multipolar world order in which no power acts alone. The United States, in contrast, insists on latitude to pursue its interests unilaterally or in concert with its allies. Chávez preaches adherence to the principle of nonintervention. The United States under George W. Bush remains determined to intervene in other countries for a multiplicity of purposes: humanitarian, legal, and diplomatic, as well as to promote democracy (Perina, 2000).

Regionally, Venezuela and the United States agree on the need for cooperation to stimulate economic development and political freedom in the Western Hemisphere, but they disagree on the measures for reaching these goals. Under Chávez, Caracas holds to the principle of nonintervention. Washington's push for strengthening representative political institutions is especially annoying to the Bolivarians, who view direct democracy as superior to the system that prevails in the United States and Western Europe. In a related matter Venezuela has expressed increasing unhappiness with pressures, coordinated by Washington, to accept unregulated participation by international election monitors. To summarize, the United States prioritizes the internal dangers faced by democratic regimes in the Western Hemisphere (from corruption, electoral fraud, and human rights violations), whereas Chávez perceives mainly external threats to the sovereignty of Latin American states (from savage capitalism, economic dependence, and unconstrained military intervention by the United States).

The bilateral dimension of relationships between Venezuela and the United States has been more conflictual since February 1999, when Hugo Chávez assumed the presidency. Analogous to the tensions that permeate relations centering on hemispheric policy, the Chávez government has voiced concern over the influence that the U.S. government and private U.S. citizens exert within Venezuela. These concerns center on efforts to assure electoral transparency, respect for civil rights and the right to dissent, and an important role for private enterprise in the national economy. U.S. concerns centering on Venezuelan foreign policy relate to the president's reservations with Plan Colombia, ambivalence toward the FARC insurgency, use of OPEC to increase petroleum prices, and efforts to exclude Washington from hemispheric security institutions (Petrásh, 2000). Before the events of April 11–14, 2002, a consensus was growing in Venezuela and the United States that President Chávez was taking positions on a broad range of foreign policy and domestic issues that would increase tensions between Caracas and Washington.

It remains to be seen whether the events of April 11–14 will lead Presidents Chávez and Bush to assign a high priority to improving relations between their two countries. In late May 2002 the White House sent a high-level diplomat to Caracas for the purpose of urging President Chávez to seek international mediation to heal the breach that had opened in Venezuelan society between supporters and opponents of his Bolivarian Revolution, and the United States subsequently supported the mediation efforts of the OAS, Carter Center, and United Nations Development Programme (UNDP) Tripartite Group. However, the most militant Bolivarians remained opposed to compromise, and their intransigence conjured up images of Cuba in the early 1960s, when Fidel Castro used the "you are pro-American" excuse to debilitate the democratic opposition, cover up administrative failures, and centralize power.

The prospects for a rapprochement with the U.S. government were dubious given the long list of unresolved issues and opposing views that have crept into relations between the two countries. For its part, the United States remained unsure about the meaning of the changes in Venezuela for its own vital interests. Although Venezuela was not a primary concern within the U.S. political scheme, Bush's new doctrine of national security and the return of the geopolitical thinking in the White House were likely to affect bilateral relations. In fact, by 2001 the "wait and see" policy had already turned to a "suspicious minds" policy, and it had the potential to be transformed into a "do the right thing" policy in terms of pressure from within Venezuela to reestablish normal strategic coincidences.

On the other hand, there was reason for optimism that many important relationships between Venezuela and the United States would persist and grow stronger. What happens between the two countries is no longer the exclusive domain of the White House and the Palacio de Miraflores. Interaction between private interests and individuals intensified during Venezuela's post-1958 democratic regime, and those relationships are proving highly resilient. Commerce between Venezuela and the United States remains strong, and many Venezuelans currently visit, reside in, or try to stay illegally in the United States. New York City's financial community is still the most likely source of foreign capital for developing Venezuela. Important connections exist between the media of the two countries. Venezuelan entrepreneurs play a dominant role in UNIVISION, the most important Spanish-language television network in the United States. Finally, strong cultural and professional ties unite the middle classes of the two countries, and these ties provide multiple avenues for cooperative activities in the future.

'APTER EIGHT

The Unraveling of Venezuela's Party System

From Party Rule to Personalistic Politics and Deinstitutionalization

José E. Molina

The political transformations through which Venezuela passed in the last decade of the twentieth century included, along with the other changes examined in this volume, a profound change in its system of political parties. The mid-1990s system of national political parties, like its immediate predecessor, had roots in the 1940s. However, the post-1993 party system differs dramatically from the configuration that persisted between 1973 and 1993. That earlier system crystallized as the consequence of agreements in 1958, 1959, and 1960 between political and economic elites. The most important of these agreements, one discussed at length throughout this volume, is the Pact of Punto Fijo.[1]

This chapter examines the evolution of Venezuela's Punto Fijo party system, the factors that facilitated its emergence, its consolidation, and its unraveling. This trajectory holds vital keys for understanding the post-1993 party system and its implications for democratic stability and governability. Understanding what happened to the party system after 1993 is especially important for identifying how and why Hugo Chávez Frías's Bolivarian Revolution triumphed, which movements were viable alternatives, and which may yet emerge as effective challengers. Finally, this account locates changes in Venezuela's party system within contemporary theorizing about party systems types and their consequences.

Modern analyses of party systems tend to focus on two dimensions that Sartori (1976) identified as basic: number of relevant parties and the ideological distance between them.[2] For Sartori (1976), the smaller the number of relevant parties in competitive systems and the smaller the ideological distance that separates them, the greater the political stability and the higher the quality of democracy. Based on these two dimensions, Sartori (1976: 131–216) classified competitive party systems in four types: *predominant-party system, two-party system, moderate pluralism,* and *polarized pluralism.*[3]

Following Mainwaring (1999: 21–60) and Mainwaring and Scully (1995:1), I add a third dimension to this analysis, level of institutionalization. For these scholars a political party system is more or less institutionalized to the extent that its component parties achieve permanence over time, with stable electoral weight; exhibit significant penetration of the society that they seek to represent; and possess solid organizations. The aspects of the party system which determine the extent of its institutionalization, then, are stability, social penetration, legitimacy, and organizational strength (Mainwaring, 1999: 21–60).

Mainwaring (1999: 321–41) argues that the level of institutionalization is a critical variable for understanding how party systems shape the political system and effect democratic stability in developing countries, especially in Latin America. Mainwaring (1999: 22–39) situates political party systems on a continuum having one pole at which the systems are weakly institutionalized (fluid), characterized by high electoral volatility, and composed of individual parties that have minimal social penetration, low legitimacy, and weak organizations (for example, Ecuador, Peru, and Brazil). Highly institutionalized party systems cluster at the other end of the continuum. They exhibit low electoral volatility, and their component parties enjoy high social penetration, elevated legitimacy, and solid organizations (such as Costa Rica, and Venezuela from 1973 until the 1993 elections). For Mainwaring (1999: 322–28), the higher the level of institutionalization, the greater will be the stability and quality of the democracy. A higher quality of democracy provides fewer possibilities of personalism and populism and greater continuity in public policies.

For the Venezuelan case it is especially important, when analyzing the level of institutionalization, to take into account the characteristics of party systems that have attained a high level of institutionalization and subsequently enter into a process of decomposition which transforms them (in Mainwaring's [1999] terminology) into unstable or fluid systems. This is the hallmark of systems that have undergone "deinstitutionalization," a process in which the traits that signified institutionalization have seriously eroded. The thesis of this chapter is that there are important differences, ones that will be discussed at length, between a party system that was never institutionalized and one that experienced institutionalization and subsequently underwent a process of deinstitutionalization, as with the Venezuela's post-1958 configuration. Mainwaring has identified the consequences with respect to democratic stability, and the party system in general, which are associated with the differences between highly institutionalized and weakly institutionalized party systems. Drawing on the Venezuelan case, this chapter discusses and analyzes the characteristics and impact of a specific type of weakly institutionalized party system, one that has experienced deinstitutionalization.

The Evolution of the Party System prior to the Pact of Punto Fijo

Political Movements Predating the First Democratic Government (October 1945)

In Venezuela, as in the rest of Latin America during the nineteenth century, the liberal and conservative political movements dominated partisan politics until they were buried by the dictatorship of Juan Vicente Gómez (1908–35). They responded to the social divisions that characterized the process of national construction after the war for independence.

The post-1935 liberalization ushered in a political opening that gave rise to political parties that dominated Venezuela for more than half a century, until the national elections of 1993. Most important were Acción Democrática (AD; Democratic Action) and Comité de Organización Política Electoral Independiente: Partido Social Cristiano (COPEI; Committee of Independent Electoral Political Organization: Social Christian Party). The former, a social democratic party founded in 1941, was led by professionals who rose to prominence in the student revolts of 1928. The latter, a Christian Democratic party, was founded in 1946. In the beginning, these two rivals took their social and doctrinal cues from the cleavages between labor and capital and between church and state. AD represented workers and peasants, favored state intervention to improve their livelihood, and extended the party o[illegible]anization to the entire national territory. COPEI, on the other hand, c[illegible]n on the opposite side of these social, cultural, and political divisi[illegible] The Christian Democrats enjoyed their strongest support in th[illegible] And[illegible] states—Táchira, Mérida, and Trujillo, where the church retained [illegible] influence (Myers, 1977: 131). Andeans, especially natives of Tá[illegible], ruled Venezuela from 1899 until 1945, when General Medina Angari[illegible] was overthrown by an alliance of AD and young officers from the armed f[illegible]es.

Two other important political parties crystallized in the post-Gómez era, Partido Comunista de Venezuela (PCV; Venezuelan Communist Party) and Unión Republicana Democrática (URD; Democratic Republican Union). PCV lost out in the competition to organize workers and peasants, but it retained important pockets of support in the capital (Caracas) and in the western oil region (Zulia). URD was a populist grouping centered on the personality of Jóvito Villalba. Although PCV remained true to its Marxist roots, URD, like AD and COPEI, became a "catch-all" party (Kirchheimer, 1966; Myers, 1998). Ideological differences between the three all but disappeared.

Predominant-Party System (1945–1948)

The military coup of October 18, 1945, ushered in Venezuela's first democratic period, one dominated overwhelmingly by AD (Myers, 1980: 247). AD received more than 70 percent of the votes in each of the three elections that took place between 1946 and 1948 (constituent assembly, presidential/congressional, and municipal). For this reason, the political party system during this three-year interregnum (the Trienio) can be characterized as a predominant-party system (Molina and Pérez, 1996: 202), following the classification of Sartori (1976: 192). Three other parties gained representation in the national Congress: COPEI, URD, and PCV; however, the central confrontation pitted AD against COPEI. This confrontation led to a high level of polarization within a fragile institutional framework (Levine, 1973).

Disagreement centered on the role of the state in the economy and on setting the curriculum in education. AD, especially in the eyes of its adversaries, loomed as intensely pro-state, determined to organize the political system along socialist lines and intent on creating a state monopoly of the educational process. This placed the party on a collision course with the Roman Catholic Church.

... political party system of this period was highly polarized and weakly institutionalized. The adversaries of mass-based politics took advantages of these vulnerabilities in 1948 when they mounted a coup to end the Trienio.

AD had succeeded in becoming the dominant political party during the Trienio because of its success in playing on two popular themes: the sociopolitical aspirations of organized labor and the peasantry on the one hand and the encompassing societal desire for democracy on the other. The leaders of AD displayed great organizational skill in establishing neighborhood party organizations throughout Venezuela. They also formed party cells among organized workers and peasants. Nevertheless, the imposition of Marcos Pérez Jiménez's dictatorship in 1948 and migration from the countryside undid many of the AD and COPEI party networks, thus preventing loyalties that had been being forged during the 1940s from consolidating. Had that support solidified, a predominant-party system, similar to the one of the 1945–48 democratic interlude, might have resurfaced at the end of the military regime. Instead, although the political parties that surfaced following the overthrow of General Pérez Jiménez were the very ones of the Trienio, events in the late 1950s quickly demonstrated that political space now existed for personalistic leadership and new organizations.

The Punto Fijo Era: Institutionalization of the Party System

Moderate Pluralism Party System in the Process of Institutionalizing (1958–1973)

On January 23, 1958, a broad-based movement overthrew Pérez Jiménez's dictatorship. This movement encompassed all basic sectors of national life, beginning with the four political parties of the transitional Patriotic Committee (Junta Patriótica): AD, COPEI, URD, and PCV. It also included the church, the unions, the private sector, and the greater part of the military officer corps in the armed forces. The victors immediately restored civil and political liberties, and they scheduled elections for December of that year. The post-1958 party system and its component political parties displayed a low level of institutionalization. The incipient party system of the Trienio, itself never fully institutionalized, had decayed because of political persecution and social changes. Between 1958 and 1973, the Venezuelan political party system exhibited a high level of electoral instability, reflecting a low level of party system

Table 8.1. Legislative Election Results, 1947–1993 (parties' share of the vote as a percentage)

	1947	1958	1963	1968	1973	1978	1983	1988	1993
AD	70.83	49.45	32.71	25.55	44.44	39.68	49.90	43.24	23.34
COPEI	16.95	15.20	20.81	24.03	30.24	39.80	28.68	31.06	22.62
MAS	—	—	—	—	5.30	6.16	5.74	10.14[a]	10.81
MIR	—	—	—	—	1.00	2.35	1.58	—	—
URD	4.34	26.76	17.38	9.25	3.20	1.68	1.91	1.44	0.56
PCV	3.65	6.23	—	2.82[b]	1.20	1.04	1.75	0.96	0.45
LCR	—	—	—	—	—	—	0.54	1.65	20.68
MEP	—	—	—	12.94	4.97	2.23	1.96	1.61	0.59
Convergencia	—	—	—	—	—	—	—	—	13.84
FDP	—	—	9.59	5.29	1.24	0.25	—	—	—
IPFN/FND	—	—	13.36	2.61	0.24	—	—	—	—
CCN	—	—	—	10.93	4.31	0.20	—	—	—
Others	4.23	2.36	6.15	6.58	3.86	6.61	7.94	9.90	7.11
Turnout	74%	92%	91%	94%	96%	88%	88%	82%	60%

Source: Consejo Supremo Electoral (1987, 1990, 1994).

[a] In 1988, the parties MAS and MIR formed an electoral alliance.

[b] In 1968, the Venezuelan Communist Party participated under the name Unión Para Avanzar (UPA).

institutionalization. Although this allowed for the rise and fall of new political groups, AD and COPEI managed to reestablish competition between them as the principal axis of political confrontation, just as it had been in the Trienio (see tables 8.1 and 8.2).

The number of relevant political parties during this period, based on voting in national congressional elections, was within the general framework of low fragmentation and limited pluralism (Sartori, 1976: 127): four in the elections of 1958 (AD, COPEI, URD, and PCV), five in the elections of 1963 (AD, COPEI, URD, Fuerza Democrática Popular [FDP; Popular Democratic Force], and Frente Nacional Democrático [FND; National Democratic Front]), and five in the elections of 1968 (AD, COPEI, Movimiento Electoral del Pueblo [MEP; Electoral Movement of the People], Cruzada Cívica Nacionalista [CCN; Nationalist Civic Crusade], and URD).[4] The effective number of parties (N) was 3.1 for 1958, 4.8 for 1963, and 6.1 for 1968 (Laakso and Taagepera, 1979).

With regard to the second dimension of party systems, ideological distance, the polarized ideological conflict that marked competition between the political parties of the Trienio moderated when they faced each other in the post–Pérez Jiménez electoral arena. Perhaps the most important developments as a consequence of this moderation were a series of formal and informal agreements—the Pact of Punto Fijo—entered into during 1958 by AD, COPEI, and

Table 8.2. *Presidential Election Results, 1947–1993 (parties' share of the vote as a percentage)*

	1947	1958	1963	1968	1973	1978	1983	1988	1993
AD	74.47	49.18	32.81	27.64	48.65	43.30	55.38	52.75	23.23
COPEI	22.40	15.18	20.18	28.68	35.35	45.28	32.66	40.08	22.11
URD	—	30.67	17.50	11.82	3.07	1.07	1.30	0.69	0.59
PCV	3.12	3.23	—	—	0.69	0.55	1.02	0.34	0.34
MAS	—	—	—	—	3.71	4.70	3.81	2.71	10.59
LCR	—	—	—	—	—	—	0.09	0.37	21.95
MEP	—	—	—	17.35	4.38	1.10	1.12	0.39	0.49
FDP	—	—	9.43	6.46	0.80	0.16	—	—	—
IPFN/FND	—	—	16.08	3.55	0.14	—	—	—	—
Convergencia	—	—	—	—	—	—	—	—	17.03
Others	—	1.74	4.00	4.50	3.21	3.84	4.17	2.67	3.67
Turnout	74%	92%	91%	94%	96%	88%	88%	82%	60%

Source: Consejo Supremo Electoral (1987, 1990, 1994).

Notes: The figures indicate the vote for the party. In some cases several parties supported the same presidential candidate. The party coalitions that supported a common presidential candidate were the following (coalitions that obtained less than 2 percent of the national vote are excluded):

1958—URD/PCV/MENI; COPEI/PST/IR
1963—URD/PSV/MENI
1968—AD/API/AIR/OPIR; COPEI/MDI; MEP/PRIN/OPINA; URD/FND/FDP/MENI
1973—AD/PRN; COPEI/FDP/MPJ/IP; MAS/MIR; MEP/PCV
1978—COPEI/URD/FDP/OPINA; MAS/VUC
1983—AD/URD/VOI; COPEI/FUN/MIO/NGD/ICC/CIMA; MAS/MIR/IRE; MEP/PCV/NA/LS/GAR/SI
1988—AD/PN; COPEI/MIN/FNP/ICC; MAS/MIR; MEP/PCV/Renovatión/MONO; URD/IRE
1993—Convergencia/MAS/URD/MEP/PCV and twelve other parties; AD/FDP and seven other parties; COPEI/PAZ/GE and three other parties

The winning candidates were Rómulo Gallegos (AD) in 1947, Rómulo Betancourt (AD) in 1958, Raúl Leoni (AD) in 1963, Rafael Caldera (COPEI) in 1968, Carlos Andrés Pérez (AD) in 1973, Luis Herrera Campíns (COPEI) in 1978, Jaime Lusinchi (AD) in 1983, Carlos Andrés Pérez (AD) again in 1988 and Rafael Caldera (Convergencia) again in 1993.

URD, the Trienio's most important electoral rivals (Caldera, 1999: 141–50, 189–96). PCV was excluded from this understanding; nevertheless, its leaders signed the 1961 constitution.[5] The Pact of Punto Fijo, and the concurrent drawing near the ideological center (and near each other institutionally) by AD and COPEI, provide the basis for characterizing the 1958–73 party system as one of moderate pluralism.

Important antisystem forces of the period reacted to their exclusion from the Pact of Punto Fijo by abandoning the institutional path of political competition and launching a guerrilla insurgency with the assistance of Cuba. PCV reversed itself and became the core institution seeking to overthrow the post-

1958 democratic system. It was joined by the Movimiento de Izquierda Revolucionaria (MIR; Movement of the Left Revolutionary), an organization that coalesced in 1960 from disillusioned members of the left wing of the AD. Thus, although one can speak of a moderate ideological distance between the political parties that were competing in elections, an important dissident movement challenged the legitimacy of the electoral system throughout the 1960s. Around 1968, and to an even greater extent during the first government of President Rafael Caldera (1969–74), the parties that took up arms against the Punto Fijo system reincorporated themselves into the institutional life of Venezuela's polity as minority forces.[6]

Electoral volatility, a critical indicator of political party system stability (and therefore of the level of institutionalization), is the third variable that this chapter uses to classify party systems. It measures the aggregate variation in electoral support for political parties between one election and the next in percentage points. The greater the electoral volatility, the less stable the political party system and the lower its level of institutionalization.[7] On the basis of the findings in the literature (Bartolini and Mair, 1990), a level of volatility below 5 percent can be classified as "low," a level between 5 percent and 15 percent can be classified as "moderate," and a level above 15 percent can be classified as "high." The volatility for Venezuelan elections of the period, using the Pedersen Index of Volatility, would be 32 between 1958 and 1963; 30 percent between 1963 and 1968; and 31 percent between 1968 and 1973. In other words, over the three national elections that followed the signing of the agreement to implement representative democracy (Punto Fijo), the political party system displayed an extremely high volatility.

Social science views the extent of party identification as an indicator of another aspect of the level of party system institutionalization: social penetration. Throughout the 1960s, the political parties that signed the Pact of Punto Fijo attempted to build followings and organizations with a national reach. AD and COPEI were successful, and URD was not. The success of AD and COPEI between 1958 and 1973 leads us to characterize those years as a time when Venezuela's political party system became institutionalized. This process advanced despite the high electoral volatility that marked voting shifts between the national elections of 1958, 1963, 1968, and 1973. Institutionalization and the reduction of the ideological distance between the period's important political parties imparted a resiliency to the fledgling democratic system. It helped the Punto Fijo regime to withstand assaults from rightists and their military supporters and from the Marxist Left. This success supports Sartori's proposition (1976), noted earlier, that the smaller the ideological distance and the fewer the number of relevant parties, the greater the likelihood of democratic stability. Similarly, Mainwaring (1999) hypothesizes that the greater the level of political party institutionalization, the higher the probability of survival and democratic consolidation.

The multiparty configuration of the 1960s gave way to the biparty arrangement of the 1970s. Many factors conditioned this transformation, among them the innovative organizational effort by both political parties which enabled them to have a presence throughout the entire country (Myers, 1977: 131); the successful ideological socialization by the two political parties which allowed them to appear as defenders of democracy (Myers, 1977:131); the marginalization of the Left, owing to its exclusion from the institutional life of the Punto Fijo system, and the defeat of its insurgent cadres; and the intensive use of incumbency to develop a clientelistic network and penetrate most sectors of civil society (Coppedge: 1994; Myers, 1977:131). The institutional dynamics of the presidential election system also proved important in the transformation to the biparty arrangement. Punto Fijo democracy had a plurality electoral system for the president in concurrent elections (presidential and legislative), and as Mainwairing and Shugart (1997) and Shugart and Carey (1992) have demonstrated, this institutional arrangement tends to be associated with a reduced number of relevant parties and a tendency toward a two-party system.[8] Another contributing factor was the victory of COPEI in 1968, which converted the Social Christian party into an "alternative electoral pole" to AD. It also generated its own special dynamic for polarization between these two political parties. Finally, the stabilizing economy of the period favored AD and COPEI, the two parties most associated with the emerging political and economic regime.

One factor, the victory of COPEI in 1968, tends to be overlooked, but it proved decisive. By the mid-1960s AD had recovered its position as Venezuela's main political party, although it was by no means hegemonic. Despite a division in 1967, AD survived as the second political force in 1968. Owing to its organizational capacity and its social penetration, this party became the principal force of the opposition during the first COPEI government (1969–74). The victory by COPEI in December 1968 forced AD to focus its opposition on COPEI and in the process to portray the democratic competition as basically a contest between the Christian Democrats and itself.

High Point of the Two-Party System (1973–1993)

This period saw two political parties, AD and COPEI, dominating the electoral scene, along with a minority "third force": Movimiento al Socialismo (MAS; Movement toward Socialism). The national congressional vote of AD during this period oscillated between 40 and 50 percent, and that of COPEI ran from 29 to 40 percent (see table 8.1). Only AD and COPEI had any realistic chance of capturing the presidency (see table 8.2), but MAS consistently garnered between 5 and 10 percent of the congressional vote. Thus, we label the party system of this period an "attenuated two-party system" (Molina and Pérez, 1996).[9] A short ideological distance separated the two main political forces, AD and COPEI: both tended to meet in the *center-right.* This is confirmed by studies of public opinion which probed the ideological positioning of their supporters. In fact, in 1973, on a scale of 1 to 3 (left, center, right), COPEI supporters were placed, on average, at 2.5, and AD supporters registered 2.3.[10] In 1983, using the same indicator, COPEI and AD supporters exhibited an average of 2.5 and 2.2, respectively.[11]

During this period, the Punto Fijo system of political parties reached its zenith of institutionalization. Electoral volatility between the elections of this period declined from the initial years of post-1958 democracy: 12 percent between the balloting in 1973 and 1978, 13 percent between 1978 and 1983, and 10 percent between 1983 and 1988. This is a moderate rate of volatility, according to criteria already mentioned, and similar to or below that displayed in other political party systems in Latin America, such as Uruguay, Colombia, Costa Rica, and Chile, all considered highly institutionalized by Mainwaring and Scully (1995: 8).

AD and COPEI organizations consolidated themselves as the only forces capable of winning presidential elections during the period; both created a wide network of party loyalists and came to dominate sociopolitical life in an arrangement known as *partidocracia* (government by the parties; Rey, 1991: 82) or "partyarchy" (extreme party domination of political life; Coppedge, 1994). This result derived from the conjunction of factors previously mentioned as the causes of bipartism. The bottom line is that AD and COPEI came to control demand making by most interest group associations, for most of these associations had been formed by the two dominant political parties as part of their efforts to dominate civil society. Important exceptions to this pattern were the business-related associations, the military institution, and the church.

Only after the infamous Black Friday economic crisis of February 18, 1983, undermined the legitimacy of COPEI and AD did political space begin to open which enabled Venezuelan interest groups to evolve into significant entities.

The attenuated two-party system remained entrenched for more than a decade despite negative reaction to the events surrounding Black Friday. Nevertheless, the long decline in the legitimacy of COPEI and AD can be traced to that economic crisis. Along with reduction in the oil-related income of the national government, the Black Friday crisis derived from unwise increases in Venezuela's external debt which were contracted during the high-income governments of Carlos Andrés Pérez (1974–79) and Luis Herrera Campíns (1979–84).

The major portion of blame for the decline in support for AD and COPEI can be laid at the feet of the governments of presidents Luis Herrera Campíns (COPEI; 1979–84), Jaime Lusinchi (AD; 1984–89), and Carlos Andrés Pérez (AD; 1989–93). These administrations handled the economy badly and were not able to shield the population effectively from the worst effect of the crisis; nor could they convince the public that they were doing the best that could be done. Their ineptitude focused attention to the corruption and clientelism that had become hallmarks of the Punto Fijo system. Nevertheless, this loss of legitimacy did not crystallize as an open crisis in the political party system until the 1989–94 constitutional period, and the massive rejection of AD and COPEI became clear only when votes were tallied following the national elections of 1993 (Levine, 1998a).

Turning to the evolution of partisanship (number of party members and sympathizers) between 1973 and 1993, we find a significant decrease. In 1973, 49 percent of Venezuelans declared themselves to be members or sympathizers of a political party, whereas this self-identification fell to 37 percent in 1998.[12]

Growing negativism toward AD and COPEI was accompanied by a sharp reduction in the capability of government institutions to maintain order and tranquility. The urban rioting that rocked Venezuela's ten largest cities in late February 1989 called into question the myth of a consolidated democratic order. The two unsuccessful military coups of February and November 1992 shattered that myth and intensified the search for alternatives to AD and COPEI. The mid-1993 impeachment and trial of President Pérez revealed deep divisions in the ruling circles of the two dominant political parties. Voter disgust with both deepened. In the presidential elections of December 1993 Rafael Caldera received a plurality of the votes in a hotly contested four-way race; it was the first time since 1958 that a candidate not supported by AD or COPEI had won the presidency (Kornblith, 1998).

Attenuated bipartism remained the order of the day between the economic debacle of Black Friday and Rafael Caldera's 1993 election victory. Throughout that decade rejection of a government run by one of the dominant political parties still led dissatisfied electors to shift to the main opposition party. In other words, the social, economic, and administrative crisis that surfaced on Black Friday did not immediately destabilize the party system. As late as the regional elections of November 1992, when victorious COPEI appeared poised to recapture the presidency, Venezuela's attenuated two-party system did not appear fatally damaged. A close look at the evidence, however, reveals pervasive decay. Voter abstention was on the rise in both the national and regional political arenas (see table 8.1).[13] Results from the national elections of 1983 and 1988 confirmed a moderate reduction in voter support for the national legislative (congressional) and regional assembly (state legislature) candidates of AD and COPEI (see table 8.1). Even as these two political parties maintained their total dominance of presidential elections (see table 8.2), the frequency of charismatic leaders increased among the emergent forces on the left. The capability of the Left to challenge the electoral dominance of AD and COPEI increased following the decentralization reforms of 1989. These reforms provided for the direct election of governors, mayors, congresspeople, and municipal councilpersons.[14]

The two unsuccessful coup d'états in 1992 signaled advanced political decay; nevertheless, results from the regional and local elections during December of that year indicated that AD and COPEI remained at the center of the political system. In these elections voter turnout increased slightly, from 45 percent to 49 percent; COPEI attained 36.5 percent and AD 31.3 percent of votes. Together these historically dominant parties received almost 68 percent of the total vote, which approximates their cumulative share of the vote in the regional elections of 1989 (71.4%). Victory in the December 1992 elections strengthened COPEI in a way that suggested that partisan competition would lead to the well-known government alternation between AD and COPEI in the presidential elections of 1993.

The event that seems to have undone Venezuela's attenuated two-party system was the decision of COPEI's founding leader, Rafael Caldera, to abandon the party and run for the presidency as an independent. As the 1993 presidential campaign unfolded, Caldera presented himself as an alternate to AD and COPEI, both of which he sharply criticized. With support from a newly minted movement (Convergencia), MAS, and the other minor leftist parties (the only exception being La Causa Radical [LCR; The Radical Cause]),

Caldera was able to convey the image of a democratic alternative for real change and rejection of the two historically dominant political parties. Had Caldera not divided the party that he founded and nurtured, it is probable that in 1993 the pattern of alternation of power between the two Punto Fijo regime-sustaining political parties would have withstood the challenge of such anti-establishment forces as LCR. On the other hand, a victory by COPEI in 1993 might only have delayed the collapse of the Punto Fijo party system, since it seems unlikely that a government of COPEI headed by Alvarez Paz over the 1994–99 constitutional period could have reversed growing alienation from the two establishment political parties.

The Rise of the Fifth Republic: A Party System of Deinstitutionalized and Polarized Pluralism (1993–)

The Unraveling of the Party System

After COPEI's division in 1993, the effects of the social and economic crisis were felt decisively at the presidential level and in the evolution of Venezuela's party system. One pole of the two-party system (COPEI) was no longer seen as the instrument of choice to throw the rascals out. Most people now wanted both parties out. The national elections of 1993 created a new party system, one of deinstitutionalized and polarized pluralism.[15] Table 8.3 reveals that AD and COPEI, whose combined vote in the 1988 congressional elections had approached 75 percent, experienced a decrease to 46 percent in 1993, 36 percent in 1998, and 21 percent in 2000 (Molina, 2000; Molina and Pérez, 1996). MAS retained its historical level of support in the first two elections but suffered loses in the most recent one: 11 percent in 1993, 9 percent in 1998, and 5 percent in 2000.

The electoral space lost by AD and COPEI was occupied partly by new center and center-right political organizations—in 1993 by Convergencia, the party of Rafael Caldera (in 2000 this organization contracted into a regional party concentrated in the state of Yaracuy); in 1998 by Proyecto Venezuela (Venezuelan Project), the party of the runner-up in the 1998 presidential elections (in 2000 this party was also reduced to its roots [in Carabobo state]); and in 2000 by several regional parties: Primero Justicia (Justice First) in the affluent areas of Caracas, Un Nuevo Tiempo (A New Time) in Zulia (the largest state), and Alianza Bravo Pueblo (Brave People Alliance) also in metropolitan

Table 8.3. Results of the Legislative Elections of 1993, 1998, and 2000 (party votes)

	Chamber of Deputies				National Assembly	
	1993		1998[a]		2000[a]	
Party	Votes (%)	Seats	Votes (%)	Seats	Votes (%)	Seats
MVR–CONIVE[b]			19.9	35	44.33	80
MAS[b]	10.8	24	8.9	24	5.12	21
AD	23.3	55	24.1	61	16.10	30
COPEI	22.6	53	12.0	26	5.10	8
Proyecto Venezuela			10.4	20	6.92	7
Primero Justicia					2.46	5
Convergencia-LAPY	13.6	26	2.5	6	1.07	4
LCR	20.7	40	3.0	5	4.41	3
PPT			3.4	11	2.27	1
Un Nuevo Tiempo					1.75	3
Alianza Bravo Pueblo					1.10	1
Puama					0.04	1
Migato					0.47	1
Apertura			1.5	3		
Renovación			1.2	2		
IRENE			1.3	3		
Others	9.0	5	11.8	11	8.86	0
Total seats		203		207		165
Parties with seats		10		21		13
Volatility	32%		41%		32%	
Effective number of parties	5.6		7.6		4.3	
Turnout	60%		54%		56.5%	

Sources: Consejo Supremo Electoral, Dirección de Estadísticas Electorales, Elecciones de 1993 (electronic file); Consejo Nacional Electoral, *Resultados Electorales 1998,* CD-ROM; Consejo Nacional Electoral–INDRA, *Elecciones* 2000, CD-ROM.

Note: For full party names, see list of abbreviations.

[a]The distribution of seats among the parties is based on a survey of members of the National Assembly by the newspaper *El Universal,* as well as on personal research. *El Universal,* January 18–22, 1999, and August 14, 2000, 1–10.

[b]For the year 2000, although in some cases the Movimiento Quinta República (MVR) and MAS presented separate candidates, they integrated an alliance of national character. For this reason it is better to understand the results as those of an electoral coalition. Under this alliance other political parties also participated without obtaining positions. These parties and their percentage of votes for the year 2000 are as follows: PCV (0.36%); MEP (0.08%); SI (0.34%); IPCN (0.17%); GE (0.11%); and NRD (0.10%). These minority parties are grouped together in the table with the rest of the parties that did not obtain positions in the category "Others." CONIVE was the denomination taken by the MVR candidates in the three single member seats for the indigenous population; therefore, the MVR won 77 seats and CONIVE 3 seats.

Caracas.[16] The remainder of the freed-up space left by the demise of AD and COPEI was taken by the new radical Left (LCR in 1993 and Chávez's party, Movimiento Quinta República [MVR; Fifth Republic Movement] in 1998 and 2000).

This fragmentation of Venezuela's party system becomes even clearer when we use the quantitative indicator for the effective number of parties. In the wake of the 1993 national elections, the effective number of parties (N), based on the legislative vote, was 5.6. It rose to 7.6 in 1998 but declined to 4.3 in 2000. The last figure suggests a reduction in the effective number of parties between 1998 and 2000 and the probable surge of a new process of party concentration. However, a closer look reveals that this apparent reduction is mainly an artifact of the increase in the share of the vote received by the government party (MVR), which is due not to its organizational strength but to the charisma of President Chávez. Actually, the Center-Right imploded in the 2000 elections: it included the weakened AD, the all-but-extinct COPEI, and the other five groupings mentioned earlier, concentrated in specific regions of the country.

The Left, always a fragile component of Venezuela's political party system, became more unstable and divided than ever. The leftist political parties that attracted significant support during the early and mid-1990s have seen their share of the vote decline severely, and their popular support has been swallowed up by a personalistic and highly unstable party: MVR. In the December 1993 national elections, LCR, a party that dates from the 1970s, garnered 21 percent of the total congressional vote, but this success exacerbated long-standing tensions between pragmatists and militants within the party. The more militant faction broke with the official LCR party in 1997 and set up a new party: Patria para Todos (PPT; Homeland for All). Several important PPT leaders had participated in the unsuccessful coup attempts of 1992, and the party supported Chávez's presidential candidacy in 1998 (Medina, 1999). In 2000, PPT broke with the president over his selection of regional candidates for governor and the state legislatures. After the December 2000 municipal council elections, a weakened PPT realigned itself with President Chávez's "Patriotic Pole." MAS, as noted earlier, saw its share of the vote reduced by half between 1993 and 2000. However, its alliance with President Chávez in the 2000 elections allowed it to increase its representation in the national legislature and to secure four governors. In 2002, President Chávez's most ardent supporters within the party broke away and formed their own organization under the name of PODEMOS, and MAS joined the opposition. The remainder of leftist support is concentrated in several microparties.

During the period under analysis, the climate of ideological convergence in the center among the relevant parties broke down. Early in the 1990s it gave way to ideological polarization with the rise to relevance of leftist parties with strong antisystem orientations: LCR from 1993 to its decline in 1998, and MVR from 1998 onward. The rise of ideological polarization among the new relevant actors of the party system is shown by the location of party supporters in the left-right scale in public opinion surveys. In a survey done in 1993, using a scale from 1 to 3 (left, center, right) the attitudes held by supporters of AD resulted in their being placed, on average, at 2.5 on the left-right continuum; COPEI supporters possessed attitudes that yielded a placement at exactly the same location.[17] Supporters of LCR in 1993 (at that time a relevant party) held attitudes that led to their placement on the left-right continuum at 1.6 (center-left). This reveals that, in the period leading up to the 1993 presidential elections, a significant increase occurred in the ideological distance that separated the party system's relevant political parties. This marked a significant change from the low ideological distance that separated AD and COPEI between 1973 and 1993 and signaled the appearance of a polarized multiparty system.

The characteristics exhibited by the party system in 1993 became more pronounced in 1998. Employing a scale that ranges from 1 (left) to 10 (right), the supporters of AD during the 1998 national election campaign placed themselves on average at 7.8, those of COPEI at 7.3, and those of MVR at 4.8.[18] This confirmed that the ideological gap that opened up in 1993 had become a permanent feature of the party system. In other words, from the perspective of the second dimension, ideological polarization, Venezuela's party system was far from the attenuated bipartism of Punto Fijo democracy.

The third dimension for classifying political party systems, level of institutionalization, changed dramatically in the 1990s. Political decay undermined institutionalization along each of the dimensions (Mainwaring, 1999: 26) commonly used to measure institutionalization: stability, social penetration, legitimacy, and organizational strength. In contrast to the 1973–93 configuration, the post-1993 system of political parties exhibited a high level of electoral volatility. Some relevant political parties blazed across the political horizon like comets and disappeared almost as quickly as they had appeared (see tables 8.3, 8.4, and 8.5). The index of volatility for each election during this period (in relation to the results of the previous one) is as follows: 1988–93: 32 percent; 1993–98: 41 percent; 1998–2000: 32 percent (between 1973 and 1988, in contrast, the volatility index of the Punto Fijo party system never exceeded 13%).

With regard to the intense social penetration exercised by system-dominant

AD and COPEI (long seen as a factor that suffocated demand making from civil society), this dimension eroded incrementally, more slowly than electoral strength. Nevertheless, by the mid-1990s new social organizations were becoming important, and the political parties were unable to co-opt them. Party identification, also viewed in the literature as an indicator of social penetration (Mainwaring, 1999), eroded in the 1990s. As discussed earlier, there was a decline in the proportion of the population which expressed a positive attachment toward AD and COPEI. This "dealignment," however, has yet to produce enduring loyalties toward the new political parties (Dalton and Wattenberg, 1993: 202; Molina, 2000: 41; Molina and Pérez, 1999: 29–30; Pérez, 2000; Vaivads, 1999).

Legitimacy is the third dimension that influences the level of institutionalization of the political party system. In general, Venezuelan party institutions retain some legitimacy, but far less than during the glory days of Punto Fijo democracy. This is an important explanation for the difficulties experienced by new parties as they attempted to build a stable base of popular support and party identification (Álvarez, 1996; Buxton, 2001). One indicator of the decline in political party legitimacy has been the increased political space occupied by charismatic leadership. The decline of party-centered politics and rise in personality-centered politics has two main causes: the decay of loyalties toward the traditional parties (due in large part to their errors, corruption, and inability to deal with the economic crisis), and the Venezuelan political reforms of 1989 which established the direct election of governors and mayors (they created new channels—different from the party bureaucracies—for recruiting national and regional political leaders).

This new importance of personality-centered politics can be seen in the fact that Convergencia never became more than an electoral vehicle for Rafael Caldera and Proyecto Venezuela was only a grouping to advance the presidential candidacy of Henrique Salas Römer. As of this writing, MVR remains nothing more than the personal property of Hugo Chávez, and its fortune rises and falls with his personal success or failure. The new regional parties are also dependent on their leaders' popularity. Even organizations that once commanded intense loyalties (AD, COPEI, and MAS) found that in the 2000 elections their capacity to resist the Chávez tide depended heavily on the success of their regional and local leaders.

The new political parties have not had the time to build organizational strength, the fourth aspect of party system institutionalization. In addition, most of them are regional and personalistic institutions not interested in creating a national political infrastructure. As for the historical parties, their organization has either been destroyed (the case of COPEI) or seriously weakened (as with AD and MAS). MAS sustained a division in 1998 when most of its founding leaders refused to support the majority decision to back Hugo Chávez's presidential candidacy. The party divided again in late 2001 over whether to remain part of the Chávez government. MAS subsequently carried on as a federation of regional leaders and national factions, but without the coherence previously provided by a common ideology and historically heroic leaders.[19]

AD and COPEI were stunned by electoral defeat and by the defection of national and regional leaders. The Caracas-based leadership of both parties fell into destructive internecine conflicts that are far from over, and their infrastructure decays at an accelerating rate. Several dissident AD regional organizations have been the source of new parties: Alianza Bravo Pueblo and Un Nuevo Tiempo. COPEI has sustained even more damaging defections. Three new parties have fed from its onetime clientele: Convergencia, Proyecto Venezuela, and Primero Justicia.

The Rise of Hugo Chávez: Inevitable or Opportune?

This chapter has examined the causes of decline in popular support for AD and COPEI which led to the deinstitutionalization of Venezuela's party system, but it has not focused on why Chávez was the beneficiary of that process. It is important to note that Chávez is a consequence, not the cause, of the party system's unraveling. The key to Chávez's success rests on the pervasive desire among Venezuelans for a profound change; most wanted to throw out AD and COPEI. A growing majority regarded these two parties as the ones to blame for the economic and social crisis that deepened during the early 1990s. In 1993 this perception led a majority of voters to cast their presidential ballots for the two candidates not associated with AD or COPEI. In the presidential elections of that year, the antiestablishment candidates were Rafael Caldera (with the support of the Center and the Center-Left) and Andrés Velásquez (from the radical Left). Many in the latter's inner circle were involved in the previous year's attempted coup d'états.

Caldera's assumption of power in 1994 inspired great expectations. His government, however, proved incapable of alleviating the economic crisis, and the resulting disillusionment proved fatal for Punto Fijo democracy. In all fairness, international events complicated Caldera's task. A sharp drop in the international price of petroleum in 1998 (an election year) undermined the economic recovery that gathered some steam in 1997. Intensifying frustration prompted the people to start again the search for radical change. For the overwhelming majority of Venezuelans, the alternative to Caldera was not to fall back on AD or COPEI. Indeed, popular support for President Caldera and his minority government declined dramatically following his entry into an informal coalition with AD in order to pass legislation in the Congress.

The disillusioned Venezuelan electorate searched for radical alternatives throughout 1998. Irene Sáez, the former Miss Universe, initially attracted widespread support. Sáez was serving as mayor of the urban municipality Chacao (an affluent zone of eastern Caracas). She had established a reputation for honesty, independence, and administrative competence. In January 1998, she was clearly the front-runner for the presidency according to opinion polls (Buxton, 2001). After three months of a confused national campaign, in early April, support for the onetime Miss Universe dipped below the level enjoyed by Hugo Chávez and Henrique Salas Römer. Support for Sáez went into a free fall for two reasons: first and most important, she accepted support from COPEI. This alliance erased linkages between her candidacy and voters' desire for radical change. Second, Sáez's own errors created an image of being insecure and ill prepared.

The saga of Sáez's downfall suggests that Chávez's triumph was not inevitable; nor was it the product of belated support for his failed 1992 coup. Rather, Chávez won the 1998 presidential election because he appeared as the only candidate who consistently and wholeheartedly rejected any role in government for the discredited AD and COPEI. This perception also explains why Hugo Chávez defeated another charismatic and independent leader, Henrique Salas Römer, the former governor of the state of Carabobo (see table 8.4). Salas Römer also presented himself as an option for radical change. However, he never was able to pass Chávez in the opinion polls, and two weeks before the election he accepted support from AD and COPEI. As in the case of Irene Sáez, the willingness of Henrique Salas Römer to negotiate with the two established political parties signaled to voters that if they wanted a complete break with the past, the Carabobo governor was not their man.

The shift to Chávez was a consequence of the desire for fundamental change. Other serious candidates who also supported change appeared half-

Table 8.4. Results of the Venezuelan Presidential Election, December 6, 1998 (candidate and party votes)

Candidate	Vote (%)	Parties Supporting the Candidate and Voting Percentage of Each One
Hugo Chávez Frías	56.20	MVR (40.17); MAS (9); PPT (2.19); PCV (1.25); IPCN (1.03): GE (0.86); MEP (0.84); SI (0.57); AA (0.29).
Henrique Salas Römer	39.97	Proyecto Venezuela (28.75); AD (9.05); COPEI (2.15); PQAC (0.02)
Irene Sáez	2.82	IRENE (1.96); FD (0.37); La Llave (0.30); INCVF (0.19)
Luis Alfaro Ucero	0.42	ORA (0.12); URD (0.08); RENACE (0.08); VU (0.05); ICC (0.05); FIN (0.03); ONDA (0.01)
Miguel Rodríguez	0.30	APERTURA (0.30)
Alfredo Ramos	0.11	LCR (0.11)
Others	0.18	
Turnout:	6,988,291 (63.76%)	Valid votes: 93.55%
Abstentions:	3,971,239 (36.24%)	Void votes: 6.45%

Sources: Consejo Nacional Electoral, *Resultados Electorales 1998*, CD-ROM (this is the last report with 99.61% of the votes tallied, on December 10, 1998).

Note: For full party names, see list of abbreviations.

hearted in their rejection of the past. It bears repeating that by the end of the 1998 presidential election campaign AD and COPEI were out of the race. Even more telling, the support given by those political parties to two of the contending candidates damaged their chances of winning, a sort of kiss of death.

The best way to view balloting in the 2000 mega-elections is as "honeymoon elections." Scholars define honeymoon elections as balloting in which a recently victorious party of government usually increases its share of the vote (Shugart and Carey, 1992). The July 2000 elections occurred twenty months after Chávez's triumph in the presidential voting of December 1998. Public opinion surveys revealed that most of the electorate felt that it was too early to assess the Chávez government, so most of the factors that were in play during the earlier election dictated a similar outcome in the latter. In addition, voters anticipated that the new constitution of 1999 and its attendant institutions would pave the way for the social and economic revolution that the president promised. The elections of 2000 ratified Chávez's 1998 victory and confirmed the Venezuelan party system as one of deinstitutionalized and polarized pluralism, the configuration that crystallized in 1993 (see tables 8.3 and 8.5).

Table 8.5. Results of the Venezuelan Presidential Election, July 30, 2000 (candidate votes)

Candidate	Vote (%)	Parties Supporting the Candidate and Voting Percentage of Each One
		Polo Patriotico Coalition:
Hugo Chávez	59.8	MVR (48.11); MAS (8.7); PCV (0.91); IPCN (0.47); GE (0.21); MEP (0.22); SI (0.70); AA (0.24); NRI (0.19)
Francisco Arias	37.5	LCR (18.95); ID (2.36); MIN (1.07); MDD (1.02); Bandera Roja (0.26); personal votes for the candidate (13.87)
Claudio Fermín	2.7	Encuentro Nacional (2.72)
Turnout:	6,600,196 (56.5%)	Valid votes: 95.3%
Abstention:	5,081,449 (43.5%)	Void votes: 4.7%

Sources: Consejo Nacional Electoral–INDRA, *Elecciones 2000,* CD-ROM (this is the last report with 99.66% of the votes tallied, August 11, 2000).

The Fifth Republic: Political Consequences of Party System Deinstitutionalization

Weakly institutionalized party systems exhibit important operational characteristics that contrast with those displayed by highly institutionalized party systems (Mainwaring, 1999:323–36). The former tend to be more personalistic, less stable, more conducive to populist movements, and more volatile. Weakly institutionalized political party systems also appear to diminish the capability of voters to force accountability from elected officials and, because of the high level of volatility, to increase levels of insecurity among social, political, and economic actors. In other words, the bundle of structures and processes associated with weakly institutionalized political party systems does not favor high-quality democracy. It appears conducive to low-quality "delegative democracy," a system that Guillermo O'Donnell (1994) sees as pivoting on a powerful presidency, weak checks and balances, and charismatic leadership (Álvarez, 2000). Building on this insight, Mainwaring (1999: 322–41) argues that although a weakly institutionalized party system is not incompatible with democratic survival it weakens the capacity of democracy to resist the slide into authoritarianism. Mainwaring views this reduced capacity as endemic to democracies possessing a party system that is weakly institutionalized and which never achieved high levels of institutionalization. Venezuela, on the other hand, has a system that once was institutionalized but lost this condition;

will this system exhibit the same characteristics or behave differently in regard to its capability to sustain democracy? Thus, the Venezuelan case raises an important question: What are the consequences for democratic development of the decay of an established party system that was once strongly institutionalized?

This chapter hypothesizes that a weakly institutionalized party system that evolved from one that was highly institutionalized will exhibit characteristics different from those of systems that have remained weakly institutionalized since their inception. There are two possible reasons for this difference: first, strongly institutionalized party systems produce streams of political socialization which create a deeper and more pervasive democratic political culture; and second, the process of delegitimating established political parties inculcates attitudes and orientations, derived from the process of delegitimation itself, which are not found in systems in which political parties have always been weakly institutionalized.

Democratic Culture

By definition, a deinstitutionalized party system was previously institutionalized. When party system institutionalization occurs in a democratic context (as in Venezuela), it is expected that, at one time or another, popular support for democratic institutions was the norm. Under such circumstances, we would expect to detect the presence of a democratic political culture (Dahl, 1998). Thus, when party system deinstitutionalization occurs, there is a high probability that orientations supportive of democracy remain entrenched in popular culture. This suggests that deinstitutionalized party systems are more resistant to the return of authoritarian government than party systems that have always been weakly institutionalized.

The Venezuelan case supports this hypothesis. To date (September 2003), democracy has survived against dismal odds and despite political, economic, and social crises. The coup attempts of 1992 and 2002 failed. In addition, in 1992, although an important segment of the population considered the coups to be justified, they sparked no popular uprising on behalf of the plotters (Myers and O'Connor, 1998). Popular support for democracy as the most desirable form of government remained strong. On the other hand, alienation toward rule by AD and COPEI decimated those political parties' electoral support in 1998 and 2000, opening the way for Hugo Chávez, the individual who had planned and implemented the unsuccessful coup d'état of February

4, 1992. The pervasive democratic culture of the country, however, forced Chávez to promise a new and different democracy in order to gain power. Once he was in power, it constrained the nondemocratic elements among his supporters. The events of April 2002 and their aftermath showed the Bolivarian Revolution protecting itself under the principles of democracy and the Democratic Charter of the Organization of American States.

Support for democracy in Venezuela reached high levels during the 1970s and has remained so despite party system deinstitutionalization (Pereira, 2000). Surveys in 1983 and 1998 asked Venezuelans: "And which one do you prefer, a democracy like the one we have, or a dictatorship"?[20] The answers both times were overwhelmingly in favor of democracy: 85 percent in 1983 and 79 percent in 1998. The World Value Survey, done in Venezuela during 1996 and 2000, asked the respondents to state whether they agree strongly, agree, disagree, or disagree strongly with this statement: "Democracy may have problems but it's better than any other form of government."[21] In the former survey 86 percent agreed or strongly agreed with that statement; the level responding positively increased to 93 percent in 2000. The data provided by Lagos (2003) from the Latinobarometer surveys also show that Venezuelans have significantly increased their support for democracy from 1996 (65%) to 2002 (78%), and in Latin America they were outscored only by Costa Rica and Uruguay in 2002.[22] To summarize, recent survey data give backing to the hypothesis that in a party system that was once institutionalized the process of deinstitutionalization does not necessarily mean a decline in support for democracy.

In Venezuela, the high level of popular support for democracy has been a significant factor for containing the danger of an authoritarian setback during the current process of political change. This orientation has strengthened democratic elements and has limited the room for maneuver open to opponents of democracy, in the government and in the opposition. The perception among Venezuelan elites that most of their compatriots favor democracy is one critical reason (the international context being the other) why the plotters of April 11–13, 2002, portrayed the overthrow of President Chávez as an effort to fill a supposed "power vacuum" by extraordinary but institutional means.

In fact, one sector in which the willingness to defend democracy has declined is political elites themselves, not to mention the economic elites that, to a large extent, openly supported the 2002 coup attempt. Following the unsuccessful military coups in February and November 1992, most of the opposition rallied against the plotters and in support of the 1961 constitution. In April

2002, few opponents of the Chávez government defended constitutional procedures following the initial coup that created an interim government. Most turned a blind eye, at least until interim president Carmona's government took on many attributes of a traditional dictatorship.

Assessment of the strength of Venezuelan democracy mandates that we examine attitudes in the armed forces. The level of support for democracy within the military appears quite low: three coup attempts in less than a decade. Nevertheless, it is also true that these coup attempts have failed, in large measure, because of lack of support within the officer corps. The fact that most Venezuelans support democracy is what probably led most officers participating in the coup of April 2002 to insist that it was not a military coup at all. They presented it as a resignation by the president, after which the military stepped in to fill the vacuum while constitutional government was being reestablished. When their chosen interim president, Carmona, took a clear path in the direction of an open dictatorship (by dissolving Congress, the Supreme Tribunal, and regional governments), support within the military crumbled. One important reason for this was the conviction even among those who disliked Chávez that it was unlikely that they could ever achieve popular backing for an authoritarian government.

Loss of Institutional Legitimacy by the Political Parties

Political party systems that are weakly institutionalized possess political parties whose legitimacy tends to be low. Few people identify with any political party, and personality-centered politics predominates. When personalism is ascendant, political party organizations play a secondary role in recruitment to political elite status and in electioneering; instead, direct linkages to popular leaders become the preferred pathway to influence and power.

In the case of deinstitutionalized party system there is a different dynamic. Party dealignment and decayed legitimacy signal negative attitudes toward the political parties that have long dominated the party system and toward parties as institutions (Dalton, 2000). Thus, it is not that parties have failed to attain a high level of legitimacy, as in party systems that have always been weakly institutionalized. Parties have forfeited the legitimacy they once had, rejected by individuals who at one point in time supported them. This rejection of institutions that once commanded widespread respect and loyalty complicates the process of party system reinstitutionalization. In other words, reinstitutionalization seems to be much more difficult than institutionalization. In addition, owing to the process of deinstitutionalization, parties would be expected to have less social penetration and lower number of stable followers and depend more on personalistic leadership than their counterparts in the antecedent system of institutionalized parties.

The current state of the Venezuelan party system supports the characterization of the effects of deinstitutionalization just discussed. In the Fifth Republic, personality-centered politics is the name of the game. The leaders of the political parties are experiencing difficulties in building up strong organizations and cementing loyalty. This problem extends across the political spectrum. On the center-right, we saw that Rafael Caldera's Convergencia and Henrique Salas Römer's Proyecto Venezuela burst on the scene in one election and almost disappeared in the next. Primero Justicia, a party that has become the main pole of attraction for the Center-Right, depends largely on the appeal of several charismatic leaders, especially television personality Julio Borges. Political parties on the left have been no less transitory or dependent on charismatic leadership. The popularity of LCR was short lived, and MVR remains totally dependent on President Chávez's popularity.

Developments in Venezuela's party system since 1993 suggest that reinstitutionalizing the party system in the aftermath of a process that led to the unraveling of the previous party system is more difficult than achieving institutionalization in the first place. During the forty-year Punto Fijo regime Venezuelans came to associate all political parties with clientelism, expediency, and corruption.[23]

The weakening of parties as the preferred vehicles of political interest representation and aggregation has led to interest associations and social movements taking on these roles (Schmitter, 2001). The mass campaign and demonstrations that asked for the resignation of Hugo Chávez and preceded the coup attempt of April 11, 2002, and also the national strike of December 2002 were led by the main labor organization (Confederación de Trabajadores de Venezuela [CTV; Confederation of Venezuelan Workers]) and the main business organization (Federación de Cámaras y Asociaciones de Comercio y Producción de Venezuela [FEDECAMARAS; Federation of Chambers of Commerce and Production of Venezuela]), along with several nongovernmental organizations of the middle class. Parties played a secondary role. This is one of the main reasons why this movement was so easily manipulated by the radical right-wing elements intent on overthrowing the Chávez government.

Conclusions

With regard to the salient dimensions of party systems considered in this chapter, the main features of the Fifth Republic's party system are multipartism, ideological polarization, and deinstitutionalization. To this picture we add the tensions that characterize an underdeveloped country that has experienced declining living standards for almost two decades. There is consensus that this mix is highly unfavorable for the functioning of democratic life (Mainwaring, 1999: 323–41; Sartori, 1976: 31–145). The frequency of events threatening the political regime since 1989 supports this consensus. Venezuela has been rocked by widespread riots, coup attempts, intensified class conflict, and institutional breakdown, problems that once appeared to have been overcome or reduced to manageable proportions.

The fact that Venezuela experienced a process of party system institutionalization, followed by deinstitutionalization, has had positive and negative consequences for the survival of democracy in the Fifth Republic. On the positive side is the persistence of a democratic political culture that crystallized during the time of party system institutionalization in the Punto Fijo regime. This democratic political culture has remained in place despite political and economic decay. It serves as a positive factor in the struggle to preserve democracy. Among the elites, this democratic political culture may have deteriorated (if one takes into account their attitude toward the 2002 coup attempt), but democracy remains the governmental system of choice for the overwhelming majority of Venezuelans.

On the negative side, the growing rejection of all political parties has increased the attractiveness of personalistic appeals and retarded the process of reinstitutionalizing the system of political parties. Venezuela seems poised for a long period of electoral instability owing, among other factors, to the disrepute into which political parties in general have fallen. Although this does not imply that Venezuelan democracy will continue to unravel, it means that the risks of sliding into authoritarianism are greater than during the era when AD and COPEI dominated the political system.

Deinstitutionalization and polarization in the party system, personalistic politics, and instability mean also that, as it is sustained in this book, the quality of Venezuelan democracy has eroded from where it was during the Punto Fijo regime. The decay of the political parties has not given way to a higher-level participatory democracy but to a period of severe instability in which democracy itself has been at risk, and the tendency toward institutional strengthening through reform which seemed to be making inroads in the 1990s has been fully reversed. Venezuelan democracy is no longer trying to improve itself; it is struggling to survive.

Part III / Policy Making and Its Consequences

CHAPTER NINE

Decentralization

Key to Understanding a Changing Nation

Rafael de la Cruz

Many Latin American countries have moved along the path of decentralization, a type of state design which normally strengthens and expands democratic institutions. Until recently Venezuela, Colombia, Chile, Argentina, Brazil, and Mexico had moved farthest in this direction. Now efforts at decentralization in other countries, such as Guatemala, Honduras, Nicaragua, Costa Rica, Peru, Ecuador, Bolivia, and the Dominican Republic, are leading to significant changes in their political systems.

Venezuela began a major decentralization experience with direct election of governors and mayors in 1989 in an effort to buoy the flagging democratic regime. A subsequent backlash began, however, under President Rafael Caldera in the mid-1990s and was intensified under President Hugo Chávez Frías. The strong centralist penchant of his political experiment casts doubts on the intention of President Chávez to abide by the intent of earlier decentralization legislation, as his government sought to undue many of the early decentralization reforms.

The bright promise of decentralization may fail if public finances are not adapted to the new model of government. Successful adaptation requires a long-term public finance model that would enable the different levels of government to be assigned responsibilities over income and expenditure, in keeping with their responsibilities, so as to increase the efficiency of the public sector and guarantee interregional equity. On the other hand, many decentralization experiences in Latin America have been set in motion through a combination of technical advice and political decision making. The resulting models sometimes display ill-designed rules regulating intergovernmental relations. Thus, although decentralization has contributed to enhancing governance in most cases, the need for improving and streamlining the structural incentives related to decentralization remains a daunting challenge.

The Meaning of Decentralization: In Search of Governance

The most important meaning of the rediscovery of federalism and the new decentralization modalities is, to a large extent, related to the very idea of democracy being the system that guarantees the greatest degree of freedom, participation by citizens, and justice in the formulation of public policies. The meaning of decentralization at the beginning of the twenty-first century is to devolve to the communities control over the state, bringing it administratively closer and making it more vulnerable to the preferences of the electorate. Decentralization is a way to enhance citizens' faith in the democracy as well as a means to improve the quality and coverage of public services.

Yet decentralization is still a work in progress. The way this governmental model is expressed in each country differs. In nations with an old federal tradition like the United States, the reinvention of government is associated with changes in the federal structure itself. In other, more centralized ones, like most Latin American countries, the fundamental challenge is to formulate public policies that will give communities a greater say in matters relevant to them and to overcome the inefficient, occasionally authoritarian, populist state model.

The state structures and administrative mechanisms being implemented in each country reflect the variety of circumstances and the wealth of cultural, economic, and political legacies. Good decisions and mistakes have been made in every country facing the challenge of designing a new intergovernmental structure. The experience accumulated has been sufficiently documented by the specialized literature showing that certain institutions are necessary to create the incentives that will enable the new wave of federalism to progress and deliver.

First, the popular election of municipal and regional authorities (the latter in the cases where regional governments exist) is a requisite for increasing the dependence of public decision makers on their communities and to enhance accountability.

On this point one must realize that there are many variants in the electoral mechanisms. The direct election of governors and mayors, or their equivalent in intermediate and local governments, is a widespread method and the most effective one to make officials personally responsible to the electorate. The greatest risk of this scheme is that the political composition of the local and regional legislative bodies, which are also elected, may be the opposite of that of the executive branch.[1] This possible distortion may be attenuated by increasing the personal responsibility of the members of the legislative bodies through electing them nominally. Under these circumstances personalized accountability to the community for their actions when a new election takes places does, in principle, encourage public officials to behave responsibly.

Another common form of election is indirect election. Through this method, the population elects the members of the local and regional legislative bodies, and they, in turn, form an electoral body, which appoints the executive authority of the respective governmental level. This method fosters a regional or local parliamentary majority favorable to the executive. Hence, in principle, it ensures that the administration is viable and expeditious. However, the less direct contact citizens have with their mayors or governors, the less incentive these officials have to meet the demands of their communities. On the other hand, if representatives are elected by slate, as is frequently the case in Latin America, the personal responsibility of those elected toward the voters is further diluted into a more abstract responsibility, that of the party behind them.

In Venezuela, municipal councillors have been elected by slate since the beginning of Punto Fijo in 1958. The proportion of votes for each slate was transferred to a similar proportion of the offices to be held. This meant that the first candidate on the slate held the first office available in the council for his or her party, and so on, with all the offices assigned to each slate being gradually filled until the respective quota was met. This system, which ended with the councillors electing the chair of the council without executive authority, discouraged accountability by local authorities to communities, delegitimizing these organizations and exposing them to the risk of becoming inefficient and corrupt. Ever since governors and mayors began to be elected in 1989, the reaction of many sectors in Venezuela was to demand that the legislative authorities be elected nominally as well.[2]

The second common aspect of any decentralization process involves the distribution of public service provision among the different territorial levels of government in each country. The election of regional and local authorities is meaningless if they lack sufficient power to formulate public policies and run the services that the communities require the state to provide. The responsibilities of each level of government in the distribution of public expenditure are defined generally taking into account externality and subsidiary principles.[3] Once these indicators are applied, a scheme of intergovernmental relations emerges whereby the national government retains public services with high externalities and low need for using the subsidiary principle, like defense, macroeconomic policy, and national legislation. Meanwhile, municipal governments absorb services with very low externalities, the costs and benefits of which can be mostly internalized within local jurisdictions and at the same time may be enhanced by the intense use of the subsidiary principle. Community services like police, transportation, and sanitation are typically municipal. Finally, state governments are often involved in education and health, services that present a certain degree of externalities but also benefit from a strong involvement of communities in their management or investment decision making or both.

The third common topic is closely associated with the previous one: distribution of responsibilities for the production of government revenue. Tax responsibilities and financial autonomy of each territorial level of government vary from one country to the next. On the one hand, there are countries in which public revenue is almost completely concentrated in the central government. In other cases, the subnational governments have considerable tax authority and provide fundamental support for the consolidated income of general government. In the first model, transfers are the most widely used mechanism for providing resources to subnational administrations; in the second, their own income is essential in helping them cover their spending requirements. In general terms, one can say that the incentives to make elected authorities accountable are conditioned by the ratio of expenditure assigned to the different governmental levels and their own income autonomy.

The vital importance of the existence of a subnational tax system is explained by the fact that communities can link their tax effort to local government performance more clearly, and this establishes a strong incentive for them to reveal their preferences and to oversee government use of funds. This fact is well understood by experts but often ignored by national politicians.

The need for the different government levels to have elected authorities that are sensitive to citizens' preferences is also sufficiently well established. If these authorities have full fiscal competencies, which means capacity to make decisions on charges and tax rates as well as on a defined share of public expenditure, politicians' sensitivity toward their electors' preferences will be very high. In turn, the less fiscal autonomy that these authorities have over income and expenditure, the less sensitivity they tend to have toward their voters' wishes and the less incentives citizens have to supervise government action. The conjunction of these factors leads to an unresponsive and inefficient allocation of public sector resources.

The Decline of Punto Fijo Democracy: Comparing Venezuela

Government revenue and spending as a proportion of the total gross domestic product (GDP) are important indicators for analyzing the state's impact on the economy. In turn, studying the intergovernmental distribution of fiscal responsibilities yields powerful indicators of the influence of special interests. Profiling this distribution also lays bare the burdens borne by each level of public sector institutions. Table 9.1 compares the government revenue and spending indexes of selected Latin American countries with those of Venezuela. This table profiles the percentage of income, expenditure, and intergovernmental transfers as a proportion of GDP, as well as the vertical equilibrium between regional and municipal governments and the central government. In other words, the statistics express the size of the public sector compared with the economy as a whole, as well as the internal geopolitical distribution of fiscal responsibilities.

The first relationship profiled in table 9.1 reveals that the total government revenue and expenditure of the industrialized countries are far higher than those of the Latin American countries selected. The average income of all governments in the industrialized countries is equivalent to 42.4 percent of their respective GDP, whereas the Latin American ones secured only 25.6 percent of GDP. Similarly, the expenditure of the industrialized countries was 47.8 percent, compared with 27.9 percent of the countries of Latin American. Venezuela's consolidated public sector consumed roughly 22 percent of GDP during most of the nineties. Recently, the national government has increased its income as a consequence of high oil prices, but most of that additional revenue has been used for special projects by the national government and for the Stabilization Fund.

Table 9.1. Intergovernmental Fiscal Data by Level of Governments: Selected Countries

	Venezuela (1997 est.)		Average Latin American Countries[a]		Average Industrialized[b]	
	Income		Income		Income	
	% GDP	% Total	% GDP	% Total	% GDP	% Total
Public sector	19.5	100.0	25.6	100.0	42.4	100.0
Central government	18.5	94.8	20.9	81.6	27.8	65.6
States (regions)	0.2	1	3.4	13.3	9.0	21.2
Municipalities	0.8	4.1	1.3	5.1	5.5	13.0
After transfers						
Central government	14.8	75.4	16.1	64.9	22.8	53.5
States (regions)	3.5	17.8	6.1	24.6	11.7	27.5
Municipalities	1.3	6.8	2.6	10.5	8.1	19.0
	Expenditures		Expenditures		Expenditures	
	% GDP	% Total	% GDP	% Total	% GDP	% Total
Public sector	22.0	100.0	27.9	100.0	47.8	100.0
Central government	17.4	79.1	18.4	65.9	27.2	56.9
States (regions)	3.3	15.0	6.9	24.7	12.6	26.4
Municipalities	1.3	5.9	2.6	9.3	8.0	16.7

Sources: Author's own calculation based on World Bank (2000); International Monetary Fund (1990–99); Secretaría de Hacienda y Crédito Público de México, Estadísticas Financieras del Sector Público (1999); Gingale and Webb (2000); de la Cruz (1998).

[a] Argentina, Brazil, Colombia, Venezuela, Mexico (1992–95).

[b] Australia, Austria, Canada, Germany, Spain, United States, (1993–96).

The second important piece of information that emerges from table 9.1 concerns the distribution of income and expenditures at each level of government (central, regional, and municipal) after deducting intergovernmental transfers. The industrialized countries average a central government income of 22.8 percent, another 11.7 percent for regional governments, and 8.1 percent of GDP for local governments. The comparable distribution for the Latin American countries is 16.1 percent, 6.1 percent, and 2.6 percent, respectively. Venezuela's case is 14.8 percent, 3.5 percent, and 1.3 percent of GDP, respectively. With regard to the proportion of income out of total public income captured by each level of government before transfers, the industrialized nations average as follows: 65.6 percent (national government), 21.2 percent (state or provincial governments), and 13 percent (municipalities); Latin America: 81.6 percent, 13.3 percent, and 5.1 percent, respectively; and Venezuela shows a less decentralized situation: 94.8 percent, 1 percent, and 4.1 percent out of total income before transfers. After intergovernmental transfers, income is less sharply differentiated, but Latin America remains far below the level of decentralization which exists in the industrialized countries, and Venezuela's performance is below the regional norm.

In regard to total public expenditure, the difference between Latin America and the industrialized countries is less marked but still substantial. In general, Latin American central governments average about 10 percentage points of spending more than their industrialized counterparts, to the detriment of local government spending. In summary, the relative figures are 56.9 percent, 26.4 percent, and 16.7 percent for the industrialized countries for central, regional, and local governments, respectively; for Latin America, they are 65.9 percent, 24.7 percent, and 9.3 percent, respectively. Venezuela again appeared more centralized, with national expenditure reaching 79.1 percent out of total public expenditure, the states 15 percent, and the municipalities 6 percent.

Exhaustion of the Punto Fijo Representative Political Model: The Basis for Reform

If we pay attention only to the indicators discussedearlier, Venezuela appears to have made minimal progress in decentralizing. As of 1998, the last year of the second Caldera government, the central government retained control over most government revenues, and total regional and local expenditures depended heavily on national transfers. However, there is more to the story. The Venezuelan state had been undergoing a profound transformation since 1989. In a process marked by as many setbacks as successes, decentralizing reforms sent a breath of fresh air throughout the political system. By the mid-1980s much of the population felt that the representative democratic model inaugurated in 1958 had become a cover for rule by Caracas-based political and economic elites. In many ways, the unleashing of decentralization in 1989, with the direct elections of state governors and municipal executives (mayors), kept the moribund system alive for a decade while newly responsive state and local politicians attempted to adapt to changing conditions.

The Impetus behind Decentralization

Venezuelan reformers, in a brave effort to change historical trends, chose to implement decentralization procedures in the late 1980s and early 1990s. Their effort was part of a broader program of mainly middle-class democrats to reconstruct and expand democratic relations between the state and society. The fact that these efforts were a departure from established practice is particularly relevant to understanding the trajectory of those reforms. This process, along with similar attempts at decentralization in Mexico and Colombia, suggests that the region's democratic regimes can find in themselves the strength and incentives for political renewal. Other countries, such as Argentina, Brazil, and to some extent Chile, have associated political decentralization with the reestablishment and deepening of democracy. These developments raise the intriguing possibility that Latin American political systems are firmly set on the path to attaining pluralist self-sustaining regimes capable of avoiding the democracy/dictatorship cycle.

Many social groups insisted on participating in numerous activities that had previously been undertaken only by the public sector. Some outcomes of this movement are the privatization of public enterprises and the transfer of national responsibilities to regional and local governments in the nineties. Although this latter point does not really amount to "destatism," it was and still is perceived as such because it redefined the functions of central government and increased the opportunities for nongovernmental organizations to involve themselves in policy making that affected their interests.

A huge devaluation known as Black Friday (February 18, 1983), reduced the capability of post-1958 political institutions to allocate resources and other valued commodities, thus widening the gap between society and the state. In 1985, the government of Venezuela created the Comisión Presidencial para la Reforma del Estado Presidential (COPRE; Commission for State Reform), composed of representatives of the different political parties, unions, professional associations, business associations, and citizen groups to review relations between the state and Venezuelan society. A consensus existed that some restructuring was necessary. The major conclusion reached by COPRE was that the legitimacy of post-1958 democratic institutions had declined and that the representative democratic political regime needed to be made more effectively representative. Specifically, COPRE proposed that citizens should elect the state governors, who until 1989 were appointed by the president of the republic. COPRE also insisted on the creation of the office of mayor, a Spanish tradition that had disappeared in Venezuela. The reform proposal sought to separate the legislative from the executive branch of government in the municipal councils. It also hoped to increase the responsiveness of legislative officeholders with a system of direct elections of congressional and council representatives. These propositions became laws between 1989 and 1993, despite a significant resistance from important elements in both major political parties. Nevertheless, the overwhelming majority of Venezuelans supported these reforms.

The greatest supporters of decentralization have been the politically mobilized sectors of society, which have discovered that this arrangement gives them more influence as they recast their relations with all three levels of state government. An important consequence of these changes is that Venezuela now functions more like a federal state (as opposed to a unitary one).

Venezuelan-Style Federalism: Major Reforms between 1989 and 1994

Beginning in 1986, when COPRE proposed holding popular direct elections for state governors and mayors in the municipalities, a significant number of legal reforms and institutional changes occurred. These can be grouped into four types: political, administrative, those that recast relations among the three levels of government, and fiscal changes.

Political Reforms

Again, the motivation for decentralization in Venezuela was political. It was underpinned by the conviction that the political control of the Caracas-based political parties had to be broken. This conviction explains the decision by civil society leaders to press for the popular election of regional and municipal officials prior to reorganizing state and local governments, which effectively happened in 1989. The sequence that most planners would have preferred—improve the administrative capabilities of state and local governments, transfer responsibilities for certain services, and only then elect the authorities—would have allowed Caracas-based party elites to operate more efficiently in the municipalities and at the regional level. This turn of events would have likely liquidated the decentralization process before it had begun. The population would not have felt represented in state and local institutions staffed by technicians whose first loyalty would have been to the national leaders who appointed them. In addition, important forces at the national headquarters of Acción Democrática (AD; Democratic Action) and Comité de Organización Política Electoral Independiente: Partido Social Cristiano (COPEI; Committee of Independent Electoral Political Organization: Social Christian Party) would have searched for (and likely found) an opportunity to discredit the reforms in view of the lack of interest the communities would have shown in them.

Decentralization as it evolved in Venezuela found its governors and mayors to be its best defenders and the driving force behind it. Polls taken since their first election consistently show broad support for decentralization, always more than 80 percent of population.

Administrative Reforms: Sharing Out the Responsibilities

The Laws on Decentralization and Transfer of Responsibilities (LOD) and the Law on the Municipal Regime (LORM) of 1989 contain the main provisions that lay out the distribution of responsibilities for services among the nation, the states, and the municipalities. The prevailing criterion when assigning concurrent responsibilities to the three levels was for central government to reserve all responsibilities with high externalities—referred to as "of a strategic nature" in the political jargon of Venezuela—as well as political decisions that affected the nation as a whole. The LOD and the LORM assigned to the states and municipalities responsibility for managing, budgeting, and staffing basic services.

An important aspect of the LOD is the gradual and negotiated nature of responsibility transfers from the central government. The state governor had to obtain the state legislative assembly's approval in order to request the total or partial transfer of any shared responsibility. Then the national executive (under the 1961 constitution) accepted the request after it passed through the Senate. The president of the republic, subject to approval from the Senate, also had authority to propose the transfer of responsibilities. The LORM, however, contained no mechanisms for the transfer of new powers to the municipalities, assuming that most of the relevant local government responsibilities were already in effect. In addition, exclusive responsibilities could be taken on by the states in response to a formal proposal from the governor and following passage of the proposal by the state legislative assemblies.[4] These responsibilities were almost entirely transferred in the early 1990s.

The LOD had fundamental shortcomings that proved to be bottlenecks for the deepening of decentralization. These defects left many governors, as well as the central government officials, with feelings of frustration. In the first place, the LOD was excessively generic to the extent that it attempted to separate out concurrent responsibilities. It mentioned, as regional governments' attributions, substantial policy areas but did not spell out which aspects of those responsibilities were to be assigned to the states. This situation is all the more limiting for operational decentralization when it is taken into account that national laws gave the central government a large number of functions in the very policy arenas that were mentioned in the decentralization legislation and that municipal law also reserved a broad set of specific powers in many of the same policy arenas for the mayors.

Neither the LOD nor the LORM delimited the shared powers of states and municipalities. Along with the LORM, the decentralization law could have been the operational blueprint for distributing concurrent competencies among the three levels of government. In contrast, the ambiguity in the decentralization and municipality laws made for a scheme of ongoing negotiation, definition, and redefinition to define the respective spaces of each territorial government. This situation at first helped the governors when they sought to transfer responsibilities that their respective constituencies wanted to be administered closer to them. Initially, therefore, the decentralization process gained credibility. Over the long run, the asymmetrical demands of the states and the enduring resistance to devolution by the central government have produced a confusing map of the allocation of responsibilities among the national, state, and local governments.

Intergovernmental Relations

Decentralization legislation in Venezuela includes a system of state coordination which enables state governors to exercise their constitutional role as an agent of the national executive (a fairly uncommon position in the legislation of other countries, where central government normally appoints its own regional representative) when it comes to aligning national, state, and municipal policies. Other coordination mechanisms were created in 1993; the most significant are the Territorial Council of Government, the Council of Governments of the Caracas Metropolitan Area, and the Intergovernmental Fund for Decentralization. The first two intended to bring representatives of the three levels of government to the negotiating tables for coordination. The fund, in contrast, crystallized as a financing mechanism in which representatives of the three levels of government participate equally.

Fiscal Reforms

The Intergovernmental Fund for Decentralization, created in 1993, was intended to complement the 1989 decentralization and municipal regime legislation. Together these three laws facilitated regular fiscal forecasts to guide the transfer of services and financing from the central government to the states and municipalities. Classical instruments were modified and new ones created, in principle, to meet the new needs of a decentralized state.

The most important intergovernmental fiscal instrument in Venezuela is the constitutional budget (*situado constitucional*), whose origin dates from 1925. According to the constitution of 1961, at least 15 percent of the national government's regular earnings were to be transferred to the states. Thirty percent were to be divided equally among the state governments, and the other 70 percent were to be distributed proportionately, based on population. According to the LOD, the budget was increased by 1 percent each year between 1990 and 1994 to achieve 20 percent of the nation's total regular income as of that year. The municipalities also received, in their transfer account, a percentage of the states' regular income, which started at 10 percent in 1990 and was mandated to reach 20 percent by the year 2000. Fifty percent of these funds were divided equally among the twenty-three states and 50 percent shared proportionately according to the size of the state population.

The LOD also envisioned that, with each shared service delivered to the states by the central government, the financial resources allocated annually by the latter for the provision of that service would also be transferred in accordance with variation of the republic's regular income. The cost of this provision to the national government during the final Punto Fijo government (Caldera, 1994–99) was estimated to have approached 20 percent of public national regular income by the time all the concurrent services had been transferred.

A wide variety of taxes are reserved exclusively for the national government, the most significant of which are the value-added tax; the income tax, including oil revenue; customs duties; the gasoline tax; excise taxes; and banking debit taxes. Rates may also be charged for public services provided. In turn, the states have the residual power to create taxes on production and consumption that have not been allocated by law to the national government. Because of the existence of a value-added tax, the states cannot levy a local consumer tax.

Service charges are another source of income for states, and the LOD transfers a series of exclusive services to state governments. These include the power to charge for the use of freeways, bridges, seaports, airports, salt marshes, oyster beds, and nonmetal mines. These levies have begun to produce significant income for certain states. Municipal regime law envisages a large number of tax competencies for local governments, among which the most important are the property tax, industry and trade license, vehicles permit, commercial propaganda, and public shows. They are also entitled to charge for improvements to urban property.

The fiscal structure crafted by Punto Fijo politicians in 1989 envisioned no interregional compensation mechanism beyond the per capita distribution of the budget.[5] Some concern was voiced over the failure to provide for any kind of redistributive system between the rich and poor areas of the country, but proposals to create a clearing fund for this purpose came to naught.[6] Finally, in 1993, upon authorization from the Congress, President Ramón Velázquez passed the Fondo Intergubernamental para la Descentralización (FIDES; Intergovernmental Fund for Decentralization), which unified the compensatory procedures and coordinated public sector investment. Almost 30 percent of FIDES funds come from value-added tax collection. For fiscal 1993, a 4 percent share of the collection was established; 10 percent in 1994; 15 percent in 1995; 18 percent in 1996; 22 percent in 1997; 24 percent in 1998; 28 percent in 1999; and up to 30 percent as of the year 2000.[7] This allocation of resources was also conditional upon the presentation of projects for evaluation and cofinancing. Management of the fund resided with an executive board composed of three representatives from the central government, two representatives of the governors, and one representative of the mayors. Membership on this board was designed to maximize the circulation of information about investment projects among the various level of government in order to facilitate coordination.

Should the existing arrangement persist, the accountability of the governors to their constituents will fall short of what reformers intended even though some states have made a serious effort to increase revenue by charging for services. However, when the population do not have to pay for state government directly with state taxes, the incentive of regional communities to monitor and seek correction of governor's policies is limited. Just as serious is the fact that budgetary pressures in the regions have led to continuous political tension between the federal government and the states. In practice, the former is reclaiming its prerogative to allocate financial resources assigned for national priorities. The deficit that the states could accumulate under these conditions may produce an unpleasant surprise for national fiscal discipline. The mayors, in contrast, have made considerable progress in taking advantage of the additional capabilities given to them by the LORM to levy and collect taxes.

In any process of institutional and political change outstanding results in the immediate aftermath of implementation are the exception. However, our analysis of the composition of Venezuelan state and municipal expenditures during the first years of decentralization reveals some interesting developments.[8] First, in the year immediately following promulgation of the reforms, the proportion of expenditures going to staffing drops on average from 39 percent to 33 percent of the total expenditures made by all subnational governments. For state governments the proportion drops from 38 percent to 34 percent and for the municipalities from 42 percent to 30 percent. This does not signal a decrease in the total number of employees. Indeed, at the state level the number of state government employees appears to have increased. In 1991 Venezuelan state governments employed 194,393, and this number rose to 212,814 (+ 9.4%) in 1993.[9] The bulk of this increase came in hires to staff the newly formed police forces that the decentralization legislation authorized.

The containment of salaries in the public sector in relation to the nominal increase in fiscal revenue partly explains the proportional decrease in staffing expenditures. Especially telling is the proportional increase in the budget line labeled "contribution to organizations" (10% in 1989, 21% in 1993). By and large these transfers were devoted to the financing of public or private organizations in charge of administering a variety of local and state programs. These programs ranged from low-cost housing and transportation infrastructure to municipal management schools. They also included funding for loans to small and medium-scale industrialists, fishers and farmers, microenterprises, and sports or tourism institutions. What all these programs have in common is that they enjoy considerable autonomy in relation to the regular administrative expenditures of the states and municipalities. The flourishing of this organizational tendency suggests an ongoing lack of confidence in the traditional "tied" public bureaucracies on the part of state and municipal managers.

On the expenditure side, as with income, the averages conceal a high degree of individual variance. In the municipality of Maracaibo (the third most important in Venezuela), for example, the decline in the proportion of spending on wages and salaries was particularly noteworthy. Roughly 52 percent of the budget went for this purpose in 1989, but three years later expenditures for salaries and wages were only 34 percent. In the nearby petroleum-producing municipality of Cabimas, an even more dramatic decline occurred, from 41 percent to 16 percent. On the other hand, over the same period in the isolated state of Delta Amacuro, comparable expenditures rose from 45 percent to 61 percent.

This variation highlights one of the reasons that advocates of decentralization argue that reducing the role of central government will make the public sector more effective. The mix of solutions developed by each leader differs depending on the geopolitical unit that he or she administers. Once the programs are under way, they are subject to evaluation by constituents who may compare them with what is occurring in neighboring states and municipalities. On the other hand, nothing suggests that a *prior* drop in spending on public sector wages and salaries is always a good thing. The perceptions of the electorate about what value they are receiving for their expenditures on bureaucracy do not always coincide with objective reality. For instance, many Venezuelans believed that the public sector is bloated and that bureaucracy in the United States is small and efficient. Yet the ratio of public employees to the total population in the United States was 7.2 for every 100 inhabitants, while in Venezuela it was 6 to every 100 in 1998.

This type of misconception can lead the uninformed to believe that cuts in expenditure on staff in the public sector must be a good thing under any circumstances. However, the real efficiency of the public sector must be measured in each case in order to judge performance. Still, few would dispute that efficient public management, whether national, regional, or local, should have relatively few well-paid but highly skilled employees.

Rise of the Fifth Republic: Centralism's Backlash

The major reforms undertaken during the glamorous first years of decentralization in Venezuela, despite some shortcomings, reflected the hope of many in Venezuelan society that they could resolve the ongoing political crisis while at the same time deepening representative democracy. In other words, advocates of decentralization believed that their reforms would strengthen representative institutions, facilitate transparency, and improve governmental accountability. The popular support for decentralization among groups in civil society during the 1990s, especially the middle sectors, suggested that most such groups viewed the weakening of central authority as the correct path to deepen democracy.

The incremental reform and modernization of Venezuela's Punto Fijo democracy, a system that had its roots in egalitarian populism, seemed possible in the early 1990s. Subsequent events suggest that although decentralization was necessary if traumatic rupture was to be avoided, decentralization in and of itself could not save the Punto Fijo system.

Governors and mayors were elected more because of their local leadership than because of their support from the national leaders of AD, COPEI, or Movimiento al Socialismo (MAS; Movement toward Socialism). These leaders never seemed to have grasped the depth of the alienation from them as political brokers which was crystallizing. Their failure to put in place an effective safety net that would cushion the poor from the most pernicious effects of economic liberalization and weak credibility of traditional politicians made Venezuela almost ungovernable. The leaders of AD and COPEI joined to oust President Carlos Andrés Pérez in 1993, but it proved a futile attempt to regain legitimacy and reinvigorate post-1958 representative democracy. They hoped that the sacrifice of Pérez would redeem the system that had lost its way. In fact, Pérez's impeachment seemed to have created a scapegoat with little effect on the core problem of Venezuelan democracy: lost faith in political parties and other representative institutions, especially the national Congress.

Moreover, the leaders of AD and COPEI never attempted to explain that many of the neoliberal economic reforms initiated in 1989 were needed if Venezuela was ever to reduce its dependence on the volatile international petroleum market. Quite to the contrary, in what appeared as confirmation that something was fundamentally amiss in the move to privatization and decentralization, the leaders of the three dominant political parties joined to cancel critical but necessary aspects of the Pérez program. Ironically, the way the political parties handled the "purge" of President Pérez ended up weakening the institutions of Punto Fijo democracy and destroying their domination over national politics.

Rafael Caldera, as discussed elsewhere in this volume, was elected president for the term 1994–99 as the candidate of a coalition that promised to end political control by AD and COPEI. His allies were a minority in the Congress, and Caldera soon sought the support of AD in order to govern. Caldera's allies had little strength in the states and municipalities, and this led him to refuse most demands for responsibility transfers that states and the municipalities anticipated under the reforms of 1989 and 1993. Caldera also reduced the share of national income allocated to FIDES while passing a law that gave state and municipal governments the powers to set salaries and standards for their civil servants. This led to crisis and deadlock in state and local governments, which in turn allowed the central government to reassert its influence in geopolitical arenas that had been given autonomy earlier in the decade. Throughout the second Caldera government governors and mayors coexisted uneasily with a national government that was actually searching for ways to reverse decentralization. A great opportunity to strengthen the representative democratic system was lost.

Decentralization in the Fifth Republic

The consequences of this loss became evident in 1999 when President Hugo Chávez moved with determination and resolve to craft a new political system that would increase the power of the national executive. Confusion has permeated President Chávez's rhetoric regarding decentralization. On the one hand, he proclaims Ezequiel Zamora, a provincial insurgent leader of the nineteenth-century Federation War who challenged domination by Caracas elites, to be one of the models for his movement. On the other hand, his government has not promulgated a single regulation that would advance the decentralization process; on the contrary, President Chávez has decreed several measures that further reduced financing to the states and municipalities.

The current constitution, drafted by a constituent assembly controlled by Chávez supporters and approved by voters in December 1999, does retain the traditional definition of the Venezuelan state as a federation. Nevertheless, several of its articles place limitations on the powers of state and local governments. In addition, the constitution abolished the senate, thus eliminating the equal representation of the states with population in the national legislature. The constitution of 1999 also leaves to national legislation the crafting of subnational powers such as the regulation of public services delivered by states and municipalities. The same is true in regard to structuring pivotal subnational institutions, such as the state legislative assemblies.

The 1999 constitution intended that the Federal Council of Government, composed of representatives of the three levels of government, would provide channels through which subnational governments could influence central policy making. As of mid-2002, however, legislation to structure the Federal Council of Government languished in the National Assembly. The 1999 constitution also established the Interregional Compensation Fund to replace FIDES, but it too has yet to take shape. Funding for FIDES derives from a set proportion of the national tax income. In contrast, the Federal Council of Government will decide the amount of resources available for allocation by the Interregional Compensation Fund on an annual basis. This means that between 20 and 30 percent of transfers from the federal government to the states and municipalities will depend on short-term political and economic conditions. Finally, the post-1999 political regime established procedures that effectively bar the public from knowing how transfers take place between the central governments, the states, and the municipalities, a level of intragovernment secrecy not seen since the dictatorship of General Marcos Pérez Jiménez (1952–58).

The general conduct of Chávez's administration spelled conflict with governors and mayors. The most prominent evidence of this conflict has been an unprecedented delay and lack of transparency regarding financial transfers from the central government. The National Association of Governors (representing, in fact, opposition governors) has denounced this situation in a number of occasions. On the other hand, there is evidence that discretionary transfers have been channeled to subnational authorities close to the president.

Despite these difficulties, decentralization continues to enjoy a high level of support. Not very surprisingly, most supporters of President Chávez in the National Assembly claim to favor advancing the decentralization process. They need to strengthen the support of their own constituency. Legislation that would increase the powers of state governments to levy taxes was discussed during 2001. Nevertheless, President Chávez instructed the leaders of his political party (Movimiento Quinta República [MVR; Fifth Republic Movement]) in the National Assembly to move this legislation to the back burner.

The economic downturn during the Chávez administration has undermined the capability of state and local governments to collect taxes and other local revenues. In practice, this undermines the autonomy of subnational governments and allows the Chávez administration to recentralize political and economic control. Additional momentum leading to recentralization comes from the tendency of President Chávez to use the military to construct public works and deliver public services.

Outcomes of Decentralization in Venezuela

The obvious deterioration of Punto Fijo democracy's legitimacy was the impetus for moving rapidly to increase the responsive capability of subnational governments through the direct election of governors and mayors. In other words, advocates of decentralization believed that it was critical to move with all deliberate speed to create a space in the polity for institutions that would be close to the people, accessible, and responsive. They saw this as the best hope for restoring credibility in the representative democratic system. This strategy led to some administrative disorder and uncertainty over how responsibilities for providing services would be allocated among the three levels of government. However, the cost of waiting until all management issues had been resolved before restructuring state and local institutions seemed even more risky given the accelerating decline of the post-1958 democratic model.

The institutions that appeared as a result of decentralization changed the shape and substance of the Venezuelan polity, especially the manner in which interest groups related to state institutions. The axis of Venezuela's federal government since the reforms of 1989 and 1993 has been characterized by permanent negotiation between the nation and the states, between the states and the municipalities, and between a multiplicity of political, economic, and social actors.

At first glance, this approach might seem chaotic, and many senior public executives undoubtedly missed the times when affairs of state were decided in small circles that rarely extended beyond the limits of Caracas. Although this pattern served to normalize Punto Fijo democracy in the 1960s, it led to institutional uncertainty and political decay in the 1980s. Broad sectors of an increasingly diverse society were ignored in matters in which public input into policy making was critical for maintaining support for the political regime. The urban riots of 1989 confirmed the necessity of consultation and comprehensive political brokering in order to safeguard the democracy and ensure economic growth. Paradoxically, the more participation and negotiation there is under federal conditions, the more stability can be expected from the institutions owing to their increased legitimacy.

The first class of elected state governors showed great interest in decentralization. Upon assuming office in 1990, many attempted to strengthen the administrative infrastructure of their state governments and to use regional resources to build a political base that was autonomous from national political party leaders in Caracas. Most also took advantage of the decentralization law to transfer services and responsibilities from national ministries controlled from Caracas to their state governments. Considered as a whole, this profound political transformation occurred at breakneck speed. During the first period of elected regional and local governments, a mandate that lasted only three years (1989–93), twelve services came under "concurrent competency" (jointly administered by state and national governments), and state governments took on eighteen exclusive competencies. At the end of 1992, negotiations were under way to transfer eighty-three concurrent and thirty-two exclusive public services.

State governors strengthened the management capabilities of their governments throughout the 1990s. Between 1989 and 1993, the National Association of Governors (then representing all governors) created fifteen state reform commissions in order to launch promising decentralization projects. Individual state governments crafted institutions that gave them the ability to deliver housing and stimulate activities that ranged from industrial development to tourism. Additional regional institutions were created to manage the new infrastructure that had been assigned to the states, specifically seaports, airports, and highways. The legal charters of these institutions evolved in keeping with their new organizational structure. In this context, it must be noted than in many instances the state governments created simple supervisory and regulatory agencies while the private sector took charge of delivering services.

The municipal sphere underwent less reorganization than its state counterpart did in the first stage of the decentralization process. As the 1990s progressed, there were an increasing number of municipal initiatives in the areas of tax collection, management training, urban planning, and policing. In the case of Caracas, the municipalities that constitute the Capital District created local police forces that quickly gained the confidence of the communities. They also took charge of critical services that included water supply, the regulation of transportation, and garbage collection. Elected state governors have demonstrated a sustained interest in strengthening the capacity of local governments and in forming institutions that linked state and municipal bureaucracy. There appeared to be a consensus among the governors that if the municipalities remained weak the capabilities of the states to act autonomously would be undermined in the long run.

Governors and mayors assigned a high priority to improving the efficiency and professionalism of service delivery because local neighborhood organizations began to act as watchdogs in matters that concerned their place of residence. Watchdog activity was aided by the newly aggressive reporting by the press and television news media in monitoring the decisions of state and local governments. Communication between elected officials and their constituents intensified, especially in the urban areas. According to one study, a direct correlation could be seen between the success of the governors when they stand for reelection and the attention they have given to developing and monitoring efficient service delivery during their term in office.[10] The ability of citizens to reward for responsiveness to community interests was impossible prior to 1989, when the president of the republic appointed the governors.

Conclusion

How can the persisting popularity of decentralization be explained? One way of understanding the phenomenon lies in understanding that broad sectors of Venezuelan society are asking for more personal accountability as a way to reconstruct a democratic social pact that possesses broad legitimacy. The decline of party influence in subnational politics which began with the election of local and regional leaders in the early 1990s is likely to continue in upcoming elections. Even in 2000, when President Chávez won what he called "relegitimization" in a landslide election, eight governors out of twenty-three were elected among opposition leaders in states that were also massively voting for Chávez. These opposition governors bucked the trend of supporting a popular charismatic leader because they had a track record of attending to local interests. Even authoritarian temptations, such as the one Venezuela experienced between 1998 and 2003, will in all probability yield to the underlying affect toward democracy which has historical roots and which grew stronger during the forty years of Punto Fijo governments.

Decentralization, although incomplete, has strengthened orientations supportive of democracy among Venezuelans. Less but more strategic central government, fewer public enterprises, more powerful regional and local governments, new vigorous accountability mechanisms, and more privately supplied goods appear to be an attractive formula for synthesizing the new public institutions required to make Venezuela truly democratic. Numerous countries in Latin America are treading this path, with considerable difficulty and resistance from old interest groups, which, quite rightly, feel threatened. Within this context, decentralization is a long-term strategy to create the conditions for a new, fairer, more democratic, and more efficient balance of power.

CHAPTER TEN

The Syndrome of Economic Decline and the Quest for Change

Janet Kelly and Pedro A. Palma

The Venezuelan economy spun out of control sometime in the 1970s after many years of stability and high growth. Successive governments applied different approaches to solving the deep problems that spread from the economic system into the very heart of the society. Their failures contributed to a malaise that undermined confidence and generated competing theories of what had gone wrong. For a quarter of a century, the country had enjoyed a stream of income from oil which should have made it possible to put Venezuela on a path to development, but by the turn of the millennium, most citizens thought that all their riches had been turned to naught. How did this come about? Would the Chávez "revolution" find a way out of the maze?

The answers to these questions require an understanding of the interplay between the economic events that marked the democratic period since 1958 and the ideas about the economy which guided policymakers. This chapter shows that, despite trends taking root in many developed and developing nations, Venezuela resisted more than most countries the idea that market processes would produce prosperity and equality. Experiments with the market, especially the short-lived effort to liberalize the economy between 1989 and

1993, generated deep and even violent conflict, thus reinforcing the traditional bias toward seeking growth and income redistribution through government action. Although most of the market reforms of that period remained intact and some were even furthered, successive governments continued to fail to achieve the stability that sustained growth would require.

The "antineoliberal" campaign and eventual political triumph of Hugo Chávez Frías in 1998 seemed once again to reveal the deep preference of most Venezuelans for letting the state take the lead and their distrust of leaving development to the forces of the unguided market. The peculiar mix of policies of the Chávez government, some profoundly interventionist and others surprisingly liberal, defied the simple conclusion that Venezuela would slide back to a reliance on government controls. The country was looking for a new formula that would permit a better balance between policies that would reduce income disparities and at the same time stimulate investment and growth. The Chávez mix promised growth with equity and, based on the record, seemed to seek growth through a continuation of the macroeconomic policies of his predecessors while ensuring equity through changes in microeconomic policies and transformation of the political system.

There was no guarantee that the country had found its way. Wishing for an innovative route to prosperity is not the same as finding it, especially in an environment of radical political and social changes that inevitably provoke resistance and uncertainty. Even in the absence of such turbulence, underlying realities of dependence on oil, volatility in basic economic variables, public impatience with unemployment and poverty, and the persistence of government inefficiency and corruption would continue to dog efforts to put the system on an even keel. In particular, popular expectations for a quick turnaround pressured the government to look for "easy" solutions and promises that would be hard to keep without endangering the solvency of the state.

Venezuela's quest for change after years of decline confronted the dilemma of reformers everywhere. Stagnation and crisis reflect deep-seated institutional problems that demand radical transformation; at the same time, radical change is inherently destabilizing and generates resistance and uncertainty in such a way as to undermine the very objectives the government seeks to achieve. The challenge for the future will be to break the syndrome of failure and to restore citizens' confidence in the ability of their governments to provide prosperity while reducing poverty and widening the possibilities of the whole population.

Long-Term Features of Economic Policy in Venezuela

Economic policy reflects the institutional and social context in which countries make decisions. Venezuelans themselves were conscious of the factors that conspired against solid and consistent economic policy: the capture of the state by powerful interests, party hegemony that blocked change, popular pressures for short-term economic results, and presidential government insensitive to the weakening of its own legitimacy.

The very stability of the Venezuelan political system created in 1958 and the progressive dominance of two main competing parties, Acción Democrática (AD; Democratic Action) and Comité de Organización Política Electoral Independiente: Partido Social Cristiano (COPEI; Committee of Independent Electoral Political Organization: Social Christian Party), forged a consensus view of economic and social policy which tended to suppress alternative models and to create a strong alliance between government and elite groups like the peak business associations organization, Federación de Cámaras y Asociaciones de Comercio y Producción de Venezuela (FEDECAMARAS; Federation of Chambers of Commerce and Production of Venezuela),and the powerful unions, particularly the Confederación de Trabajadores de Venezuela (CTV; Confederation of Venezuelan Workers). This consensus favored the protection of both industry and workers through trade protectionism, state-owned industries, subsidies, controls, and a comprehensive labor law. In effect, Venezuela closely resembled the kind of polity described by Mancur Olson in *The Rise and Decline of Nations* (1982), in which long periods of stability give rise to entrenched coalitions of groups in society which institute policies that favor their interests but which gradually undermine the forces of renewal and change necessary for a country to adapt and compete in a dynamic world.

The Influence of the Oil Economy

The case of Venezuela might well reveal how a democracy enters into decline and fails to deliver the very economic results that voters want. But an additional factor specific to the country contributed to the phenomenon: oil. Production of oil in Venezuela was important since almost the beginning of the twentieth century but became even more so as a result of the spectacular rise in oil prices which began around 1973.

Perhaps it was not inevitable that Venezuela should have failed to convert its oil wealth into sustained development, but such was not to be the case. In

Venezuela, the dominant obsession since at least the 1930s had been centered on how to avoid turning over to foreigners the bulk of the substantial profits the industry produced. Until the nationalization of the industry in 1976, most oil was produced by large multinational companies, and Venezuelans were universally aware that they did not control the exploitation of their most precious asset. The idea voiced by the young intellectual Arturo Uslar Pietri in the thirties that Venezuela should "sow the oil" became the common aim of the whole country, in the sense that oil should be the seed of development and investment in the future. This idea informed a positive developmentalist ideology that would push the country first to increase taxes on the foreign companies, then to make common cause with other petroleum producers in the founding of the Organization of Petroleum Exporting Countries (OPEC) in 1960, then to form a state-owned oil company as the eventual base for local knowledge of operations and technology, and, finally, to mandate the state takeover of the entire industry.

Venezuela's long, and even heroic, struggle for control was based fundamentally on a view of the world which corresponded to that of the dependency theorists of the 1960s and 1970s: development required gaining autonomy from the economic currents of the developed world; injustice and inequality resulted not from the national failure to give equal opportunities to the whole population but from asymmetries of power; the market should be firmly regulated by the state so that oligopolistic power should not be used against the interests of citizens. Around this set of beliefs a strong consensus developed in Venezuela. As could be expected, some voices of dissent could be heard, particularly from business interests that felt squeezed by the growth of state-owned enterprises in much of the economic system, but the paternalistic state made room for just about everyone, guaranteeing protected markets for the private sector.

The Statist Consensus

By the time of the nationalization of the Venezuelan oil industry in 1976, the wave of optimism in the country reached an unprecedented level. Economic growth was high and unemployment low; investment in industry presaged a new future for diversification of the economy, and little doubt existed that the nation was now on the route to closing the gap with the most developed countries. Students were sent abroad in huge numbers to absorb the knowledge that such development would require. Everything indicated that the consensus reached on how to achieve success was correct. In fact, within only two or three years, evidence accumulated that all was not well. Growth began to falter, the balance of payments weakened, and prices started rising. Occasional booms in the oil market convinced Venezuelans that such problems were temporary, but the truth was that the country began a long decline at the end of the 1970s which was marked by repeated crises and failed attempts to deal with them. As Fernando Coronil said (1997: 368), "The myth of Venezuela as a wealthy democratic nation steadily advancing toward modernity continued to hold into the 1990s despite problems that had become evident by 1978."

Yet the consensus about economic policy and the role of the petroleum state in ensuring the welfare of every citizen failed to break down, despite the record of poor economic performance. Two brief periods of liberalization, during the government of Carlos Andrés Pérez (1989–93) and during the last part of the government of Rafael Caldera (1996–99), although promising in terms of economic recovery, ended with popular rejection and calls for reining in the market. Hugo Chávez's presidential campaign in 1998 repeated the traditional rhetoric of distrust of the market—"savage capitalism" in the candidate's repeated words—and called for a restoration of state leadership and of the reinforcement of government control over the oil industry. As demonstrated later in this chapter, the Chávez government did not always apply its own rhetoric, yet its need to insist on the old formulas hostile to the market and liberalization reveals the force of popular conceptions of the optimum balance between the state and the market.

A key factor that the new government did not take into account was its administrative capacity to take over the state and redirect its energies. Good intentions might not be enough if inexperience, corruption, and incompetence were to get in the way. What would impede the repetition of the same patterns in the Chávez period? In Venezuela, the yearning for change had become irresistible, but it was unlikely that the syndrome of decline could be reversed without real changes in economic policy, especially in maintaining fiscal balance and stability.

The Record of Economic Performance until 1998

Four key variables sum up the evolution of the Venezuelan economy in the democratic period leading up to the political changes that were to mark the start of the Chávez era. In the first place, income per capita gradually eroded between 1978 and 1998. Another variable, inflation, started to rise in the 1970s and accelerated thereafter. The exchange rate, stable for many years, also began a long depreciation that steadily reduced the value of the currency after the crisis of 1983. Finally, oil prices imposed a stop-go pattern of boom and bust which imposed great uncertainty on policy makers and contributed to capital flight and low investment. Efforts to stabilize these variables and restore growth met with popular and political resistance that seemed always to return economic policy to traditional solutions based on state controls.

The Fall in Income per Capita

The best measure for understanding the drama of the Venezuelan economy in the democratic period is real income per capita. As figure 10.1 shows, income per capita rose steadily for many years until about 1978, when it began its progressive decline. Venezuelans in 1999 had slipped back to commanding a per capita gross domestic product (GDP) that was about the same as it was in 1962, and the purchasing power of their average salary was only 33 percent of that in 1978.

The Surge in Inflation

A second variable, inflation, tracks the failure of economic policy with equal force. Venezuela, long a haven of price stability in Latin America—where other countries often suffered hyperinflation—also faced disturbing peaks in inflation which took citizens by surprise, eroding the purchasing power of their salaries and causing grave uncertainty (see fig. 10.2). Under the circumstances, people tried to protect the value of their assets by investing abroad, thus contributing to capital outflows.

Figure 10.2 shows how inflation had remained modest during the 1960s; with the oil boom of the 1970s, however, prices began to rise slightly. The response at the time was simply to declare price controls on basic goods and services, particularly those affecting consumers, such as food and rents and, of course, public services such as telephones, electricity, and the like. Even producers were favored in that the prices of inputs produced by state-owned companies—steel, energy, cement, and fertilizers—were kept low. Low prices also meant low returns, however, and the private sector naturally pressed for protection from cheaper imports, access to low-cost credit, and diverse subsidies. The government generally obliged, often absorbing losses through public enterprises that constantly needed injections of capital from the state and

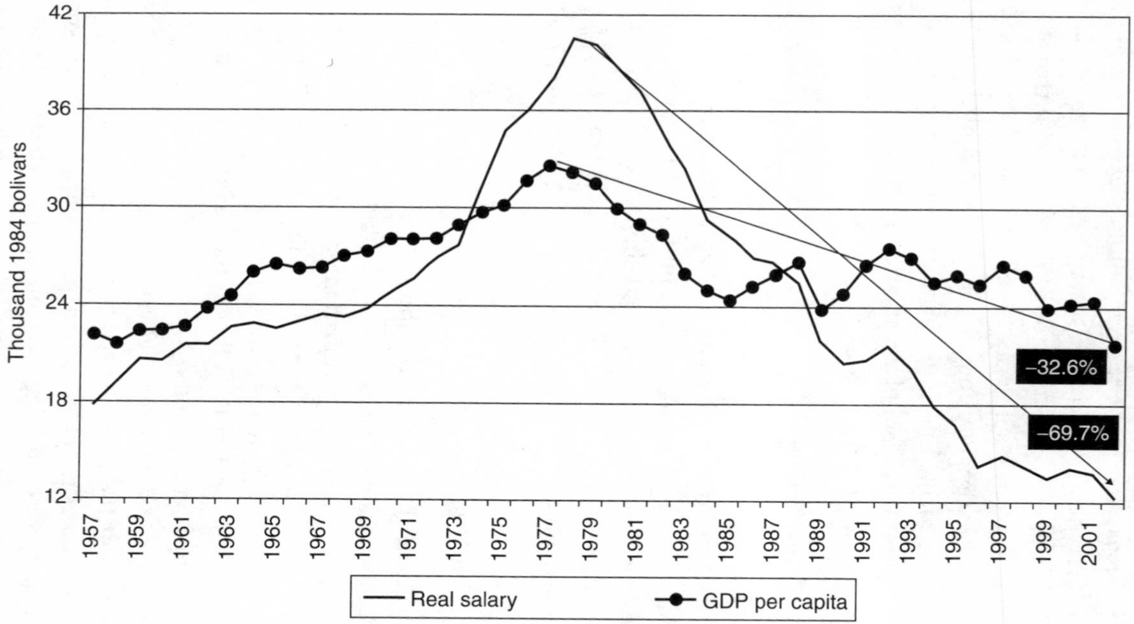

Fig. 10.1. GDP per capita and average real salary. *Sources:* Central Bank of Venezuela, Central Office of Statistics and Information, and MetroEconómica.

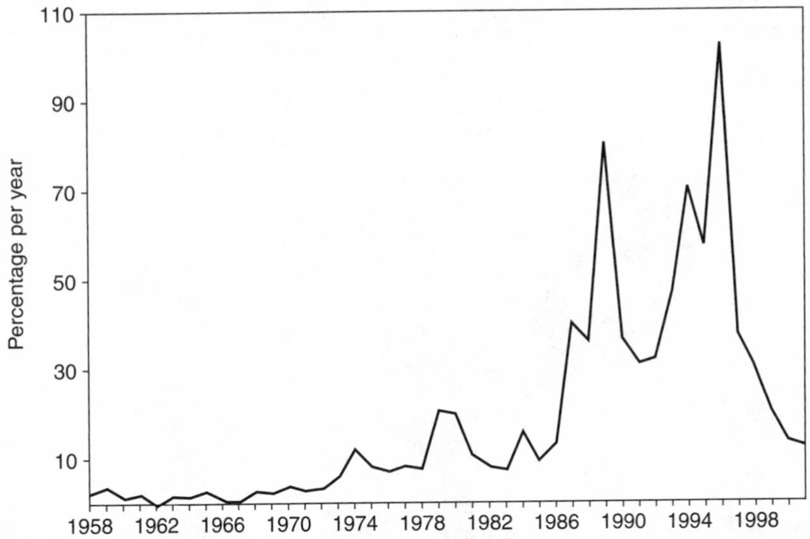

Fig. 10.2. Inflation, 1958–2001. *Source:* Central Bank of Venezuela.

often sacrificed good management in the face of financial pressure. The government, in turn, took advantage of the availability of foreign credit to pay for its increasingly unsustainable pattern of spending.

The Loss of Control over the Exchange Rate

No country can maintain a fixed exchange rate in the long run if its rate of inflation differs significantly from that of its trading partners because that disparity overvalues the currency, making imported goods cheaper and deteriorating the trade balance. This in turn leads to devaluation expectations and capital outflows as people try to protect the value of their assets. If, in addition, the country accumulates debt abroad, uncertainty about its ability to service those obligations compounds the problem. In the end, devaluation becomes inevitable, although governments often try to put off the moment of truth by implementing restrictive monetary policies and by sacrificing their international reserves. This cycle began in Venezuela with the inflation of the late 1970s and continued to repeat itself throughout the 1980s and 1990s. Venezuela maintained a fixed exchange rate for most of the period until 1983, when the bolivar was devalued and exchange controls were put into effect until early 1989. Despite efforts to return to stability, the inflation-devaluation cycle

Table 10.1. The Exchange Rate, 1982–2001 (bolivars per dollar, end-year)

Year	Bs/$	Rate of Depreciation (%)
1982	4.30	
1983	10.87	152.8
1984	12.10	11.3
1985	13.80	14.0
1986	22.20	60.9
1987	28.20	27.0
1988	34.02	20.6
1989	43.79	28.7
1990	50.79	16.0
1991	61.63	21.3
1992	79.60	29.2
1993	106.00	33.2
1994	215.33	103.1
1995	334.12	55.2
1996	476.75	42.7
1997	504.25	5.8
1998	564.50	11.9
1999	648.25	14.8
2000	699.75	7.9
2001	763.00	9.0

Sources: Central Bank of Venezuela and MetroEconómica.

Note: The exchange rates indicated refer to the estimates of the end-of-period value in the free market, including periods of exchange control.

proved difficult to break, especially when the world oil market entered a downturn.

The constant depreciation of the bolivar constituted external evidence of the economic failures of the democratic regime in Venezuela.

The Volatility of Oil Income

Making economic policy is never easy; many factors conspire to thwart the most careful plans, and, as we have seen, politicians are often tempted to sacrifice the long-term health of the economy in favor of short-term benefits. In Venezuela, the problem of economic policy is complicated by the powerful impact of oil prices on the rest of the economy. Venezuelan governments have always given in to the temptation to spend excessively during periods of high oil prices, without saving for the inevitable reversal of the positive trend.[1] The

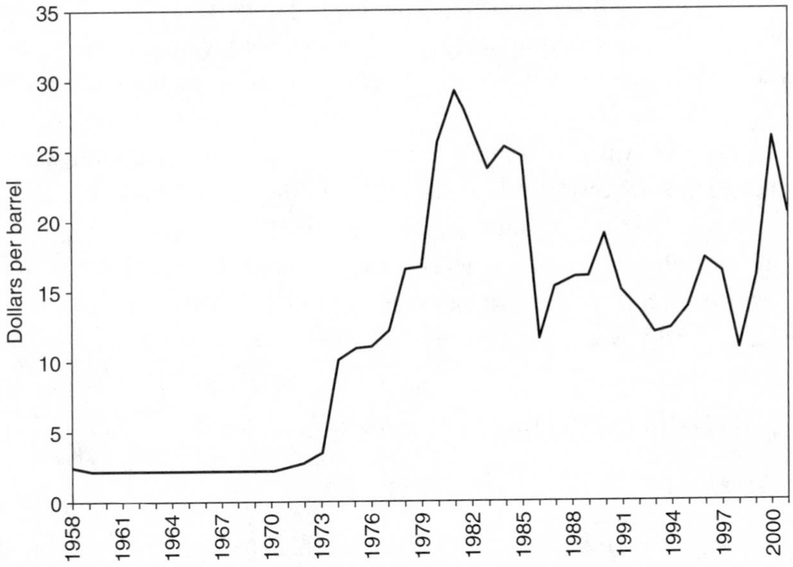

Fig. 10.3. The price of Venezuelan oil, 1958–2000. *Source:* Venezuela, Ministry of Energy and Mines.

costs of volatility are considerable. According to a study carried out by the Inter-American Development Bank (IDB) (1995), the more volatile an economy, the lower will be its growth over time, especially because of negative effects on certainty which scare off investment and make long-term decisions highly risky. According to the theory of the economic management of uncertainty, government policy should be designed to smooth out irregularities (Newbery and Stiglitz, 1981).

As figure 10.3 shows, the price of Venezuelan oil underwent a long cycle of extreme instability after 1973. War in the Middle East, revolution in Iran, and invasion in Kuwait produced high peaks in the oil price in 1973, 1979–80, and 1991. Likewise, economic declines in the industrialized countries brought down prices as demand fell off; the Asian crisis also contributed to the steep decline of the oil market in 1998. Venezuela suffered serious ups and downs with each change in the market.

Under the liberal regime of Carlos Andrés Pérez in the early 1990s, the need to establish a well-functioning stabilization fund appeared on the public agenda, but political pressures impeded its approval. The idea was still alive, however, so that the government of Rafael Caldera, chastened by its own experience with falling oil prices during 1998, decided to create the Fondo de Estabilización Macroeconómica (FEM; Macroeconomic Stabilization Fund), whose only purpose was to ensure a regularization of public spending and avoid the tendency of governments to spend more in times of plenty and then find themselves without resources in times of hardship. This fund was not created in time to leave a cushion of savings for the next fall in the price of oil, however, leaving the incoming Chávez regime with little margin when it faced the historically low prices at the beginning of 1999. Thereafter, and with the recovery of world oil prices, savings accumulated in the fund, thus providing a cushion in the downturn of 2001–2.

The Decline of the Punto Fijo Regime

The First Crises, 1983–1988

The combination of a weakened oil market, high level of imports due to the overvaluation of the bolivar, massive capital outflows, the outbreak of the debt crisis, and the lack of a sound economic policy led to a crisis in February 1983 which the government could not control.[2] Its response was to institute a system of exchange and price controls which would be maintained by the succeeding government of Jaime Lusinchi until 1989. This marked the end of the fixed exchange rate system that prevailed for several decades. Those controls, which led to unprecedented levels of corruption, permitted the government to satisfy major groups of consumers and producers, since they constituted an implicit subsidy for all, at least until the money ran out.

Even though the exchange rate volatility that followed sounded a warning that the pattern of debt, protection, and subsidies was unsustainable, it was not until 1989 that the country had to face the truth. Oil income simply could not cover the cost of maintaining an artificial economy, and international reserves were insufficient to pay the accumulated public debt of some $27 billion. Even so, in the 1988 presidential campaign, voters chose Carlos Andrés Pérez as president for the second time without any suspicion that crisis was once again about to break out.

The Short Liberalization Experiment of Carlos Andrés Pérez

Pérez assumed the presidency for the second time in February 1989 after a comfortable victory, but his popularity would not last for long. Elsewhere in this book, the story is told of the violent riots that shook the country shortly after his inauguration. As important as the announcement of price increases to come were the severe shortages in basic foodstuffs which had been growing in the preceding months.[3]

Pérez had little choice but to accept the conditions of the International Monetary Fund for a major stabilization program that mandated a sharp reversal of the interventionist policies that had been applied in former years. His team of technocrats led the way, convinced that the country had to break its pattern of subsidization and dependence on oil income. Prices had to be freed up, the exchange rate needed to be adjusted regularly to avoid overvaluation of the currency, trade protectionism needed to be reduced and the rules of international commerce set by the General Agreement on Tariffs and Trade (GATT; later the World Trade Organization) accepted, and unprofitable public enterprises needed to be privatized.

The Pérez reform program was an instant disaster that quickly turned into what looked like a success. The disaster was so great, however, that the incipient signs of success were insufficient to undo the political harm. In 1989, real incomes fell precipitously, and inflation surged above 80 percent in the wake of a massive devaluation and the liberalization of prices. When growth returned—the economy grew by 4.4 percent in 1990, 9.7 percent in 1991, and 6.7 percent in 1992—little credit was accrued by a government that had carried out such a violent adjustment in 1989.

In addition, the reduction in protective tariffs created resentment in a group of businesses threatened by foreign competition. Opposition groups delayed or blocked approval of some key parts of the reform program, such as the institution of a value-added tax that would balance government accounts, and a financial reform aimed at increasing competition in the banking system and granting more autonomy to the Central Bank. Likewise, the labor law reform that was to be a step toward reducing distortions in salaries was sabotaged in the Congress and left essentially as it was. The government made no progress toward modernizing the system of social insurance, which was underfinanced and of poor quality, both in pensions and in health care.

It is impossible to say what might have happened in Venezuela had there not been two unsuccessful coup attempts in February and November 1992. However, what is undeniable is that the political unrest of 1992 contributed to a weakening of Venezuela's economy. The government continued to fight for its reforms, but with less capacity, as political pressures forced the president to incorporate into his cabinet politicians opposed to his neoliberal policies. He also bent and restored subsidies that had eased living conditions for the urban poor. In addition, he rescinded the increase in gasoline prices. Privatization also caused discord, especially the sale of CANTV, the telephone company, which was turned over to a consortium led by GTE (now Verizon). This privatization would be recognized as highly successful only long after Pérez was gone.

The Path to Another Crisis: Caldera and the Collapse of the Banking System

Despite the excellent record of economic growth from 1990 to 1992, serious problems still plagued the Venezuelan economy. In particular, inflation was by no means under control. In 1992, prices rose by almost 32 percent and in 1993 by 46 percent. One policy of the Pérez government, continued by his interim successor, President Ramón Velázquez, seemed to feed the inflationary process: the strategy of continuous devaluation under the so-called crawling peg. Encouraged by the International Monetary Fund, Pérez's chief economist and planning minister, Miguel Rodríguez, defended the policy as the correct way to allow the economy to escape its dependence on oil, permitting exporters a competitive environment to develop alternative industries and limiting excessive imports. If prices in Venezuela were rising, therefore, the currency should be devalued by at least an equivalent amount. From 1989 to 1993, the currency went from 43 bolivars per dollar to 106 bolivars per dollar (see table 10.1).

The problem with devaluation is that it has a direct impact on inflation, especially in Venezuela, where imports and their cost are a vital part of the economic system. Thus, a devaluation immediately raises the price of imports and, to the extent that such imports have no easy substitute produced at home, increases the prices within Venezuela. Of course, when imported goods rise in price, there is a tendency for all prices to rise over time, since even barbers want to raise the price of a haircut so that they can pay for their imported bread or their imported televisions. Devaluation in many countries stimulates the foreign demand for exports, but in Venezuela, this effect is minor, since the price of oil is set in dollars in international markets and is unaffected. What is more, oil income in dollars is translated into more bolivars after a devaluation, so that the government may actually be able to spend much more after a devaluation because of its increase in fiscal revenues from oil exports. For these reasons, devaluation in Venezuela tends to have an especially inflationary effect. This suggests the importance of keeping inflation low through monetary and fiscal discipline in order to minimize the need for depreciating the currency.

Political uncertainty coupled with a lower price of oil in 1993 compounded economic problems. Interim president Velázquez achieved approval for a modest value-added tax in that year, which might have signaled that Venezuela was finally getting serious about raising taxes and putting government finances on a more solid base. But the tax stimulated popular opposition, and presidential candidate Caldera took advantage of the resistance by promising to do away with it. Rather than signaling responsible policy, therefore, Caldera inadvertently sent the message that Venezuela's problems were not over and that bigger deficits might lie ahead.

Confidence disintegrated, and huge capital outflows followed in the wake of Caldera's victory. This forced the Central Bank to implement a tight monetary policy.[4] Interest rate on loans at commercial banks jumped to more than 80 percent, which implied real rates of 40 or 50 percent. Since no business can generate enough profits to pay that kind of interest rate, banks found themselves hard pressed to offer depositors a sufficient rate to persuade them to leave their money in Venezuela. The banking crisis was about to start, just at the moment when a new government was coming into power, unprepared to deal with the threat of a general banking collapse.

Once again, poor economic policy and political uncertainty plunged the country into a downward spiral. Instead of containing the banking crisis that started with the collapse of one of the largest institutions, the Banco Latino, in early 1994, the government closed the bank and set off a chain of further bankruptcies that continued throughout the year. The president of the Central Bank resigned in frustration. Bailouts failed to staunch the failures, and huge amounts of liquidity were injected into the monetary system, stimulating capital flight even further. Exchange controls were put into effect once again, lasting for two years. Other negative economic developments between 1994 and 1996 included yearly devaluations of more than 70 percent and annualized inflation reaching 150 percent.

The Caldera Correction and the Second Liberal Experiment, 1996–1999

President Caldera's policies of returning to state-centered economic growth failed miserably. By the end of 1995, with his popularity at a historical low (57%

of the population expressed little or no confidence in his ability to manage the country; Datos, 1995), Caldera faced a dilemma similar to that of President Pérez in 1989. He could accept the only alternative available, implementation of a severe adjustment program, or continue with a failing strategy. President Caldera's statement "We are in bad shape, but getting better" served to win public patience with a reversal of policy which was hardly understood by voters who had placed their confidence in a leader whom they thought would give them something different.

Caldera's second round of policies included an even more daring aspect than had been undertaken by Carlos Andrés Pérez. Convinced by Luis Giusti, the charismatic president of Petróleos de Venezuela Sociedad Anónima (PDVSA; Venezuelan Oil Company, Incorporated), the state-owned oil firm, Caldera approved the move toward opening up the oil industry to limited private investment, for the first time since the nationalization of the industry in the 1970s. He also downplayed Venezuela's loyalty to OPEC by launching a frank expansion of oil production and ambitious plans for investment in new capacity for the future. PDVSA designed a ten-year plan that would have doubled oil production by 2006.

Following a massive devaluation of the bolivar, the exchange controls were eliminated and replaced by a band system in early July 1996, according to which the exchange rate would fluctuate within a band defined by upper and lower limits. The administration had come to the conclusion that devaluations were not part of the solution but rather part of the problem. The government decided to try to limit the rate of devaluation, keeping it well below the inflation rate so as to act as a brake on prices. Inflation did start to recede but stayed well above that of Venezuela's trade partners, causing the overvaluation of the commercial bolivar to exceed 35 percent by the end of 1998.

Rise of the Fifth Republic

Hugo Chávez's presidential campaign in 1998 left many observers in the dark with respect to the kind of economic policy he preferred. Indeed, he was often vague about his specific intentions, which only contributed to uncertainty. Expectations around his presidency were largely limited to speculation about the orientations of his closest collaborators, many of whom came from the Venezuelan Left.

Economic Thinking

The most important group advising Hugo Chávez on economic matters reflected the thinking of Professor Jorge Giordani of the Universidad Central de Venezuela (UCV; Central University of Venezuela). Giordani sat at the center of a circle called the "Garibaldi group," which included future ministers José Rojas (Finance), J. J. Montilla (Production and Commerce), and Héctor Navarro (Education). Giordani himself became minister of planning, a post from which he would exert considerable influence over the president and the cabinet. The Garibaldi group, inexperienced in practical policy, shared the president's hostility to the liberalizing policies implemented by both Carlos Andrés Pérez and Rafael Caldera. This team prided itself on offering an alternative route to development, one that would contrast with the liberal, or "neoliberal," approaches advocated by the International Monetary Fund, the World Bank, and, by extension, the United States. The Garibaldi group was socialist, with little time for reformist experiments with market forces. Its ascendancy awakened doubts in the business community about what was to come.

Chávez also enjoyed the support of the military sector, where economic nationalism tends to thrive as a component of national security doctrine, although differences certainly exist among officials. Significantly, Francisco Arias Cárdenas, a former comrade in arms who became a rival to Chávez and ran against him in the presidential campaign of 2000, presented a platform that placed him in the liberal camp, with the natural support of important business interests. Yet the Movimiento Bolivariano Revolucionario 200 (MBR-200; Bolivarian Revolutionary Movement 200), the original group that encompassed all the coup plotters of February 1992, was later revealed to have had long-standing contact with the remnants of the old guerrilla leadership of the 1960s through the intermediation of Adán Chávez, the future president's brother (Garrido, 1999).

Much of the history of the circle close to Chávez was unknown during the campaign, and Chávez himself defied easy definition. One of the best sources of his thinking, a series of long interviews carried out by Agustin Blanco Muñoz published in 1998, revealed Chávez as a person who borrowed from whatever sources caught his attention. He tried to present himself as a person who wanted to construct an original Venezuelan position, based on traditional historical figures like Simón Bolívar, Ezequiel Zamora (a populist of the nineteenth century), and Simón Rodríguez, who was Bolívar's teacher. Since Bolívar was an aristocrat and Zamora a rebel who promised land to the peasants, it was unclear what Chávez was about at all.

Chávez rarely expanded on his plans beyond this level of generality. His interests were concentrated on political change more than economic programs. His words sounded vaguely threatening to the business community and to many who thought that Venezuela needed less direct state intervention in the economy and more modern and efficient regulation. Optimists thought that he would soon learn the impracticality of his ideas and that the best strategy was to seek contact with the candidate so as to educate him about the realities of running an economy.

The Fifth Republic Defines Itself

The First Semester: Economic Caution

What would economic policy look like under Chávez? Two problems confronted the government and constrained its freedom to institute significant policy initiatives. In the first place, the oil price had reached its lowest level in years by the end of the Caldera government. Second, the noise surrounding the presidential campaign and reports of the candidate's incendiary rhetoric against "savage capitalism" and neoliberal policies, together with his references to the problem of the foreign debt—which became increasingly watered down over time—led to pessimistic projections by the national and international financial communities. Chávez first showed his pragmatic side by confirming President Caldera's minister of finance, the Christian Democrat Maritza Izaguirre, as his own minister. This was an undeniable sign that Chávez was willing to do whatever was necessary to calm the markets and signal that he was no danger. The FEM was confirmed as government policy. Izaguirre's presence also guaranteed the continuation of the Caldera exchange rate policy, which permitted flexibility but also tried to minimize the depreciation of the currency, in order to bring down inflationary pressures.

The problem of the oil market was critical. In early 1998, oil production (excluding gas) had reached 3.3 million barrels per day, a level that had risen gradually since its average of about 2 million barrels per day at the start of the 1990s. PDVSA's plan had envisioned doubling oil production to 5.7 million barrels per day by 2005, with foreign investors accounting for about 28 percent of production under the new arrangements for joint ventures between PDVSA and private companies. It was a bold policy to capture a greater world market share, but 1998 was a year of low demand and, it seems, low tolerance for such a policy on the part of Saudi Arabia, the most powerful member of OPEC, which was willing to let the price fall to punish Venezuela (Morse and Richard, 2002). OPEC's cooperative reaction came too late to avoid a total crash in the oil market.

Economists predicted that if the oil price remained below $10 per barrel in 1999, the fiscal deficit could be enormous, opening once again the possibility of a major loss of control. Chávez had blamed the fall in the world oil price on Venezuela's own policy of expanding oil exploration and production under the ambitious plans developed by Giusti and his predecessors. Even though the Caldera government had already recognized the problem by cutting oil production by more than a half a million barrels and delaying the expansion plan, 1998 saw on average the lowest real prices for Venezuelan oil exports since the early 1970s (see fig. 10.3), combined with the highest production reached during the same period.[5]

Giusti resigned days before Chávez was sworn in. Roberto Mandini, an experienced oil executive who had been at odds with Giusti over issues other than the company's market strategy, was appointed PDVSA's new president. Chávez also named a prominent critic of Giusti, Alí Rodríguez, as minister of energy and mines, with the mission of bringing PDVSA firmly under government's control. Negotiations continued within OPEC to order further reductions by agreement of all members. The expansion plan was frozen, and Venezuela played a stronger leadership role in achieving unity among OPEC members, which had often produced above the agreed-upon quotas (including Venezuela).

Higher oil demand in response to the Asian countries' recovery, combined with lower oil supply, made the world petroleum price recover from its slump within a relatively short time. From a low price of $ 8.43 per barrel for Venezuelan oil in February 1999, when Chávez assumed the presidency, the price rose steadily to $22.77 in December. OPEC mandated another production cut in March 2000, bringing the Venezuelan quota down to 2.7 million barrels and reducing total OPEC country production to 23 million barrels per day. From then on, the market strengthened, and OPEC once again increased production, at least until the end of 2000, when Venezuela could produce 3 million barrels per day. By January 2001, concern reappeared that a possible recession in the United States could slow world demand, and prices were already sliding. OPEC reduced production again on January 17 and March 17, with Venezuela's quota reduced to 2.8 million barrels per day.

Of course, in the first months of the Chávez government, no one was sure that the price would recover as it did, and dire action was needed to avoid an unsustainable deficit in the budget. This was the critical moment for an untested government. Perhaps in a more established administration, it might have been possible to cover the deficit with foreign borrowing, on the grounds that the problem was unlikely to last for a long time. For Chávez, however, such an option was hardly open. The distrust he had generated in international markets made borrowing there highly unattractive. His economic team, perhaps with the exception of Finance Minister Izaguirre, failed to impress observers, especially since it included many newcomers without experience in managing economic crises. What is more, a question mark hung over the country as the result of the president's announcement that he would call a constituent assembly to overhaul the political and economic system—with results that might prove negative for the economy if the worst predictions about Chávez's ideological orientation were to come true.

It was at this point that Chávez revealed some surprises. To prove that he was no irresponsible demagogue, the president announced a series of actions designed to gain confidence. In the first half of 1999, the Congress approved an enabling law that gave the president wide decree powers to manage the emergency. The following actions were swiftly taken:

- The value-added tax was officially established at 15.5 percent, lowering the rate by 1 percent in comparison with the old wholesale tax it replaced.
- A temporary emergency tax was placed on financial transactions, at a 0.5 percent rate.
- The budget was cut across the board by more than 7 percent.
- FEM, created by the previous government, was converted in May into the Fondo de Inversión para la Estabilización Macroeconómica (FIEM; Investment Fund for Macroeconomic Stabilization), basing the saving rule on a very conservative oil price base of $9 per barrel.

With unemployment on the rise and a weakening economy, the government accompanied these measures with actions designed to alleviate the worsening social situation. Additionally, President Chávez decided to support further emergency actions by the armed forces within a project called Plan Bolívar 2000, whereby military personnel would provide direct services in poor areas and relieve unemployment with short-term hiring of civilians in some of the operations.

Thus, the Chávez government consciously made an attempt to combine harsh macroeconomic policies with direct programs for the poor. He complemented his strategy with his constant presence in the media and his appeals to the people to be patient. He was sufficiently convincing to maintain his popularity despite the poor economic conditions. Indeed, he argued repeatedly that the problem was the result of the "forty years" of corrupt party rule, poor oil policy, and inhuman neoliberal ideology. This rhetoric, plus the promise of social action oriented toward the poor, was enough to assuage potential resistance to the cutbacks.

Although President Chávez surprised many with his decisive action, it was not enough to gain approval abroad, where his antimarket rhetoric continued to raise doubts. To send a further positive message in the United States, the president gave the green light to final approval of a bilateral tax treaty with that country, despite the doubts of some of his more radical followers. However, the government did not go so far as to finish negotiations on the stalled Bilateral Investment Treaty with the United States, although it did approve a new law for the protection of foreign investment in general which went a long way toward establishing a commitment to providing security under Venezuelan law. Chávez would visit New York and Houston in June 1999, meeting with financial and petroleum industry leaders, with the clear intention of communicating assurances that he was willing to do business.

Another aspect of continuity was the exchange rate policy, which was similar to that implemented by Caldera since mid-1996. This policy was controversial—many businesses complained that they were being forced into bankruptcy because of high imports stimulated by the bolivar's overvaluation—but the Chávez government decided that controlling inflation was a high priority. From a level of 30 percent in 1998, inflation fell to 20 percent in 1999, still high by world standards but a measurable improvement from the point of view of the Venezuelan consumer. Critics claimed that inflation was receding only because of the recession and that the country would pay later for its increasing overvaluation of the bolivar, but the government undoubtedly reaped political benefits from this policy, which would continue to reduce price increases to more bearable levels over the next two years.

The Second Semester: The Constituent Assembly and Chávez Economics

President Chávez promised a new constitution in his electoral campaign and swore on his inauguration in February to go ahead with a constituent assembly. As the organization of the constituent assembly proceeded in 1999, fears rose that the newly elected representatives might write a constitution that would finally confirm the radical economic ideas of Chávez and his followers. Some information seemed to point in this direction as proposals emerged from some of his more radical followers (Kelly, 2000). The Movimiento Quinta República (MVR; Fifth Republic Movement), which won an overwhelming majority in the constituent assembly, clearly included representatives who would vote for a constitution that would reduce the market and increase the role of the state. As the constituent assembly began its task, President Chávez, assisted by a commission he had appointed, presented a draft of the concepts that he would suggest to the assembly on August 5.[6] Although the document contained some controversial articles that prompted quick responses from business sectors, it also tended to calm many doubts because its economic clauses were little different from traditional statist approaches to the economy. In any case, the final version of the constitution hardly confirmed the claim that the Chávez government planned to socialize the economy or diverge greatly from traditional economic strategies.[7]

The debate leading up to the popular referendum approving the constitution was short, since the government was insistent on ending the somewhat chaotic process as soon as possible. For this reason, the referendum was set for December 15, 1999, less than a month after the draft was completed. The main opposition to the document came from the business organization FEDECAMARAS. Given that the constitution was likely to be approved easily in an electorate that still supported the government by an overwhelming majority, some thought that outright business opposition would be foolhardy and might prejudice future business-government relations. Indeed, President Chávez began to see the business elites as enemies, and, with some exceptions, they returned the favor. This conflict would continue unabated until the violent events of April 2002, by which time a formidable alliance had been built linking FEDECAMARAS with unions, oil workers, human rights defenders, and a large number of common citizens.

In contrast to the FEDECAMARAS opposition, other economic interests were more circumspect in expressing their doubts. The binational Venezuelan-American Chamber of Commerce and Industry (VenAmCham) issued a businesslike report on the constitution which avoided political judgments, and American ambassador John Maisto privately expressed the view that the constitution meant no particular danger for international investors.[8]

The Year 2000: Normalcy or Something New?

The close of the debate over the constitution provided a measure of political stability, and early in 2000 the government turned to the task of economic recovery. The budget, severely restrained in that year, could be expanded, and indeed the government proposed an increase of 13 percent in real terms for 2001. As oil prices rose, spending plans grew as well. President Chávez solicited extra spending authority that would have permitted an even larger increase in spending, although, at year's end, it became clear that the executive had not been able to carry out a significant portion of total authorized spending (Bs. 23.6 trillion). Instead, the government spent 20.7 trillion, or 21.4 percent of GDP, with a deficit of 1.8 percent of GDP.

The economy grew in 2000 at a rate of 3.2 percent in real terms, an improvement over the rate of 6.1 percent in 1999. Inflation continued to decline, leveling off at 13.4 percent at year's end. What most concerned the analysts, despite the visible improvement in most indicators, was the dependence of the government's economic strategy on the assumption of a strong world market for oil.

The ambiguous character of the Chávez economic strategy left room for important initiatives that pointed toward modern approaches to the economy. For instance, investors praised innovative policies in high technology. The Comisión Nacional de Telecomunicaciones (CONATEL; Telecommunications Commission) pressed for competition and opened up new services to bidding. This sector showed the highest growth rate in 2000, the last year in which the privatized telephone company would enjoy its monopoly in basic services.

Doubts about government plans for the oil industry surfaced when President Chávez named the controversial Héctor Ciavaldini as president of PDVSA in mid-1999. A period of conflict ensued, with the resignations of many experienced oil executives, leading to accusations that the industry was being politicized. But in 2000, after a botched negotiation of a labor dispute, Ciavaldini was himself replaced by Guaicaipuro Lameda, a respected general who reinstated a modified plan for expanded production and investment which initially reassured private investors. This policy would eventually lead to Lameda's dismissal in 2002, which in turn led to the strike by oil executives in April which challenged the very legitimacy of the Chávez government. Plans for opening the gas industry to private investment also went ahead despite a long debate on what price commitments would be necessary to stimulate interest in investment projects. A new electricity law adopted forward-looking concepts designed to permit competition in generation and distribution, although its implementation was put off and the industry would soon face the effects of insufficient investment.

The Chávez government used diverse means to provide credit to small enterprises—through a "People's Bank" (Banco del Pueblo Soberano) and, later, a National Development Bank (a transformation of the Venezuelan Investment Fund) and a Women's Bank. The People's Bank quickly ran into difficulties as a result of administrative failures and an unclear objective; a new law would be approved in 2001 to provide easier rules for these socially oriented banks—rules that might end up ensuring their dependence on government subsidies. Given a very high unemployment and an informal sector of workers that exceeded 50 percent of the labor force, however, it is not surprising that the government sought to provide direct assistance to poorer groups. In these projects supporting "microenterprise," Chávez was seeking to solve the problem of poverty by giving help to people who wanted to work.

The Unraveling of 2001–2002

Considerable optimism accompanied the Chávez government at the start of 2001. Most macroeconomic indicators supported the official economic strategy, and the projections provided by the minister of planning pointed to further gains on inflation, better economic growth, and strong international reserves. Storm clouds were forming at home and abroad, however, and excessive confidence led to plans for government spending based on oil price expectations that were not to materialize. Indeed, the political radicalization of the government during 2001 owed much to unfounded arrogance based on what would be only fleeting economic success.

The U.S. economy was entering recession, which would weaken the world economy in general and the oil price in particular. Already by the first quarter of 2001, Venezuela's average oil price had fallen by 22 percent over the average price of the previous year. And after the terrorist attacks of September 11 on the United States, the price fell almost by an additional 20 percent, far below the budget forecast.

By the final quarter of 2001, there seemed to be no alternative to admitting that a new economic policy would be necessary, although the end-of-year figures still showed positive, if weakening, growth of 2.7 percent overall. But the drop in the public oil sector would soon spill over into the rest of the economy, repeating the cycle that Venezuelans had suffered for several decades.

How did the Chávez government react to the classic problem of the Venezuelan economy? Certainly, his revolutionary regime no longer enjoyed the huge popularity that had once supported it. Convinced that the traditional business, labor, and ecclesiastical elites were responsible for the long decline of the country, the president attacked. Empowered by an enabling law, he issued a series of controversial decree-laws: a hydrocarbons statute that disappointed those who hoped for a return to the expansive oil policies of the 1990s, a land law that raised doubts about the protection of private property, a civil service act that turned public employees against him, and other sectoral laws that brought new groups into the opposition. The national strike of December 10, 2001, revealed the depth of the opposition. The political climate turned nasty, worsening the economic situation and stimulating unsustainable capital outflows that led to a fall ofmore than $3 billion of international reserves in the first eleven weeks of 2002.

Once again, the government faced a situation similar to the crisis of 1999. One factor that alleviated the impact of falling oil prices was the existence of the FIEM, in which more than $7 billion had been accumulated since 1999. The government changed the formula for drawing from the fund in October 2001 and in so doing reinforced doubts about its willingness to adhere to fiscal discipline. The budget shortfall was so great that only a vigorous recovery of the oil market could prevent the crisis from deepening. Local governments increased their borrowing, which drove the public debt to more than 14 trillion bolivars at the end of 2002, an amount five times larger than that of 1999. The national debt rose from 4 percent of GDP in 1999 to 12 percent in 2002.

Faced with an untenable situation and a looming fiscal deficit, President Chávez announced a major change of policy in February 2002. The Central Bank would abandon its defense of the exchange rate, letting the bolivar float to a new level, in effect devaluing the currency. Spending would be cut and taxes increased, in particular through the reimposition of the same emergency financial transaction tax that had been used in 1999. To assuage his disappointed supporters, especially among the poor and lower middle classes, the president promised to maintain spending on health, education, and welfare and to expand small business loan programs.

An unexpected oil respite materialized in March, when OPEC production cuts and the U.S. military campaign in Afghanistan drove up oil prices. Higher petroleum revenues, combined with higher excise tax rates, heavy local borrowing, and intensive use of the FIEM resources, allowed the government to continue its expansionary fiscal policy throughout 2002 despite lower tax receipts (due to the economic slowdown). Nevertheless, it was a year of devaluation, recession, high unemployment and underemployment, inflation, and impoverishment. Political turmoil, combined with social tensions and uncertainty, led to additional capital flight, channeling abroad resources that had been injected into the economy through public spending. That forced the Central Bank to implement a restrictive monetary policy, which drove interest rates up to very high levels.

The banking sector also felt pressure. Nonperforming assets increased substantially. Borrowing declined as a consequence of the deep recession, limiting the possibilities of using monetary policy to manage the crisis. Since devaluation expectations made dollar purchases very attractive to the banks, the Central Bank imposed limitations on the amount of foreign exchange they could hold; nevertheless, exchange profits from the dollar's appreciation were plentiful during 2002. In addition, the Central Bank restricted its financial assistance, leaving the banks with few options on how to use the funds they received as deposits. That situation, in conjunction with the considerable fiscal gap the government was facing, explains why the banks bought massive amounts of public bonds during this period, causing the ratio of investments to total assets to grow steadily.

Inflation and recession were two major problems during 2002. The bolivar's devaluation, higher excise taxes and salaries, and high financial costs were among the reasons for the inflation rate's jumping to 31 percent, causing real salaries to decline. The level of economic activity also fell as a result of reductions in oil production, in response to cuts ordered by OPEC in 2001, and a severe contraction in nonoil sectors. Devaluation, higher interest rates, lower consumption, and plummeting investment due to uncertainty and negative expectations explain the severe GDP contraction of 6.4 percent during the first three quarters of that year. The situation worsened during the fourth quarter because of the national strike of December, which paralyzed the oil industry and severely restricted other economic activities. This caused total GDP to decline 8.9 percent for the year as a whole, a historical record.

The Devastation of 2003

Radicalization and confrontation are only two of the features that characterized 2003. The continuation of the general strike into February 2003 had devastating effects on the whole economy. The firing of more than eighteen thousand PDVSA employees, mainly top and middle managers and highly skilled workers, had and would continue to have such far-reaching consequences as declining production capacity, environmental degradation, and severe deterioration of some oil fields and industrial infrastructure.

A dramatic contraction of real wages during the first half of the year, combined with massive layoffs due to downsizing or simply the bankruptcy of several firms, worsened the already adverse situation of the labor force, causing reported unemployment to surpass 18 percent and underemployment to approach 55 percent. As a consequence, poverty increased substantially, affecting more than 70 percent of all Venezuelan households.

The extremely adverse political and economic conditions prevailing in January 2003 induced capital flight to surge out of control, causing the bolivar to depreciate by 47 percent in just one month and the international reserves to decline deeply. On January 22 all Central Bank foreign exchange transactions were suspended, and two weeks later severe exchange controls were imposed. That move was followed by strict controls on prices, setting several prices at levels below cost; this condemned many producers to work with very narrow margins or simply to lose money, forcing them to shutdown.

During the first four months of the exchange controls, the system was totally inoperative. The Comisión de Administración de Divisas (CADIVI; Exchange Control Agency) authorized the delivery of only $30 million for private imports, a figure totally divorced from the country's foreign currency needs. In addition, the government made massive duty-free imports of basic food products, mainly from Cuba and Brazil, imposing unfair competition on the private producers. This reflected the official objective of taking revenge on political opponents such as entrepreneurs who had supported the strike.

Although some improvements in the approval of official dollars for imports and debt service took place in the third quarter, the situation was still far from normal as of early November 2003. Economic activity remained depressed. In fact, after a devastating 27 percent GDP contraction during the first quarter of the year, the second quarter continued showing a deep recession, with sales contractions on the order of 20 to 40 percent in some sectors. That has constrained inflation at the consumer level, though at the wholesale and producer levels price adjustments due to the bolivar's depreciation were very intense. Shrinking purchasing power among the population prevented those higher wholesale prices from being passed along to the consumers, leading to a repressed inflation.

Ongoing economic decline led to demands for ending the Chávez presidency through the constitutionally delineated process of the revocatory referendum. In response, the government ordered a substantial fiscal expansion during the third quarter of 2003. Coming in the face of declining oil prices and lower tax receipts, this action increased the deficit. President Chávez ordered the Central Bank to finance the deficit by artificially creating profits through the manipulation of exchange rate differentials. His action had the intended effect of inducing local financial institutions to purchase public bonds in large amounts. All of this provoked multiple concerns: about the future viability of public finance, the inflationary impacts of the Central Bank financing, and the effects on the banks with high exposure to public sector obligations, particularly several small and weak banks with low levels of equity.

Fiscal expansion in the second half of 2003 did not lead to revitalization of the public infrastructure. Hospitals, schools, public transportation, and highways were in a serious state of disrepair because of low capital formation and deferred maintenance. They continued to deteriorate throughout 2003 as public disbursements were concentrated in salaries and other current expenditures.

Conclusions

After four years of the Chávez revolution, many Venezuelans were still at a loss to define the economic policy of the regime they had elected at the end of 1998. Once again, policies that failed to establish fiscal responsibility and stability had ushered in a severe economic and political crisis. After his near ouster in April 2002, the president replaced his economic team. The new ministers of finance, planning, and production held orthodox credentials but questionable political clout. They attempted to restore credibility with local and international business interests by proposing a traditional package with higher taxes and cuts in government spending. But political resistance to the regime was so intense that even those who had been calling for such policies refused to support any initiative by the government. Chávez found himself trapped between his dazed supporters, who had not banked on further impoverishment, and his opponents, who would settle for nothing less than the installation of a new government.

In many ways, the Chávez formula meant the implementation of reforms that had been promoted previously, especially in the area of regulation of public services and the financial sector. Rather than reversing plans for the expansion of the petroleum industry and the development of downstream and related activities in gas and petrochemicals, the government liberalized some areas in the energy sector but maintained the traditional insistence on restricting oil production within the OPEC framework, even risking destabilizing its own industry when conflict broke out over oil strategy.

Equally, the effort to control inflation with exchange rate stability represented the continuation of the policy initiated by the Caldera government, although this turned out to be just as fragile as previous policies when the rest of the economy weakened. Practically no important changes were made in trade policy; the government resisted returning to the protectionism of the 1980s but also refused to consider any deepening of commercial liberalization, either with Latin American neighbors or within the proposed Free Trade Area of the Americas.

Perhaps the greatest doubts with respect to the economic future of Venezuela rested precisely on the lack of change that Chávez was to bring about. The economy showed no signs of freeing itself from its dependence on oil, which continued to mean the dominance of the state in the economy. Social commitments, particularly in health and pensions, could once again put Venezuela back into the dilemma of its Punto Fijo predecessors: excessive promises for government subsidies that would surpass the country's ability to pay for them. It was yet to be seen if progress could be made toward an effective tax system, which the government promised to achieve but failed to implement effectively.

The most serious problems of the Venezuelan economy, however, might have little to do with economic policy as such. Thus, President Chávez's foreign policy, resistant to the perceived dominance of the United States in the world, and in Latin America in particular, sent signals of alert to investors unsure about the stability of a country at odds with plans for a free trade area in the Americas, doubtful about globalization, and openly critical of markets. In addition, the arrival of a government weak in administrative experience and careless with the formalities of bureaucratic controls opened the possibility of new sources of corruption and inefficiency which could defy the best intentions. Reports of chaotic implementation of social programs like the Plan Bolívar 2000 and the Unified Social Fund, among others, fueled the doubts and contributed to a sense of disorder. Politically, the president's continuous attacks on traditional leadership groups and the press created a level of social tension which would undermine the best of economic policies, not to speak of those that repeated the mistakes of the past.

Venezuela, then, seemed to cling to economic strategies followed for decades which had failed to produce the kind of results necessary to raise the income and quality of life of the population. The Fifth Republic promised that, somehow, political changes would be sufficient to make the economy work. Yet in the face of another failure, as evidenced by the political and economic crises of 2002 and 2003, Venezuelans would have to think again about how to achieve prosperity, this time with real changes in economic policies that would go beyond wishful thinking and grandiose rhetoric.

CHAPTER ELEVEN

Public Opinion, Political Socialization, and Regime Stabilization

José Antonio Gil Yepes

This chapter examines the relationship between public opinion, political socialization, and regime stability in post-1958 Venezuela by addressing four puzzles. The first asks how the innovative policies pursued by those who founded the Punto Fijo polity created opinions that facilitated regime normalization and political stability. The second analyzes how and why support for that political regime decayed and when this occurred. The third puzzle is to identify the political attitudes that post-1958 democracy bequeathed to the Fifth Republic and assess the efforts of President Hugo Chávez Frías to build upon and transform them. Finally, this research explores whether existing attitudes toward the Bolivarian Revolution's performance are positive enough to ensure its viability. Public opinion surveys, focus group research, and electoral results provide the data for the analysis that follows.

Innovative Policies and Normalization of Representative Democracy

The founders of Venezuela's Punto Fijo regime crafted a political regime in which power was highly centralized. In this respect, they took the road traveled by their predecessors, including General Marcos Pérez Jiménez. They also held egalitarian attitudes that led them to support free elections based on universal suffrage as the preferred procedure for political participation and renewing the political leadership. On the other hand, the founding fathers of Punto Fijo democracy (Rómulo Betancourt, Rafael Caldera, and Jóvito Villalba), viewed many liberties and pluralism based on the open expression of demands to be the prerogative of political elites. They reserved the exercise of these dimensions of power for party executives, the president of the republic, high-level bureaucrats, and congressional leaders. In other words, Punto Fijo's pluralism was highly limited.[1]

Party leaders and government officials discouraged interest groups from articulating their demands when political elites were engaged in rule making. Groups tied to the political parties were expected to support the policies and priorities on which party leaders had reached agreement. Interests that enjoyed autonomy from the political parties (and sometimes the groups tied to the political parties themselves) were allowed to participate in policy-implementing decisions. Again, however, they had minimal influence in deciding the content of public policy.

The mechanisms favored by the dominant political parties (Acción Democrática [AD; Democratic Action] and Comité de Organización Política Electoral Independiente: Partido Social Cristiano [COPEI; Committee of Independent Electoral Political Organization: Social Christian Party]) for distributing instrumental rewards varied. They reflected the structural complexity of the polity. But for all, elites as well as the masses, the rewards for working within guidelines established by the political elite were substantial. Supportive groups received generous allocations from the abundant oil money that flowed into the state's coffers from the mid-1960s until the late 1980s.

Symbolic rewards complemented instrumental rewards. Punto Fijo democrats were sensitive to the importance of symbolic rewards in gaining and retaining support. The symbolic rewards that AD and COPEI leaders dangled before the economic and social elites were support for anticommunism, influence for the church, nationalism, and political liberties. To the masses they offered unity and democracy, which translated into direct, secret, and universal suffrage; limited freedom of political expression for individuals; and anticommunism. *Unity* and *democracy* became the buzzwords to symbolize all that was good. *Dictatorship* and *communism* symbolized the bad, along with *peculado,* or official corruption.

Table 11.1. Components of Social Mobilization to Induce Political and Economic Legitimacy

	Democracy 1958	Import Substitution 1960s	Market Economy 1989–92	Decentralization 1984–93
Existing crisis	Repression	Unemployment	Deficit	Government inefficiency
Shared goal	Reestablish democracy	Substitute imports create jobs	?	Better public services
A clear message	"Unity"	"Buy Venezuelan"	None	"Decentralization"
A common motivation	Liberty	Nationalism	?	Accountability
Public opinion	Mobilized	Mobilized	Not mobilized	Mobilized
Leadership	Party and sectorial leaders	Rómulo Betancourt	Carlos Andres Pérez	(Pressure from all sectors and the masses for decentralization)
Intermediary leaders	Eugenio Mendoza (business)	Alejandro Hernández (business)	None	COPRE's presidents
Specialized institution for elite mobilization	Junta Patriótica	ProVenezuela	Consejo Nacional de Concentración	COPRE Presidential Commission for State Reform
Use of massive political communication	Very intensive	Very intensive	Very low	Moderate
Level of success	Very high	High	Low	Medium

The symbolic rewards offered by Venezuela's post-1958 democratic politicians to shape mass and elite political attitudes constituted an indigenous (criollo) political technology. Internalization of positive affect toward the approved symbolic rewards was intended to impart legitimacy to the political regime. Initially, the official symbolic rewards advanced by party leaders were democracy and import substitution industrialization; later on they sought to create positive affect toward the market economy and decentralization. Positive affect toward the first two symbolic rewards dominated political socialization when Punto Fijo democracy enjoyed great support. The last two entered into the mix in the late 1980s, when political decay was setting in. Table 11.1 compares the components of social mobilization which AD and COPEI leaders attempted to manipulate when they were creating positive affect toward regime supportive political symbols. The eight components are nature of the existing crisis, shared goal, clearly supportive message, common motivation, status of public opinion, leadership, prominent intermediary leaders, and specialized institution for elite mobilization.

The most important message revealed by comparing the table 11.1 symbolic components of political mobilization is that the level of success of each is related to the extent that it affirms the components that are identified as instrumental in building regime-supportive political symbols. Table 11.1 reveals that the most successful mobilizations were the internalization of democracy into the political culture and the legitimation of the Import Substitution Policy through the nationalistic call *Compre venezolano* ("Buy Venezuelan made goods").

Marketization of the economy proved highly unpopular. Criticized initially because of the shock approach with which it was implemented by President Pérez, the neoliberal experiment foundered in large measure because the government failed to explain why it chose an approach that its predecessors had rejected. Marketization introduced an individualized competition that was foreign to Venezuelan political culture. It was opposed by party leaders, bureaucratic managers, the masses, and even some entrepreneurs. Moreover, Pérez failed to offer even symbolic rewards that would justify the new policy. Promises that market forces would eventually allow Venezuela to overcome the economic difficulties brought on by falling petroleum prices rang hollow. Prevailing attitudes associated "market economies" with "savage neoliberal capitalism," and even under the best of circumstances most Venezuelans saw the market economy as demanding a great deal of sacrifice before there would be any economic payoff.

In the case of decentralization, support for this policy came from below (rather than from party or government elites). In 1984 President Jaime Lusinchi (1984–89) created the Comisión Presidencial para la Reforma del Estado (COPRE; Presidential Commission for State Reform), viewing it as window dressing that would allow him to delay or derail decentralization and other political reforms. However, the commissioners of COPRE took it upon themselves to build support for political reforms, and by and large they succeeded. The resignation in 1988 of COPRE's president, Senator Ramón J. Velásquez, led to widespread dissatisfaction. Velásquez accused the Lunsichi government of sabotaging political reform, a charge that former president Pérez echoed in his successful campaign to wrest control of the AD presidential nomination from Lusinchi's anointed successor in 1987. Two years later, in his second presidency, Pérez implemented decentralization.

In retrospect it is clear that reforms to Punto Fijo institutions came slowly. Political elites could have begun to redistribute and decentralize political power after 1972, when the guerrilla movement collapsed. However, meaningful decentralization only got under way after the urban riots of February 1989. This suggests that those who crafted post-1958 democracy were wedded to central control of the state. It took a crisis of the magnitude of the 1989 riots to prod them to experiment with the more fluid political dynamics that normally accompany market economies. However, unease with regional and local political power resurfaced in the Fifth Republic, when President Hugo Chávez undermined decentralization provisions of the 1999 constitution.

Stages in the Unraveling of Representative Democracy: The Decay of Punto Fijo

Sixteen years of frustrating delays in implementing reforms (1973–89) undermined the efficiency, efficacy, and legitimacy of post-1958 democracy. In addition, the regime's unraveling derived from the effects of changes in oil policy implemented in 1973–74. Figure 11.1 reveals that until then oil prices had been low and stable for decades. When petroleum-exporting countries wanted more income from oil, they had to produce a greater volume. This condition was economically healthy because moderate profit margins avoided the inflationary impact of a high rent, and oil production increases were automatically transmitted to the rest of the economy through creation of new jobs.

After the 1973 the global market for petroleum changed. More oil income was no longer to be obtained from higher production but through price manipulations by the Organization of Petroleum Exporting Countries (OPEC), which could operate as a cartel. Initially, the consequences of this change were misunderstood. Analysts viewed the OPEC countries as asserting their sovereignty and "liberating" themselves from imperialist exploitation by the large multinational oil corporations. The nationalization of oil industries in OPEC countries, price increases, and greater flexibility in cutting production were portrayed to the leaders of these countries as liberation from economic exploitation.

The true impacts of this new policy (which remains in effect as of this writing) include loss of macroeconomic stability due to high fluctuations of oil prices; reduction of the oil industry's capability to stimulate growth in the rest of the economy; weakening of the linkages between government expenditures and local tax burdens; and enrichment of the state vis-à-vis an increasingly

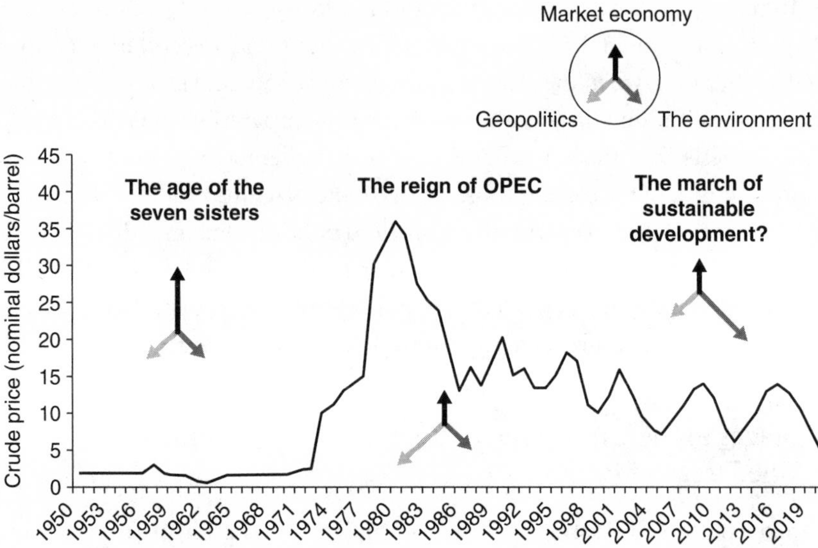

Fig. 11.1. Key forces shaping the oil industry through 2020. *Source:* Ross, 1999.

impoverished population. In other words, the oil production and pricing policies that OPEC adopted in 1973, ones that President Chávez endorses, have a track record of retarding economic growth and distorting the political democracy.

The Turning Point and the "Schizophrenic" Stage

Punto Fijo democracy's loss of legitimacy and its decay relate to the traditional elites' refusal to implement political reforms and to their insistence on pursuing an oil policy that was self-serving and short-sighted. The roots of political decay go back beyond Black Friday to the early 1970s, a time when the first Caldera government (1969–74) was making halting attempts to distribute power more broadly. The previously noted change in oil policy at the end of that government derailed those efforts and led to even greater centralization of state power. This development set in motion the process whereby state managers became richer while the people reaped few benefits.

A tension between the ingrained preference for socialism and the lack of material resources needed to create a socialist state marked post-1974 Venezuela. Economic policy, as a consequence, was schizophrenic. It oscillated between the preferred interventionist approach and incoherent efforts to create a market economy. Support for one alternative or the other rose and fell with the revenue the state received from foreign oil sales. Government planners detested this volatility. They wanted a more stable source of income, or at least one less dependent on the vicissitudes of the global petroleum market. Among these planners one faction, usually a minority, favored replacing the interventionist state with reliance on the market. This faction argued that only a market economy could generate capital based on domestic economic activity and that this was the most obvious path to reducing dependence on oil. Calls for a market economy were usually accompanied by plans for political reforms intended to deepen democracy. Programs to deepen democracy called for two specific changes: inviting certain excluded political interests to participate in public policy making, and restructuring the national bureaucracy so that it would be able to operate public services more efficiently.

Events during 1980 reveal the interplay of these dynamics. At that time, Venezuela's economy was in recession, and the distributive system on which the political regime's legitimacy rested was stretched to the breaking point. This condition led former president Rómulo Betancourt (AD) to propose that the dominant political and economic elites rally behind President Luis Herrera Campíns in a *concertación* (literally, a coming together). Betancourt envisioned this *concertación* as including the top leaders of AD and COPEI, the Confederación de Trabajadores de Venezuela (CTV; Conferation of Venezuelan Workers), and the Federación de Cámaras y Asociaciones de Comercio y Producción de Venezuela (FEDECAMARAS; Federation of Chambers of Commerce and Production of Venezuela). These organizations would form an institutional pact that would guide Venezuela through the current difficulties. However, most COPEI and AD leaders rejected this idea. COPEI especially resisted sharing the spoils of power. Most elites, economic as well as political, assumed that petroleum prices would rebound quickly. This would bail the government out of its economic difficulties. Prices in fact did recover, and President Herrera removed the issue of *concertación* from the political agenda.

Each of the three Punto Fijo regime presidents who followed Luis Herrera proposed some form of government by *concertación* when economic difficulties surfaced. However, none could craft the pluralistic decision mechanisms that *concertación* implied. During the second Caldera administration (1994–99) there was some agreement between government, organized labor, and the business community. It resulted in reforms to the labor law, including the sticky issue of defining the norms that would govern severance payments.

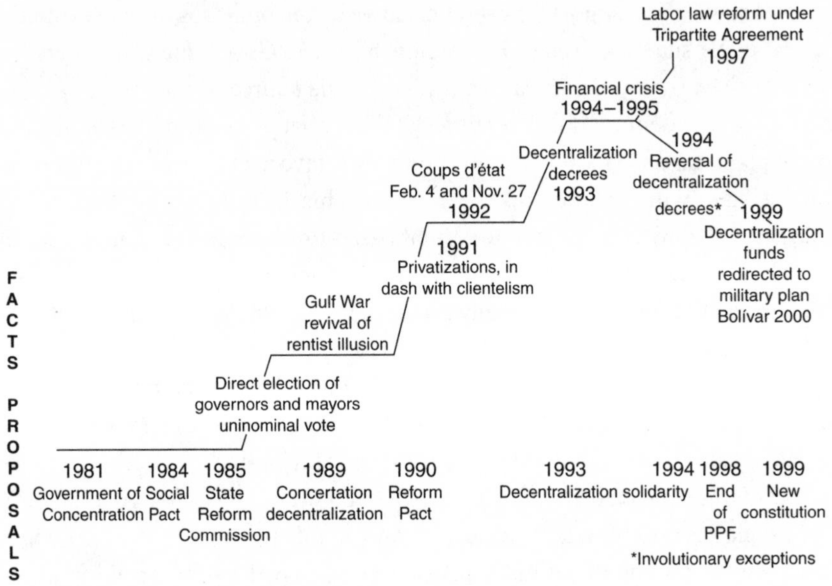

Fig. 11.2. Stop-go decentralization of political power.

These reforms passed at a time when advocates of market competition held the upper hand.

Openings toward expanded participation by the new diversity of interest groups that emerged in the 1980s and 1990s tended to stall when oil prices increased and state revenue recovered. On the other hand, once an opening was in place, it was seldom repealed. Figure 11.2 profiles this stop-go overall pattern of political reform during the Punto Fijo years, although it also reveals some exceptions.

The most important exceptions occurred when political decay was advanced, early in the second Caldera government. At that time, President Caldera suspended the decentralization decrees approved by his immediate predecessor, interim president Ramón J. Velásquez (May 1993–February 1994). Caldera insisted that resource allocation remain centralized because his ruling political party, Convergencia, did not control any important regional or local governments. Subsequently, during the transition from Punto Fijo democracy to the Fifth Republic, President Hugo Chávez retained the Caldera policy of ignoring legislation that allocated resources to regional and local governments. Moreover, Chávez has continued to divert to the army funds to which mayors

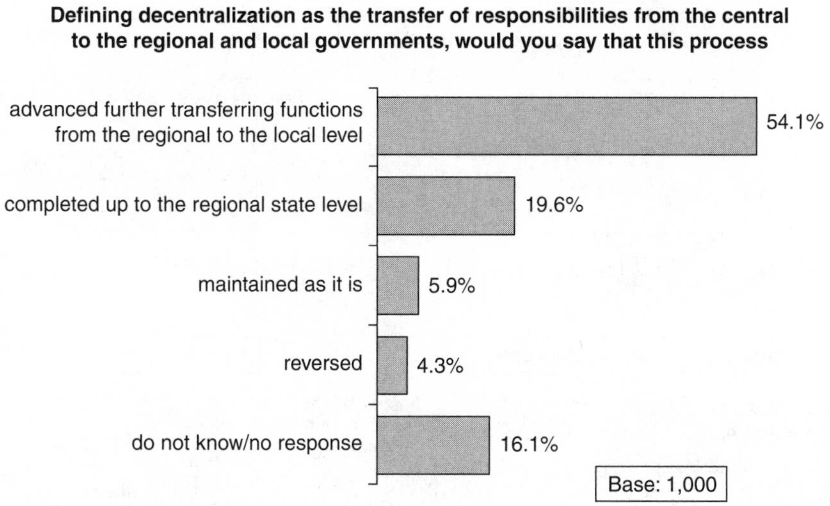
Defining decentralization as the transfer of responsibilities from the central to the regional and local governments, would you say that this process
advanced further transferring functions from the regional to the local level
54.1%
completed up to the regional state level
19.6%
maintained as it is
5.9%
reversed
4.3%
do not know/no response
16.1%
Base: 1,000

Fig. 11.3. Attitudes toward decentralization. *Source:* Datalanisis, C.A., National Omnibus Survey, December 1994.

and governors are legally entitled. Garrison commanders currently allocate these funds to localities under their command through a specially created program, Plan Bolívar 2000.

During the 1990s, decentralization helped to stem the tide of alienation from Punto Fijo democracy by demonstrating that elected officials could be made accountable and public sector investment more efficient. Decentralization was the most widely approved political reform of the 1990s. Figure 11.3 reveals that 80 percent of the population supported this process in 1994.

Other administrative reforms—especially privatization and payment for public services and highway tolls-were surprisingly popular. Economic reforms—price, exchange, and interest rate liberalization—commanded less support, as shown in figure 11.4.

The attitudes summarized in figures 11.3 and 11.4 suggest that during the final years of the Punto Fijo regime Venezuelans displayed some willingness to accept changes away from policies of state control. These supportive attitudes remained in the same range as of late 2003. In other words, the general public is not now more negative toward a market economy even though the flow of political communication in the Fifth Republic has included much propaganda that attacked the private sector. This argues that the so-called political costs of privatization and the shift to a market economy that was attempted in the

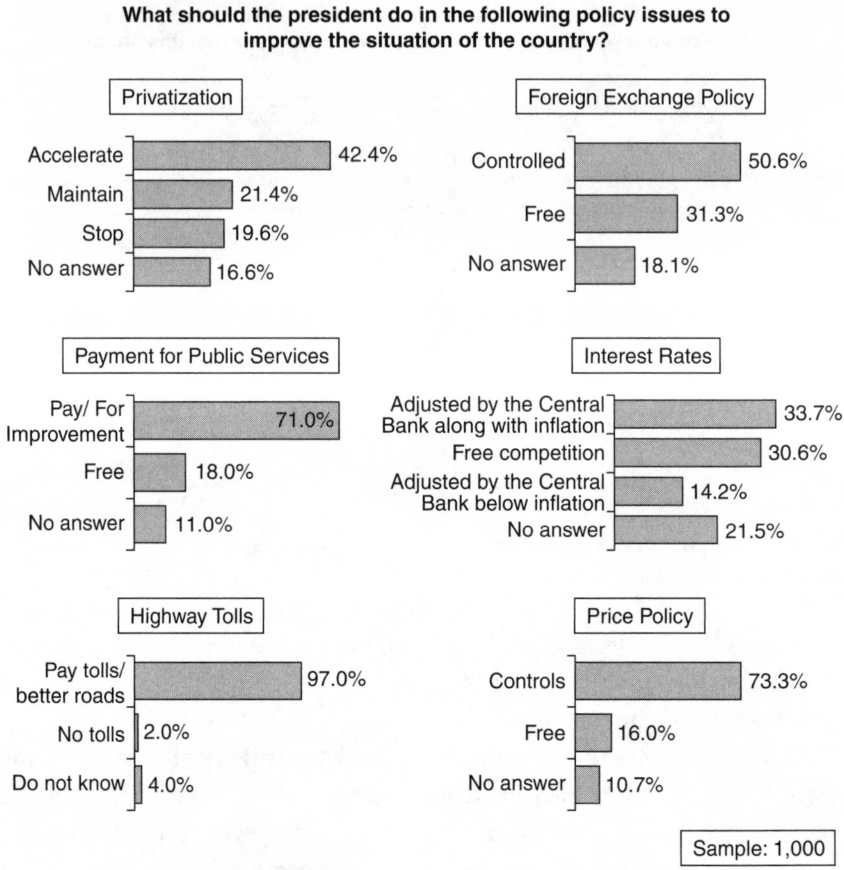

Fig. 11.4. Attitudes toward presidential policy alternatives. *Source:* Datanalisis, C.A., National Omnibus Survey, October 1996.

1990s might have been bearable had the Pérez and Caldera governments better explained what they were attempting and why.[2]

The failure of party, business, and labor leaders to leverage potentially supportive attitudes into actual changes had fatal consequences for Punto Fijo democracy. The political regime ossified, the quality of life deteriorated, and the two establishment political parties received the blame. Alienation oozes from this often repeated chant:

> Venezuela is a rich country because it has oil
> I am Venezuelan, and the oil belongs to the people.

The oil wealth should be distributed to all of us; therefore, we should all be rich.
But the fact is that the majority of the population is very poor.
Thus, those who should have distributed the oil wealth must have stolen it.

Evidence in support of this chant's sentiments surfaced in the Datanalisis national survey of public opinion in September 1996. This survey probed attitudes about who was responsible for the economic and political crisis. Respondents identified "political elites" and the "national government" as the chief villains. They saw the most important reasons for the crisis as "corruption" (58 percent) and "poor public administration" (24 percent). Figure 11.5 summarizes these responses.

Figure 11.5 reveals that 88 percent of respondents viewed the government and political elites as most responsible for the crisis of 1994–95. It also suggests that the "scapegoat campaign" mounted by Rafael Caldera in the 1993 national election campaign, and sustained during the first half of his government, was unsuccessful. Caldera, as discussed in Chapter 4, had attempted to blame bankers (many of whom had fled the country) and speculation by merchants for the crisis.

In September 1996 Datanalisis also probed other salient issues: corruption, the reasons why people did (or did not) hold politicians accountable, and when respondents thought that things would improve. The corruption question asked, "Which factor is more conducive to corruption?" Sixty-six percent replied that it was due to the practice of "clientelism" by the political parties; 14 percent blamed "the capitalist economy"; and 13 percent answered that it was due to "state controls over the economy." In reply to the question as to why the people had not confronted politicians, 36 percent replied that it is "useless, a waste of time," and 24 percent answered that "they are corrupt and govern only in their self interest." Other answers included "they have too much power" (10 percent) and "I am afraid to confront them, they may strike back" (19 percent). Datanalisis also asked the same sample, "When do you think that the situation in Venezuela will improve?" Pessimism predominated: 21 percent said "never," 18 percent said "between 5 and 10 years"; 12 percent replied "in more than 10 years"; and 18 percent answered that "they did not know when things would improve." Finally, the economic condition of our respondents was a powerful reason for these negative perceptions: average real (monthly) salary per worker had fallen from US$1,300 in 1979 to US$600 in 1988; disguised unemployment hovered around 35 percent.

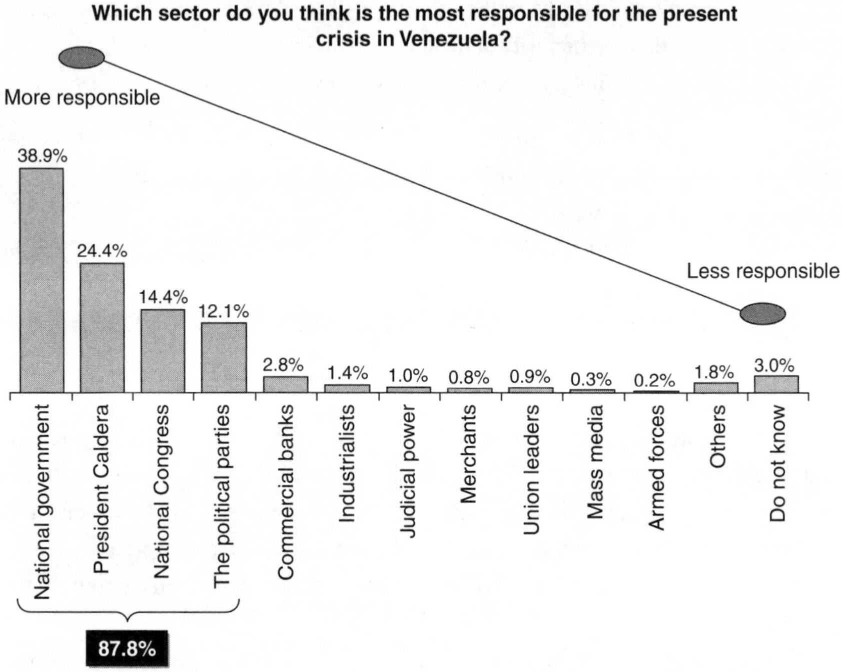

Fig. 11.5. Perceptions of responsibility for the Venezuelan crisis. *Source:* Datanalisis, C.A., National Omnibus Survey, September 1996.

More than a decade of frustration with the rentier state's performance alienated the electorate from the dominant political parties. The final years of Punto Fijo democracy evidenced lower voter turnout and success by presidential candidates on the fringes of the regime. Carlos Andrés Pérez's second successful run for the presidency, against the will of his AD party's ruling elite, was perhaps the first warning that there was strong support for antiregime leadership. However, Pérez had been an AD politician for his entire political life, and voter turnout remained high, at 82 percent. The failure of Pérez's second government discredited AD, but COPEI proved unable to capitalize on the dissatisfaction. In December 1993 Rafael Caldera's antiestablishment electoral campaign, as discussed in Chapter 8, returned him to the presidency as the candidate of the personalistic Convergencia. The COPEI presidential candidate, Oswaldo Alvarez Paz, finished third, and voter participation fell to less than 60 percent. Only 31 percent of voters chose Caldera. Figure 11.6 profiles decline in voter support for AD and COPEI candidates from 1993 onward. This trend tracks closely with depressed oil prices.

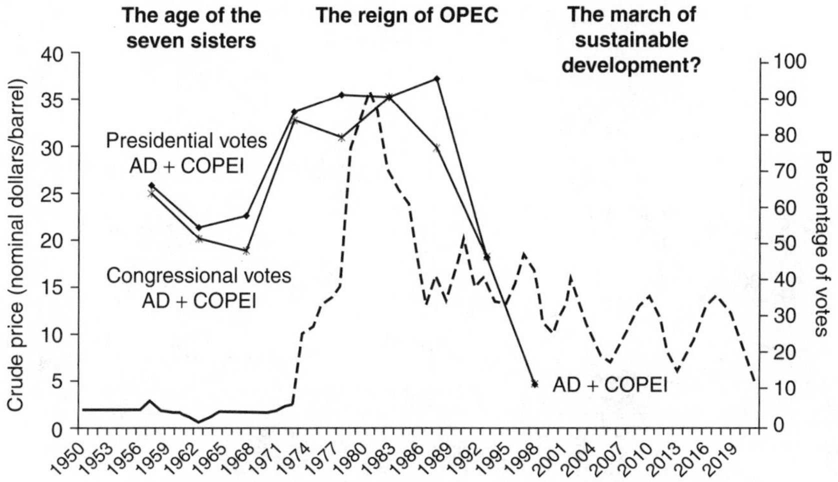

Fig. 11.6. Oil prices and votes for AD and COPEI. *Sources:* Consejo Nacional Electoral, 1999; Consejo Supremo Electoral, 1987, 1990, 1994; Ross, 1999.

The pessimism that permeated Venezuela in the late 1990s was a far cry from the optimism that prevailed during the 1970s. In the national elections of 1973 voters ended the party system fragmentation that had retarded democratic consolidation for ten years. An overwhelming majority voted for either AD or COPEI (Myers, 1977: ch. 5); twenty years later, as noted above, Rafael Caldera won the presidency for the second time by opposing these longtime dominant institutions.

It was two decades before the frustrations of ordinary Venezuelans crystallized into votes that ended the electoral dominance of AD and COPEI. Party identification with the two system-sustaining political parties remained high until fallout from the two unsuccessful military coups in 1992 confirmed high levels of dissatisfaction with both. This fallout also revealed unanticipated levels of alienation from Punto Fijo democracy. Until then, roughly 30 percent of Venezuelans identified with the AD and 20 percent with COPEI. Five percent identified with the militantly leftist Movimiento al Socialismo (MAS; Movement toward Socialism). Thirty-five percent identified themselves as independents. After 1992, identification with AD dipped below 20 percent, and only 10 percent identified with COPEI. The proportion viewing themselves as independents grew to 57 percent (Datanalisis, C.A., 1990–98).

Abstention is a pivotal indicator of dissatisfaction with the established political alternatives. In the post-1958 political regime voting was obligatory, and

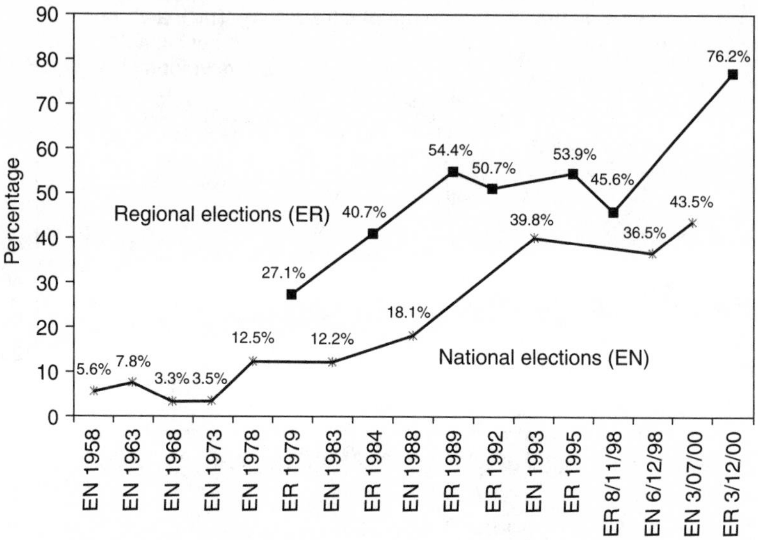

Fig. 11.7. Levels of abstention, 1958–99. *Source:* Consejo Nacional Electoral, 1999: 18.

abstention in presidential elections remained below 15 percent until 1988. Figure 11.7 reveals that in the 1990s the level of abstention in presidential elections increased dramatically, and in regional elections they exceeded 60 percent.

Public opinion polling in early 1989 indicated that the major reasons for not voting in the December 1988 presidential election were motivational: "I did not like any of the candidates" (22 percent), "I lost faith in the Democratic System" (18 percent), and "We all knew that Carlos Andrés Pérez was going to win" (14 percent). Other reasons were instrumental (e.g., "I changed my residence"). However, 8 percent responded that they preferred a military government (Myers, 1995: 62). Five years later, Hugo Chávez's call for abstention in the national elections may have been a factor in the failure of 39.5 percent of eligible voters to cast a ballot, and his presidential candidacy in 1998 likely contributed to the small reduction in levels of abstention. Finally, focus group interviews conducted by Datanalisis revealed that electoral abstention in the 1990s reflected embedded systemic dissatisfaction, not lack of motivation to participate due to confidence in the system.

Over the four decades of the post-1958 political regime, support for democracy remained high among Venezuelans. A mid-1992 national poll, following the failed coup attempt by Lieutenant Colonel Hugo Chávez, found that only 8 percent favored a military government, and rejection of the coup d'état as a mechanism to gain political power hovered near 75 percent (Njaim, Combellas, and Álvarez, 1992: 33). Forty-three percent favored democracy with the AD and COPEI political parties, and 40 percent favored a democracy without them. Support for democracy as a system of government ran at around 85 percent, and this level of support continued into the 1998 national election campaign, the last of the Punto Fijo period.

The first and only instance (until Hugo Chávez's 1998 run for office) in which a third-party candidate, one from a party other than AD and COPEI, captured the Venezuelan presidency occurred in December 1993. This was the case of Convergencia and Rafael Caldera. Caldera's success as the candidate of his own personalistic movement was made possible by destruction of the political myth that AD and COPEI represented different political alternatives and held each other in check. Since the presidential election of 1968, the first victory by COPEI over AD, most voters believed that the country's ills could be cured by substituting one of these political parties for the other in national elections (*voto castigo*).

Two events proved crucial in undermining the myth that AD and COPEI provided meaningful alternatives. One was the identification of COPEI and its leader, Eduardo Fernández, with the second Pérez administration. The week after the February 1992 coup by Chávez, COPEI became part of a coalition government to "support democracy." The visible manifestation of support was integrating two prominent members of COPEI into the Pérez cabinet. This was an unselfish act, for there was little to gain by identifying COPEI with a government that had become highly unpopular. It proved a disastrous choice for the presidential ambitions of Eduardo Fernández and for perceptions of COPEI as a distinctive alternative to power. The presence of COPEI in an AD government effectively ended the *voto castigo* myth. It led a majority of the electorate either to abstain from voting or to support parties other than AD and COPEI. Indeed, Caldera's rise in the polls began immediately following his February 5, 1992, televised speech to Congress. In that discourse he criticized COPEI's entry into the Pérez government, whose neoliberal policies he attacked for impoverishing the country. Caldera also uttered the often repeated line: "Poverty can hardly be a supportive basis for democracy."

Damage to AD as a responsible governing party occurred during the second Caldera administration. At the beginning of Caldera's presidential term AD presented itself as the most important opposition political party. But nothing was further from the truth. Luis Alfaro Ucero, the secretary general of AD (nicknamed "El Caudillo" [The Chieftain]), had seen an opportunity to secure patronage for his party in return for quietly supporting President Caldera in the Congress. During the first three years of Caldera's government this strategy worked well. Alfaro Ucero bided his time. He planned to move into open opposition in the final eighteen months of the presidential period, appear as the obvious alternative to govern, and regain the presidency for AD.[3]

For reasons that remain unknown, Alfaro Ucero abandoned this strategy in mid-1997. At that time, he intervened to stop impeachment proceedings against Caldera's minister of finance, Luis Raúl Matos Azócar. AD then moved into open support for the government, whose unpopularity was increasing. This move created dissention within AD. Alfaro Ucero then made the mistake of attempting to restore unity by imposing his presidential candidacy on the party. Support during the 1998 presidential campaign for Alfaro Ucero, at that time an uncharismatic seventy-five-year-old patriarch, never climbed above 5 percent in public opinion polls. Two weeks before the December elections AD terminated his candidacy and expelled him from the party. AD then threw its lot behind the presidential bid of Henrique Salas Römer in a last-ditch attempt to prevent the election of Hugo Chávez. COPEI did the same. In the wake of this development, Chávez's advantage over Salas Römer increased from 5 percent to 16 percent. Postelection focus groups conducted by Datanalisis confirmed that Salas Römer's decline was attributable largely to rejection after he received the endorsement of AD and COPEI.

The most salient explanation of Salas Römer's defeat, despite the votes he lost because of endorsements from AD and COPEI, was not his mistaken strategies of alliance. It lay in the attitude of the overwhelming majority that the time had come to gamble on voting for the candidate most hostile to the existing state of affairs.[4] To a lesser extent this desire influenced earlier voting decisions: in 1988 (on behalf of Carlos Andrés Pérez) and in 1993 (on behalf of Rafael Caldera). In 1998 Hugo Chávez personified rejection of post-1958 democracy as it had evolved under the tutelage of AD and COPEI. Voters perceived Salas Römer as located in the center, a moderate option that the intensely dissatisfied electorate rejected. Instead, they embraced Hugo Chávez, the failed *golpista* who, after his release from prison, was trying his hand at electoral politics.

Transforming the Attitudes Inherited from Representative Democracy

The legacies from forty years of Punto Fijo democracy are legion. The Fifth Republic inherited some of its basic political attitudes, but the Chávez government crafted new institutions, most of of them intended to modify these inherited political attitudes. The chances that political socialization in the Fifth Republic will achieve its goals are linked closely to the personal charisma of Hugo Chávez, father of the Bolivarian Revolution.

The founders of Punto Fijo democracy were successful at the beginning in creating broad popular support for democracy as a procedural form of government. This attitude survived the discrediting of AD and COPEI and was passed on to the Fifth Republic. Even while rejecting the democracy that they knew best (the regime dominated by AD and COPEI), Venezuelans viewed universal elections as the only acceptable procedure for choosing political leaders. However, the election of Hugo Chávez to the presidency in 1998 proclaimed that the electorate demanded more than procedural democracy. Chávez won in large part by promising a new and different democracy, one that would be more efficient, less corrupt, and highly participatory.

Venezuelans wanted a different economic system in 1998, and this preference is the second attitude inherited from post-1958 political regime. Respondents to Datanalisis polls in the late 1990s consistently blamed deteriorating economic conditions on the Paquete Económico (economic adjustment program that implemented neoliberal reforms), on mismanagement, and on corruption. Viewed in light of other opinions that suggested some flexibility of attitude toward market reforms, the assigning of blame by Datanalisis poll respondents suggests that the economic challenge facing the Fifth Republic is to create a hybrid economy. This hybrid should be one that efficiently allocates resources while softening the most unforgiving characteristics of neoliberalism. It must also be distinct from the so-called liberal economy that the second Pérez and Caldera governments imposed in 1990 and 1996. Those economic regimes proved politically unsustainable. They failed to provide for the social and economic needs of the urban poor, an interest that is now the country's single largest socioeconomic grouping.

The liberal economies advocated by Pérez and Caldera also ignored the interests of national entrepreneurs. They exposed these entrepreneurs to debilitating macroeconomic forces (high inflation, high interest rates, and de-

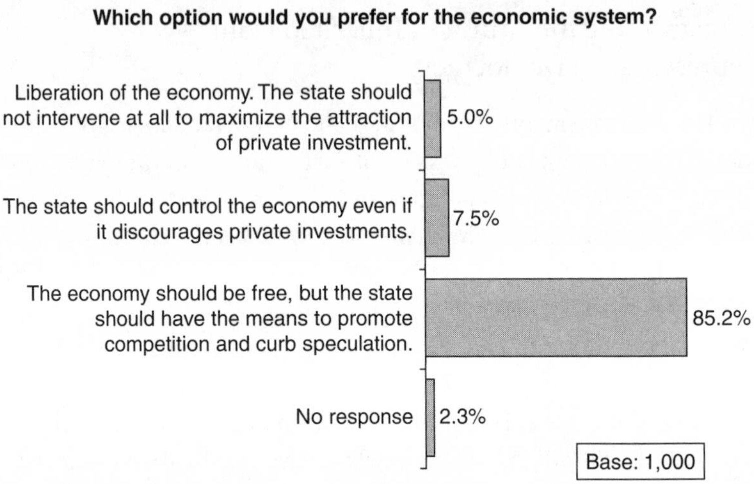
Which option would you prefer for the economic system?
Liberation of the economy. The state should not intervene at all to maximize the attraction of private investment.
5.0%
The state should control the economy even if it discourages private investments.
7.5%
The economy should be free, but the state should have the means to promote competition and curb speculation.
85.2%
No response
2.3%
Base: 1,000

Fig. 11.8. Economic system preference. *Source:* Datanalisis, C.A., National Omnibus Survey, December 1994.

valuation) and to extreme competition from the lowest-cost goods produced anywhere, all with no preparation. Many entrepreneurs went bankrupt. Nevertheless, as of late 2003 neither entrepreneurs nor the urban poor could expect a return to the populist clientelism of earlier times. Datanalisis surveys suggest that this message is percolating through public opinion. Figure 11.8, like figure 11.4, hints that Venezuelans may be amenable to an alternative economic configuration located between state subsidies/controls and extreme liberalization.

The third important attitude passed on from post-1958 democracy is social and cultural. It is the desire to make the state less paternalistic and more accountable to ordinary citizens. Responding affirmatively to this attitude mandates that politicians limit the state's financial autonomy. They must also empower taxpayers. In the final decade of Punto Fijo, as we have seen, progress was made along these lines. Civil society groups increased accountability by crafting programs to decentralize public administration, reduce the power of national party elites, and privatize selected components of the petroleum industry.

Fifth Republic leaders campaigned in 2000 with promises that they would build on the success of civil society groups in the 1990s. However, President Chávez's propaganda in this regard misleads. He portrays his policies as increasing popular participation. In practice, however, they shield public officials from the pressures of public opinion with respect to deepening democracy, expanding the market economy, restoring decentralization, and increasing accountability. In addition, despite superficial differences from the policies of Punto Fijo democracy, important similarities exist. Both political regimes concentrate political power, favor state ownership of the major sources of wealth, and depend on populist appeals to gain and maintain support. It is easy to make the case that the performance of Fifth Republic institutions and leaders will prove just as disappointing as that of their predecessors. Before we rush to judgment, however, the new regime deserves a close look, especially as to its capabilities to undertake successful political socialization.

Two ideological components of democracy which official political socialization sought to inculcate during the Punto Fijo regime, political equality and political liberty, have taken on a different meaning in the Fifth Republic. The 1999 Bolivarian constitution stresses equality far more than its predecessor; it contains multiple articles that increase the means by which citizens can participate in elections and referenda. These changes have the potential to enhance the role of public opinion in politics. In terms of the exercise of political liberty, the Bolivarian Revolution's attitudes are nuanced. Here two dimensions of political liberty merit special analysis: individual liberties and the freedom of groups to make demands (pluralism). The Fifth Republic is less enthusiastic about pluralism than was its predecessor. President Chávez and his inner circle appear uncomfortable with the idea of powerful and autonomous groups lobbying the state in pursuit of their special interests. More so than Punto Fijo, the Fifth Republic favors the establishment of an official umbrella institution to aggregate the interests of all groups. These institutions are intended to link interest group leaders with government. President Chávez's preference for corporatist-style organization extends to empowering neighborhood councils tasked with assisting national bureaucracies in distributing resources aerially. In contrast, the Bolivarians have been tolerant, even supportive, of the individual's freedom of speech.

The institutional designers of Fifth Republic Venezuela envision the army as having the pivotal role in mobilizing and socializing citizens. They are uncomfortable with the competitiveness and diversity of opinion which are innate to strong political parties and competitive party systems. Indeed, the public statements of many of Chávez's closest collaborators over the past two years suggest that they are distrustful even of their own political party, the Movimiento

Quinta República (MVR; Fifth Republican Movement). On the other hand, there is little doubt that President Chávez himself is more suspicious of the armed forces than he was prior to the coups of April 11–14, 2002. He continues, nevertheless, to use the military for political mobilization and public administration. These functions are the central task of a program known as Plan Bolívar 2000.

Plan Bolívar 2000 has allocated resources directly through the regional military commanders, thus bypassing the national bureaucracy, the political parties, regional public administration, elected mayors and governors, and neighborhood councils. The results of this management strategy are mixed. The armed forces have built and repaired important works of infrastructure, but corruption appears to be creeping into military decisions that allocate resources. As an institution, however, the armed forces enjoyed the highest level of public approval (Datanalisis, C.A., 2000). The military's popularity, however, has undermined the role of governors, mayors, and neighborhood councils, institutions that prior to 1998 were a source of new political leaders and innovative procedures to hold elected officials accountable.

Perhaps the farthest-reaching change accompanying efforts to consolidate Fifth Republic political institutions has been the weakening of AD and COPEI and the destruction of what was once one of Latin America's most consolidated political party systems. The 1998 election campaign confirmed that AD and COPEI had lost much of their appeal; and over the five years that President Chávez has been in office he has used the national executive to undermine and discredit these once dominant institutions further. Most Venezuelans now view AD and COPEI as selfish and incapable of offering new and acceptable political ideas. These once vigorous institutions are but a faint shadow their former selves.

President Chávez's political party system is intended to be less intrusive than its Punto Fijo predecessor. The Bolivarians see political parties as necessary evils, facades that they use in order to please democrats abroad and win elections at home. The political party system, however, is not to be the primary locus of public policy decision making. The preferred Bolivarian political party system would have one dominant institution, MVR, and a group of smaller ones, none of which would be capable of mounting an effective challenge for national power. The possibility of crafting such a system existed in 1999 and 2000, but subsequently the window of opportunity appears to have closed. As of late 2003, supportive attitudes toward all political parties are volatile. Still, this condition fits well into President Chávez's preferred vision of the new Venezuela, a political regime in which he reaches out directly to the masses while the military and paramilitary groups support his rule by mobilizing the anonymous and dependent masses.

The 1999 constitution stipulates the preferred Bolivarian procedures for citizen participation in politics: referenda at the national, regional, and local levels. These referenda provide for ongoing popular consultation by Fifth Republic leaders and for remedies to intense popular dissatisfaction. The government can ask citizens to approve a new law or even the constitution, as occurred on December 15, 1999. Two other kinds of referenda are intended to reinforce the power of citizens over elected officials. The first, the abrogatory referendum, provides for the repeal of laws or regulations (Article 74). The revocatory referendum allows citizens to recall elected officials from office, including the president of the republic (Articles 72 and 172).

The Bolivarians portray replacing participation through pluralism (demand making by special interest groups) with the referenda as a major advance for holding government accountable. This position sparks intense debate. The disparity in power between individual citizens and government is far greater than that between organized interests and government. Nevertheless, as the events of early 2004 demonstrated, when elected officials alienate a significant segment of the electorate it is possible to fulfill the conditions necessary to force a recall election.

Mass public opinion is intended to be more important in the Fifth Republic than in Punto Fijo. President Chávez cultivates approval from the "people" by means of frequent public appearances, multiple speeches, and constant reference to the "sufferings" of the downtrodden. He claims to be communicating directly with the people (*el soberano*), sending the message that he is attending to their long-neglected basic needs. This message fulfills the same purpose (political socialization and social mobilization to induce desired regime-supportive attitudes) that the theme of cross-class unity (*democrácia polyclasista*) served during the 1960s, when AD and COPEI sought to legitimate Punto Fijo democracy (see table 11.1).

Findings from focus group interviews conducted by Datanalisis during the first half of 2001 suggest that the social mobilization sought by President Chávez is being undercut by the lack of clarity in his message.[5] The opinions expressed in those groups supported this conclusion when they were assessed in terms of the components of the social mobilization paradigm presented in table 11.1. Indeed, most focus group participants lacked a clear idea of the Bolivarian Revolution's goals. Some volunteered that the purpose of the revolution was to gain more support for Hugo Chávez, but there was little consensus on how this could be accomplished. A few volunteered that the president wanted Venezuelans to back the army as a way of supporting him. Most were confused with regard to the purpose of the Bolivarian political party (MVR). Most important, focus group participants perceived that the "existing crisis" was unresolved. They were frustrated because they still thought of Venezuela as a rich country while they themselves remained poor. We saw that this scenario of frustration built after 1983 and undermined Punto Fijo democracy. It remains a threat to political stability in the Fifth Republic.

Focus group participants were also confused by fuzziness in the "message" that purported to explain the kind of changes the Bolivarians wanted. The message that focus group respondents most often associated with President Chávez was revenge against those who controlled and profited from Punto Fijo democracy. This negative message has limited utility for institution building, although it does cultivates a bonding that allows the charismatic leader to lead. President Chávez understands that he must disseminate a more positive message, and throughout 2003 his weekly television appearances in "Aló Presidente" (The President Speaks) repeat the message that the Bolivarian Revolution will eliminate poverty no matter how long this may take. Nevertheless, confusion remains with respect to the goals of gaining revenge, growing the economy, and changing the country's class structure. The Bolivarians have not sorted this out. Thus, everything depends on the ability of Hugo Chávez to retain his charismatic authority and his symbolic identification with the underclass. This is no easy task given that during the first five years of the Fifth Republic this group has become poorer.

Bolivarian Revolution in Power: Bases of Support

National surveys of public opinion taken by Datanalisis reveal that support for President Chávez's performance between February 1999 and November 2003 fell from extremely high levels to a moderate range (fig. 11.9).

Positive assessment of Chávez's performance as a leader peaked at 91.9 percent in the wake of his first inauguration (February 1999). His rate of

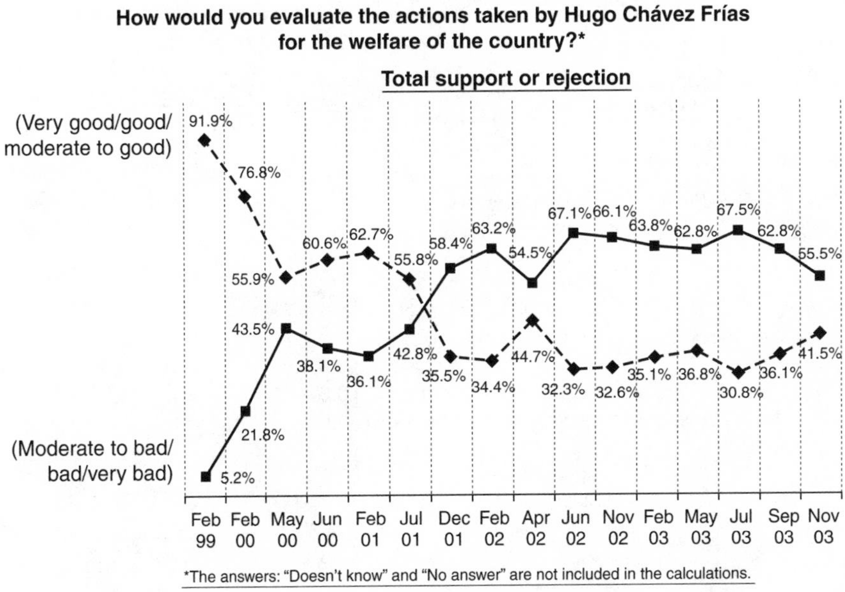

Fig. 11.9. Evaluation of actions by Hugo Chávez. *Sources:* Datanalisis National Polls. Samples of 1,300, stratified by region, sex, age group, and socioeconomic status; home interviews.

approval varied between 56 and 76 percent throughout 2000. A significant rise occurred in late 2000 (and lasted into early 2001), when support for his performance in office increased from 55.9 to 62.7 percent. This increase appears to have been the result of the presidential electoral campaign for the mega-election of July 30, 2000 (which Chávez won handily) and the electoral campaign for municipal and neighborhood councils (which were swept by the Bolivarians in December 2000). From early 2001 onward the president's popularity has declined. It reached its nadir in July 2003 (30.8% rate of approval). This deterioration was the product of the conflictive political climate, declining private investment, and high levels of unemployment and crime.

Chávez's job approval rating rose from 30.8 to 41.5 percent in the second half of 2003. Several factors explain this increase. First, the government was mounting an election-style publicity campaign on behalf of President Chávez, who anticipated that he would have to fend off a recall attempt. An important component of this effort by the government was to increase funding for a wide range of social and economic programs that appealed to potential voters. As of late 2003, however, Datanalisis polls found that in free and open balloting the

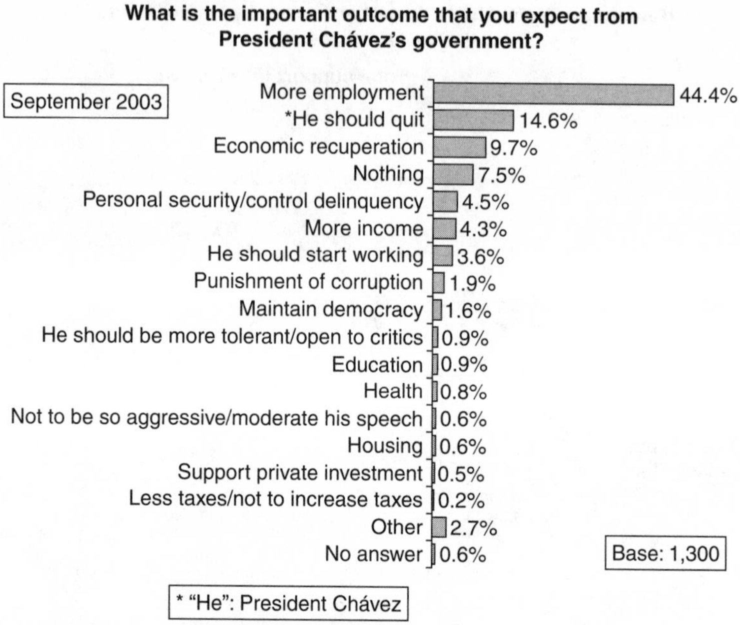

Fig. 11.10. Anticipated outcome of the Chávez government. *Sources:* Datanalisis National Polls. Samples of 1,300, stratified by region, sex, age group, and socioeconomic status; home interviews.

president would be recalled. Second, opposition leaders, still reeling from the failure of their massive demonstrations during January 2003 to dislodge the government, have adopted a pacifist strategy in the face of official provocations. Third, the tolerance of opposition leaders reflects their calculation that any protest (or even judicial demands) against the government will only serve the latter's purposes, namely, to delay the recall referendum. However, this approach is not well understood by rank-and-file opponents of the government, who tend to view their leaders' apparent passivity as weakness.

Datanalisis public opinion polls provided respondents with options describing the most important outcomes that they could expect from the Chávez government. Choices included: "employment," "income," "attract private investment," "improve personal security," "upgrade education," "provide access to health care," "punish corruption," and "maintain democracy." Figure 11.10 profiles the replies of respondents to four Datanalisis surveys in 2000 and 2001.

Respondents were also asked to assess their satisfaction with the progress the Fifth Republic had made in achieving the outcomes just listed. Most respondents, including those who identified with the government political party

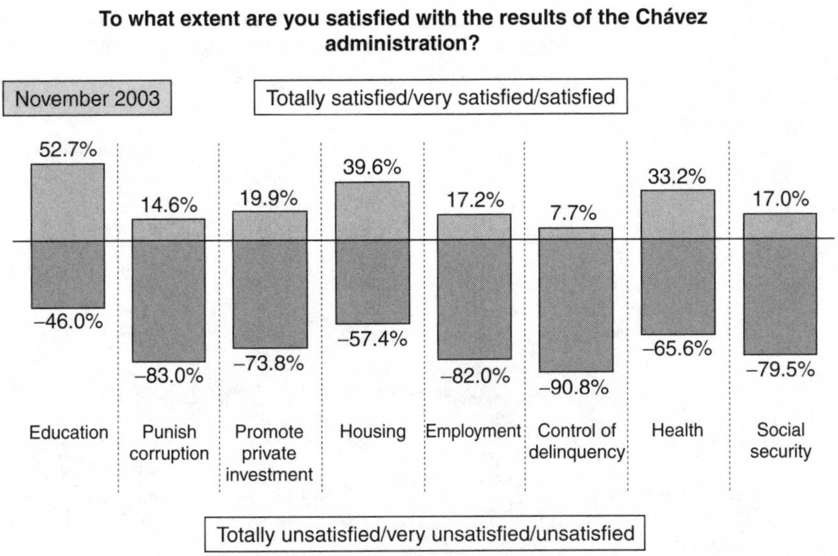

Fig. 11.11. Satisfaction with the Chávez government. *Sources:* Datanalisis National Polls. Samples of 1,300, stratified by region, sex, age group, and socioeconomic status; home interviews.

(MVR), were not satisfied with the progress made by President Chávez's administration in achieving those outcomes. Figure 11.11 profiles the extent of this dissatisfaction.

Figure 11.12 reports the perceptions of respondents concerning whether fourteen influential institutions, and President Chávez, are performing in ways that contribute to the well-being of the country. It reveals that, at least until November 2003, the view of the president (with respect to other institutions) was becoming more negative.

Several important messages stand out in figure 11.12: (1) all institutions associated with the government rank on the lower (or predominantly negative view) range of the scale; (2) all the nongovernment interests, including organizations openly identified with the opposition, such as the church and the media, rank in the range that signals that they are viewed more positively than negatively; (3) government actors from decentralized institutions (such as governors and mayors) are viewed more positively than central government institutions; (4) the political institution most identified with opposition politicians, the Coordinadora Democrática, is viewed a bit less positively than President Hugo Chávez himself. Thus, despite widespread dissatisfaction with the Bolivarians, dislodging Chávez from the presidency remains a formidable challenge.

How would you qualify the performance of these sectors for the well-being of the country?
% of positive responses: summation of "very good, good and fair"

Feb 99	Feb 01	Apr 02	Aug 02	Feb 03	Jul 03	Sep 03	Nov 03
Chávez 91.9	Mass media 85.4	Civil society 83.7	Church 76	Church 78.2	Church 78.4	Church 80.5	Church 74.6
Mass media 89.3	Church 81.1	Church 81.2	Mass media 71.9	Banks 66.1	Mass media 70.5	Mass media 71.9	Mass media 66.1
A.A.F.F 87.9	A.A.F.F 76.5	Commerce 80.8	A.A.F.F 66.7	Commerce 65.8	Commerce 67.4	Commerce 70.8	Commerce 63.2
Church 81.4	Commerce 75	Industrialists 74.8	Commerce 62.1	Mass media 64.5	Industrialists 61.6	Banks 70.3	Banks 62.2
Government 79.3	Industrialists 74.9	Mayor 72	Banks 58.4	Civil society 62.6	Banks 57.9	Industrialists 63.9	Industrialists 60.8
Governors 70.7	Banks 74.8	Banks 71.3	Industrialists 58	Industrialists 60.5	"Gente del Pertróleo" 57.3	A.A.F.F 58.8	A.A.F.F 54.8
Entrepreneurs 70.4	Civil society 72.7	Governors 70.4	Mayor 57.7	"Gente del Pertróleo" 56	Civil society 55.7	Civil society 58.5	CNE 53.8
Commerce 68.9	Governors 66.7	A.A.F.F 63.6	Civil society 57.4	"C. Democrática" 49	A.A.F.F 52.4	"Gente del Pertróleo" 56.2	Civil society 53.4
Industrialists 67.9	Ombudsman 64.2	Mass media 62.0	Governors 49.7	Mayor 48.3	Mayor 51.6	"C. Democrática" 51.7	Governors 51.3
Banks 67.6	Mayor 62.9	Ombudsman 49.9	Judicial power 46.7	Governors 46.2	Governors 47.4	Governors 51.5	Mayor 50.8
Mayor 59.2	Chávez 62.7	National Assembley 49.9	"C. Democrática" 40.4	Labor unions 42.4	"C. Democrática" 45	Mayor 51.4	"Gente del Pertróleo" 48.7
Judicial power 41.3	Attorney general 57.3	Attorney general 46.2	Labor unions 39.7	A.A.F.F 42	Labor unions 36.7	CNE 51.4	Chávez 41.5
Congress 38.6	Government 56.1	Judicial power 45.4	Ombudsman 39.7	Political parties 36.7	CNE 33.2	Judicial power 46.1	Labor unions 40.9
Political parties 24.1	National Assembley 54.8	Chávez 44.7	National Assembley 37.6	Chávez 35.1	Ombudsman 33.2	Labor unions 45.8	"C. Democrática" 39.6
Labor unions 21.9	Comptroller 53.5	Comptroller 44.5	Chávez 32.7	CNE 34.7	National Assembley 31.6	National Assembley 43.2	National Assembley 38.8
	Judicial power 51.7	Government 44.5	CNE 32.5	National Assembley 34.4	Political parties 31.6	Political parties 39.9	Government 38.7
	MVR 39.2	CNE 42.4	Political parties 32.3	Government 32.3	Chávez 30.8	Ombudsman 37.4	Judicial power 37.8
	Labor unions 24.6	MVR 35.2	Attorney general 29.8	Ombudsman 31.6	Judicial power 30.5	Chávez 35.9	Attorney general 34.5
	Political parties 16.7	Labor unions 42.3	Comptroller 29.1	Judicial power 31.3	Attorney general 28.6	Attorney general 34.7	Ombudsman 33.8
		Political parties 29.4	Government 28	Comptroller 30.4	Government 27.2	Comptroller 34.2	Comptroller 33.4
			MVR 27.2	Attorney general 29.3	MVR 26.7	Government 34	MVR 33.0
			"Circulos Bolivarianos" 26.2	"Circulos Bolivarianos" 28.5	Comptroller 26.5	MVR 30.4	Political parties 30.0
				MVR 28.3	"Circulos Bolivarianos" 23.8	"Circulos Bolivarianos" 28	"Circulos Bolivarianos" 29.8

Fig. 11.12. Performance of institutions. *Sources:* Datanalisis National Omnibus Surveys.

One outcome of protracted confrontation between government and the opposition, from the standpoint of public opinion, has been a polarization of both groups. Figures 11.13 and 11.14 profile the extent of this polarization.

Figures 11.13 and 11.14 reveal that extremist views have grown, while the moderate or "ambivalent" attitudes have diminished. This is an important indication that Venezuela is moving toward a confrontation that centers on the personality and policies of Hugo Chávez. This concern led Datanalisis to conduct its national surveys using the technique of cluster analysis. The results of this probe reveal the presence of five distinct views of President Chávez in July 2001. These are shown in figure 11.15.

The five distinct views of President Chávez which emerged from the application of the cluster analysis technique to the poll of public opinion for July 2001 became three when the technique was repeated for the poll of May 2003. *Chavistas* who in 2001 "repented" over having voted for him in the July 2000 presidential elections had disappeared as a viable cluster by 2003. Some from

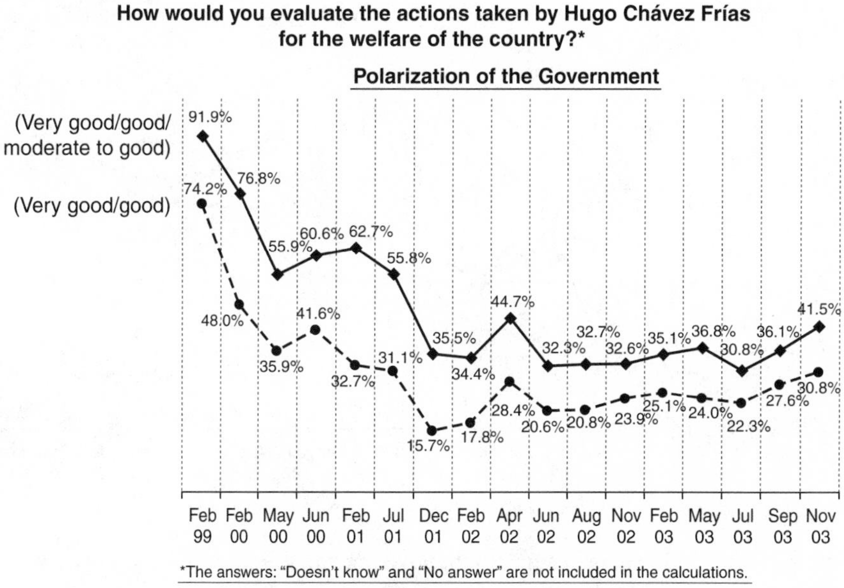

Fig. 11.13. Evaluation of support for the government. *Sources:* Datanalisis National Polls. Samples of 1,300, stratified by region, sex, age group, and socioeconomic status; home interviews.

this cluster were incorporated into the cluster of "light" Chávez supporters as of June 2002, but this cluster disappeared in May 2003. By then most "light" *chavistas* appear to have become "hard core" supporters of the president. Between July 2001 and May 2003 the cluster containing "hard core" opponents of the president increased from under 20 percent of the Datanalisis sample to 36 percent. The cluster encompassing "light opponents" of the *chavistas* rose from one-quarter to slightly more than 30 percent. Thus, figure 11.15 reveals that the president's policies after mid-2001 polarized public opinion, with roughly one third strongly supporting his Bolivarian Revolution and two-thirds opposed as of May 2003. Only half of those opposing the government's policies were strongly opposed, confirming that the opportunity exists for President Chávez's supporters to regain their majority position.

The Chávez government's failure to respond to popular demands throughout its first four years in office led to popular protests in December 2002 and January 2003. The most dramatic of these protests were the almost daily marches by up to a million people in Caracas. Similar marches occurred in the interior cities of Maracaibo, Valencia, and Puerto La Cruz, and these attracted hundreds of thousands of protesters. Four factors shed light on why President

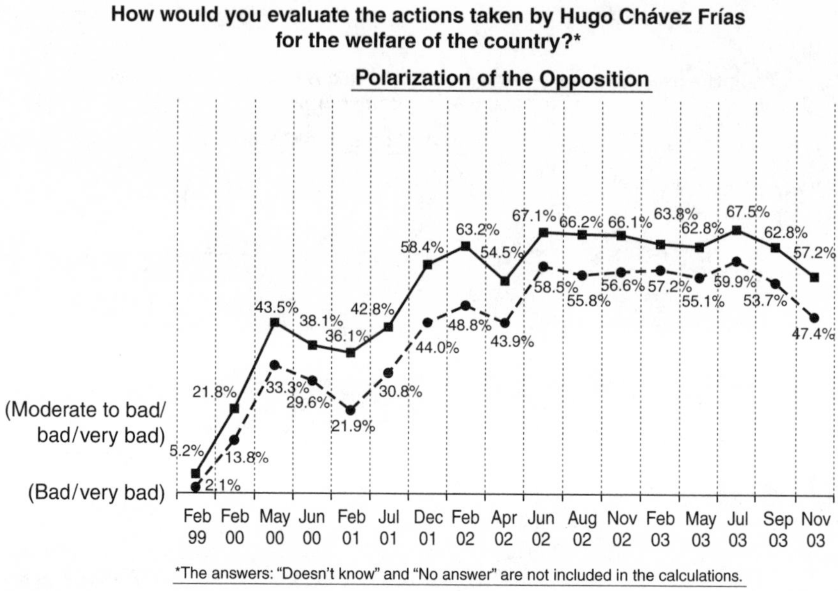

Fig. 11.14. Evaluation of opposition to the government. *Sources:* Datanalisis National Polls. Samples of 1,300, stratified by region, sex, age group, and socioeconomic status; home interviews.

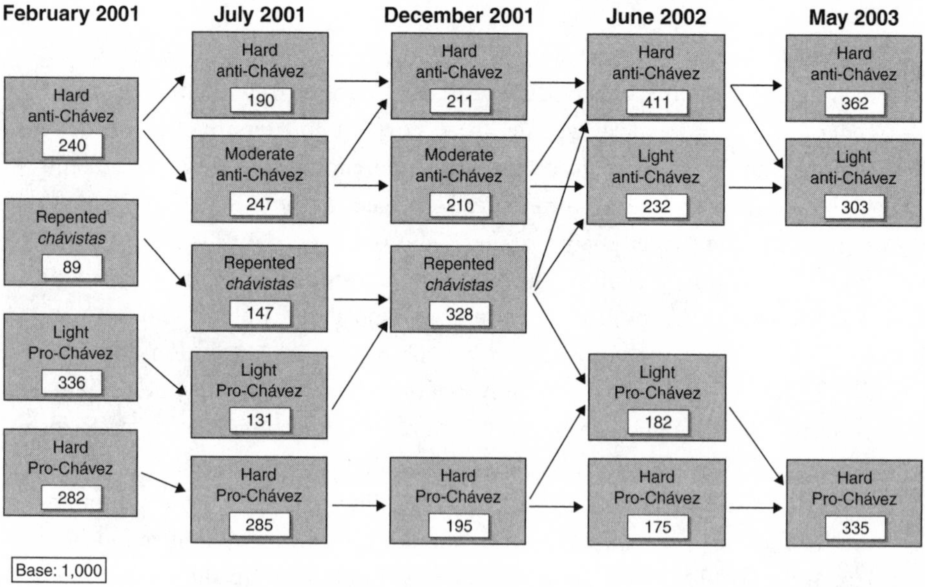

Fig. 11.15. The evolution of the segments of the population.

In which way would you prefer that the political crisis be solved?

Response	Total	Pro-Government	Opposition	Independent
Recall referendum	43.6%	15%	**52.7%**	**50.7%**
The president should be allowed to govern	20.1%	**67.4%**	0.4%	15.2%
The president should resign	11.7%	1.1%	17.8%	10.9%
Constitutional amendment elections without Chávez	7.8%	0.3%	12.5%	6.7%
Constitutional amendment elections with Chávez	4.3%	5.8%	5.0%	2.4%
Impeachment	2.1%	0.5%	3.2%	1.7%
Peaceful protest	1.6%	0.3%	2.5%	1.3%
Civil disobedience	1.6%	–	3.0%	0.7%
Other	4.6%	6.6%	2.2%	6.6%
No answer	2.5%	3.2%	0.6%	3.7%

Base: 1,300

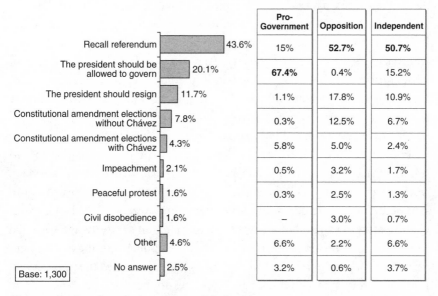

Fig. 11.16. Preferred resolution of the political crisis. *Sources:* Datanalisis National Polls. Samples of 1,300, stratified by region, sex, age group, and socioeconomic status; home interviews.

Chávez was able to remain in power given this enormous pressure: (1) public transportation workers did not join the strike; (2) the banks worked half-time; (3) the marginal classes perceived the media's communication strategy as so harsh and unfair that they became more supportive of the government; and (4) the military high command threw its weight behind the president and against the marchers.

The events of 2002 and 2003 convinced most opponents of the Bolivarian Revolution that military coups and pressure from the street stood little chance of dislodging the Chávez government. Indeed, respondents to a Datanalisis survey of September 2003 (figure 11.16) replied that they wanted the political crisis to be solved through legal, democratic, and pacific means.

Conclusions

The policies of political socialization pursued by President Chávez have consolidated the negative image that most Venezuelans held of Punto Fijo democracy in 1998. His revolutionary government, however, remains suspended between classical Western democracy that seeks to represent diversity and a quasi-Marxist democratic vision that relies on the state to impose equality. Bolivarian revolutionaries have always viewed as disloyal opponents those who reject their formula for equality. They have yet to define their vision of what constitutes a loyal opposition within the Fifth Republic. Yet most Venezuelans view the presence of a loyal opposition as a necessary condition for meaningful democracy.

The forty-year reign of Punto Fijo democracy helped to fix democracy as a basic orientation of the Venezuelan people. This political socialization had important implications for the signature process that occurred over four days, from November 28 to December 1, 2003. At that time, millions turned out to sign petitions requesting a revocatory referendum to recall President Chávez. Controversy over the validity of one million signatures favoring the recall led to a process of "repairs" in early May (2004). Opponents of the government turned out in large numbers, and President Chávez conceded that those favoring his ouster had secured enough signatures to force a recall referendum, which the National Electoral Council scheduled for August 15. However, in order for the president to be removed from office through the recall referendum, those favoring his ouster would have to obtain more votes than the 3.78 million votes that President Chávez received in winning the July 2000 election, and the number of voters calling for the President's removal would have to be greater than the number favoring his retention in office. A national survey of public opinion by the firm of Greenberg, Quinlan, and Rosner, for which fieldwork was completed during the last week of June, showed 48 percent of Venezuelans supporting the president's ouster and an equal percent favoring his retention in office. Thus, the electorate was closely divided, and as of this writing (mid-July 2004) the outcome of the August 15 revocatory referendum appeared too close to call.

Polling by Datanalisis between 2001 and 2003 confirmed that Venezuelans view the provision of the 1999 constitution that facilitates the revocatory referendum to be an important component of the post-1999 political regime. In this context, the acceptance by Chavista and anti-Chavista forces of the revocatory referendum as a mechanism to reinforce their legitimacy provides strong evidence that democratic norms continue to orient political behavior as Venezuelans seek to craft new political institutions and processes.

Part IV / Conclusion

CHAPTER TWELVE

From Representative to Participatory Democracy?

Regime Transformation in Venezuela

Jennifer L. McCoy

The conditions that facilitated the institutionalization of the Punto Fijo system during the 1960s had changed by the 1990s. The dramatic transformation from a poor, rural society to one that was urbanized and characterized by a highly unequal distribution of wealth between an expanded upper middle class and slum dwellers was not unlike developments that accompanied economic modernization and structural differentiation elsewhere in Latin America, even though it was influenced by oil. Globally, the cold war had passed, and a new era of globalization and integration promoted trade and economic liberalization. Yet a backlash to the negative consequences of these developments was emerging around the world in new forms of political mobilization by those who perceived themselves to be excluded from the benefits of the new era.

Venezuela was no exception. As political elites struggled to adapt to the conditions of relative scarcity of the 1990s, citizens grew angry and frustrated at growing impoverishment and viewed their leaders as increasingly unresponsive and isolated. They looked elsewhere for leadership, and with the election of Lieutenant Colonel Hugo Chávez Frías as president in 1998 they sealed their rejection of Punto Fijo representative democracy.

This volume has examined the failure of the Punto Fijo democracy to adapt to structural changes, both nationally and globally, and described the political regime that replaced it. We are interested in drawing out the lessons of this transition, which left in ruins one of the few second-wave limited democracies surviving the reverse wave of authoritarianism that swept over most of Latin America in the mid-1960s. What does it tell us about the pitfalls and dangers that confront the region's newer third-wave democracies? We also seek to identify the conditions of change from one political regime to another within the "gray zone" of regimes that are neither fully liberal democracies nor outright dictatorships.

We started with the assumption that several kinds of polyarchies exist and that each may have its own unique embedded vulnerabilities. These vulnerabilities explain how a regime that appears to be well established can deteriorate or enter into disequilibrium.

As elaborated in the following sections, our explanation for the unraveling of Venezuela's representative democracy under Punto Fijo and the inability of its elites to restore the status quo ante or to revitalize the representative democracy draws on three theoretical approaches: structural approaches emphasizing the political economy; institutional approaches emphasizing political choices; and cultural explanations emphasizing mediating political orientations and political learning. The structural, institutional, and cultural characteristics of the regime included embedded vulnerabilities that eventually led to crises in the areas of distribution and representation.

The first vulnerability was an overreliance on distributive policy. As described in Chapter 1, the founders of Punto Fijo assumed that revenue from foreign petroleum sales would continue at high levels into the indefinite future. Therefore, they relied inordinately on the state's distributive capability to maintain stability and legitimacy and manage conflict. This choice made the regime heavily dependent on the global petroleum market, and so when the price of oil fell and remained low, stress intensified on one of the regime's points of vulnerability.

The second vulnerability derived from the neglect of regulative and redistributive capabilities. The Punto Fijo founders had learned from the regime of General Marcos Pérez Jiménez that regulative measures could be met with destabilizing resistance. They learned from their Trienio experience that redistributive policies could be even more dangerous, as they caused the backlash of a military coup that ended the first short-lived democratic experiment in Venezuela. The weakness in regulative capability impeded the government's ability to allocate basic services when state income declined and hard choices had to be made, and it complicated attempts to control corruption, contributing to the distribution crisis.

The democratic regime remained highly centralized while a supposedly temporary power-sharing pact from 1958 failed to generate consensus on longer-term forms of political and economic decentralization, creating the third vulnerability of Punto Fijo. A tutelary political culture and an overriding concern with survival of the fragile democratic regime led central party leaders to block the ascension of a new generation of leaders and to keep regional leaders dependent on central control.

The fourth vulnerability derived from the very pacts that enabled party leaders, business leaders, and unionized labor to stabilize the regime initially. As structural and demographic changes brought new groups to the fore, the original power-sharing arrangements failed to include them, contributing to the crisis of representation. These groups, including middle-class civil society, the urban poor, intellectuals, and junior ranks of the military, became increasingly resentful and eventually deserted the regime.

The distribution crisis refers to the weakened capability of the public bureaucracies to administer the state, extract revenues through sources other than externally derived oil rent, and distribute those resources effectively. The representation crisis refers to the lost confidence of citizens that their political leaders would represent the collective interests over private interests and to the lack of access to the centralized decision-making structures for regional leaders and newer social and economic groups.

The crises of representation and distribution intertwined to weaken the Punto Fijo model. As the representation crisis eventually weakened central party control, the capacity to administer the public bureaucracy eroded further; at the same time, falling oil prices and weak managerial competency contributed to popular perceptions of nonperforming political institutions and politicians representing the needs of the few over the many. Together, these twin crises eventually produced the collapse of the Punto Fijo model of representative democracy in Venezuela.

The social polarization produced by the distribution crisis and exemplified by growing income inequality and poverty rates was compounded by the representation crisis whereby new middle-class nongovernmental organizations (NGOs), intellectuals, and even some business representatives joined with the marginalized poor to vote for a leader promising radical change.[1] Hugo Chávez's crosscutting electoral support and 90 percent approval ratings immediately after taking office belie the notion that his election was the product of class conflict.

Explaining the Demise of Punto Fijo Democracy (1983–1998)

We date the visible beginning of the decline of Punto Fijo from an economic event: Black Friday, February 18, 1983, when the currency was devalued for the first time in two decades. Rising foreign debt and falling oil prices after 1982 made especially visible the regime's weaknesses derived from its overreliance on distributive politics and underdeveloped regulatory capacity. Structural/economic, political/institutional, and cultural/learning factors all contributed to the demise of Punto Fijo's limited pluralism.

Structural/Economic Factors

Scholars like Karl (1997) in *The Paradox of Plenty* see the impact of the international political economy of oil as primary in shaping the structures of Punto Fijo democracy. Our contributors differ in that they see it as only one of several factors.

Janet Kelly and Pedro Palma's analysis in Chapter 10 of the economic factors contributing to the fall of Punto Fijo, in fact, resembles a diagnosis of many developing countries: capture of the state by powerful interests, party hegemony that blocked change, popular pressures for short-term economic results, and presidential government insensitive to the weakening of its own legitimacy, all leading to poor economic policy. In Chapter 4, Nelson Ortiz further demonstrates the symbiotic relationship between, on the one hand, a private sector dependent on high levels of protection in an economy increasingly dominated by the state and, on the other, politicians who formed alliances with competing private sector groups. Eventually the failure to deliver the promise of growth and equity underscored the distributive crisis and doomed the Punto Fijo regime.

Oil, of course, played a role, making the state the primary engine of the economy and absolving Venezuelans for some time of the necessity of paying taxes in exchange for goods and services from the public sector. Decades of increasing oil revenues helped reassure Venezuelans of continued income and sustain the myth of a rich country, creating resistance to government attempts to liberalize or rationalize the economy. Oil income, in this sense, has always provided a cushion that prevented Venezuela from hitting bottom, especially with hyperinflation, and making the hard choices that outsiders believed were needed, very much like fellow oil producer Ecuador. Nevertheless, the pattern of rising average real salaries after 1958 peaked in 1978, after which inflation escalated and salaries declined. Purchasing power of average salaries in 1999 was only 33 percent of what it had been in 1978 (Chapter 10 in this volume). Further, by the late 1990s, after forty years of Punto Fijo governments, Venezuela's per capita gross domestic product was only 80 percent of what it had been in 1950 (Wanted: A New Agenda, 2003: 28).

Pernicious consequences of oil include the impact on the private sector, as an overvalued currency in the 1960s and 1970s meant that the tradable sector of the economy had to be protected and subsidized to become internationally competitive and even domestically competitive. State capitalism as a development strategy limited the scope of action of the private sector.

Entrepreneurs, always participants in decision making through consultative mechanisms and cabinet appointments, began to split as new economic groups favored by government policies emerged to challenge traditional economic leaders in the 1970s. When the distributive crisis became manifest from 1983 onward, the policy decisions supported by the private sector—devaluation and differential exchange rates—affected the country and the private sector in the long term, as discussed later in this chapter. From a vibrant, strong sector in the mid-twentieth century, the private sector severely contracted near the end of the Punto Fijo partially as a result of the short-lived economic opening of the Pérez administration (1989–92) and subsequent banking failure in 1994 (see Chapter 4 in this volume).

The urban poor were even more highly vulnerable to the volatile oil economy and the growing distribution crisis in the 1980s and especially the 1990s. The percentage of Venezuelans employed in the informal sector increased from 40 percent in 1992 to 55 percent in 2002, with an additional 15 percent unemployed (Datanalisis, C.A., 2002b). Poverty rates doubled during the 1990s (see note 1). As described by Damarys Canache in Chapter 2, the urban poor played a leading role in the bloody riots of 1989, giving a new political role to this sector and heightening their concern with public policy. Likewise, the downward slide of the middle sectors in standard of living contributed to their withdrawal of support from Punto Fijo.[2]

Political/Institutional Factors

Political/institutional factors emerge clearly in the collapse of Punto Fijo. Two of the embedded vulnerabilities identified earlier in this chapter fall in this category: First, the democratic regime remained highly centralized while a supposedly temporary (five-year) power-sharing pact from 1958 failed to generate consensus on longer-term forms of political and economic decentralization. Second, the power-sharing arrangements that set Punto Fijo in motion and which were crystallized in the institutional pact between Acción Democrática (AD; Democratic Action) and Comité de Organización Política Electoral Independiente: Partido Social Cristiano (COPEI; Committee of Independent Electoral Political Organization: Social Christian Party) and the corporatist relations between the government, business, and organized labor failed to incorporate groups that gained influence as economic and political modernization unfolded. These groups became increasingly resentful and eventually found a voice. As Canache shows with the urban poor (Chapter 2), Richard Hillman with the intellectuals (Chapter 6), Luis Salamanca with the middle-class civil society movements (Chapter 5), and Harold Trinkunas with junior ranks of the military (Chapter 3), the failure to provide representation and a share of the resources eventually led important sectors of these groups to desert the Punto Fijo regime. These intrinsic weaknesses began to be revealed in the 1980s and became quite visible in the 1990s, leading to the final collapse of the Punto Fijo model of representative democracy in 1998.

The most dramatic change and evidence of a representation crisis, belying the expectations of the scholars writing in the early 1990s, was the demise of the party system dominated by AD and COPEI. Even while reform of electoral rules and decentralization of political power unleashed a new dynamism and competitiveness within the parties, this sort of political tinkering was too little, too late, to save the Punto Fijo regime. José Molina argues in Chapter 8 that the highly institutionalized party system under Punto Fijo began to lose its legitimacy as a result of errors by party leaders and the opening of political space with political decentralization. This decline accelerated when they refused to curb corruption and failed to attenuate the post-1983 economic crisis.

The institutional reform leading to the direct election of governors and creation of the office of directly elected mayor after 1989 produced greater electoral competitiveness. These reforms also opened up new career paths outside the control of central party hierarchies for politicians. Those taking advantage of these opportunities included governors such as Henrique Salas

Römer, Francisco Arias Cárdenas, Enrique Mendoza, and Andrés Velásquez, as well as mayors Claudio Fermín, Irene Sáez, and Antonio Ledesma, all of whom became eventual presidential precandidates.

By 1993 the party system appeared to be a polarized and deinstitutionalized multiparty system with new parties surging and disappearing in each electoral cycle. This institutional decay also opened space to charismatic leaders and led to the personalization of political parties, evident in the 1998 elections with the emergence first of Irene Sáez and subsequently of Henrique Salas Römer and Hugo Chávez as leaders of new personalistic movements.

At the same time, electoral reform intended to make the legislature more accountable also failed to salvage the system. Punto Fijo Congresses were traditionally subservient to the president and the party hierarchy, with strict party discipline maintained by closed-list proportional representation formulas and concurrent elections with the president. In fact, contrary to the expectation in the political science literature, proportional representation in Venezuela reinforced a two-party system, rather than a multiparty system. The change to a mixed system in 1993 did little to improve relations with constituents, as the new single-member, winner-take-all districts (called uninominal in Venezuela) also practiced a centralized candidate selection process controlled by the party headquarters and the elected representatives proved little more accountable to their constituents than the proportional representation legislators (Kulisheck, 1996). The result was an ineffective Congress, a weak civil society penetrated by the parties, and policy making dominated by a powerful president who occasionally consulted labor and business in devising a state-led development strategy based on external rents, protection of domestic interests, and heavy social commitments to the lower and middle classes.

Organized business, labor, and many professional associations had access to policy making by the executive branch through consultative commissions and participation on governing boards of state enterprises, financial institutions, and regional development corporations. These three interest groups dominated the participation of civil society in policy making and implementation (Crisp 2000; McCoy, 1987, 1989). The centralized nature of political decision making and the influence of protected and rentier classes meant that Venezuela continued to pursue an inward-oriented development strategy long after it proved unproductive. This contributed to the distribution crisis and also fueled the representation crisis as other sectors perceived themselves to be excluded from policy making and the distribution of benefits.

The representation crisis hit the urban poor particularly hard. Canache

(Chapter 2) points out that, despite subsidy programs and early competition for support among this sector by the political parties, its collective interests were not well represented for several reasons: lower-income citizens generally tend to participate less in politics; in the early years they bet on the wrong horse (parties other than AD and COPEI); and subsequently their loyalties were divided between AD and COPEI, which acted as catch-all parties. The capability of AD and COPEI to dispense patronage declined after 1983, although during his administration Jaime Lusinchi (1984-89) commanded enough patronage to satisfy the clientelistic needs of the governing AD. Nevertheless, Lusinchi reduced subsidies to the urban poor; and in response slum dwellers began to engage in new forms of political participation—primarily street protests. In February 1989 the urban poor responded to austerity measures with three days of rioting (Caracazo). They also began to support new political actors such as La Causa Radical and expressed post hoc approval for Hugo Chávez's unsuccessful coup of February 4, 1992. But the urban poor never successfully organized politically.

On another front, civilian presidents sought to use the military to help sustain a decaying regime as regime legitimacy declined. Trinkunas argues in Chapter 3 that Punto Fijo leaders had achieved civilian control of the armed forces "by containment" by the early 1970s. That is, governments ceded control of defense policy to the armed forces while barring them from participation in other areas of policy making. The politicians successfully reoriented the military's mission from the internal one of defeating guerrillas in the 1960s to an external one of protecting Venezuela against its neighbors. Punto Fijo leaders further managed the ambitions of the armed forces through legislative oversight of promotions and the dissolution of the joint command that coordinated military activity by the four services and by rapidly rotating and retiring senior officers.

From the mid-1970s through the early 1990s, however, the high command began to lose the respect of a new generation of junior officers trained in civilian universities and recently accredited military academies emphasizing professionalism, leadership, and nationalism, as well as a more populist and egalitarian perspective toward democracy. Moreover, oil wealth and a practice of co-opting military loyalty through the purchase of advanced weaponry had created opportunities for corruption among senior military officers and civilian politicians, to the dismay of the junior officers.

The military generational split was laid bare following the 1989 riots in which the armed forces were called upon to play a deadly internal security role. The split between junior and senior officers widened when a nationalistic group of junior officers led by Hugo Chávez and opposing partisan promotions and corruption attempted a coup against the elected government on February 4, 1992. In retrospect, it appears that inattention on the part of civilian politicians to the issues that divided junior and senior officers meant that the growing alienation of captains, majors, and lieutenant colonels had gone undetected and the coup attempt came as a surprise.

Ironically, a subsequent government's attempt to distract the armed forces from the political crisis involved reinitiating an internal mission for the armed forces. Thus, as Trinkunas argues (Chapter 3), President Rafael Caldera's use of the military to help solve the public policy and distribution crisis by deploying soldiers to maintain emergency services during public sector strikes in the mid-1990s actually foreshadowed the Fifth Republic's renewed emphasis on an internal orientation for the armed forces.

Venezuelan exceptionalism does stand out when it comes to nonpolitical actors in the society and the stunted civil society in Venezuela. After 1958, Venezuela had escaped the authoritarian governments that in other Latin American countries spurred the development of human rights groups, self-help neighborhood organizations, and church and intellectual opposition as political parties were destroyed or pushed underground in those countries. (This situation changed in Venezuela after 1998, as discussed later in this chapter.)

In Punto Fijo democracy, political parties mediated between state and society to such an extent that autonomous, nonpartisan civil society organizations scarcely existed. The political parties penetrated the large social organizations representing the labor unions, peasants, and professional associations (though business organizations remained comparatively independent). The parties served as intermediaries between these groups and the state and ran slates to compete for the leadership positions within these organizations. The participation of citizens in public policy making was largely through the sectoral bureaus of the political parties or through direct incorporation of the labor and business confederations in tripartite decision-making mechanisms, state enterprise boards, and consultative commissions. This control of participation and restriction to certain interest group participation exacerbated the crisis of representation as excluded sectors felt increasingly marginalized from decision making regarding distribution of resources.

Neighborhood associations, small businesses groupings, and professional organizations that were autonomous from the political parties began to emerge in the early 1980s. As Salamanca points out in Chapter 5, these groups formed in reaction to the party-dominated civic and social organizations of the Punto Fijo model and explicitly rejected party control. Working to increase citizen participation in social problem solving, these emerging groups generally did not play a political role. One exception was their successful push for the decentralization reforms of the late 1980s, which in turn helped spur their own growth.

In Chapter 9, Rafael de la Cruz describes how decentralization reforms, leading to direct election of mayors and governors in 1989 and a subsequent negotiated transfer of administrative responsibilities to subregional governments, had the potential to revitalize Punto Fijo democracy and mitigate both the distribution and representation crises. The reforms brought elected leaders closer to constituents and provided for more accountability. One of the motivations to decentralize was in fact to break the political control of the Caracas-based parties. The decentralization effort was short lived, however, as the political parties repudiated the second administration of Carlos Andrés Pérez (1989–92), which had supported the reforms, and the second Caldera administration (1994–99) reversed some of the reforms.

Ironically, this backlash from the central parties led to a weakening of Punto Fijo institutions and party domination over national politics, rather than a reassertion of central party control. The effect of stunting decentralization reforms was thus to exacerbate both the distribution crisis, as neither local nor national governments could effectively manage the sustained economic crisis, and the representation crisis as voters reacted against the attempt of party elites to reassert their hierarchical control. The 1998 elections brought regional leaders to the forefront of the presidential race and confirmed this trend. The national political elites' resistance to decentralization limited the reforms' ability to strengthen the accountability and representativeness of elected leaders and thus deepen representative democracy; at the same time the inability to reassert effectively the central control practiced in the original Punto Fijo model meant they could not stem its decay.

Political Culture/Learning Factors

A utilitarian culture produced by an oil-fed economy, a tutelary approach to democracy, and the nature of political learning all help explain the demise of

Punto Fijo and rise of the Fifth Republic. A utilitarian culture emphasizing the myth of a rich country and a birthright to access that wealth has been noted by Anibal Romero (1997), Fernando Coronil (1997), and José Antonio Gil Yepes (Chapter 11 in this volume), among others. In *The Magical State: Nature, Money and Modernity in Venezuela,* Coronil analyzes the mediating orientations of Venezuelans toward a state that "magically" acts as a caregiver. These orientations predisposed policy makers to choose distributive policies over regulative or redistributive ones, even when the latter may have been more efficient or productive. As the oil boom transformed Venezuelan society into a modern culture with easy access to material goods, those who were left behind, or who lost their benefits as the economy deteriorated, easily fell into the refrain noted by Gil Yepes in this volume (Chapter 11): the country is rich from oil; I am a Venezuelan and am entitled to a share of its riches; if I am not benefiting, it must be because someone is stealing my share.

The rifts among major economic groups and affiliated political figures contributed to perceptions of social breakdown and corruption. According to Ortiz, short-term utilitarian viewpoints contributed to an economic elite that favored a policy of devaluation to finance fiscal deficits, and corresponding exchange controls, for the personal benefits those policies would provide to those with dollars abroad and access to differential exchange rates while ignoring the long-term contraction of domestic consumer purchasing power. The distribution crisis was thus deepened.

The second cultural factor is the tutelary nature of Venezuelan democracy. In *Tutelary Pluralism,* Luis Oropeza (1983) argues that prior to 1958 there was no "civic culture" predisposing the country toward democracy and that the political values of the society could have supported either authoritarian or democratic alternatives. After pointing out that cultural pluralism in Venezuela was not historically based on racial, linguistic, religious, or regional antagonisms, he argues that Venezuelan political culture exhibits a dualism of democratic pluralism and military autocracy. Oropeza does identify three traits within Venezuelan political culture which shaped the nature of the democracy that evolved after 1958: a corporatism in which groups organized and participated in policy making in a voluntary manner, through formal corporatist mechanisms provided by the state; a centralism emanating from Simón Bolívar's preference for a strong executive to protect itself against the other powers in a republic; and a predilection toward consensus in which prior agreement among established parties in the form of pacts was seen as crucial to avoid conflict by removing contentious issues from political debate. Any consensus resting on these facets diminishes the effectiveness of participatory institutions by restricting participation in the name of the higher goal of political stability. Coppedge (1994) and Gil Yepes (1981) also discuss the implications of limited pluralism in Venezuela.

The authors in this volume confirm the tutelary nature of Punto Fijo limited pluralism. The strong executive, elite pacts, and tripartite decision-making mechanisms highlight the priority given to political stability through consensus-based centralism. The early concern with democratic survival was addressed by removing contentious issues from the political arena. This eventually gave way to concern with the political survival of individual political parties and leaders. Elite tutelage of democracy by hierarchical political parties and peak organizations excluded marginal sectors, much of the middle class, and the junior military officers from decision making. Participation became more and more restricted, and policy-making competency declined, exacerbating the twin problems of distribution and representation.

As the distribution crisis worsened after 1983, Venezuelan political elites showed little capacity to engage the society in consensus building on how to adjust resource distribution to the new reality of scarcity. The second administration of Carlos Andrés Pérez attempted to steer the economy toward a market opening in the "Grand Turnaround," but with little thought to developing a prior political consensus for this dramatic change. In a similarly imperious vein, the second administration of Rafael Caldera reversed some of the neoliberal and decentralizing policies of the prior administration, but without a clear alternative plan. He then had to reinstitute the discredited austerity policies of Pérez. Tutelage thus became more remote and unresponsive as the consensus-based elite decision making of the earlier tutelary years gave way to the unilateral imposition of controversial policies by weakened governments led by aging politicians. Social and political deterioration accelerated.

The third factor related to political culture is that of political learning. Although Venezuelan leaders learned important lessons from the failed Trienio and applied those lessons to ensure that the Punto Fijo democracy survived severe challenges from the Right and the Left in the first decade, they also overlearned. In other words, after 1983 they relied on the pact-making strategy and distributive politics that had served them well during the 1960s (Jácome, 2000; McCoy, 2000). The fear of a return to autocracy and the lessons learned from the participatory explosion of the Trienio led to elite-imposed limits on opportunities for conflict and controversy, as indicated earlier in this chapter (Oropeza, 1983). Nevertheless, the failure of the same generation to learn new strategies (and the comfortable position of entrenched interests) inhibited their ability to adapt to a changed demographic and economic context in the 1970s and 1980s. The resistance and delayed response by political leaders to the demand for decentralization and electoral reform are examples of this, with the consequences noted earlier. The failure of AD and COPEI to learn and adapt to a new electoral climate was further evident in their (mis)handling of the 1998 and 2000 election campaigns.

Choice of policy strategies by the signatories of the Pact of Punto Fijo was also a product of political learning. The intrasocietal tensions stemming from redistributive policy making during the short-lived Trienio democratic experiment (1945–48) led post-1958 democrats to avoid redistribution whenever possible. The inept attempt of the autocratic Pérez Jiménez government to enforce regulations, such as control of internal migration and the collection of rents in the large-scale housing projects, not to mention the decrees that slum dwellers should abandon the *ranchos* (slum shacks) and move to the housing projects in Caracas and Maracaibo, made the slums of the large cities hotbeds of opposition. Resistance to these regulations motivated the urban poor to join in the rebellion that forced General Pérez Jiménez to flee and taught Punto Fijo democrats to use distributive policy making, rather than regulatory or redistributive, at every opportunity. The preferred method of governing became "throwing enough money" at the problem to solve it.

One consequence of this type of learning was that, even as oil revenues increased in the 1970s and early 1980s, corruption returned to levels not seen since the Pérez Jiménez regime and the ability of the government to distribute effectively declined. Eroding state administrative capacity, of course, was exacerbated with the volatility of revenues throughout the 1980s and 1990s. Further, the prioritizing of political development and stability over economic development and redistribution of wealth meant that the fundamental social and economic changes needed to confer continued legitimacy on the democratic system became more and more distant. As Oropeza predicted, if the ruling elites were not capable of maintaining the tutelary consensus approach, Venezuelan democracy would not have the supportive cultural capacity to survive. It would unravel, unable to withstand open social conflict or to address the pressures for social and economic change (1983: 40).

The Rise of the Fifth Republic: Bolivarian Participatory Democracy (1998–2000)

The meteoric rise of Hugo Chávez during the election campaign of 1998, along with the grouping of his political supporters in the Movimiento Quinta República (MVR; Fifth Republic Movement), was the consequence of being in the right place at the right time. Venezuelans' desire for change in their political party system and larger political economy first surfaced in the 1993 elections with the victory of Rafael Caldera on his own ticket, after splitting with COPEI, which he had founded decades earlier, and the high showing of La Causa Radical. By 1998, Venezuelans wanted an even deeper change, but this did not necessarily mean it had to be Hugo Chávez. Two candidates promised moderate but significant reforms; the third promised radical economic and political change. All proclaimed their independence from the traditional political parties that had dominated the Punto Fijo regime.

Former independent mayor and beauty queen Irene Sáez was the first choice of almost 70 percent of Venezuelans for president in the final national poll of public opinion in 1997. Six months later, despite having spent millions of dollars in media publicity, she slipped below 15 percent. Her decline came in two phases: first, in her public pronouncements she gave an impression of lack of preparation to serve as president; and second, her acceptance of support from COPEI raised fears that she would be no different from other Punto Fijo presidents. Henrique Salas Römer, the governor of the industrial state of Carabobo and leader of the new party Proyecto Venezuela, finished second to Chávez and for a brief time appeared to be a credible challenger. However, his star also fell when AD and COPEI threw their support behind him just prior to the election.

After leading the failed coup in 1992, Hugo Chávez reappeared on the political scene in 1997 and appealed directly to the refrain that corrupt elites had stolen Venezuelans' birthright of oil wealth. Chávez had been pardoned by President Rafael Caldera in 1994 and spent the intervening years quietly building a political base in the country, under the tutelage of old leftist thinkers Luis Miquilena and José Vicente Rangel. Choosing the electoral route this time, Chávez mobilized large sectors of the lower classes which felt excluded by established parties and did not possess institutionalized forms of political self-expression. In this sense, Chávez represented the first credible alternative with enough popular appeal to effect a change of political regimes. (Caldera's victory in 1993 was the first time that a candidate not backed by AD or COPEI won the presidency. The perception that AD and COPEI could be beaten was important in establishing Chávez as a viable challenger.) As Przeworski (1986) noted, regimes change not when they lose legitimacy but when a viable, preferable alternative becomes available.[3] With the Punto Fijo model of democracy losing legitimacy since the 1980s, the exact timing of its collapse may be accounted for by the appearance of a preferable alternative in the form of Hugo Chávez and his Bolivarian Revolution.

Structural/Political Economy Factors

Venezuelans had indicated their displeasure with the old system, but what exactly did they want a new system to look like? Above all, Venezuelans were frustrated at the inability (or unwillingness) of Punto Fijo elites to address the slide in living standards and to curb corruption, which the public blamed for its deteriorating lifestyles. The distribution crisis was reflected in the fact that real per capita income in the presidential election year of 1998 had slipped to the same level as in 1963, representing a one-third drop from the peak in 1978 (Chapter 10 in this volume). Venezuelans wanted to eliminate the mismanagement, corruption, and extreme centralization, but few favored a neoliberal market economy.[4] Instead, as Gil Yepes (Chapter 11) and Kelly and Palma (Chapter 10) note, most Venezuelans wanted some type of social market economy which would continue the kind of paternalistic state to which they had grown accustomed since the dramatic post-1973 increase in petroleum income. But they wanted that state to be more fair and effective.

The private sector had been so severely weakened by the banking collapse, internal rifts, and political accusations during the second Caldera administration that it was unable to help address the distribution crisis once Caldera adopted his own economic adjustment program. As Ortiz shows (Chapter 4), market capitalization declined from $13 billion in 1990 to $8 billion in 2000, and the number of major economic groups was reduced to two.

Ironically, the Chávez administration did not initiate a radical change in economic policy. Rather, the first two years were dominated by the efforts to achieve political change. The new 1999 constitution maintained the basic economic lines of the Punto Fijo regime, protecting private property rights but also giving responsibility to the state for the social well-being of its citizens. Private sector critics feared that the 1999 constitution reversed progress in the labor and social security provisions which had been made during the 1990s.

The 1999 constitution reinstated onerous employee dismissal compensation and all but eliminated the option of private pension plans. It also obligated the Central Bank to report to the National Assembly, raising fears among some of reduced Central Bank autonomy. Finally, it protected the petroleum industry from privatization, though it allowed other sectors to be privatized.[5]

Economic policy in 1999–2000 focused on containing the economic recession through orthodox austerity measures and cementing an agreement within the Organization of Petroleum Exporting Countries (OPEC) and with other major oil producers to reduce production in order to raise prices. This latter policy paid off as the average price of a barrel of oil shot up from $11 in 1998 to $16 in 1999 and $27 in 2000 (McCoy and Neuman, 2001). The government used the oil revenues to fund its Plan Bolívar 2000 in 1999–2000, employing the armed forces in the provision of social services, disaster relief, and a jobs creation program. The government also announced plans to privatize telecommunications further, move forward on the stalled aluminum privatization, and reform the tax code and enforce tax collection. Criticisms arose, however, that the oil stabilization fund was not being properly capitalized in times of surplus and that it was used instead to finance the budget improperly.

Subsequent declines in oil prices in 2001 put increasing pressure on a government that had raised expectations higher than it was capable of reaching. The government continued to distract attention from the economic problems with a controversial foreign policy and political attacks on social and political opponents.

Institutional/Political Factors

As Gil Yepes shows (Chapter 11), in voting for change in the political system, Venezuelans also expressed their desire for a state that was less autonomous and more accountable to citizens. This preference reflected their disgust with the perceived massive corruption and poor public administration. They desired more citizen participation, rebelling against the hierarchical party control of Punto Fijo and supporting recent decentralization efforts. Finally, they wanted to retain a democratic system, suggesting that a democratic political culture had begun to take shape sometime during the brief democratic interlude of the 1940s and strengthened during the Punto Fijo era. On the other hand, they rejected the post-1958 model of limited pluralism, with its emphasis on elections as the main form of participation and control by centralized party apparatuses.

Although perceived exclusion from effective political representation and a growing distribution crisis led the urban poor toward anomic and other nonconventional channels of political participation in the late 1980s and early 1990s, the rise of Hugo Chávez and the Fifth Republic opened a new electoral option. Canache (Chapter 2) shows that voter participation among the poor increased more than among the nonpoor between 1993 and 1998. Likewise, 55 percent of the poor indicated support for Chávez in the 1998 elections compared with 45 percent of the nonpoor. The disarray in the traditional parties and the emergence of new actors thus opened up political space for a new level and type of political participation by this previously marginalized sector, helping to bring Hugo Chávez to power.

Once in power, Chávez began a systematic attack on institutional structures and organized interests. Fulfilling his campaign promise, he held a referendum on April 1, 1999, to approve the election of a constituent assembly to write a new constitution. The electoral formula selected to choose the members in July, although approved by all the parties, disadvantaged the disorganized opposition and advantaged the governing coalition, which won control of 94 percent of the seats. The constituent assembly that took power in August 1999, with Chávez's backing, dismantled the Congress elected in 1998 and assumed legislative powers in addition to the writing of a constitution. The constituent assembly also intervened in the court system, examining and disbarring a number of judges deemed to be corrupt. The constituent assembly threatened to unseat the elected governors, mayors, and state assemblies until a local and international outcry persuaded the government to back away from this move.

The 1999 constitution both reassured and alarmed people. In many respects, it was not as radical as some had predicted; nevertheless, it brought far-reaching changes. The 1999 constitution maintained and even deepened centralized, presidential control over the country, along with a statist approach to economic affairs, while reducing civilian control over the military. In contrast to the 1961 constitution, the Bolivarian constitution allowed for the immediate reelection of the president and expanded the presidential term from five to six years; this raised the possibility that Hugo Chávez could remain in office for thirteen years. The 1999 constitution also changed the legislative power from a bicameral Congress to a unicameral National Assembly and created a new appointed vice president. It maintained the federal structure with elected governors and mayors but created the Federal Council to manage the distribution of national resources to the states and municipalities while further restricting revenue-raising authority of those entities.

The new constitution gave the military the right to vote, removed congressional oversight over military promotions, and, perhaps most significant, omitted the previous obligations for the military to remain an apolitical and nondeliberative force. Finally, it created two new public powers (the Electoral Power and the Citizens' Power to control corruption) and provided for more direct democracy through the creation of popular referenda with the power to revoke legislation and recall elected officials. All these provisions had implications for the political developments and growing tensions over the following three years, as discussed in the following paragraphs.

Recentralization

One of the ironies of the new constitution celebrating "participatory democracy," and of Chávez administration policies in the first two years, was the weakening of the one Punto Fijo institutional reform that had begun to bring more accountability and participation to local citizens—decentralization. As de la Cruz points out (Chapter 9), the 1999 constitution not only eliminated the Senate—the basis of equal state representation in the legislature—but it also changed the funding formulas for transfer to state and local governments, making them more ad hoc and less transparent. Laws to carry out decentralization functions under the 1999 constitution had yet to be approved three years later, and Chávez's tendency to rely on the military to carry out public works and deliver public services eroded the decentralization reforms of the 1990s.

Expanded Military Mission

In the Fifth Republic, the armed forces became openly political for the first time since the regime of General Marcos Pérez Jiménez, with individual officers not only speaking out for and against the Chávez administration but also accepting increasing levels of participation in government decision making and policy implementation. From his inauguration in February 1999 until the unsuccessful coup of April 2002, President Chávez favored the military as an institution, relative to public bureaucracies and political parties that he viewed as corrupt. The president appointed active and retired military officers as top-level decision makers in his government, employed the armed forces in massive disaster relief and development programs, and intervened in the promotion process to advance the careers of his supporters.

These practices led to growing tensions within the military, between generations, and between Chávez loyalists and opponents, which played out in dramatic terms in 2002. Perhaps most damaging for democratic governance in the long term is the legacy of dismantling institutionalized civilian control over the Venezuelan armed forces. As it now stands, the Fifth Republic deprives elected officials of the institutional means to assert their authority or prevent military intervention in politics. In Chapter 3 in this volume, Trinkunas points out that the Punto Fijo democracy achieved civilian control by containment and, after the defeat of the guerrillas, by narrowing the mission of the armed forces to external defense. The Fifth Republic, however, reinstated and expanded that mission to a broad focus on internal security and development and replaced institutional control with direct personal control by the president.

Institutional Weakening

The creation of a new Citizens' Power composed of attorney general, ombudsman, and comptroller general was aimed at rooting out corruption and bringing more integrity to public administration. Its original name, in fact, was the Moral Power, until that was deemed too theocratic. This new Citizens' Power was tasked to nominate the Judicial and Electoral Powers from slates presented by civil society groups, thus creating a new confidence in the independent checks and balances of public institutions in Venezuela.

The reality, however, was different. After the adoption of the new constitution in December 1999, the constituent assembly closed and left in its place a small legislative committee (Congresillo) to run things until new elections could be called (which eventually occurred in July 2000). In one of its last acts before dissolution, the constituent assembly appointed, by decree, the Supreme Court's members as well as the Citizens' Power troika and the new National Electoral Council, most of whom were widely considered to be *chavista* partisans.

None of these appointments followed the provisions of the new constitution, which required that civil society groups nominate these positions, the Citizens' Power present a slate to the National Assembly in the case of the Supreme Court and Electoral Council, and the National Assembly confirm them. The government argued that these would be temporary appointments only until a National Assembly could be elected in July 2000. In fact, however, the new government-dominated National Assembly confirmed all these appointments (with support from opposition parties), again without following constitutional procedures for their nomination, and the maintenance of those individuals in their posts led to a serious erosion of confidence in the independence of the public institutions and their ability to serve as a check on presidential power.

Organized Interests

The Fifth Republic further sought to revamp civil society in its own image. Arguing that existing organizations, which were growing increasingly vociferous, did not represent the citizenry of the country, the administration began an effort to create an official version of civil society. The most blatant was the effort to create a new labor confederation. After a devastating oil workers strike in October 2000, the administration quickly presented to the voters a referendum on whether to suspend trade union leadership and call new, direct, secret votes for all labor union leadership. The Supreme Court rejected arguments that, constitutionally, the unions are not subject to government intervention and that only workers, not the general populace, can vote on such questions. International trade union organizations threatened sanctions against Venezuela. Nevertheless, the referendum passed in December 2000, with a low voter turnout, and elections for trade union leaders were finally held in October 2001. The government sponsored a slate that was soundly defeated by a slate tied to the traditional parties controlling the labor movement. The election was marred, however, by contentions of fraud, leading to an inconclusive result that contributed to the unrest of 2002.

As early as 1999, relations between President Chávez and the Roman Catholic Church began to crumble during the debate over the new constitution. The issues of abortion and restrictions on private education led to name-calling and Chávez references to the church as the devil. The church moved to the opposition as the personal attacks escalated in 2000. President Chávez's plan to create Bolivarian schools brought clerical and public educators together in opposition to the specter of ideological intervention by the Bolivarians in the school curricula.

Likewise, Chávez's relationship with the media became increasingly hostile. Venezuela has long enjoyed a free-wheeling, competitive media, with ties to various political parties and economic groups. By and large this has continued under the Chávez administration. Nevertheless, Chávez's relationship with the media deteriorated in late 2000, after the press and radio and television stations became stridently critical of the government. Chávez responded to these criticisms with new attacks on newspaper, radio, and television owners. These media entrepreneurs viewed the president's personal attacks as open invitations for Chávez supporters to harass and threaten them and journalists. The tension escalated in 2001 and 2002 when verbal harassment turned to physical assaults and when the government began to abuse its right of access to television by requiring coverage of multiple hours of presidential speeches. This culminated in the government intervening in television coverage of the massive April 11, 2002, opposition marches, cutting off access to the airwaves, and subsequent accusations by the government that the media refused to cover the counterprotests against the ouster of Chávez. By the summer of 2002, Chávez was claiming that the media were his most significant political opponents.[6]

Finally, Chávez's foreign policy provoked concern particularly in the United States and neighboring Colombia. Although commercial relations continued as normal, the strategy of reducing OPEC oil production to raise prices had a significant impact on prices in the United States. In addition, differences over antiterrorism policy also surfaced, particularly in Chávez's rhetorical (and suspected material) support for Colombian guerrillas and in criticism of U.S. intervention in Afghanistan after September 11, 2001.

Political Cultural/Learning Factors

Venezuelan representative democracy under the Punto Fijo system, particularly its party system, unraveled in the 1990s. Nevertheless, basic democratic values survived and permeated the Fifth Republic. According to Gil Yepes (Chapter 11), after the failed coup attempt by Lieutenant Colonel Hugo Chávez in 1992, only 8 percent of the population favored a military government. Support for democracy as a system of government was at 85 percent, though this was split almost evenly between those who favored democracy with AD and COPEI and those who favored a democracy without them. These levels of support for a democratic system continued into the 1998 election campaign and beyond.[7]

Venezuelan intellectuals (journalists, writers, academicians) contributed to the erosion of Punto Fijo democracy's legitimacy. Hillman discusses(Chapter 6) how this stratum seemed to delight in pointing out the political regime's failures and shortcomings. Initial intellectual support for Chávez's Bolivarianism came particularly from the old Left, and some of his principal advisers were university professors who followed various tenets of Marxism, and state-led development, and favored a tutelary approach that would impose direct democracy. They helped draft the 1999 constitution, with its emphasis on new forms of participatory democracy under the guidance of a strong executive with direct links to the populace.

Nevertheless, the commitment to democratic principles among Venezuelan intellectuals meant that critics of Punto Fijo also became critics of the Fifth Republic as democratic deficits surfaced. Hillman (Chapter 6) argues that the divide in intellectual support for Chávez, in fact, rested on the interpretation of his contribution to democracy—whether he was deepening it through new forms of participation or weakening its representative functions. Some of Chávez's earliest intellectual supporters, in fact (such as Alfreda Peña and Jorge Olivarria), became some of his fiercest critics within the first two years of his regime.

Hugo Chávez's rise with support from the urban masses and his subsequent emphasis on class differences raise the further question of whether and when Venezuela developed a class-based political rift. Venezuelan political culture, as noted earlier, displays a divide between democractic and authoritarian ideals but manifests little evidence of racial, linguistic, or religious cleavages. Class-based polarization has appeared only sporadically in Venezuela politics, although it permeated the political agenda during the Trienio.

Canache (Chapter 2) demonstrates that this absence of an open class rift with regard to preferences on the economy and the role of the state persisted into the 1990s. The poor, however, as documented in surveys between 1995 and 1998, expected more from the government in terms of economic intervention, jobs, and health care, and they preferred radical over gradual change. These small but significant differences in policy preferences took on new importance in 1998 when Hugo Chávez's campaign messages gave them great prominence.

The ideological confusion of the Bolivarian Revolution contributed to the difficulty in discerning where Venezuelan democracy was headed. Gil Yepes points out that Bolivarian ideology stressed both political equality and political liberty but favored direct citizen participation over pluralist interest group mediation. Thus, freedom of speech was protected, but organized groups were attacked. Chávez asserted repeatedly that "civil society organizations" do not in fact represent citizens but constitute a small, self-anointed elite. As discussed earlier, Chávez carried out a systematic attack on organized interests that he portrayed as representing the old order—political parties, labor unions, the church, NGOs, economic elites, and the media. He referred to them as the "squalid ones" and the old oligarchy that had to be eliminated to make way for the new republic.

The attack on civil society organizations was reflected in the new constitution. Salamanca (Chapter 5) argues that the 1999 constitution raised a new confusion in that it bestowed constitutional rank on civil society (for example, it gave civil society "co-responsibility for the security of the nation" and a role in postulating names for the National Electoral Council), but it failed to define what civil society is. Consequently, a fight over who represents civil society emerged, with the Chávez administration attempting to create its own Bolivarian civil society organizations while simultaneously arguing that there is no such thing as civil society representation. MVR thus aspired to provide revolutionary direction for all of Venezuelan society, much as AD did during the Trienio.

The Course of Democracy in the Fifth Republic (2001–2003)

Venezuela is moving from one type of limited democracy to another type of regime within the gray zone—a regime not yet fully defined but exhibiting tendencies of hybrid regimes or dominant-power regimes. Venezuela consolidated a limited pluralist democracy in the Punto Fijo regime, with institutional patterns both supportive of and inimical to liberal democracy.[8] Early successes obscured embedded weaknesses that made Venezuelan representative democracy susceptible to the twin crises of representation and distribution.

In some measure the embedded weaknesses of the Punto Fijo regime are present in other democracies throughout Latin America. Is the Fifth Republic, then, reforming democracy in Venezuela with the new forms of participation so clearly needed in Latin America?[9] Or is it institutionalizing a modern variant of an old form of Latin American populism centered on a strong presidency with authoritarian undertones, either Guillermo O'Donnell's delegative democracy or Ken Roberts' neopopulism?[10] Roberts argues that in any era populism emerges "in contexts where substantial sectors of the lower classes are available for political mobilization but are not effectively represented by established parties and do not possess institutionalized forms of political self-expression" (2000: 2). Political exclusion thus generates populism.

As we have seen, Venezuelan democracy under Punto Fijo was based on a centralized, presidentialist political model. It relied on the distribution of externally derived rents, rather than redistribution through domestic taxation, to ameliorate social conflict and gain the support of hostile elements. Despite a strong electoral system, vertical accountability was weak, as the party system and legislature answered to party elites rather than citizen constituents. In other words, the Punto Fijo regime was deficient in accomplishing democratization in the sense of greater equity and participation. Instead, in the forty years of Punto Fijo, income inequality grew, living standards rose and then declined, and political party leaders became removed from the citizens. Alienation was reflected in growing voter abstention, which rose to 18 percent in the 1988 national elections and skyrocketed to 40 percent in 1993. Voters were clearly alienated because governments proved administratively incapable of solving basic policy problems.

In assessing the quality and future direction of Venezuelan democracy in the Fifth Republic, we again turn to the three analytic approaches of the previous sections.

Structural/Political Economy Factors

Four years into the Chávez presidency, the former lieutenant colonel's promises to create a more efficacious and responsive democracy were unfulfilled. Dissatisfaction with the performance of the government on key policy problems such as crime, unemployment, and corruption was above 70 percent in mid-2001 and continued to rise above 80 percent in mid-2002 (Gil Yepes, Chapter 11, and Datanalisis, 2002a). Further, the Chávez administration had failed to formulate a clear economic strategy four years into his administration, beyond raising oil prices through curtailing production. In fact, the surprising thing, as Kelly and Palma note (Chapter 10), is that the Chávez administration had not strayed far from the consensus established by the Punto Fijo regime about an underlying strategy of development based on the action of an enlightened state that would distribute oil wealth for the benefit of the people. In fact, Fifth Republic economic policy appeared to be dependence on oil without the diversification plans of the 1970s.

During his 1998 election campaign, Chávez called for a change in the political system to drive out corrupt and parasitical forces, but he did not explicate a change in economic policy. Instead, his first year was one of austerity and pragmatism. The Bolivarian constitution of 1999 was not radically different from the statist 1961 constitution in economic policy, and throughout the second year of his government Chávez worked toward economic recovery and modernization of the economy. A moderate dip in oil prices and a global recession in his third year forced new belt-tightening in year four. Nevertheless, by 2003 (the fifth year of the administration), facing the buildup toward a recall referendum, Chávez expanded fiscal policy and initiated a number of new social programs to bring medical care, literacy programs, and supermarkets into poor neighborhoods. The most significant change in policy was the Chávez administration's attempt to assert greater government control over the nationalized oil company, Petróleos de Venezuela Sociedad Anónima (PDVSA; Venezuelan Oil Company), and therefore over its revenues. President Chávez had long opposed PDVSA's strategy of maximizing market share through increased production, reinvestment of profits abroad, and lower prices, rather than using oil revenues to fund domestic social programs. The president first attempted a change with a decree-law in November 2001 to modify the system of taxation and royalties in the hydrocarbon sector. The purpose of this shift was to reduce PDVSA's ability to hide its revenue from the state, thus carrying out one of the most important pillars of the Bolivarian Revolution.[11]

He then attempted to take control of PDVSA's board of directors and fired the PDVSA president in early 2002, leading to a strike by PDVSA executives and precipitating the massive march and April coup. Although the president temporarily backed down after being reinstated in office, he took advantage of another oil strike eight months later (December 2002–Janary 2003) to fire eighteen thousand oil workers and executives, replace the board, and restructure the organization.

Kelly and Palma (Chapter 10) argue that most fears about Chávez's economic policy stem from the continuity of Punto Fijo economic policies: dependence on oil, unsustainable social commitments, and weak bureaucratic controls and capacity. All of this was exacerbated by Chávez's rhetoric, which at times frightened investors, foreign and domestic. Popular dissatisfaction with Chávez's inability to promote private investment, in fact, rose to 77 percent by mid-2002 (Datanalisis, 2002a). After more than four years under the Fifth Republic, Venezuela seemed unable to abandon the failed economic strategy of dependence on the vagaries of the world oil market, a condition that helped to undermine its predecessor.

Political/Institutional Factors

The Fifth Republic concentrated power even further in the national executive, to an extent not seen since Rómulo Betancourt mobilized the state to fight leftist guerrillas in the 1960s. The political regime over which President Chávez presided possessed a weakened and fragmented party system, a legislature dominated by the executive branch, and fiscally dependent regional and local governments. Independent institutions (courts, legislature, comptroller general, electoral authority) that could provide for public accountability were politicized. Regime legitimacy relied on the personal charisma of President Chávez, his neopopulist rhetoric, and a new role for the military to sustain the regime in the face of curtailed oil rents and economic deterioration. Political participation rested on plebiscitarian forms of mass participation and mobilizational politics to engage those who were previously excluded from political decision making.

Direct democracy and mass participation were encouraged through elections and referenda, enhancing the role of public opinion and creating a direct link from the president to the people while weakening the intermediaries of political parties and interest groups. Does the more direct form of participation of the masses through elections and referenda constitute an advance in holding government accountable and making democracy more efficacious and beneficial for the people? Not necessarily. As Gil Yepes notes (Chapter 11), the disparity in power between individual citizens and the government is much greater than that between organized interest groups and the government. The ability to hold governing authorities accountable through recall elections and revocatory referenda to repeal legislation depends on an incredible organizational effort on the part of the people, unless the president himself calls for the referenda, as the new constitution allows. (It was not until the end of 2003 that the opposition to the Chávez administration had regrouped enough to organize a recall effort against the president midway through his term.)

As Gil Yepes points out, the need for a loyal opposition was clearly recognized by post-1958 elites but not by the Bolivarian leaders. Collapse of the Punto Fijo party system and the failure of a new party system to crystallize in the Fifth Republic (partially a consequence of policies pursued by President Chávez) meant that initially grievances had to be channeled through alternate routes. The most important vehicles to express opposition to the policies of the Chávez government were institutions that made up the resurgent and newly autonomous civil society—the labor unions, business organizations, professional associations, and NGOs. These institutions filled the void left by the demise of the traditional political actors and evolved into mechanisms of representation, citizen participation, and interest aggregation.

Entrepreneurs became alarmed as President Chávez excluded them from the access to policy making to which they had grown accustomed during Punto Fijo. The private sector moved into open opposition in December 1999 when business organizations opposed the referendum to approve the new constitution. NGOs played a critical role in persuading the Supreme Court to postpone the May 2000 elections. In November 2001 a series of forty-nine decree-laws approved by Chávez under his delegated authority from the National Assembly galvanized labor unions and the private sector to organize in protest. NGOs subsequently joined with labor unions and the business federation to call for political action, including strikes and marches to protest government policies on land reform, reorganization of the state petroleum agency, and the sale of oil at subsidized prices to Cuba. A series of demonstrations in late 2001 and early 2002 culminated in the march of April 11, 2002, on Miraflores, the seat of presidential power. That march ended in violence, convinced the armed forces to depose President Chávez, and led to the designation of businessmen Pedro Carmona as interim president. However, confusion in the military and in the opposition resulted in the generals and admirals switching their support back to Chávez after less than forty-eight hours.

The chaotic four days of April 11–14 demonstrated the continued inability of political parties to regroup and assume leadership positions while media, labor, and business leaders took the lead in challenging the direction in which the Fifth Republic was heading. If the political actors had been more capable, perhaps the politically inept domination of the short-lived interim government by the radical Right would have been averted. Even after the coup, the weakness of the political opposition remained evident, as public opinion polls failed to identify a clear opposition leader able to challenge Chávez.[12] Work in this volume by Gil Yepes (Chapter 11) confirms that AD, COPEI, and Movimiento al Socialismo (MAS; Movement toward Socialism), the traditional Punto Fijo political parties, continued to be viewed negatively by most Venezuelans.

Nevertheless, an incipient organized opposition in the form of the Coordinadora Democratica (CD; Democratic Coordinating Committee) in mid-2002 began to redress the imbalance in organizational power between the president and individual Venezuelans. The opposition political parties, NGOs, business, and labor came together to form a coalition aimed at ousting Chávez one way or another. Street mobilization, court challenges, and constitutional means to reach early elections through a recall referendum or constitutional amendment to shorten the mandate were some of the methods attempted to remove the president. The sense that Chávez was driving the country bankrupt or transforming it into another Cuba had gained credence since December 2001, and many in the opposition now argued for the president's immediate ouster. Still, the government had its supporters, and the country divided over the question of whether to characterize the April 11–14 events as a coup.

Division in the opposition undermined its effectiveness. In the months after the events of April one faction favored pursuing an extended legal process or referendum scenario. Another argued for a more immediate forced ouster of President Chávez through demonstrations, strikes and work stoppages, and even military force if he continued on his divisive course. The CD pursued both strategies in the second half of 2002. On the one hand, it entered into negotiations with the government at the Mesa de Negociaciones y Acuerdos (Negotiating Table) facilitated by the Organization of American States (OAS), United Nations Development Programme (UNDP), and Carter Center. On the other, CD leaders organized street demonstrations and their ultimate card—a devastating oil strike in December 2002.

Political Culture/Learning Factors

As Molina, Canache, Gil Yepes, and Salamanca demonstrate (Chapters 8, 2, 11, and 5, respectively), the perception of betrayal and incompetence on the part of the traditional Punto Fijo political parties led Venezuelans to look for something different. Rather than transfering their loyalties to new parties, they turned to charismatic leaders, social movements, and civic associations. Chávez's support continued among the urban poor, in particular, resting on the hope he provided them in populist appeals based on his charismatic personality. As Max Weber argued (Guenther and Wittich, 1979), citizens responding to charismatic political authority identify with the leader's personal qualities and political vision and do not necessarily make new organizational commitments. Such identification with a charismatic leader can last a lifetime. (Witness the loyalty to Juan Perón and his movement in Argentina fifty years later.)

Yet the question remains, Will poor Venezuelans remain pragmatic, as Canache (Chapter 2) demonstrated they were at the end of Punto Fijo, shifting their loyalty once again if their expectations go unfulfilled? Or will they retain a lifetime identification with the charismatic figure of Chávez, whom they identified as one of their own? Although it is too early to answer this question definitively, the early evidence suggests that the attitudes of the urban poor do not differ greatly from those of other Venezuelans. Slum dwellers' evaluations of Chávez were highly positive at the time of his inauguration, in February 1999, but began to fall soon thereafter. Following the coup events of April 11–14, 2002, approval of the president stabilized at roughly 30 percent of all

Venezuelans, with his hardcore support concentrated in the urban poor.[13] Nevertheless, the urban poor became the most polarized sector of the population in 2002, as their sentiments divided while the upper classes united in their rejection of Chávez.[14] Subsequently, government initiatives in the slums of the ten largest cities, coupled with the opposition's inability to articulate a clear alternative program, led to a situation in the final quarter of 2003 in which President Chávez's approval rating reached 42 percent among the lower social strata (Consultores 21 S.A, 2003).[15]

President Chávez and his opposition behaved in ways during 2002–3 which suggested that political learning had occurred. The president drew the lesson from the short-lived coup against him that he was too tolerant and permissive.[16] Consequently, he attempted to consolidate his position within the armed forces by purging disloyal officers, intimidate the private media by threatening administrative and financial sanctions if they continued to overstep the line in opposing him, and take advantage of the year-end (December 2002–February 2003) petroleum strike by reasserting national political control over a petroleum agency that he believed had become a "state within a state." Throughout all these changes President Chávez continued on a more or less constitutional path, suggesting that he had learned the pitfalls of behaving in ways that outraged international opinion or went against the grain of Venezuela's democratic political culture.

The opposition also drew important lessons from the failed coup. The CD learned that the president was willing to use all the resources at his disposal to remain in power. The national strike of December 2002 began in the wake of a contentious debate within the CD over the wisdom of calling such a strike. Initially less extensive than anticipated, the national strike began to look like a failure until petroleum workers joined on its third day. President Chávez, defying all odds, began importing gasoline and food to meet the nationwide shortages. He tolerated long-term damage to the oil fields in his firing of the skilled workers and his refusal to back down. After two months of shortages, a bleak Christmas, and the collapse of innumerable small business, the opposition called off the strike. It had failed to meet the minimum goal of forcing a nonbinding consultative referendum on Chávez government, much less its leaders' escalated demand for the president's immediate resignation.

The CD shifted gears in the wake of this reverse. Hard-line labor and business leaders went into a voluntary exile to escape arrest, and the political parties began to reassert their role. Opponents of the government focused on the constitutional provision for a recall referendum halfway through the presidential term (August 2003), following the course that much of the international community had long advised. Thus, the majority faction in the CD drew the lesson that the public had grown tired of polemics and confrontation. However, a militant faction, the Bloque Democrático, split from the CD to continue the call for civil disobedience as the only means to force Chávez from power. It enjoyed little public support.

As 2003 drew to a close, the tug-of-war between Chávez and his opponents focused, then, on the ability of each to use legal mechanisms to annihilate the other. The opposition banked on winning a referendum to remove the president from power, and Bolivarians counted on weakening the opposition into submissiveness by preventing the referendum or defeating them at the polls. Neither side acknowledged the possibility, much less the necessity, of coexistence. Neither did they demonstrate a willingness to work together to meet the challenges of addressing the underlying problems stunting Venezuela's development: dependence on oil, income inequality, eroded public infrastructure, and the incapacity of the state to provide basic human services.

Conclusions: Lessons for Democratic Theory and Venezuela

This work confirms that political economy and political culture variables contribute to explaining political change in Venezuela. It also suggests that institutional variables are even more central to explaining the unraveling of post-1958 representative democracy and the nature of the current political regime. Cultural and structural factors helped to shape Venezuelan political institutions, but the institutions themselves had an even more important impact on determining how the distribution and representation crises unfolded in the Punto Fijo era and how since 1999 they have prevented normalization of the Bolivarian polity.

The institutional hypotheses generated from this analysis of a half century of Venezuelan politics can be summarized as follows:

- Dominant political actors, once ensconced in power, resist reforming their own system when it entails surrendering a share of that power (i.e., failure of Punto Fijo party elites to incorporate newly important interest groups and President Chávez's reluctance to make space for a democratic political opposition).

- After one form of democratic regime unravels, it is difficult to gain support for alternative democratic institutions (parties, legislatures, courts, corruption controls). This difficulty derives from the psychological fallout of the unraveling process. Unraveling creates skepticism toward the political institutions necessary to normalize any new political regime. Therefore, even when the dominant political culture is democratic, a new democratic political regime will not be easily institutionalized.
- Deinstitutionalization of a strong party system leads to negative attitudes toward all political parties. This impedes the formation of loyalties to any political party and delays institutionalization of a new party system.
- Nevertheless, deinstitutionalization of a party system contrasts with systems that have never been institutionalized in that an institutionalized party system contributes to a democratic culture that provides greater resistance to the dismantling of democracy.
- The demise of a party-mediated model of state-society relations opens the path to a direct confrontation between the state and society. In this situation newly mobilized interest groups seek to fill the gap left by the decline of political parties and become interest aggregators as well as interest articulators. The effects of this development, the absence of a specialized institution to aggregate interests, may lead to a destabilizing direct confrontation between state and citizens.
- Dismantling institutionalized civilian control over the military may increase the authority of the political executive over the armed forces, but it deprives other branches of government (especially the legislative branch) of institutional means by which to assert their authority over those charged with managing violence in the political regime. In the medium term this increases the likelihood of open military intervention in politics.
- The urban poor are most susceptible to mobilization by a personalistic movement when their quality of life has declined and they perceive themselves to be excluded or discriminated against in the policy-making process of the existing political regime. These two conditions prevailed in 1998, when slum dwellers flocked to the Chávez candidacy.

What, then, does Venezuela tell us about regime change in an institutionalized limited democracy located in the gray zone? Above all, we learn that such regimes have their own embedded vulnerabilities and, when stressed, can succumb. In the Venezuelan case, the twin crises of representation and distribution emanated from the structural, institutional, and cultural characteristics of post-1958 Venezuela: an oil economy and a centralist, elite-consensus-seeking political culture shaped a political institutional system based on distributive policies and elite settlements. The strong emphasis on centralism and conflict management through elite consensus outside the public realm led eventually to a representation crisis as excluded sectors rebelled.

At the same time, the public institutions tasked with regime maintenance by this approach to politics contributed to a distribution crisis because Punto Fijo leaders had been reluctant to rebuild the state's deteriorated regulative and redistributive capacities. Thus, when distributive capabilities eroded, Punto Fijo democracy's other capabilities (redistributive and regulative) were so weak that they could contribute little to stabilizing the regime.

The Fifth Republic has not changed these basic traits of post-1958 Venezuelan politics: structurally, dependence on oil continues; demographic trends continue to accelerate as the population grows, urbanization increases, and poverty remains pervasive. Institutionally, it maintains a highly centralized decision-making structure, even though a new set of privileged actors have emerged. It is now the traditional elites who are excluded, much like in the Trienio of 1945–48. The Bolivarian regime continues to rely on the distribution of oil rents and has failed to restore the regulative and administrative capacities of the state.

What *has* changed? Culturally, the Fifth Republic has emphasized class divisions rather than seeking to develop cross-class alliances, the strategy pursued during the early Punto Fijo years. The revolutionary sense that truth and justice are on the side of the Bolivarians and that all who oppose it are enemies is reminiscent of the rhetoric of the revolution of 1945. Institutionally, the attempt to dismantle and discredit the representative democratic institutions has impeded the creation of legitimate replacements. In addition, the tactic used by the new ruling class to replace existing institutions unilaterally with procedures intended to establish a direct relationship between leader and citizens, state and society, has fueled confrontation. Thus, the avoidance of conflict which characterized Punto Fijo was replaced by a seeking out of such confrontation in order to effect social change.

Political order hung by a slender thread as President Hugo Chávez began his fourth year in office in early 2002. Two mutually antagonistic groupings, the Bolivarians and their opponents, viewed each other as illegitimate. These perceptions fostered a political climate in which the two forces played a zero-sum game. They became unwilling to coexist and instead sought to annihilate each other, even at the price of destroying the country. The resulting crisis of governability raised the specter of regime collapse, civil war, or anarchy.

During 2003, the fifth year of the Bolivarian Revolution, both sides had reverted to constitutional mechanisms in their struggle to defeat the other—the government using all sorts of legal appeals and delay tactics to put off a recall referendum, as well as traditional social spending to shore up support, while the opposition attempted to garner popular support to remove the president from office through the constitutional provision of a recall referendum and thus to end the revolution.

Venezuelan politics remained unconsolidated and in the gray zone. The country appeared to be in the process of a regime transformation from one form of limited democracy to a new, inchoate and uninstitutionalized form. The emerging political regime was a hybrid—neither liberal democracy nor outright dictatorship. The regime eroded the checks and balances of autonomous democratic institutions by asserting governing party control over the courts, electoral authority, attorney general, ombudsman, and comptroller general. It weakened representative institutions while strengthening direct democracy mechanisms. It involved the military extensively in policy making and implementation. Its legitimacy relied on the authority and centralized decision making of its charismatic leader and on populist spending programs of an ever growing number of social programs for the poor.

With the embedded vulnerabilities of the Punto Fijo democracy in stark relief, the Venezuelan case provides important clues of how apparently institutionalized representative democracies can unravel when stressed. These clues, which have been identified and discussed in this conclusion, suggest that no political regime is ever immutably consolidated. Any political regime can unravel when stressed, a lesson of great importance for leaders seeking to normalize the political regime in the more recent democracies that took root in the 1980s in many countries of the developing world.

Epilogue

Jennifer L. McCoy and David J. Myers

On August 15, 2004, Hugo Chávez defied his opposition to resoundingly defeat a recall referendum seeking to end his term early. The shocked opposition refused to accept the 59 percent to 41 percent vote favoring Chávez and searched for evidence of fraud. Meanwhile, governments in the Western hemisphere and around the world accepted the results, endorsed by the international observer missions of the Organization of American States (OAS) and the Carter Center, and withdrew the intensive international involvement in the country that began after the April 2002 coup and counter-coup. In the October 31, 2004 election for regional governors and mayors, President Chávez's political party, the Bolivarian Revolutionary Movement (*Movimento Revolucionaio Bolivariano*), and its allies elected 21 of the 23 regional governors and 270 of the 337 mayoralties. Thirteen months later, on December 4, 2005, the same supportive alliance captured all 167 seats in the National Assembly. The magnitude of these victories led Hugo Chávez to declare that his Bolivarian Revolution would reorder Venezuela's polity, economy, and culture toward the end of building "twenty-first-century socialism."

The recall vote capped a two-and-a-half-year effort by the opposition to remove Chávez from office by any means possible.[1] In May 2003, the opposition settled on the recall as its last legal chance to remove the president before the end of his term on February 2, 2007. Former U.S. president Jimmy Carter had proposed an agreement between the administration and the opposition in January 2003 on how to carry out a recall referendum as provided for in the constitution. Carter's proposal included a voting date of August 19, 2003 (the earliest one eligible), as well as commitments by all concerned to accept international electoral supervision, human rights safeguards, new members for the National Electoral Council, and a new attorney general, comptroller general, and national ombudsman.

In the accord that the two sides reached under OAS facilitation in May 2003, they agreed that a recall referendum could help to defuse the crisis but reached no consensus on a time frame or provisions for carrying it out. This accord merely accepted the right to petition for a recall referendum; it did not guarantee that the referendum would take place or specifically address Carter's proposals. The accord, however, affirmed Venezuela's commitment to nonviolence and human rights while acknowledging an offer from the OAS, the Carter Center, and the United Nations Development Programme to furnish technical help, election observation, and follow-up to the agreement.[2]

The recall referendum as a means of conflict resolution raised expectations that could not be met. Militants in each camp desired that it would signal the other's total defeat. The less partisan simply wanted it to solve the crisis. But a yes-or-no referendum question is an inherently divisive process and offers poor prospects for resolving deeper issues of the kind troubling Venezuela. Nonetheless, many hoped that a recall vote could at least let the country gauge how much support Chávez and his agenda enjoyed and then peacefully move forward on the basis of that information.

The different ways in which the government and its opponents approached the recall reflected their differing time horizons. The government took the longer view, systematically consolidating its power and riding out challenges in order to survive and press the Bolivarian Revolution forward. The opposition was gripped by the desire to remove the government immediately. Their strategy echoed the television-influenced approach to politics in which the immediacy of the moment commands all attention and the media decisively shape political messages and public opinion. This shorter horizon ruled out efforts to organize at the grassroots level in ways capable of winning voter trust or changing the accountability institutions (the courts, the electoral council, and the offices of the attorney general, comptroller general, and ombudsman), all of which were led by government sympathizers.

Repeated delays in scheduling the recall hurt the opposition's chances. Venezuela's GDP had contracted more than 9 percent in the first half of 2003 due to the oil strike and widespread disorder. This decline reduced the popularity of the government. However, the economy began to recover as the world price of petroleum climbed to $29 per barrel in August 2003 and $41 per barrel in August 2004. President Chávez used the resulting windfall to channel more money into his popular "missions," programs he personally controlled that distributed resources directly to the urban poor. These programs provided medical clinics, subsidized food markets, housing, and adult education programs. In addition, the government initiated a broad national-identification campaign, naturalizing immigrants (including many illegal immigrants) and issuing identification cards to those (mostly the poor) who previously had none. Government officials expected that these newly naturalized citizens would vote "no" overwhelmingly on recalling the president. The voter rolls swelled from 12 to 14 million people in the weeks before the balloting.

The opposition, in contrast to well-coordinated efforts by the government, formed a unified electoral command only in the final two weeks of campaigning to revoke the mandate of President Chávez. Part of this delay derived from prolonged but ultimately unsuccessful negotiations to select a unity presidential candidate to challenge the president, should the recall referendum succeed. Such disarray and bickering among opposition forces left voters with no clear alternative to the Chávez presidency.

With all of these factors at work, the president's approval ratings rose steadily in the months leading up to the August 15 referendum. The share of voters who told pollsters that they would vote to recall him dropped from 69 percent in July 2003 to 44 percent in the first week of August 2004. Correspondingly, approval of President Chávez steadily increased, from 31 percent to 56 percent. The final results of the balloting in the recall referendum—59 percent voting to retain Chávez and 41 percent voting to remove him—were consistent with these trends.[3]

The turnout was high at 70 percent of registered voters—the average over the last three presidential elections had been 60 percent. The absolute numbers voting were the highest ever, not surprising given the growth of the voter rolls. The OAS and the Carter Center concluded that, delays and controversies aside, the vote was a true reflection of the electorate's intent. Nevertheless, militant opponents asserted that fraud had taken place. The observer missions disagreed based on their observation of simulations before the voting, their application of three different tests of the new electronic voting system on or near the day of the recall, and their assessment of fraud charges leveled after the vote.

More Rounds of Elections

The voters' rejection of the recall referendum presented the opposition with a serious dilemma. On one hand, the Coordinadora Democrática (the umbrella organization of opposition political parties) had charged fraud and voiced distrust of the electoral authority, thereby painting the electoral process as unreliable at best and an outright sham at worst. On the other hand, opposition leaders interested in resurrecting their party's prospects still needed to motivate voters to take part in the late-October elections for governors, mayors, and state assemblies. Attacking the credibility of the electoral process would only lead to greater abstention of opposition supporters.

Victory in the regional and local elections of October 31, 2004 proved an important milestone in President Chávez's drive to consolidate a "different democracy." His allies captured all but two of the regional governorships (and the office of "high mayor" of Greater Caracas) and 80 percent of the other mayoralties. Government candidates also scored a resounding triumph in the municipal council elections of August 7, 2005. The opposition, bitter and dispirited, was not shocked by these defeats. Disillusionment and lingering doubts over the validity of the electoral process did indeed lead many registered voters to abstain from the elections of October 2004 and August 2005, though those processes themselves received very few complaints.

The results of elections between August 15, 2004 and August 7, 2005 weakened President Chávez's opponents dramatically. The next electoral contest, to choose a National Assembly, took place on December 4, 2005. The publicly stated goal of the opposition for the National Assembly elections was conditioned by their anemic showing in the August 7 elections for the municipal councils and by public opinion polls indicating lowered support. Their goal was to elect one-third of the deputies in the National Assembly, the number needed to prevent the government alliance from changing the constitution and approving measures with quasi-constitutional status, known as organic laws. However, President Chávez and his allies won all 167 seats in the National

Assembly. This outcome completed the marginalization of those who had ruled Venezuela between 1958 and 1998.

The lopsided outcome came after the opposition decided to boycott the election during the week leading up to it. The opposition had continued to question the electoral process, due to the absence of an internationally verified voters list, a hole in the law allowing the majority party to win a number of seats higher than its proportion of votes, and continued suspicions about the electronic voting machines.

One of the main controversies to emerge from the strategies of the pro-Chávez forces in the elections for governors, mayors, and municipal council was their use of so-called "twin" voting, first used by an opposition governor in the 2000 elections. This strategy involved encouraging voters to vote for the MVR party on the party vote and for the candidate nominated by the UVE (Unity of Electoral Conquerors), an organization controlled by the Chavistas that had a separate legal identity from the MVR. The voting system of the Fifth Republic is a mixed electoral system modeled after the one in Germany, in which each voter receives the opportunity to choose a party and a candidate. The results are then tabulated so that the seats are distributed according to proportional representation on the party vote, which accounts for 40 percent of the seats, and according to majority vote for the individual candidates in single-member districts, which constitute 60 percent of the seats in the legislative body.

The MVR-UVE twin voting enabled pro-Chávez forces to win more seats in the municipal council elections than if voters had just voted for the MVR. Had the latter been the case, the winning MVR candidates would have been counted against the proportional vote that the party obtained. With public opinion polls in September 2005 suggesting that at least 60 percent of the electorate favored the MVR and its allies, retention of this "twin" strategy all but insured that the opposition would elect fewer than 20 percent of the members of National Assembly on December 4.

The opposition argued that the "twin" strategy was unconstitutional, but neither the Supreme Court nor the National Electoral Council (CNE) forbade it. Distrust of the CNE by the opposition had been especially intense since the recall referendum of August 2004. Conventional wisdom among middle-class opponents of the government was that individuals who had voted to remove the president in that election subsequently found it difficult to secure employment in the public sector and that medical and social security benefits for their relatives were bogged down in red tape or denied altogether. Opposition supporters were especially distrustful of the new voting system that used technology based on fingerprints to determine if a prospective voter was legally entitled to cast a ballot. The opposition became convinced that with this system the government would be able to know how individual electors voted and that this information would be used against them in the future.

The CNE agreed on additional pre-electoral audits and election-day recounts of the paper voting receipts, and invited the Organization of American States and European Union to send observers to monitor the elections. Additional negotiations facilitated by the international observers led the National Electoral Council to meet the conditions of the opposition to continue their participation, primarily removing the fingerprint machines and adding safeguards for the electronic voting machines to guarantee the secrecy and accuracy of the vote. Nevertheless, and to the surprise of the observers, the opposition parties withdrew one by one in subsequent days, apparently in reaction to continued lack of trust of citizens in the process, and projections that they could win at most twenty percent of the seats. After the elections, the opposition charged that the 75 percent abstention rate delegitimized the entire process.

The OAS and European observers verified in a public news conference after the vote that the voting had been honest and that President Chávez's allies had indeed captured all 167 seats in the National Assembly. However, they also stated that distrust of the CNE was widespread and urged the government to name a new council in which all Venezuelans could have greater confidence. President Chávez reacted with some irritation to this recommendation, but in general the government and the opposition made little effort to engage each other in the aftermath of the National Assembly elections. Both withdrew to contemplate the course of events in 2005 and plan their strategies for the presidential election year of 2006.

Regime Transformation?

After six years in power, the Bolivarian Revolution of Hugo Chávez had consolidated its dominance over key institutions: the national oil company PDVSA, the military, the National Assembly, elected local and regional officials, the National Electoral Council, and the Supreme Court. The National Electoral Council saw its membership change slightly in January 2005 when the Supreme Court added two new members to it and moved one existing member up to replace the retiring president (who moved to the Supreme Court). As a result, the partisan balance now appeared to be four to one pro-government versus pro-opposition members.

The National Assembly expanded the Supreme Court in December 2004 from twenty to thirty-two members, ostensibly to reduce the backlog of work of the magistrates. Authority to increase the number of justices came from the Assembly's rewriting of the organic law in ways that increased its powers to shape the Supreme Court. This action changed the partisan balance of the Court from one perceived as evenly divided in 2004 to one with a pro-government majority in 2005.

The Chávez government began to define a new economic model in 2005, a model it described as "twenty-first-century socialism." It included co-management of enterprises between managers and workers, cooperatives, and a mixed economic system of private and state capitalism. In practical terms, the government began to reshape the economy through two major initiatives: a controversial land reform and reform to the petroleum policy. Implementation of the land reform act passed in 2001 became a high priority in 2005 as the National Land Institute sought to identify unproductive private lands and haciendas without proof of title, going back as far as the War of the Federation in the 1850s. In collaboration with regional governors belonging to the government party, the central government challenged the titles of selected private estates and expropriated lands deemed idle. Portions of these estates were to be redistributed to landless rural workers or those who were already squatting on the land. President Chávez also proclaimed that his power to expropriate unproductive land included industrial food processing plants deemed to be insufficiently productive. This escalated the conflict between the government and billionaire Lorenzo Mendoza, whose Polar Group dominated food production and distribution in Venezuela.

Petroleum policy continued the strategy of tightly controlling supply in order to support high oil prices, which reached $66 per barrel in October 2005. The high price of crude on the international market also led Venezuela to rewrite the contracts of foreign oil companies, requiring the payment of larger royalties on the production of viscous or heavy oil produced from the Orinoco Tar belt and a majority state control in joint ventures. In addition, President Chávez opened talks with China and India to explore construction in Asia of a new facility capable of refining heavy Venezuelan oil. This reflected the president's desire to develop an alternative market for Venezuelan petroleum to the United States, whose Houston, Texas, Lake Charles, Louisiana, and Delaware Valley refineries remained, along with those located in Curaçāo, the only ones in the world capable of refining Venezuelan crude on a large scale.

Finally, control of the private media was enhanced with the Social Content Law, approved in December 2004. The stated aim of this law was to reduce the violence and pornography to which children were subjected by television, and to increase the amount of Venezuelan programming on television. Critics claimed, however, that the law muzzled the private media and impinged on free speech. Severe administrative fines and sanctions included in the law seemed to push the private media to voluntarily reduce the government critiques prevalent in television and radio programming, and the change from the media's previous confrontational tone was quite notable.

The media law combined with changes to the penal code in 2005 worked to curtail political dissent. The penal code increased the penalties for insulting public officials (contradicting the broader trend in the Western hemisphere and rulings of the Inter-American Court of Human Rights) and for certain kinds of nonviolent protest.

Despite these concerns over restrictions of political, civil, and property rights, President Chávez's approval ratings oscillated between 60 and 70 percent in the second half of 2005. High oil prices, and perhaps the continued very noisy dispute with the United States, buoyed his ability to increase public spending and ride the wave of anti-imperialist nationalism. High oil prices also allowed the government to expand its influence in the Caribbean basin and South America as it signed new energy and commercial deals with neighboring countries and offered them oil at discounted prices.

Prospects

As President Chávez neared completion of his first term in office under the Constitution of 1999, he appeared to be consolidating a kind of electoral democractic regime—that is, support for rules of a political game that holds minimally acceptable elections but lacks some crucial dimensions of liberal democracy. These crucial dimensions that became deficient include the failure to fully respect requirements that the rule of law be applied equally to all citizens through a system of impartial justice, and curtailment of some basic freedoms of organization and expression, at least for some groups. Also, in

Venezuela the erosion of horizontal accountability mechanisms accelerated in 2004 and 2005 as all five powers of the state (executive, legislative, judicial, electoral, and "citizen") increasingly came under partisan control of the Bolivarian Revolution, which blurred the lines that normally separate these powers.

Venezuela could stay in the "gray zone" of electoral democracies with serious deficits preventing it from reaching full, liberal democracy. Or it could digress further to some form of electoral authoritarian regime, in which the minimal conditions of competitive and inclusive elections and their associated basic liberties come into question. The elections of December 4, 2005 for National Assembly suggest a tilt toward electoral authoritarianism, although the presidential election of 2006 will be even more important in determining how the Bolivarian regime evolves.

As in the past, the international environment will play a major role in shaping Venezuelan politics. Moderate rises in petroleum prices allowed the Chávez government to compensate for capital flight in 1998 and 1999 and to invest modestly in 2000. Events between 2001 and 2005 made it all but impossible for President Chávez to convince Venezuelan businessmen to repatriate funds they had transferred out of the country, or for him to entice foreigners to invest large amounts of new capital. However, the spike in petroleum prices that began in 2003 provided more funds than the government could have hoped to obtain from capital repatriation or foreign investment. It also allowed the national executive to dominate all aspects of the economy to an extent not seen since the petro-bonanza years of the 1970s. Abundant resources to expand the regime's distributive capability at that time gave representative democracy (the Punto Fijo regime) a legitimacy that lasted for more than two decades. It is likely that the current favorable position of Venezuela in the international political economy will consolidate the Bolivarian Revolution's hold on power for some time to come.

Notes

Introduction

1. The post-1958 political regime is known popularly by the name of the house (Puntofijo) in which Venezuela's previously antagonistic elites reached agreements on how to organize the fledgling democracy. For whatever reason, Puntofijo is commonly referred to as Punto Fijo in the English-speaking world, a convention that we observe in this volume.

2. Robert Dahl (1971, 1989) argues that all polyarchies share seven characteristics: (1) elected officials; (2) free and fair elections; (3) inclusive suffrage; (4) the right to run for office; (5) freedom of expression; (6) alternative information sources; and (7) associational autonomy. Dahl (1989) further argues that these institutions are necessary for representative democracy on a large scale (the nation-state), but they may not be sufficient for all the attributes of classical democracy, including full participation and the pursuit of the common good.

As Collier and Levitsky (1997) demonstrate, there are various regime subtypes, including diminished subtypes of democracy. O'Donnell (2002b) disaggregates the political regime from the broader political system when he defines democracy more broadly than the formal regime (rules of accession to government). For O'Donnell, democracy also encompasses the state (bureaucracies, rule of law, and collective identity) and socioeconomic context. O'Donnell goes on to argue that a country may have a democratic political regime (with elections as the route to accession to power) without a fully democratic state (2002a). This volume explores the dynamics of political regime change; it does not focus on some potentially broader context of democratic development.

3. The movement away from dictatorial rule and toward more liberal and democratic governance in southern Europe, Latin America, and post-Communist Eastern Europe has, thanks to Samuel Huntington (1991), become known widely as the "Third Wave of Democracy." Huntington also discusses an earlier "Second Wave of Democracy"; it began with the Allied victory over the Axis powers in 1945 but retreated before a "reverse wave" of bureaucratic authoritarianism which swept away most second-wave democracies. In Latin America second-wave democracies survived in Colombia, Costa Rica, and Venezuela.

4. This is similar to Carother's "feckless democracy" (2002) and draws on Gil Yepes (1978).

5. This shares some characteristics with Carother's "dominant-power syndrome" (2002), O'Donnell's "delegative democracies" (1994), and Diamond's twilight zone democracies (1999).

6. Distributive crisis refers not only to declining state income but also to administrative, extractive, and managerial capacity.

CHAPTER ONE: The Normalization of Punto Fijo Democracy

1. This theme permeates reporting by the *New York Times* (December 17 and 18, 1961) of President John F. Kennedy's visit to Venezuela.

2. For example, see Levine, 1994, and Karl, 1995.

3. Carrasquero and Welsch, 2001: 69–88.

4. Brewer-Carías (1988: 383–84) also discusses the existence of a Document of Motives.

5. The Bicameral Commission for Constitutional Reform was never the innovator in these discussions. Venezuelan constitutions have always incorporated the idea of limitations and restrictions through law, although less directly. The 1961 constitution simply clarified and strengthened the economic rights of the Venezuelan citizens.

6. URD broke with President Betancourt after twenty-one months over his support of the United States against Fidel Castro. For an informative account of URD's role in the Betancourt government, see Alexander, 1964: 98–100.

7. Most URD leaders professed loyalty to the 1957–59 elite settlement, and Ojeda was expelled from the party.

8. Policy types, as used throughout this chapter, are classified according to perceptions of how likely it is that coercion will have to be employed in order to implement the outcome produced by the policy process. Regulatory policy significantly increases the probability that coercion must be employed, when compared with decisions that can be implemented through distribution. For a more complete analysis of the implications of policy types for political stability, see Lowi, 1964, 1972, and Myers, 1994.

CHAPTER TWO: Urban Poor and Political Order

1. This development has been examined closely by social scientists. See, for example, García-Guadilla, 1992; Gómez Calcaño, 1987, 1998; Levine, 1998b; Levine and Crisp, 1995; Navarro, 1995; and Salamanca, 1995b.

2. One organization warrants specific mention. The Centro al Servicio de la Acción Popular (CESAP; Center for the Service of Popular Action), which predates much of Venezuelan civil society, has sponsored a wide array of programs designed to aid many sectors of Venezuelan society, including the urban poor.

3. For a detailed account of the origins and development of LCR, see López Maya, 1997.

4. The data sources are from the 1995 Venezuelan survey (conducted under my supervision by the Universidad Católica Andrés Bello; urban sample—Caracas and Maracaibo—N = 897) and DATOS 1998 (national sample; N = 1,500; this survey was conducted under the auspices of the National Network of Political Culture, REDPOL).

5. All variables have been coded so that they range in value from 0 to 1.

6. Classic studies on economic voting include Kiewiet, 1983; Kinder and Kiewiet, 1979; and Lewis-Beck, 1990. Studies of economic voting in Latin America include Remmer, 1991, 1993, and Weyland, 1998.The indicators of economic perceptions have been recoded so that a score of 0 means that the respondent expects economic conditions to worsen, and a 1 means that conditions are expected to improve.

7. Respondents also had the option to say that there should not be change, but very few respondents selected this option. Consequently, I limit the analysis that follows to those respondents who chose between radical and gradual change.

8. Molina does not examine differences within or between rural/urban sectors; thus we cannot conclude from his analysis whether the urban poor in particular were as loyal to Hugo Chávez in 2000 as they were in 1998. We can affirm, though, that during the first year and a half in office Chávez maintained and solidified his electoral support among the poor.

9. On populism in Latin America, see the various reports in Conniff, 1999, and especially Ellner's discussion of populism in Venezuela (1999).

10. Data are from Datanalisis. See Datanalisis, C.A., 2003.

11. Data are from Datanalisis. Martínez, 2003.

CHAPTER THREE: The Military

1. Gustavo Tarre Briceño, chair of the Finance Committee in the lower legislative house, interview with author, Caracas, September 30, 1994.

2. General Alberto Müller Rojas, interview with author, Caracas, January 20, 1995.

3. General Carlos Celis, Noguera, director emeritus of the Instituto de Altos Estudios de la Defensa Nacional, interview with author, Caracas, October 10, 1994.

4. Rojas interview.

5. José Machillanda Pinto, retired army lieutenant colonel and political scientist, interview with author, Caracas, March 10, 1995.

6. Amalio Belmonte, chair of the Department of Sociology of the Universidad Central de Venezuela, interview with author, Caracas, October 6, 1994.

7. The second report by the Venezuelan army on its activities under the Plan Bolívar 2000 includes projections to the year 2005. Plan Bolívar 2000, number 2, Comando General del Ejercito, Impresos Mundo Gráfico, CA, 2000.

8. Roberto Bottome, editor of VenEconomía, interview with author, Caracas, July 28, 1999.

9. General Martin García Villasmíl, minister of defense under President Rafael Caldera, 1969–72, interview with author, Caracas, April 19, 1995. General José Radamés Soto Urrútia, professor at the Venezuela Air Force General Staff School, interview with author, Caracas, October 7, 1994.

10. Plan Bolívar 2000, number 2. Soto Urrútia interview.

11. Alberto Quiróz Corradi, former president of Maraven, interview with author, Caracas, August 17, 1992.

12. General Jacobo E. Yépes Daza, former director of planning for Joint Chiefs of Staff, interview with author, Caracas, March 6, 1995.

13. Plan Bolívar 2000, number 2.

14. General Gonzalo García Ordoñez, commander of Comando Unificado de la Fuerza Armada Nacional (CUFAN; National Armed Forces Unified Command), meeting, Caracas, May 27, 2000.

CHAPTER FOUR: Entrepreneurs

1. The Pacto de Punto Fijo was a power-sharing agreement designed to maintain democracy. It was signed in 1958, after the fall of the Pérez Jiménez dictatorship, by the

three main parties in the country: AD, COPEI, and URD. It was called Punto Fijo after Rafael Caldera's house, where it was signed. Punto Fijo is also the term used to describe the forty years of government beginning in January 1959 and ending in February 1999, when Hugo Chávez came to power.

2. "Punto Fijo era" and "Fifth Republic" are used in reference to political regimes. The Fifth Republic is the period after December 1998 when Hugo Chávez was elected president and turned Venezuela into a dominant power system (see McCoy and Myers, 2003).

3. For an excellent and detailed comparison, see Torres, 2000.

4. On February 18, 1983, Venezuela abandoned its policy of several decades (except for a brief period in 1961) of a free and fixed exchange rate. This date is known as black Friday.

5. It is estimated that in the period 1973–2003 Venezuela had a free cash flow of more than $100 billion (after its payment for imports of goods and services, tourism, immigrant remittances, and servicing of the public and private external debt). This figure is derived from the cumulative current account of the balance of payments plus the net external debt for this period.

6. "Dutch disease" is the term used to describe the effect that oil, when it represents an important share of the economy, has on other sectors. Usually, only sectors that are not subject to international trade remain competitive. The term was coined following the major effect of the discovery of gas on the Dutch economy.

7. *Rabo de paja* and *bozal de arepa* are two Venezuelan expressions. The former refers to the fact that nearly all the individuals involved found themselves implicated in corrupt practices to some extent. In the face of even greater wrongdoing, they thus had no choice but to keep their mouth shut. The latter expression is equivalent to "sticking one's head in the sand."

8. In 1978, José Antonio Gil Yepez, in his book *El Reto de las Élites,* was already warning of the cracks that were starting to appear in the Venezuelan elites and their likely consequences.

9. "The process" was the name coined for the Chávez Bolivarian Revolution during 1998 electoral campaign.

CHAPTER FIVE: Civil Society

1. It is beyond the scope of this chapter to discuss the different positions on the notion of civil society (Cohen and Arato, 2000; Diamond, 1994; Gellner, 1996; Keane, 1992; Walzer, 1998). Of late a great amount of literature has been written on this topic internationally.

2. We speak of power rather than the state as the pole opposite civil society because civil society may confront not only the state but also other varieties of power. Certainly the state is the most important object of confrontation, but it is not the only one. The distinction between state and civil society is the easiest to posit, but it is insufficient for establishing a theory of civil society.

3. The movement Primero Justicia provides an important example of the recent politicization of civil society. This organization went from being an NGO dedicated to the reform of the judiciary to being a political party.

4. The lineage of civility in Venezuela can be traced to the political and legal attempts to establish secret, direct, universal suffrage as the modality by which the

governing are chosen as a replacement for military means, the typical way of access to power. In this light, a number of events stand out: the weak attempts to introduce direct suffrage into the constitution; the student protests against the dictatorships that preceded Gómez; the pro-democracy uprising in 1928; the protests that followed the death of Juan Vicente Gómez; and the post-Gómez process of union and professional association (1936–48) which shaped what might be called the first expressions of civil society in Venezuela. In any case, these first modern associations express a society that strove to make itself civil but which was absorbed by political power (parties and state). I refer to this phase as traditional civil society.

5. From this point on, I use the number provided in the study by CISOR and IESA in 1999, referred to earlier.

6. The CNE's own recognition of the difficulties in realizing an unquestionable electoral process was decisive in the decision to suspend the elections.

7. The Comisión Legislativa Nacional (Legislative Committee) was a transitory legislative power that replaced the National Constituent Assembly. The members of the committee, which was popularly known as the "Congresillo" (little Congress), were designated by the ANC to legislate until a new National Assembly was elected.

8. Both the Committees for the Evaluation of Candidates and the Republican Moral Council are organs created by the 1999 constitution. The name of the Moral Council was changed to Citizens' Power and constitutes a fifth branch of government (the other four being executive, legislative, judicial, and electoral). It is composed of the offices of the Fiscalía General de la República (Prosecutor General of the Republic), the Contraloría General de la República (Controller General of the Republic), and the Defensoría del Pueblo (Public Defender).

9. On August 27, 2000, in his Sunday radio show, Chávez stated, "Mr. Santana, I am calling you to battle. Come, come. Call your civil society to one corner and I will call mine to another. We will see who's boss."

CHAPTER SIX: Intellectuals

I appreciate Elsa Cardozo's and Steve Ellner's comments, three anonymous reviews, and David Myers' editorial guidance.

1. Later editions were less critical of the United States and more hostile to the "Third International."

2. Protests and rioting in Caracas spread to other parts of the country, causing a "social explosion."

3. Comments at the Universidad Central de Venezuela in 1989.

4. Reply by Orlando Albornoz to Montilla during a televised exchange between politically involved academics on VeneVision, Sunday morning, April 13, 1997.

5. Survey of 2,000 Venezuelans: 83 percent supported democracy; 57 percent demanded a non-AD or -COPEI government (Myers, 1995: 126). Ewell (1993) reported that 97 percent preferred democracy to military government.

6. Television interview, November 11, 2000. Uslar Pietri died in February 2001.

7. They published *Encounter and Alternatives, Venezuela.* Caracas: UCAB, 1994.

8. Kenneth Roberts analyzes depoliticization of class cleavages in the Punto Fijo regime and depoliticization of class under Chávez, recognizing that the underlying cleavages were already there prior to the "social revolution" (2003: 63).

9. Inaugural address, February 4, 1999.

10. Summary of planning documents generated from jail (Hillman, 1994: 136–37).

11. "The energy flows much less from constitutional formalism . . . than from ideologies, policies, and theories drawn from a wide range of sources" (Lombardi, 2003: 5).

CHAPTER SEVEN: The United States and Venezuela

1. The Tripartite Working Group was composed of the Organization of American States (OAS), the Atlanta-based Carter Center, and the United Nations Development Programme (UNDP).

2. The OAS–Carter Center–UNDP–sponsored negotiations lasted from November 2002 to May 2003, when an accord was signed recognizing the constitutional provisions for a recall referendum. The Group of Friends was formed to support the OAS secretary general's efforts in facilitating those negotiations and was composed of the foreign ministers of the United States, Spain, Portugal, Mexico, Chile, and Brazil.

CHAPTER EIGHT: The Unraveling of Venezuela's Party System

This research is based on work financed by the Consejo de Desarrollo Científico y Humanístico of the University of Zulia. I would also like to thank the Department of Political Science of the University of Michigan, where, as a visiting professor (2000–2003), I have enjoyed optimal conditions for writing this chapter.

1. As indicated in Caldera (1999:141), the designation for this pact derives from the name of the house in which he was then residing, "Puntofijo." This is also the name of a site near the city of San Felipe (Yaracuy), Rafael Caldera's birthplace.

2. A relevant party is a party that, given its share of the vote and the political context, is likely to become a government party (alone or in coalition) or has the potential to influence the behavior of the governing parties significantly (blackmail potential) (Sartori, 1976: 121–23).

3. In the predominant-party system, only one party has the potential to win the elections, but the rules of democratic competition are respected (Sartori, 1976: 192). By definition, with only one party, ideological polarization is not possible. In a two-party system, only two parties have the potential to win government or to influence the behavior of the governing party significantly (Sartori, 1976: 185). Because the parties tend to converge in the ideological center, ideological distance is low. Within the moderate pluralism type Sartori (1976: 127) includes party systems with low fragmentation (three to five parties) and what he calls segmented party systems (more than five parties but low ideological distance between them). In polarized pluralism, there are more than five parties, one or more of them are antisystem parties, and the ideological distance between them is large (Sartori, 1976: 131).

4. FDP was a personalistic party formed around the personality of Admiral Wolfgang Larrazábal, the first president of the 1958 provisional government that replaced the Pérez Jiménez dictatorship. In the December 1958 elections, Larrazábal ran as the presidential candidate of URD and PCV. In 1963, FDP attracted many voters who had supported PCV in 1958. FND was formed to support the presidential candidacy of the writer Arturo Uslar Pietri, who had been minister of education in the government of

General Isaías Medina (1940–45). Uslar's candidacy attracted support from the middle classes, especially in Caracas and Valencia. CCN was a political party of the Right organized by supporters of ousted dictator General Marcos Pérez Jiménez.

5. Because of that exclusion, the Left considered the pact as one of the most pernicious vices of the nascent democracy. That thesis has been adopted by Chávez and MVR as an argument for classifying Punto Fijo democracy as a "false democracy."

6. PCV participated under the label Union para Avanzar (UPA; Union for Advancement) in the 1968 elections and under its own name subsequently. In 1970 the party divided, and from this division sprang the Movimiento al Socialismo (MAS; Movement toward Socialism), which until 1989 (regional elections) was the only significant electoral organization of the Left and the country's third electoral force. Its share of the vote (legislative elections) oscillated between 5 and 10 percent (see tables 8.1 and 8.3). MIR participated in elections between 1973 and 1983 with a level of voting which never reached 3 percent and subsequently merged into MAS.

7. The most common measure of electoral volatility is the Index of Volatility popularized by Mogens Pedersen (1979). The Pedersen index profiles the percentage of votes which some parties lose and others gain between two elections. It is calculated by adding the differences in the percentage of votes of all parties between one election and the next and then dividing this result by two. This index oscillates between 0 (no variation in the parties' share of the vote) and 100 (complete variation—the political parties that obtained votes in the earlier election no longer have any votes in the latter).

8. Congressional, regional, legislative, and municipal election results were determined by proportional representation among party lists.

9. The number of "effective" political parties (N), also based on voting for the national legislature, is 3.4 for 1973, 3.1 for 1978, 3.0 for 1983, and 3.4 for 1988.

10. National survey directed by Enrique Baloyra and John Martz (1979) during November 1973; N = 1,521.

11. National survey (BATOBA 83), fieldwork undertaken in November 1983 under the direction of Enrique Baloyra and Arístides Torres; N = 1,789.

12. National survey conducted by Enrique Baloyra and John Martz in 1973; total cases N = 1,521 (Baloyra and Martz, 1979). National survey REDPOL 98 (N = 1,500) by the University Network of Political Culture in November 1998 (fieldwork by DATOS C.A.). The level of confidence in the political parties seen as an institution also tends to be low, as revealed by the survey, in which only 4.9 percent professed to have much confidence in political parties, 37.8 percent had little confidence in parties, and 57.3 percent did not have any confidence at all. Still, we should be careful when we interpret these numbers as indicators of a total rejection of the political party institution, since they show a reduction in legitimacy but not a generalized rejection of their role in democracy. Indeed, 75 percent considered that political parties are necessary for democracy.

13. In the regional and local elections, the electoral participation was 73 percent in 1979, 59 percent in 1984, 49 percent in 1992, and 46 percent in 1995.

14. An indicator of declining bipartism in 1989 was the victory in regional elections of nominees of MAS and the La Causa Radical. These political parties won the governorships in the important states of Aragua and Bolívar. In addition, MAS candidates occupied second place in gubernatorial elections in the states of Zulia, Lara, and Táchira.

15. *Pluralism* is used as synonym of multipartism (three or more parties).

16. Un Nuevo Tiempo split from AD and became the personalistic party of Manuel Rosales, the winning candidate for the governorship of Zulia in 2000. Alianza Bravo Pueblo also split from AD. It was the personalistic party of the former mayor of Caracas, Antonio Ledezma, in its unsuccessful bid for reelection in 2000.

17. National survey directed by the Political Studies Institute and Public Law of the University of Zulia in June 1993. Fieldwork by CIEPA/DOXA (N = 1,500).

18. Survey REDPOL 98.

19. The two surviving founders of MAS, Teodoro Petkoff and Pompeyo Márquez, abandoned the party in 1998.

20. National survey conducted by Enrique Baloyra and Arístides Torres in 1983 (BATOBA 83) with a sample of 1,789 people. Survey REDPOL 98.

21. "World Value Survey," a worldwide study directed by Ronald Ingelhart, University of Michigan. In 1996, it was conducted in Venezuela by researchers of Universidad Simón Bolívar and Universidad del Zulia. In 2000 it was conducted by the University Network of Political Culture. In both cases, the sample was 1,200 people.

22. The percentages are calculated excluding those who did not answer. The question asks the respondents which of the three statements they most agree with: (1) democracy is preferable to any other kind of government; (2) under some circumstances, an authoritarian government can be preferable to a democratic one; (3) for people like me, it does not matter whether we have a democratic or a nondemocratic regime.

23. In the national survey REDPOL 98, the respondents were asked whether they thought the political parties could be fixed. Out of the valid answers, 64.4 percent answered "no."

CHAPTER NINE: Decentralization

1. Local legislative bodies shall be taken to mean town halls, town councils, and municipal councils. The regional legislative organizations refer to state, provincial, or departmental assemblies. In this context, the terms *legislative* and *executives* are used within the limits of each country's local and regional authorities.

2. For an analysis of the political and administrative aspects of decentralization in Venezuela, the following, among others, may be referred to: Brewer-Carías and Ayala Corao, 1990; de la Cruz, 1992a; Sánchez Meleán, 1992.

3. For the purpose of this chapter, let us define *externalities* as the spreading effects that the provision of a given service by a territorial administration has beyond its administrative boundaries. One of the main objectives of fiscal federalism is to understand how to distribute responsibilities and source of revenues among different level of governments in such a way that they are able to internalize benefits and costs of public services they provide. Subsidiarity is a common administrative postulate, which advises allocating decision-making power to authorities/managers as close as feasible to citizens/costumers in order to enhance accountability.

4. See Brewer-Carías, 1994; Linares, 1992.

5. On the per capita compensatory effect of the constitutional budget, see Bruni Celli, 1995; CORDIPLAN, 1991; and Freire, 1992.

6. See Acedo, 1992, and de la Cruz, 1992b.

7. Intergovernmental Fund for Decentralization Law, Caracas, November 25, 1993.
8. See de la Cruz, 1998.
9. Budget Laws of the States, 1991 and 1993. Compiler: OCEPRE, General Sectoral Directorate of Regional Budgets.
10. See Veneconsultores, 1993.

CHAPTER TEN: The Syndrome of Economic Decline and the Quest for Change

1. For an excellent review of the history of oil, see Yergin, 1991. For the early history of the oil industry in Venezuela, see Tugwell, 1975.
2. See Palma, 1989.
3. For an excellent account of the situation at the start of 1989, see Kornblith, 1998.
4. For an account of the financial crisis by the president of the Central Bank, see Krivoy, 2000.
5. Venezuela accepted a reduction in OPEC quotas for production of 200,000 barrels per day in March 1998 and a further reduction of 325,000 barrels in June 1998, reducing its allowed production to 2.85 million barrels from a base production level of 3.3 million barrels per day in February. See www.opec.org.
6. Chávez and the Comisión Presidencial Constituyente, 1999.
7. The final text approved by referendum on December 15, 1999, was published on December 30 in the *Oficial Gazette*. It was republished on March 24, 2000, after correction for errors. Some conflicts emerged over the validity of the texts with respect to the votes carried out in the constituent assembly, the corrections made for style in the "final version," and the additional corrections published in March. These differences did not affect the economic clauses in any substantial way.
8. Venezuelan-American Chamber of Commerce and Industry, 2000.

CHAPTER ELEVEN: Public Opinion, Political Socialization, and Regime Stabilization

1. Gil Yepes, 1978: ch. 5. This work was translated as *The Challenge of Venezuelan Democracy* (1981).
2. Evidence to support this supposition appears in all the Datanalisis Omnibus surveys of the mid-1990s, although results from only a few appear in this chapter's tables. Anecdotal evidence also backs this position. For example, Antonio Ledezma, the mayor of Caracas (1997–2000), removed peddlers from the streets and dismantled jerry-built shacks on public land, thus ending subsidies for "marginal" commercial establishments. He also moved the city's major bus terminal to a location from which it could more efficiently offer public transportation. Approval among Caracas residents for these decisions approached 85 percent despite protest from clients of the municipal government whose interests were served by maintaining the status quo (Datanalisis, C.A., 1997 and 1998).
3. Escenarios Datanalisis, September 1996 to end of 1998, thoroughly described this process.
4. On the "overwhelming majority," see Scammon and Wattenberg, 1971.
5. Most focus groups were conducted in the *ranchos* (marginal areas) of eastern Caracas (Petare), although several were conducted in working-class areas of western

Caracas (Catia). In addition, two focus groups probed the perceptions of middle-class respondents in the metropolitan area of Caracas. These focus groups took place between December 1, 2000, and April 30, 2001. Two hundred and fifteen Caraqueños participated.

CHAPTER TWELVE: From Representative to Participatory Democracy?

1. An article in the *Economist* (Stubborn Survival, 2003, 37) cites World Bank statistics to show an increase in income inequality in Venezuela from the early 1990s to the end of the decade. Critical poverty rates doubled from 12 percent living on less than US$1 per day in 1989 to 23 percent in 2000, and estimates of those living under the national poverty line grew from 25 percent in 1970 to 34 percent in 1990 and to 67 percent by 1997. The statistics for those living on less than $1 per day came from UNDP, 1999 (figures for 1989), and from the World Bank Web site (figures for 2000). National poverty rates are quoted in ECLAC, 1997 (for the 1970 and 1990 figures), and in the CIA Web site (for 1997 figures). Neither of these sources defines the national poverty line.

2. The volume compiled by Ellner and Hellinger (2003) emphasizes the role of social polarization in bringing about the collapse of Punto Fijo.

3. Penfold (2001) points this out for the Venezuelan case.

4. Ellner and Hellinger (2003) emphasize the social deterioration and backlash to neoliberal policies in their explanation of the rise of *chavismo*.

5. Mommer (2002: 141) points out that although the constitution protects PDVSA from privatization, the company itself is only a holding company, and its subsidiaries that actually produce the oil are not protected from privatization. The 2001 hydrocarbon law does require a majority shareholding by the state in any joint ventures for exploration and production, however.

6. Chávez, conversations with the author, Miraflores Palace, June and July 2002.

7. Latinobarometer polls support these findings. They show that from 1995 to 2001 a strong majority of Venezuelans consistently said that democracy is preferable to any other kinds of government, with averages in the midrange for Latin America, whereas a relatively small minority contended that in certain circumstances an authoritarian government can be preferable to a democratic one. The answers to the first question have ranged from 60 percent to 64 percent since 1995, with a slight dip in 2001 to 57 percent. The answers to the second question have ranged from 17 percent to 25 percent since 1995, again in the midrange for Latin America (cited in Alarm Call, 2001).

8. Jonathan Hartlyn (2002) notes a convergence in the literature around the idea that Latin America is now full of persisting "unconsolidated democracies" or "informally institutionalized polyarchies." Furthermore, consolidation is no longer seen as unidirectional—democracy inevitably leading to its consolidation in positive terms; instead, countries may consolidate incomplete democracy or may never consolidate some aspects of democracy.

9. Oxhorn (2000) analyzes the shrinking of the public sphere that connects state to society and allows citizens to influence policy making. Traditional forms of representation and aggregation of interests—political parties and unions—have lost their bearings in the neoliberal economic revolution. McConnell and McCoy (2001) conclude that the diagnosis of Latin America's low-quality democracies is based in the erosion of the transmission belts between the state and society. Citizens organize in new ways, but governments become suspicious and afraid of a critical civil society.

10. O'Donnell (1994) contrasts representative democracies with delegative democracies, in which a president relies on an election mandate (vertical accountability) to govern as he sees fit, appealing directly to the people for support and ignoring checks and balances and representative institutions (horizontal accountability). Delegative democracies tend to emerge in times of economic and social crisis in newly democratizing countries and an enduring set of existing democracies, which have "no imminent threat of an open authoritarian regression, nor advances toward institutionalized representatives" in sight (O'Donnell, 1994: 4–5).

Ken Roberts (2000) fears that current-day Latin American democracy has recreated conditions for the reemergence of populism as part of a bid for political inclusion. Whether it is labeled populism, neopopulism, "delegative democracy," Caesarism, or plebiscitarianism, Roberts asserts that the reemergence of political leaders who mobilize mass support while bypassing representative institutions and suppressing checks and balances (i.e., neopopulism) has serious implications for democratic governance in Latin America.

11. For a superb analysis of the Chávez administration thinking on oil policy, see Mommer, 2003.

12. Although a majority would vote against Chávez in a recall referendum, in mid-2002 polls indicated that Chávez would win a plurality against a divided opposition in a single round election (Datanalisis, 2002a). For this reason, some in the opposition began to push the notion of a second-round election, requiring a runoff if no candidate won more than 50 percent in the first round, since polling showed that some candidates could beat Chávez in a two-person race.

13. A June 2002 poll by Datanalisis showed that Chávez had fallen precipitously in the evaluation of his efforts to improve the well-being of the country, from 4.89 (on a scale of 2 to 5) in February 1999 to 2.63 in June 2002. His hard-core support also declined dramatically from 74 percent who gave him an evaluation of good or very good in 1999 to only 20 percent in June 2002, while his hard-core critics rose from 2 percent in February 1999 to 58.5 percent in 2002 (Datanalisis, 2002a). Furthermore, although the positive evaluations of Chávez declined across the board after the short-lived coup of April 2002, the biggest drop occurred within the poorest quintile, from 55 percent in April to 39 percent in June 2002.

14. A July 2002 poll by Alfredo Keller showed that the poorest Venezuelans were split on the question of whether they would vote for Chávez (35%) or another candidate (44%) if elections were held then. In contrast, the highest class was unanimous in its rejection of Chávez as a candidate (Keller, 2002).

15. Likewise, a September 2003 poll by Mercanalisis showed the poorest strata (E) split at 42 percent self-identifying as *chavista,* 33 percent as anti-*chavista,* and 21 percent netural, while working-class respondents (D) were 31 percent pro-*chavista,* 48 percent anti-*chavista,* and 19 percent neutral; upper-middle-class respondents (ABC) were 16 percent *chavista,* 57 percent anti-*chavista,* and 24 percent neutral.

16. Hugo Chávez, conversations with the author, November 2003.

Epilogue

1. Methods attempted by the opposition during this period included multiple mass marches to demand the president's resignation, a short-lived coup in April 2002, a nonbinding recall referendum effort, a campaign to change the constitution in order to

secure early elections, public protests by active duty military officers and a two month strike by petroleum workers.

2. See "Agreement of the Forum for Negotiation and Agreement in Venezuela," 23 May 2003, www.cartercenter.org/doc1338.htm.

3. Data are from Datanalisis, See Datanalisis C.A., 2004. Polling carried out by the U.S. firm Greenberg, Quinlan, Rosner for the opposition found similar numbers and the same trend line. Data from both polling firms were provided to the authors.

Glossary

Banco del Pueblo. People's Bank.

bolivar. The Venezuelan currency.

Bolivarian Revolution. Revolución Bolivariana; designation for Hugo Chávez's popular movement

caracazo. Urban riots that began in Caracas and spread to other large cities in February 1989.

Casa Amarilla. "Yellow House"; the Foreign Ministry.

chavismo. Alternative designation for the popular movement centered around the personality of President Hugo Chávez Frías.

chavistas. Supporters of President Hugo Chávez Frías.

Círculos Bolivarianos. Bolivarian Circles; state-sponsored neighborhood- or community-based associations that defend the Bolivarian Revolution or provide assistance to the urban poor (or both).

Convergencia. Convergencia Nacional (National Convergence). Political movement founded in 1993 by Rafael Caldera.

Coordinadora Democrática. Democratic Coordinator; an umbrella organization that includes the CTV, FEDECAMARAS, political parties, and civil society organizations.

criollo. In colonial times, a person of purely Spanish descent, born in the New World. Used by President Hugo Chávez Frías to describe the ruling elite that exploited the poor during Punto Fijo.

The Fifth Republic. Term used to define the ruling political regime after January 1, 2000, when the constitution of 1999 entered into force.

golpe(s). Coup(s) d'état.

Guardia Nacional. The National Guard; a militarized national police.

guerrillero. A member of a guerrilla group.

Maraven. The operating affiliate of PDVSA dominated by operations established by Royal Dutch Shell.

Miraflores. Term used to describe the business office of the president, as distinct from his residence (La Casona).

Opina. Opinión Nacional (National Opinion).

Pact of Punto Fijo. A cluster of power-sharing agreements designed to maintain democracy after the fall of Pérez Jiménez in 1958. Adherents included AD, COPEI, URD, and FEDECAMARAS.

Plan Bolívar 2000. A project designed by Chávez whereby military personnel and sometimes short-term hired civilians would provide direct services in poor areas.

Podemos. "We Can"—political party composed of leaders of Movimiento al Socialismo who refused to break with the Chávez government in 2002.

rancho. Makeshift housing in the urban slums, often constructed illegally by squatters.

República Bolivariana de Venezuela. Bolivarian Republic of Venezuela. New name of the country under the 1999 constitution.

situado constitucional. Constitutional budget. Constitutionally mandated allocations from the national treasury to the budgets of state and local governments.

the soberano. The people; this is the way President Chávez refers to the people.

Tribunal Supremo de Justicia. Supreme Court of Justice in the Fifth Republic.

Trienio. Democratic experiment that lasted between1945 and 1948.

Unión. Union; political party presided over by Francisco Árias Cárdenas, the presidential candidate defeated by Hugo Chávez in the mega-elections of July 30, 2000.

References

Acedo, Alfredo. (1992). El Fondo de Compensación Territorial. In Rafael de la Cruz (ed.), *Descentralización, Gobernabilildad, Democracia.* Caracas: Nueva Sociedad–COPRE–UNDP.

Agüero, Felipe. (1993). Las Fuerzas Armadas y el Debilitamiento de la Democracia en Venezuela. In Andrés Serbin, Andrés Stambouli, Jennifer McCoy, and William Smith (eds.), *Venezuela: La Democracia Bajo Presión.* Caracas: INVESP, North-South Center (University of Miami) and Nueva Sociedad.

———. (1995). Crisis and Decay of Democracy in Venezuela: The Civil-Military Dimension. In Jennifer McCoy, Andrés Serbin, William C. Smith, and Andrés Stambouli (eds.), *Venezuelan Democracy under Stress.* Coral Gables, Fla.: North-South Center at the University of Miami.

An Alarm Call for Latin America's Democrats. (2001). *Economist,* July 26.

Alexander, Robert J. (1964). *The Venezuelan Democratic Revolution.* New Brunswick, N.J.: Rutgers University Press.

———. (1969). *The Communist Party of Venezuela.* Stanford, Calif.: Hoover Institution Press.

———. (1982). *Rómulo Betancourt and the Transformation of Venezuela.* New Brunswick, N.J.: Transaction Books.

Álvarez, Ángel. (1996). La Crisis de Hegemonía de los Partidos Políticos Venezolanos. In Ángel Álvarez (ed.), *El Sistema Político Venezolano: Crisis y Transformaciones.* Caracas: Instituto de Estudios Políticos, Universidad Central de Venezuela.

———. (2000). Modelo de Democracia y Sistema de Partidos en el Nuevo Diseño del Sistema Político Venezolano. Paper presented at the XXII International Congress of the Latin American Studies Association, Miami, Florida.

The Ambitions of Hugo Chávez. (2000). *New York Times,* November 6.

Amerson, Robert. (1995). *How Democracy Triumphed over Dictatorship: Public Diplomacy in Venezuela.* Washington, D.C.: American University Press.

Ball M., Carlos A. (1992). Venezuela: El Triste Caso de un Gobierno Rico y un País Paupérrimo. In Barry B. Levine (comp.), *El Desafío Neoliberal: El Fin del Tercermundismo en América Latina.* Caracas: Grupo Editorial Norma.

Baloyra, Enrique A., and John D. Martz. (1979). *Political Attitudes in Venezuela: Social Cleavages and Political Opinion.* Austin: University of Texas Press.

Baptista, Asdrúbal. (1991). *Bases Cuantitativas de la Economía Venezolana: 1830–1990.* Caracas: Ediciones Corporativas.

Bartolini, Stefano, and Peter Mair. (1990). *Identity, Competition, and Electoral Availability: The Stabilization of European Electorates, 1885–1985.* Cambridge: Cambridge University Press.

Betancourt, Rómulo. (1956). *Venezuela: Política y Petróleo.* Mexico: Fondo de Cultura Económica, Sección de Obras de Política.

Bigler, Gene. (1981). *La Política y el Capitalismo de Estado en Venezuela.* Madrid: Editorial Tecnos.

Brewer-Carías, Allan R. (1988). Commentary. In Robert A. Goldwin and Art Kaufman (eds.), *Constitution Makers on Constitution Making: The Experience of Eight Nations.* Washington, D.C.: American Enterprise Institute for Public Policy Research.

———. (1994). *Report of the Minister of State for Decentralization.* Caracas: Editorial Arte.

Brewer-Carías, Allan R., and Carlos M. Ayala Corao. (1990). *Leyes para la Descentralización Política de la Federación.* Caracas: Editorial Jurídica Venezolana.

Bruni Celli, Josefina. (1995). *El Efecto Redistributivo del Situado Constitucional en Venezuela.* Caracas: IESA.

Buque Cargado de Alimentos Llega el Viernes a la Guaira desde Colombia. (2003). *El Universal,* January 13.

Burggraff, Winfield J., and Richard L. Millet. (1995). More than Failed Coups: The Crisis in Venezuelan Civil-Military Relations. In Louis W. Goodman, Johanna Mendelson Forman, Moisés Naím, Joseph S. Tulchin, and Gary Bland (eds.), *Lessons of the Venezuelan Experience.* Washington, D.C.: Woodrow Wilson Center Press.

Burton, Michael G., Richard Gunther, and John Higley. (1992). Introduction: Elite Transformations and Democratic Regimes. In John Higley and Richard Gunther (eds.), *Elites and Democratic Consolidation in Latin America and Southern Europe.* London: Cambridge University Press.

Burton, Michael G., and John Higley. (1987). Elite Settlements. *American Sociological Review* 52(3): 295–307.

Buxton, Julia. (2001). *The Failure of Political Reform in Venezuela.* Aldershot, United Kingdom: Ashgate.

Caldera, Rafael. (1999). *Los Causahabientes de Carabobo a Punto Fijo.* Caracas: Punapo.

Camel Anderson, Eduardo. (2002). Venamcham Denuncia Terrorismo de Estado Contra el Empresariado. *El Universal,* January 23.

———. (2003). Reducción de Nómina en PDVSA se Acerca a 50%. *El Universal.* March 1.

Camel Anderson, Eduardo, and Mónica Castro. (2002). Buques Siguen en Conflicto. *El Universal,* December 20.

Canache, Damarys. (2002). *Venezuela: Public Opinion and Protest in a Fragile Democracy.* Coral Gables, Fla.: North-South Center at the University of Miami.

Capriles, Ruth, ed. (1992). *Diccionario de la Corrupción en Venezuela.* Vol. 3, 1984–1992. Caracas: Consorcio de Ediciones Capriles C.A.

Capriles Ayala, Carlos, and Rafael del Naranco. (1992). *Todos los Golpes.* Caracas: Consorcio de Ediciones Capriles C.A.

Caracas Practicará Politica Cooperativa. (2000). *El Universal,* December 5.

Cardona Marrero, Rodolfo. (2000). Relanzan PB2000 el 27 de Febrero. *El Universal Digital,* February 14.

———. (2002). Alto Mando Modificó Nueva LOFAN. *El Universal,* May 30.

Cardozo de Da Silva, Elsa. (1992). *Continuidad y Consistencia en Quince Años de Política Exterior Venezolana, 1969–1984.* Caracas: CDCH-UCV.

Carothers, Thomas. (2002). The End of the Transitions Paradigm. *Journal of Democracy* 13(1): 5–21.

Carrasquero, José Vicente, and Friedrich Welsch. (2001). ¿Revolución en Democracia o Retorno al Caudillismo? In José Vicente Carrasquero, Thais Maigon, and Friedrich Welsch (eds.), *Venezuela en Transición: Elecciones y Democracia, 1998–2000*. Caracas: REDPOL.

Cartaya, Vanessa, and Yolanda D'Elia. (1991). *Pobreza en Venezuela: Realidades y Políticas.* Caracas: CESAP-CISOR.

Casas, Cenovia. (2000). Chávez: Las Relaciones con EE.UU. Están Condenadas a Ser Buenas. *El Nacional,* November 7.

Chávez, Hugo, and the Comisión Presidencial Constituyente. (1999). Ideas Fundamentales para la Constitución Bolivariana de la V República. Draft. Caracas, August 5.

Chávez at Bay. (2002). *Economist,* May 2.

CISFEM-UNICEF (Centro de Investigación Social, Formación, y Estadios de la Mujer–United Nations Children's Fund). (1992). *Situación de la Mujer en Venezuela.* Caracas: Miguel Ángel García e Hijo.

Civit, Jesús, and Luis Pedro España. (1989). Análisis Sociopolítico a Partir del Estallido del 27 de Febrero. *Cuadernos del Cendes* 10:35–46.

Cohen, Jean, and Andrew Arato. (2000). *Sociedad Civil y Teoría Política.* Mexico City: FCE.

Collier, David, and Steven Levitsky. (1997). Democracy with Adjectives: Conceptual Innovation in Comparative Research. *World Politics* 49 (April): 430–51.

Colomine, Luisana. (2000). Militares Activos no Deben Optar a Elección Popular. *El Universal Digital,* March 1.

Conferencia Episcopal Venezolana. (1994). *Encuentro Nacional de la Sociedad Civil.* Caracas: Conferencia Episcopal Venezolana.

Conniff, Michael F. (1999). *Populism in Latin America.* Tuscaloosa: University of Alabama Press.

Consejo Nacional Electoral. (1999). Elecciones 99. Caracas.

Consejo Supremo Electoral. (1987). *Los Partidos Políticos y sus Estadísticas Electorales, 1946–1984.* Caracas: Consejo Supremo Electoral.

———. (1990). *Elecciones 1989.* Caracas: Consejo Supremo Electoral.

———. (1994). Elecciones 1993. Mimeograph.

Consultores 21 S.A. (1996). Cultura Democrática en Venezuela: Informe Analítico de Resultados. January. Caracas: Consultores S.A.

———. (2003). Encuesta Nacional de Opinión Pública: Estratas Sociales CDE. November. Caracas: Consultores S.A.

Converse, Philip E., and Georges Dupeux. (1962). Politicization of the Electorate in France and the United States. *Public Opinion Quarterly* 26(1): 1–23.

Coppedge, Michael. (1994). *Strong Parties and Lame Ducks: Presidential Patriarchy and Factionalism in Venezuela.* Stanford, Calif.: Stanford University Press.

CORDIPLAN (Oficina Central de Coordinación y Planificación). (1991). Efectos Fiscales de la Descentralización. Mimeo.

Coronil, Fernando. (1997). *The Magical State: Nature, Money, and Modernity in Venezuela.* Chicago: University of Chicago Press.

Coronil, Fernando, and Julie Skurski. (1991). Dismembering and Remembering the Nation: The Semantics of Political Violence in Venezuela. *Comparative Studies in Society and History* 33:288–337.

Cortés, Adriana. (2000). Tormenta en Amazonas por Denuncias de Irregularidades en Plan Bolívar. *El Nacional,* September 4.

Crisp, Brian F. (1997). Presidential Behavior in a System with Strong Parties: Venezuela, 1958–1995. In Scott Mainwaring and Matthew Shugart (eds.), *Presidentialism and Democracy in Latin America.* Cambridge: Cambridge University Press.

——. (2000a). *Democratic Institutional Design: The Powers and Incentives of Venezuelan Politicians and Interest Groups.* Stanford, Calif.: Stanford University Press.

——. (2000b). Institutional Rules and Legislative Entrepreneurship in Colombia and Venezuela. Paper presented at the XXII International Congress of the Latin American Studies Association, Miami, Florida.

Crisp, Brian F., Daniel H. Levine, and Juan Carlos Rey. (1995). The Legitimacy Problem. In Jennifer McCoy, Andrés Serbin, William C. Smith, and Andrés Stambouli (eds.), *Venezuelan Democracy under Stress.* Coral Gables, Fla.: North-South Center at the University of Miami.

Dahl, Robert A. (1971). *Polyarchy: Participation and Opposition.* New Haven: Yale University Press.

——. (1989). *Democracy and Its Critics.* New Haven: Yale University Press.

——. (1998). *On Democracy.* New Haven: Yale University Press.

Dalton, Russell. (2000). The Decline of Party Identifications. In Russell Dalton and Martin Wattenberg (eds.), *Parties without Partisans: Political Change in Advanced Industrial Democracies.* Oxford: Oxford University Press.

Dalton, Russell, and Martin Wattenberg. (1993). The Not So Simple Act of Voting. In Ada Finifter (ed.), *Political Science: The State of the Discipline.* Washington, D.C.: American Political Science Association.

Datanalisis, C.A. (1990–98). Encuesta Nacional Ómnibus de Opinión Pública.

——. (1997 and 1998). Caracas Surveys for the City Mayor.

——. (2000). Encuesta Nacional de Opinión Pública.

——. (2002a). Encuesta Nacional de Opinión Pública. June.

——. (2002b). Venezuela una Vision del Entomo. July.

——. (2003). Encuesta Nacional Ómnibus. May. Retrieved from Datanalisis, C.A., Web site: www.datanalisis.com/publicaciones.

——. (2004). Encuestra Nacional Ómnibus. August.

Datos, C.A. (1995). *Pulso Nacional.* National survey carried out between September 6 and 27, 1995. Caracas: Datos C.A.

de la Cruz, Rafael, ed. (1992a). *Descentralización, Gobernabilidad, Democracia.* Caracas: Nueva Sociedad–COPRE–UNDP.

——. 1992b. La Estrategia de la Descentralización en Venezuela. In Rafael de la Cruz (ed.), *Descentralización, Gobernabilidad, Democracia.* Caracas: Nueva Sociedad–COPRE–UNDP.

——. (1998). *Descentralización en Perspectiva.* Caracas: IESA.

Designado Manuel Rosendo al Frente del Cufan. (2003). *El Universal Digital,* August 26.

Diamond, Larry. (1994). Toward Democratic Consolidation. *Journal of Democracy* 3:4–17.

——. (1999). *Developing Democracy: Toward Consolidation.* Baltimore: Johns Hopkins University Press.

——. (2002). Thinking about Hybrid Regimes. *Journal of Democracy* 13(2): 21–35.

Diamond, Larry, Jonathan Hartlyn, and Juan J. Linz. (1999). Introduction: Politics,

Society, and Democracy in Latin America. In Larry Diamond, Jonathan Hartlyn, Juan J. Linz, and Seymour Martin Lipset (eds.), *Democracy in Developing Countries: Latin America*, 2nd ed. Boulder, Colo.: Lynne Rienner Publishers.

Doyle, Joseph. (1967). Venezuela 1958: The Transition from Dictatorship to Democracy. Ph.D. diss., George Washington University.

Duarte, Alejandro. (1999). Nueva Constitución Eliminará Carácter no Deliberante de las FAN. *El Nacional*, September 19.

Duno, Pedro. (1975). *Los Doce Apóstoles*. Caracas: Vadel Hermanos.

Easton, David. (1966). *Comparative Politics: A Developmental Approach*. Boston: Little, Brown.

EcoNatura. (1993). *Directorio de Organizaciones Ambientales No Gubernamentales de Venezuela*. Caracas: Impresos Raga.

ECLAC (Economic Commission for Latin America and the Caribbean). (1997). *Social Panorama of Latin America*. New York: United Nations.

EE.UU. No Compara a Chávez con Castro. (2000). *El Nacional*, November 3.

El Gobierno Debe Aclarar Cómo Financia Plan Bolívar 2000. (1999). *El Nacional*, September 12.

Ellner, Steve. (1988). *Venezuela's Movimiento al Socialismo: From Guerrilla Defeat to Innovative Politics*. Durham, N.C.: Duke University Press.

——. (1993). *Organized Labor in Venezuela, 1958–91: Behavior and Concerns in a Democratic Setting*. Wilmington, Del.: SR Books.

——. (1997). Recent Venezuelan Political Studies: A Return to Third World Realities. *Latin American Research Review* 32:201–18.

——. (1999). The Heyday of Radical Populism in Venezuela and Its Aftermath. In Michael E. Conniff (ed.), *Populism in Latin America*. Tuscaloosa: University of Alabama Press.

Ellner, Steve, and Daniel Hellinger, eds. (2003). *Class, Polarization, and Conflict in the Chávez Era*. Boulder, Colo.: Lynne Rienner Publishers.

Ewell, Judith. (1993). Venezuela in Crisis. *Current History* 92:120–25.

——. (1996). *Venezuela and the United States: From Monroe's Hemisphere to Petroleum's Empire*. Athens: University of Georgia Press.

Fishbach, Nora. (2000). Análisis al Documento "Estudios Económico de América Latina: El Caribe 1988–1999." Mimeo.

Fossi, Victor. (1984). Desarrollo Urbano y Vivienda: La Desordenada Evolución Hacia un País de Metropolis. In Moisés Naím and Ramón Piñango (eds.), *El Caso Venezuela: Una Ilusión de Armonía*. Caracas: Ediciones IESA.

Francés, Antonio, and Moisés Naím. (1995). The Venezuelan Private Sector: From Courting the State to Courting the Market. In Louis W. Goodman, Johanna Mendelson Forman, Moisés Naím, Joseph S. Tulchin, and Gary Bland (eds.), *Lessons of the Venezuelan Experience*. Washington, D.C.: Woodrow Wilson Center Press.

Freire, Mila, coord. (1992). *Venezuela: Public Administration Study*. Washington, D.C.: World Bank.

Friedmann, John. (1965). *Venezuela: From Doctrine to Dialogue*. Syracuse, N.Y.: Syracuse University Press.

Galicia, Hernán Lugo. (2000a). Asamblea Nacional Define Hoy Integración de Comisiones. *El Nacional*, September 6.

——. (2000b). El Polo Patriótico Busca su Razón de Ser. *El Nacional*, July 12.

Gallegos, Rómulo. (1948). *Doña Bárbara.* New York: Peter Smith.
García-Guadilla, María Pilar, ed. (1991). Ambiente, Estado y Sociedad. Caracas: Universidad Simón Bolívar and Cendes.
———. (1992). The Venezuelan Ecology Movement: Symbolic Effectiveness, Social Practices, and Political Strategies. In Arturo Escobar and Sonia Alvarez (eds.), *The Making of Social Movements in Latin America.* Boulder, Colo.: Westview Press.
Garrido, Alberto. (1999). *Guerrilla y Conspiración Militar en Venezuela.* Caracas: Fondo Editorial Nacional.
———. (2000). *La Historia Secreta de la Revolución Bolivariana.* Mérida: Editorial Venezolana.
Gellner, Ernest. (1996). *Conditions of Liberty: Civil Society and Its Rivals.* New York: Penguin Books.
Gil Yepes, José Antonio. (1978). *El Reto de las Élites.* Madrid: Editorial Tecnos.
———. (1981). *The Challenge of Venezuelan Democracy.* New Brunswick, N.J.: Transaction Books.
Gilbert, Alan. (1981). Pirates and Invaders: Land Acquisition in Urban Colombia and Venezuela. *World Development* 9:657–78.
Giugale, Marcelo, and Steven Webb, eds. (2000). *Achievements and Challenges of Fiscal Decentralization: Lessons from Mexico.* Washington, D.C.: World Bank.
Giusti, Roberto. (2002). El 71% del País Rechaza a Chávez. *El Universal,* November 3.
Gómez Calcaño, Luis. (1987). Los Movimientos Sociales: Democracia Emergente en el Sistema Político Venezolano. In J. A. Silva Michelena (ed.), *Venezuela hacia el 2000: Desafíos y Opciones.* Caracas: Nueva Sociedad–ILDIS.
———. (1998). Civic Organization and Reconstruction of Democratic Legitimacy in Venezuela. In Damarys Canache and Michael R. Kulisheck (eds.), *Reinventing Legitimacy: Democracy and Political Change in Venezuela.* Westport, Conn.: Greenwood Press.
Gómez Calcaño, Luis, and Thanalí Patruyo. (2000). Entre la Esperanza Popular y la Crisis Económica: Transición Política en Venezuela. *Cuadernos del Cendes* 17:199–246.
González, David. (2003). Dispersaron con Bombas Lacrimógenas Nueva Marcha Opositora en Los Próceres. *El Nacional,* January 13.
González, Rosa Amelia, ed. (1998). El Sector sin Fines de Lucro en Venezuela. Mimeo.
———. (2000). Organizaciones Ciudadanas no Pueden Pretender Reemplazar al Estado. *El Nacional,* June 19.
Goodman, Louis W., Johanna Mendelson Forman, Moisés Naím, Joseph S. Tulchin, and Gary Bland, eds. (1995). *Lessons of the Venezuelan Experience.* Washington, D.C.: Woodrow Wilson Center Press.
Gott, Richard. (2000). *In the Shadow of the Liberator: Hugo Chávez and the Transformation of Venezuela.* London: Verso.
Granier, Marcel, and J. A. Gil Yepes. (1987). *Más y Mejor Democracia.* 2nd ed. Caracas: Cromotys.
Gruson, Alberto. (1993). Las Disparidades en las Condiciones de Vida de la Población de Venezuela. *Socioscopio* 1:25–61.
Guenther, Roth, and Claus Wittich, eds. (1979). *Max Weber, Economy and Society: An Outline of Interpretative Sociology.* Berkeley and Los Angeles: University of California Press.

Guerón, Eva Josko de. (1983). La Formulación y Ejecución de la Política Exterior como un Problema en la Agenda. In *La Agenda de la Política Exterior de Venezuela.* Caracas: Instituto de Estudios Políticos, Universidad Central de Venezuela.

———. (1992). Cambio y Continuidad en la Política Exterior de Venezuela: Una Revisión. In Carlos A. Romero (ed.), *Reforma y Política Exterior en Venezuela.* Caracas: Instituto de Estudios Sociales y Políticos and Nueva Sociedad.

Hartlyn, Jonathan. (2002). Democracy and Consolidation in Contemporary Latin America: Current Thinking and Future Challenges. In Joseph Tulchin (ed.), *Democratic Governance and Social Inequality.* Boulder, Colo.: Lynne Rienner Publishers.

Hausmann, Ricardo. (1995). *Shocks Externos y Ajuste Macroeconómico.* Caracas: Banco Central de Venezuela.

Hellinger, Daniel H. (1991). *Venezuela: Tarnished Democracy.* Boulder, Colo.: Westview Press.

Herrera Campíns, Luis. (1977). Transición Política. In J. L. Salcedo Bastardo, *1958 [i.e. Mil Novecientos Cincuenta y Ocho]: Tránsito de la Dicdadura a la Democracia en Venezuela.* Barcelona: Editorial Ariel.

Higley, John, and Michael G. Burton. (1989). The Elite Variable in Democratic Transitions and Breakdowns. *American Sociological Review* 54(1): 17–32.

Higley, John, Michael G. Burton, and G. Lowell Field. (1990). In Defense of Elite Theory: A Reply to Cammack. *American Sociological Review* 55(3): 421–26.

Hillman, Richard S. (1994). *Democracy for the Privileged: Crisis and Transition in Venezuela.* Boulder, Colo.: Lynne Rienner Publishers.

Huizi Clavier, Rafael. (2000). Si Estamos Amenazados. *El Nacional,* June 18.

Huntington, Samuel. (1991). *The Third Wave: Democratization in the Late Twentieth Century.* Norman: University of Oklahoma Press.

Inter-American Development Bank (IDB). (1995). *Economic and Social Progress in Latin America, Report: Overcoming Volatility.* Washington, D.C.: IDB.

International Monetary Fund. (1990–99). *Government Finance Statistics Yearbook: 1990–99.* Washington, D.C.: IMF.

Jácome, Francine. (2000). Venezuela: Old Successes, New Constraints on Learning. In Jennifer L. McCoy (ed.), *Political Learning and Redemocratization in Latin America: Do Politicians Learn from Political Crises?* Coral Gables, Fla.: North-South Center at the University of Miami.

Janssens, Armando. (1997). La Participación de la Sociedad Civil Organizada en el Quehacer Público de Nuestro País. Mimeo. Caracas.

Jeréz, Ariel, ed. (1997). *¿Trabajo Voluntario o Participación? Elementos para una Sociología del Tercer Sector.* Madrid: Editorial Tecnos.

Karl, Terry Lynn. (1987). Petroleum and Political Pacts: The Transition to Democracy in Venezuela. *Latin American Research Review* 22:63–94.

———. (1995). The Venezuelan Petro-State and the Crisis of "Its" Democracy. In Jennifer McCoy, Andrés Serbin, William C. Smith, and Andrés Stambouli (eds.), *Venezuelan Democracy under Stress.* Coral Gables, Fla.: North-South Center at the University of Miami.

———. (1997). *The Paradox of Plenty: Oil Booms and Petro-States.* Berkeley and Los Angeles: University of California Press.

Keane, John. (1992). *Democracia y Sociedad Civil.* Madrid: Alianza Editorial.

Keller, Alfredo. (2002). *Encuesta Nacional de Opinión Pública*. Caracas: Keller and Associates.

Kelly, Janet. (1995). The Question of Inefficiency and Inequality: Social Policy in Venezuela. In Louis W. Goodman, Johanna Mendelson Forman, Moisés Naím, Joseph S. Tulchin, and Gary Bland (eds.), *Lessons of the Venezuelan Experience.* Washington, D.C.: Woodrow Wilson Center Press.

———. (2000). Thoughts on the Constitution: Realignment of Ideas about the Economy and Changes in the Political System in Venezuela. Paper presented at the XXII International Congress of the Latin American Studies Association, Miami, Florida.

Kelly, Janet, and Carlos A. Romero. (2002). *The United States and Venezuela: Rethinking Relationship.* New York: Routledge.

Kiewiet, Roderick. (1983). *Macroeconomics and Micropolitics: The Electoral Effects of Economic Issues.* Chicago: Chicago University Press.

Kinder, Donald R., and Roderick Kiewiet. (1979). Economic Discontent and Political Behavior: The Role of Personal Grievances and Collective Economic Judgments in Congressional Voting. *American Journal of Political Science* 11:29–61.

Kirchheimer, Otto. (1966). The Transformation of West European Party Systems. In Joseph La Palombara and Miron Weiner (eds.), *Political Parties and Political Development*. Princeton, N.J.: Princeton University Press.

Klarén, Peter F., and Thomas J. Bossert. (1986). *Promise of Development: Theories of Change in Latin America.* Boulder, Colo.: Westview Press.

Kornblith, Miriam. (1995). Public Sector and Private Sector: New Rules of the Game. In Jennifer McCoy, Andrés Serbin, William C. Smith, and Andrés Stambouli (eds.), *Venezuelan Democracy under Stress.* Coral Gables, Fla.: North-South Center at the University of Miami.

———. (1998). Legitimacy and Reform Agenda in Venezuela. In Damarys Canache and Michael R. Kulisheck (eds.), *Reinventing Legitimacy: Democracy and Political Change in Venezuela.* Westport, Conn.: Greenwood Press.

Kornblith, Miriam, and Thais Maingon. (1984). *Estado y Gasto Público en Venezuela, 1936–1980.* Caracas: Universidad Central de Venezuela.

Krivoy, Ruth. (2000). *Collapse: The Venezuelan Banking Crisis of 1994.* Washington: Group of Thirty.

Kulisheck, Michael R. (1996). Placebo or Potent Medicine? Electoral Reform and Political Behavior in Venezuela. Paper presented at the conference Compromised Legitimacy? Assessing the Crisis of Democracy in Venezuela. Caracas.

Laakso, Markku, and Rein Taagepera. (1979). Effective Number of Parties: A Measure with Application to West Europe. *Comparative Political Studies* 12:3–27.

LaFranchi, Howard. (1999). Neo-Nazi Rhetoric. *Christian Science Monitor,* September 11.

Lagos, Marta. (2003). A Road with no Return. *Journal of Democracy* 14:163–73.

Lanza, Eloy. (1980). *El Sub-Imperialismo Venezolano.* Caracas: Fondo Editorial Carlos Aponte.

La Rotta Morán, Alicia. (2000). Dividen el Litoral en Diez Campamentos de Seguridad. *El Universal Digital,* January 10.

Lastra Veracierto, Rafael. (2000). No Cesan los Saqueos a la Propiedad Privada. *El Universal Digital,* February 3.

Leal, Adela. (1999). Chávez Anunciará el Viernes Plan Cívico-Militar de Desarrollo. *El Nacional,* February 8.

Levine, Daniel H. (1973). *Conflict and Political Change in Venezuela.* Princeton, N.J.: Princeton University Press.

———. (1994). Good-by to Venezuelan Exceptionalism. *Journal of Interamerican Studies and World Affairs* 36:145–82.

———. (1998a). Beyond the Exhaustion of the Model: Survival and Transformation of Democracy in Venezuela. In Damarys Canache and Michael R. Kulisheck (eds.), *Reinventing Legitimacy: Democracy and Political Change in Venezuela.* Westport, Conn.: Greenwood Press.

———. (1998b). Civic Organization and Reconstruction of Democratic Legitimacy in Venezuela. In Damarys Canache and Michael R. Kulisheck (eds.), *Reinventing Legitimacy: Democracy and Political Change in Venezuela.* Westport, Conn.: Greenwood Press.

Levine, Daniel H., and Brian F. Crisp. (1995). Legitimacy, Governability, and Institutions in Venezuela. In Louis W. Goodman, Johanna Mendelson Forman, Moisés Naím, Joseph S. Tulchin, and Gary Bland (eds.), *Lessons of the Venezuelan Experience.* Washington, D.C.: Woodrow Wilson Center Press.

Levitsky, Steven, and Lucan Way. (2002). The Rise of Competitive Authoritarianism. *Journal of Democracy* 13(2): 51–65.

Lewis-Beck, Michael S. (1990). *Economics and Elections: The Major Western Democracies.* Ann Arbor: University of Michigan Press.

Lijphart, Arend. (1984). Democracies: Patterns of Majoritarian and Consensus Governments in Twenty-One Countries. New Haven: Yale University Press.

Linares, Gustavo. (1992). Instrumentos Legales para Avanzar en la Descentralización. In Rafael de la Cruz (ed.), *Descentralización, Gobernabilidad, Democracia.* Caracas: Nueva Sociedad–COPRE–UNDP.

Lombardi, John V. (2003). Prologue: Venezuela's Permanent Dilemma. In Steve Ellner and Daniel Hellinger (eds.), *Class, Polarization, and Conflict in the Chávez Era.* Boulder, Colo.: Lynne Rienner Publishers.

López, Edgar. (2000a). La Contraloría Debe Investigar Uso de Recursos para la Reconstrucción de Vargas. *El Nacional,* November 18.

———. (2000b). Madre y Esposa de un Desaparecido Acusan a Grupo de Paracaidistas. *El Universal Digital,* January 21.

López, Odalis. (2001). La Enfermedad Holandesa y la Economía Venezolana: El Período 1973–1982 y el Colapso del Capitalismo Rentístico. *Revista Venezolana de Economía y Ciencias Sociales* 2:67–110

López Maya, Margarita.(1997). The Rise of Causa R in Venezuela. In Douglas Chalmers, Carlos M. Vilas, Katherine Hite, Scott B. Martin, Kerianne Priester, and Monique Segarra (eds.), *The New Politics of Inequality in Latin America.* Oxford: Oxford University Press.

Lowi, Theodore J. (1964). *At the Pleasure of the Mayor.* New York: Simon and Schuster.

———. (1972). Four Systems of Policy, Politics, and Choices. *Public Administration Review* 32(4): 298–310.

Mainwaring, Scott. (1999). *Rethinking Party Systems in the Third Wave of Democratization: The Case of Brazil.* Stanford, Calif.: Stanford University Press.

Mainwaring, Scott, and Timothy R. Scully. (1995). *Building Democratic Institutions: Party Systems in Latin America.* Stanford, Calif.: Stanford University Press.

Mainwaring, Scott, and Matthew Shugart. (1997). Conclusion: Presidentialism and the Party System. In Scott Mainwaring and Matthew Shugart (eds.), *Presidentialism and Democracy in Latin America.* Cambridge: Cambridge University Press.

Manrique, Miguel. (1996). *La Seguridad en las Fuerzas Armadas Venezolanas.* Caracas: Fondo Editorial Tropykos.

Maracara, Luisa Amelia. (1999). Gobernadores Pedirán a Chávez Reforma del FEM. *El Universal Digital,* June 30.

Márquez, Humberto. (2000). El Presidente Hugo Chávez Dejó Clara Posición de Venezuela. *El Nacional,* September 2.

Martínez, Eugenio. (2003). Rechazo Mayoritario. *El Universal.* www.eluniversal.com/2003/09/02/2003.

Martz, John D. (1966). *Acción Democrática: Evolution of a Modern Political Party in Venezuela.* Princeton, N.J.: Princeton University Press.

Martz, John D., and David Myers, eds. (1977). *Venezuela: The Democratic Experience.* New York: Praeger.

——. (1983). Understanding Latin American Politics: Analytic Models and Intellectual Traditions. *Polity* 16 (Winter): 215–41.

——. (1994). Political Parties and Technological Elites: The Professional Community in Venezuelan Politics. *Latin American Research Review* 29(1): 7–27.

Mascareño, Carlos, ed. (2000). *Balance de la Descentralización en Venezuela: Logros, Limitaciones y Perspectivas.* Caracas: PNUD, Nueva Sociedad, ILDIS.

Maso, Fausto. (2000). El Happening del Año. *El Nacional,* July 8.

Mayorca, Javier Ignacio. (2000a). Comisión de Defensa Rechaza Instauración de Nuevas Denominaciones para Generales. *El Nacional,* December 26.

——. (2000b). Comité Estratégico de la FAN Analiza Consecuencias del Plan. *El Nacional,* September 1.

——. (2000c). El Presidente: FAN Está Ganada para el Proceso Revolucionario. *El Nacional,* February 5.

——. (2000d). Min-Defensa Ordenó Revisar Anteproyecto de Ley de la FAN. *El Nacional,* March 10.

——. (2000e). Nueva Estructura de la FAN Consolida Poder Presidencial Sobre la Milicia. *El Nacional,* October 31.

McConnell, Shelley, and Jennifer McCoy. (2001). Making Democracy Meaningful in Latin America. Paper presented at the American Political Science Convention, San Francisco, August.

McCoy, Jennifer. (1985). *Democratic Dependent Development and State-Labor Relations.* Ph.D. diss., University of Minnesota.

——. (1987). The Politics of Adjustment: Labor and the Venezuelan State. *Journal of Interamerican Studies and World Affairs* 28(4): 103–38.

——. (1988). The State and the Democratic Class Compromise in Venezuela. *Journal of Developing Countries* 4(1): 85–104.

——. (1989). Venezuela: Labor and the State in a Party-Mediated Democracy: Institutional Change in Venezuela. *Latin American Research Review* 24(2): 35–68.

——. (1999). Chávez and the End of "Partyarchy" in Venezuela. *Journal of Democracy* 10(3): 64–77.

——. (2000). The Learning Process and Comparative Lessons. In Jennifer McCoy (ed.), *Political Learning and Redemocratization in Latin America: Do Politicians Learn from Political Crises?* Coral Gables, Fla.: North-South Center at the University of Miami.

McCoy, Jennifer, and Laura Neuman. (2001). Defining the Bolivarian Revolution: Hugo Chávez's Venezuela. *Current History* 100(643): 80–85.

McCoy, Jennifer, Andrés Serbin, William C. Smith, and Andrés Stambouli, eds. (1995). *Venezuelan Democracy under Stress.* Coral Gables, Fla.: North-South Center at the University of Miami.

Medina, Pablo. (1999). *Rebeliones.* Caracas: Corpográfica.

Molina, José Enrique. (1998). Electoral Systems and Democratic Legitimacy in Venezuela. In Damarys Canache and Michael R. Kulisheck (eds.), *Reinventing Legitimacy: Democracy and Political Change in Venezuela.* Westport, Conn.: Greenwood Press.

——. (2000). Comportamiento Electoral en Venezuela, 1998–2000: Cambio y Continuidad. *Cuestiones Políticas* 25:27–67.

——. (2002). The Presidential and Parliamentary Election of the Bolivarian Revolution in Venezuela: Change and Continuity (1998–2000). *Bulletin of Latin American Research* 21:219–47.

Molina, José Enrique, and Carmen Pérez. (1996). Los Procesos Electorales y la Evolución del Sistema de Partidos en Venezuela. In Ángel Álvarez (ed.), *El Sistema Político Venezolano: Crisis y Transformaciones.* Caracas: Instituto de Estudios Políticos, Universidad Central de Venezuela.

——. (1999). La Democracia Venezolana en Una Encrucijada: Las Elecciones Nacionales y Regionales de 1998. *América Latina Hoy* 21:29–40.

Mommer, Bernard. (2003). Subversive Oil. In Steve Ellner and Daniel Hellinger (eds), *Venezuelan Politics in the Chávez Era.* Boulder, Colo.: Lynne Rienner Publishers.

Monaldi Marturet, Francisco. (1999). El Novedoso Fondo para la Desestabilización: ¿Jugada Maestra del Presidente Chávez? *Venezuela Analítica* 3 (41). www.analitica.com.

Morse, Edward L., and James Richard. (2002). The Battle for Energy Dominance. *Foreign Affairs* 81(2): 16.

Myers, David J. (1977). The Venezuelan Party System: Regime Maintenance under Stress. In John Martz and David Myers (eds.), *Venezuela: The Democratic Experience,* rev. ed. New York: Praeger.

——. (1980). The Elections and the Evolution of Venezuela's Party System. In Howard Penniman (ed.), *Venezuela at the Polls. The National Elections of 1978.* Washington, D.C.: American Enterprise Institute for Public Policy Research.

——. (1993). Percepciones de una Democracia Bajo Presión: ¿Decadencia Inevitable o Refundación?" In Andrés Serbin, Andrés Stambouli, Jennifer McCoy, and William Smith (eds.), *Venezuela: La Democracia Bajo Presión.* Caracas: INVESP, North-South Center (University of Miami) and Nueva Sociedad.

——. (1994). The Emergence and Implications of Regularized Variation in Venezuelan Policy-Making during the Consolidation of Reconciliation Democracy. *MACLAS Latin American Essays* 7:173–95.

——. (1995). Perceptions of a Stressed Democracy: Inevitable Decay or Foundation for Rebirth? In Jennifer McCoy, Andrés Serbin, William C. Smith, and Andrés Stambouli (eds), *Venezuelan Democracy under Stress.* Coral Gables, Fla.: North-South Center at the University of Miami.

——. (1996). Venezuela: Shaping the New Democracy. In Howard J. Wiarda and Harvey F. Kline (eds.), *Latin American Politics and Development,* 4th ed. Boulder, Colo.: Westview Press.

——. (1998). Venezuela's Political Party System: Defining Events, Reactions and the Diluting of Structural Cleavages. *Party Politics* 4(4): 495–521.

Myers, David J., and John D. Martz. (1997). Political Culture Theory and the Role of Professionals: Data from Venezuela. *Comparative Political Studies* 30(7): 331–55.

Myers, David J., and Jennifer L. McCoy. (2003). Venezuela in the Gray Zone: From Feckless Pluralism to Dominant Power System. *Politeia* (Universidad Central de Venezuela) 30:41–74.

Myers, David J., and Robert E. O'Connor. (1998). Support for Coups in Democratic Political Culture: A Venezuelan Exploration. *Comparative Politics* 30(2): 193–212.

Naím, Moisés.(1984). La Empresa Privada en Venezuela: ¿Qué Pasa Cuando se Crece en Medio de la Riqueza y la Confusión? Mimeo.

——. (1993) *Paper Tigers and Minotaurs: The Politics of Venezuela's Economic Reforms.* Washington, D.C.: Carnegie Endowment.

——. (2001). The Real Story behind Venezuela's Woes. *Journal of Democracy* 12(2): 17–31.

Naím, Moisés, and Ramón Piñango, eds. (1985). *El Caso Venezuela: Una Ilusión de Armonía.* Caracas: Ediciones IESA.

Navarro, Juan Carlos. (1995). Venezuela's New Political Actors. In Louis W. Goodman, Johanna Mendelson Forman, Moisés Naím, Joseph S. Tulchin, and Gary Blands (eds.), *Lessons of the Venezuelan Experience.* Washington, D.C.: Woodrow Wilson Center Press.

Neuhouser, Kevin. (1992). Democratic Stability in Venezuela: Elite Consensus or Class Compromise? *American Sociological Review* 57(1): 117–35.

Newbery, David, and Joseph Stiglitz. (1981). *The Theory of Commodity Price Stabilization: A Study in the Economics of Risk.* Oxford: Clarendon Press.

The Next Fidel Castro. (2000). *Washington Post,* November 2.

Njaim, H., R. Combellas, and A. Álvarez. (1992). *Opinión Política y Democracia en Venezuela.* Caracas: Universidad Central de Venezuela.

Norden, Deborah L. (1996). The Rise of the Lieutenant Colonels: Rebellion in Argentina and Venezuela. *Latin American Perspectives* 23(30): 74–86.

Ochoa Antich, Enrique. (1992). *Los Golpes de Febrero.* Caracas: Fuentes.

O'Donnell, Guillermo. (1994). Delegative Democracy. *Journal of Democracy* 5(1): 55–69.

——. (2002a). Debating the Transition Paradigm: In Partial Defense of an Evanescent "Paradigm." *Journal of Democracy* 13(3): 39–45.

——. (2002b). Notes on the State of Democracy in Latin America. Unpublished ms., UNDP.

Olson, Mancur. (1982). *The Rise and Decline of Nations: Economic Growth, Stagflation and Social Rigidities.* New Haven: Yale University Press.

Oposición Convocó a Paro Nacional el 2 de Diciembre. (2002). *El Nacional,* December 3.

Oropeza, Luis J. (1983). *Tutelary Pluralism: A Critical Approach to Venezuelan Democracy.* Cambridge: Center for International Affairs, Harvard University.

Oxhorn, Phil. (2000). When Democracy Isn't All That Democratic: Social Exclusion and the Limits of the Public Sphere in Latin America. Paper presented at the conference Challenges to Democracy in the Americas, the Carter Center, Atlanta, October. Retrieved from the Carter Center Organization Web site: www.cartercenter.org/peaceprograms on November 1, 2002.

Palma, Pedro A. (1989). La Economía Venezolana en el Período 1974–1988: ¿Últimos Años de una Economía Rentista? In Grau-Sierra et al., *Venezuela Contemporánea, 1974–1988.*Caracas: Fundación Mendoza.

Pedersen, Mogens. (1979). The Dynamics of European Party Systems: Changing Patterns of Electoral Volatility. *European Journal of Political Research* 7:1–26.

Peeler, John A. (1989). Deepening Democracy and Democratic Consolidation in Latin America. Paper presented at the XV International Congress of the Latin American Studies Association, Miami, Florida.

———. (1992). Colombia, Costa Rica, and Venezuela. In John Higley and Richard Gunther (eds.), *Elites and Democratic Consolidation in Latin America and Southern Europe*. Cambridge: Cambridge University Press.

———. (1998). *Building Democracy in Latin America.* Boulder, Colo.: Lynne Rienner Publishers.

Penfold, Michael. (2001). El Colapso del Sistema de Partidos en Venezuela: Explicasión de una Muerte Anuciada. In José Vicente Carrasquero, Thais Maingon, and Friedrich Welsch (eds.), *Venezuela en Transición: Elecciones y Democracia, 1998–2000.* Caracas: CDB Publicaciones.

Pereira, Valia. (2000). Las Actitudes Políticas del Venezolano en el Nuevo Escenario de los Años 90. Ph.D. diss., Universidad del Zulia, Venezuela.

Pérez, Carmen. (2000). Identificación Partidaria. In Instituto Interamericano de Derechos Humanos, Centro de Asesoría y Promoción Electoral (ed.), *Diccionario Electoral,* Tomo II. San José, Costa Rica: Instituto Interamericano de Derechos Humanos, Centro de Asesoría y Promoción Electoral.

Pérez Alfonzo, Juan Pablo. (1976). *Hundiendonos en el Excremento del Diablo.* Caracas: Lisbona.

Petrásh, Vilma. (2000). *Venezuela y los Estados Unidos: Orígenes y Evolución de una Relación Especia*l. Caracas: EXD.

Perina, Rubén. (2000). El Régimen Democrático Interamericano. In Arlene Tickner (ed.), *Systema Interamericano y Democracia.* Bogotá: Universidad de Los Andes.

Pierre Tapia, Oscar. (2000). Jurisprudencia del Tribunal Supremo de Justicia. Caracas: Editorial Pierre Tapia.

Planchart Manrique, G. (1988). The Making of the Venezuelan Constitution. In Robert A. Goldwin and Art Kaufman (eds.), *Constitution Makers on Constitution Making: The Experience of Eight Nations.* Lanham, Md.: Rowman and Littlefield.

Poleo, Patricia. (2002). Factores de Poder. *Nuevo País,* April 17.

Powell, John D. (1971). *Political Mobilization of the Venezuelan Peasant.* Cambridge: Harvard University Press.

Presidente Chávez Ofrece su Apoyo a Puerto Rico. (2001). *El Nacional,* January 3.

Przeworski, Adam. (1986). Some Problems in the Sudy of the Transition to Democracy. In. Guillermo O'Donnell, Philippe Schmitter, and Laurence Whitehead (eds.), *Transitions from Authoritarian Rule: Latin America.* Baltimore: Johns Hopkins University Press.

Rangel, Domingo Alberto. (1972). *La Oligarquía del Dinero en Venezuela.* Caracas: Fuentes.

Ranking de las Mayores Empresas de Latino America 2003. (2003). *América Economía,* July 4–31.

Ray, Talton F. (1969). *The Politics of the Barrios of Venezuela.* Berkeley and Los Angeles: University of California Press.

Reinoso, Víctor Manuel. (2000). Acusación Fiscal a Dos Militares Desbloquea Impunidad en Vargas. *El Nacional,* August 31.

Remmer, Karen L. (1985–86). Exclusionary Democracy. *Studies in Comparative International Development* 20 (Winter): 64–85.
——— (1991). The Political Impact of Socioeconomic Crisis in Latin America in the 1980s. *American Political Science Review* 85:770–800.
———. (1993). The Political Economy of Elections in Latin America, 1980–1991. *American Political Science Review* 87:393–407.
Rey, Juan Carlos. (1989). *El Futuro de la Democracia en Venezuela.* Caracas: Instituto Internacional de Estudios Avanzado.
———. (1991). El Papel de los Partidos Políticos en la Instauración y Mantenimiento de la Democracia en Venezuela. In G. Murillo and M. Villaveces (eds.), *Conferencia Interamericana sobre Sistemas Eectorales.* San José, Costa Rica: International Foundation for Electoral Systems (IFES).
Reyes, Ascensión. (2000). El Gobierno Divide a la Sociedad Civil. Caracas. *El Nacional,* May 9.
Rodríguez, Miguel. (1984). El Verdadeno Origen del Endeodamiento Externo de Venezuela. Caracas: IESA.
Roberts, Kenneth. (2000). *Populism and Democracy in Latin America.* Paper presented at the conference Challenges to Democracy in the Americas, the Carter Center, Atlanta, October.
———. (2003). Social Polarization and the Populist Resurgence in Venezuela. In Steve Ellner and Daniel Hellinger (eds.), *Class, Polarization, and Conflict in the Chávez Era.* Boulder, Colo.: Lynne Rienner Publishers.
Romero, Aníbal. (1988). Aspectos Estratégicos en las Relaciones entre Venezuela y los Estados Unidos. *Política Internacional* 10:8–16.
———. (1994). *Decadencia y Crisis de la Democracia: A Dónde va la Democracia Venezolana?* Caracas: Editorial Panapo.
———. (1997). Rearranging the Deck Chairs on the Titanic: The Agony of Democracy in Venezuela. *Latin American Research Review* 32(1): 7–36.
———. (2000). Explicando los Ascensos Militares. *El Nacional,* July 5.
Romero, Carlos A. (1986). Las Relaciones entre Venezuela y Estados Unidos: Realidad Histórica u Opción Política? *Política Internacional* 1:11–14.
———. (1998a). EE.UU-Venezuela: Después de la Visita. Draft. Caracas.
———. (1998b). Las Relaciones entre Venezuela y los Estados Unidos durante la Era Clinton: Coincidencias Estratégicas y Diferencias Tácticas. In Andrés Franco (ed.), *Estados Unidos y los Países Andinos, 1993–1997: Poder y Desintegración.* Bogotá: Centro Editorial Javeriana, CEJA.
———. (2001). Las Secuelas de Quebec. *Carta Internacional* 9 (May): 2.
Romero, Dubraska. (2002a). Más Enredos en la FAN. *Tal Cual,* May 8.
———. (2002b). Sin Guáramo no Hay Golpe que Valga. *Tal Cual,* April 17.
Ross, Christopher E. H. (1999). The Energy Industry at the Start of the New Millennium. Prism A. D. Little. Third quarter.
Ruiz Pantin, Efraín. (2002). Asociación de Alcaldes Rechaza Intervención de la Metropolitana. *El Nacional,* November 19.
Salamanca, Luis. (1989). 27 de Febrero de 1989: Política por Otros Medios. *Politeia* (Universidad Central de Venezuela) 13:187–217.
———. (1995a). El Sistema Político: Una Lectura Desde la Sociedad Civil. In Andrés Serbin, Andrés Stambouli, Jennifer McCoy, and William Smith (eds.), *Venezuela: La*

Democracia Bajo Presión. Caracas: INVESP, North-South Center (University of Miami) and Nueva Sociedad.

——. (1995b) The Venezuelan Political System: A View from Civil Society. In Jennifer McCoy, Andrés Serbin, William C. Smith, and Andrés Stambouli (eds.), *Venezuelan Democracy under Stress.* Coral Gables, Fla: North-South Center at the University of Miami.

——. (1997). *Crisis de la Modernización y Crisis de la Democracia en Venezuela.* Caracas: ILDIS/UCV.

——. (1998). *Obreros, Movimiento Social y Democracia en Venezuela.* Caracas: UCV.

——. (2000) La Constitución Venezolana de 1999: De la Representación a la Hiperparticipación. *Revista de Derecho Público* (Editorial Jurídica Venezolana, Caracas), no. 82 (April–June): 85–105.

Salamon, Lester M., and Helmut K Anheier. (1999). *La Sociedad Civil Global: Las Dimensiones del Sector no Lucrativo.* Madrid: Fundación BBVA.

Salgado, Rene L. (1987). Economic Pressure Groups and Policy Making in Venezuela: The Case of FEDECAMARAS Reconsidered. *Latin American Research Review* 22(3): 91–105.

Sánchez Meleán, Jorge. (1992). *Reforma del Estado y Descentralización.* Maracaibo, Venezuela: Publicaciones de la Gobernación del Estado Zulia, Comisión para la Reforma del Estado Zulia.

Sartori, Giovanni. (1976). *Parties and Party Systems: A Framework for Analysis.* Cambridge: Cambridge University Press.

Scammon, Richard M., and Ben J. Wattenberg. (1971). *The Real Mayority Choice.* New York: Cobbard McCann and Geoghegan.

Schael, María Sol Pérez. (1993). *Petróleo y Poder en Venezuela.* Caracas: Monte Ávila.

Schedler, Andreas. (2002). The Menu of Manipulation. *Journal of Democracy* 13(2): 36–50.

Schmitter, Philippe. (2001). Parties Are Not What They Once Were. In L. Diamond and R. Gunther (eds.), *Political Parties and Democracy.* Baltimore: Johns Hopkins University Press.

Shugart, Matthew, and Carey, John. (1992). *Presidents and Assemblies. Constitutional Design and Electoral Dynamics.* Cambridge: Cambridge University Press.

Simic, Charles. (2003). Tsvetaeva: The Tragic Life. *New York Review of Books,* February 13.

SINERGIA (Asociación Nacional de Organizaciones de la Sociedad Civil). (1998). Relaciones Estado-Sociedad Civil en el Próximo Gobierno (1999–2003). Mimeo.

Sonntag, Heinz, and Thaís Maingón. (1992). Venezuela: 4-F—Un Análisis Sociopolítico. Caracas: Nueva Sociedad.

Soto, Gioconda. (2000a). Hrinak Excusa a Funcionario de EE.UU. *El Nacional,* December 8.

——. (2000b). Venezuela Propone al Hemisferio Nuevo Sistema de Seguridad. *El Nacional,* November 11.

Stambouli, Andrés. (1979). La Actuación Política durante de la Dictadura y el Rechazo del Autoritarianismo. Paper presented at the International Congress of the Latin American Studies Association, Pittsburgh, Pennsylvania.

Stevens, Paul. (2003). Resource Impact-Curse or Blessing? A Literature Survey. Dundee University, Centre for Energy, Petroleum, and Mineral Law and Policy.

The Stubborn Survival of Frustrated Democrats. (2003). *Economist,* October 30, 36–37.
Tarre, Marcos. (2003). No Sea Usted la Próxima Víctima. *El Nacional,* May 19.
Tarre Briceño, Gustavo. (1994). *El Espejo Roto: 4F 1992.* Caracas: Editorial Panapo.
Toro Hardy, Alfredo. (2000). La Relación Económica EE.UU.-Venezuela. *El Universal,* March 30.
Torres, Gerver. (2000). *Un Sueño para Venezuela.* Caracas: Banco Venezolano de Crédito.
Trinkunas, Harold A. (1999). Crafting Civilian Control of the Armed Forces in Emerging Democracies. Ph.D. diss., Stanford University.
———. (2002). The Crisis in Venezuelan Civil-Military Relations: From Punto Fijo to the Fifth Republic. *Latin American Research Review* 37(1): 41–76.
Tugwell, Franklin. (1975). *The Politics of Oil in Venezuela.* Stanford, Calif.: Stanford University Press.
UNDP (United Nations Development Programme). (1999). *Human Development Report 1999.* New York: Oxford University Press.
Uslar Pietri, Arturo. (1989). *De Una a Otra Venezuela.* 6th ed. Caracas: Monte Ávila Editores.
Vaivads, Henry. (1999). La Teoría del Realineamiento Partidista: Una Aproximación Explicativa para el Caso Venezolano. *Cuestiones Políticas* 22:133–46.
Vallenilla Lanz, Laureano. (1983). *Cesarismo Democrático: Estudio Sobre las Bases Sociológicas de la Constitución Efectiva de Venezuela.* Caracas: Monte Ávila Editores. (Previous edition, 1983).
Veneconsultores. (1993). *Informe sobre las elecciones de 1992.* Caracas: Veneconsultores.
Venezuelan-American Chamber of Commerce and Industry. (2000). Informe para los Aflilados sobre los Aspectos Económicos de la Constitución Aprobada en el Referendum del 15 de Diciembre de 1999. Mimeo. Caracas.
Vethencourt, Fabiola. (1999). Las Ferias de Consumo del Estado Lara. In Henry Gómez Samper, Fabiola Vethencourt, and Virgilio Armas Acosta (eds.), (1999). *Gobernabilidad y Democracia: Participación Comunitaria y Cambio Social.* 4 vols. Caracas: Ministerio de la Familia, Banco Mundial, PNUD.
Villegas Poljak, Ernesto. (1996). Caldera ha Callado el Ruido de Sables. *El Universal Digital,* August 5.
——— (2000). Fidel Cree Viable Nuevo Polo de Poder. *El Universal,* October 26.
Walzer, Michael. (1998). Democracia y Sociedad Civil. In Fernando Vallespín (ed.), *La Democracia en sus Textos.* Madrid: Alianza Editorial.
Wanted: A New Regional Agenda for Economic Growth. (2003). *Economist,* April 26–May 2, 27–29.
Weffer Cifuentes, Laura. (2002). ¿Por qué Fracasó el Golpe? *El Nacional,* April 21.
Weyland, Kurt. (1998). Peasants or Bankers in Venezuela? Presidential Popularity and Economic Reform Approval, 1989–1993. *Political Research Quarterly* 51:341–62.
Wiarda, Howard J., and Harvey F. Kline, eds. (1996). *Latin American Politics and Development.* 4th ed. Boulder, Colo.: Westview Press.
Yergin, Daniel. (1991). The *Prize: The Epic Quest for Power, Money and Oil.* New York: Touchstone.
Zago, Angela. (1998). *La Rebelión de los Angeles.* 4th ed. Caracas: Warp Ediciones, S.A.
Zakaria, Fareed. (1997). The Rise of Illiberal Democracy. *Foreign Affairs* 76 (November): 22–43.

Contributors

Damarys Canache. Assistant professor of political science at Florida State University. Her research focuses on public opinion and mass political behavior. Her most recent publication is *Venezuelan Public Opinion and Protest in a Fragile Democracy.* Her articles have appeared in such leading academic journals as *Political Research Quarterly* and *Latin American Politics and Society.*

Rafael de la Cruz. Senior economist with the Inter-American Develpment Bank; formerly a senior economist with the World Bank, director of the Public Policy Center of the Instituto de Estudios Superiores de Administración in Caracas, and director of decentralization of the Presidential Commission for State Reform (COPRE) of the Government of Venezuela. He has published extensively on matters of decentralization, intergovernmental fiscal relations, political economy, governance, and competitiveness.

José Antonio Gil Yepes. President of Datanalisis, a polling firm located in Caracas, Venezuela. He was also professor of sociology, research methodology, and public administration at the Instituto de Estudios Superiores de Administración, visiting professor of political science at Pennsylvania State University, Universidad Simón Bolívar, and Universidad Católica Andrés Bello; director of the Economic and Political Analysis Department of PDVSA (Petróleos de Venezuela), and assistant director of CORDIPLAN. Among his numerous published works, the study of Venezuelan government-business relations in the 1970s, *El Reto de las Elites,* remains a classic.

Richard S. Hillman. Professor of political science at St. John Fisher College and director of the Institute for the Study of Democracy and Human Rights. He has served as a consultant to the Department of State and other government agencies. His research and publications focus on political change in

Latin America and human rights issues. He is the author of *Democracy for the Privileged: Crisis and Transition in Venezuela.* His most recent work on Venezuela has appeared in a variety of book chapters.

Janet Kelly. Until her death in 2003, director of the Public Policy Institute and professor of political economy at the Instituto de Estudios Superiores de Administración. She served as a consultant to numerous Venezuelan private and public sector organizations. Her research focused on the international political economy, Venezuelan policy making, and administrative reform. Her most recent book (with Carlos Romero) is *The United States and Venezuela: Rethinking a Relationship.*

Jennifer L. McCoy. Professor of political science at Georgia State University and director of the Americas Program of the Carter Center. Her research focuses on democratization, international norms of democratization and anticorruption, and elections. Her most recent publication is *Political Learning and Redemocratization in Latin America: Do Politicians Learn from Political Crises?* Her articles have appeared in leading disciplinary and interdisciplinary journals, including *World Politics* and *Journal of Democracy,* and in numerous book chapters.

José E. Molina. Professor emeritus of political science at the University of Zulia's Instituto de Estudios Políticos y Derecho Público. He has also been a visiting professor at the University of Michigan (2000–2004). His research focuses on political parties and voting behavior, and his most recent books are *El Sistema Electoral Venezolano y Sus Consecuencias Políticas* and *Los Sistemas Electorales de América Latina.* Molina's work has appeared in disciplinary and cross-disciplinary journals, including *Electoral Studies* and the *Bulletin of Latin American Research,* and in numerous book chapters.

David J. Myers. Professor of Political Science at Pennsylvania State University. He was visiting professor of urban politics at the Central University of Venezuela and the Instituto de Estudios Superiores de Administración in Caracas. His research focuses on comparative urban politics, political parties, and public opinion. His most recent publication is *Capital City Politics: Democratization and Empowerment* (with Henry A. Dietz). His articles have appeared in leading disciplinary and interdisciplinary journals, including *Comparative Politics* and the *Latin American Research Review,* and in numerous book chapters.

Moisés Naím. Editor of *Foreign Policy.* He was a fellow at the Carnegie Institute of Peace and has served as minister of trade and development in the administration of Carlos Andrés Pérez and as dean of Instituto de Estudios Superiores de Administración (IESA). His research interests include government-business relations and politics of economic reform. He has written numerous books and articles dealing with these subjects, including *Paper Tigers and Minotaurs: The Politics of Venezuela's Economic Reform.* His work has appeared in a broad range of academic and policy outlets including *Journal of Democracy* and *Venezuela Analítica.*

Nelson Ortiz. President of the Caracas Stock Exchange, president of the National Council for Investment Promotion (CONAPRI), and a member of the board of directors of some of Venezuela's largest private corporations. He has taught macroeconomics and international finance at some of Venezuela's leading universities. He holds an M.A. in economics from Yale University and an M.P.A. from Harvard University.

Pedro A. Palma. Professor of economics at the Instituto de Estudios Superiores de Administración and founding partner of *MetroEconómica,* a macroeconomic consulting firm based in Caracas. He is a former president of the Venezuelan-American Chamber of Commerce and Industry (VenAmCham), a member of the Latin American Executive Board of the Wharton School, and a Founder Fellow of the Venezuelan National Academy of Economic Sciences.

Carlos A. Romero. Professor of political science in the Institute of Political Studies at the Central University of Venezuela. His research focuses on international relations and Venezuelan foreign policy. He has been visiting research scholar at the University of Pittsburgh, Columbia University, and the Universidad de Salamanca and AIETI, Spain. His most recent book is *El Factor Trabajo como Tema en la Agenda Global.* His work has appeared in scholarly journals throughout Latin America and in numerous book chapters.

Luis Salamanca. Professor of Political Science and Director of the Institute of Political Studies at the Central University of Venezuela His research focuses on civil society and interest group politics. His most recent publication is *Crisis de la Modernización y Crisis de la Democracia en Venezuela.* His work has appeared in such leading academic journals as *Politeia* and the *Revista de la Facultad de Ciencias Juridicas y Políticas* and in numerous book chapters.

Harold Trinkunas. Assistant professor in the Department of National Security Affairs at the Naval Postgraduate School in Monterey, California. His research focuses on democratization and the military as an interest group and as government. He has published articles in *Latin America Research Review* and *Journal of Interamerican Studies and World Affairs* and is currently working on a book on civilian control of the armed forces in emerging democracies.

Index

Numbers in *italic* denote illustrations; those in **boldface** denote tables.